The
Moment
of the Rose

The Moment
of the Rose

The Story of
Miami, Karoi and Tengwe

Wendy Herbst Lapham

Published by:
Wendy Herbst Lapham, Harare, Zimbabwe.
E-mail: <doublel@mango.zw>

Cover paintings by Tawny Stidolph.

Maps designed and compiled by K. Philip of *Street Savvy*.

ISBN 978–0–7974–6080–5

Typeset by TextPertise, Harare, Zimbabwe.
Zimbabwe edition printed by Sable Press, Harare.

Contents

By Way of Introduction

I was six years old when Karoi was opened up to ex-servicemen in 1947. The Western world was at peace once more, but many of the colonies had begun to agitate for their own independence, and, having left one war behind, they continued with another.

My parents and I, along with countless others, were escaping from a violent India, which had erupted into anarchy following Partition.

The ship *The Empress of Scotland* had been equipped to cater only for troops, so families were separated – men sleeping in dormitories, and women and children sharing cabins. The war had lingered a little longer in the east, and my father was there because he was an RAF chaplain stationed at DumDum – famous for its bullets; my mother and I had been allowed to join him for the last months there before he was demobbed. The return journey to Britain took six weeks.

Partition was just what the word suggests. It followed months of political wrangling between Muslim and Hindu leaders, each wanting more power than the other. Finally, Britain agreed that India should be divided into three parts. The western and eastern pieces would be known as Pakistan (East Pakistan later becoming Bangladesh) and would be Muslim homelands. Between these two was India, which would retain that name and be ruled by a Hindu government.

Through the eyes of a child, India was neither safe nor comfortable, and this, I realise now, was because of its political rumblings. I remember the smells as they wafted over the city, smells of strong spices cooking on open hearths and mingling with sweaty humanity, effluence and rotting garbage. It was a country of alarming contrasts, of searing heat that brought the monsoons that flooded the arid plains and caused indescribable discomfort for pale, delicate-skinned Europeans, who fled to the hills of Darjeeling where it was cool and fresh, leaving the rising waters to rid the city below of all its detritus.

Just before it left the country, the train on which my mother and I had travelled up to the foothills of the Himalayas was attacked by bandits, but they were soon driven off by the Gurkhas. When we arrived, everyone walked, for the roads were narrow – no more than pathways – and not conducive to anything other than a jeep, so a pony was rented for me to travel on.

Britain, in contrast, was peaceful at last, but noticeably grey and in disorder. The effects of six years of war made a depressing sight. The ruins of bombed cities were still being cleared up, and the population was noticeably malnourished: ration books continued to control one's shopping.

When I went to boarding school, family members and friends donated their sweets coupons so that I could fill my tuck box. Housing was short and families doubled up to share accommodation. Air-raid shelters still stood in place, abandoned and used only by tramps, stray dogs, and perhaps lovers wishing for privacy.

We were luckier than most, as my father settled into parish life again. For five years we stayed put in a rambling, draughty Victorian vicarage that fifty years earlier had accommodated at least three servants in a wing of their own above the kitchen, accessible by a second flight of stairs.

Originally there had been a well in the scullery – the only water supply. Outside a manhole opened up to a chute that carried coal deliveries to the cellar. Needless to say, my mother was having none of this and refused to move until the well had been covered over and the place modernised. Despite all the rooms and space, we continued to live in cosy comfort in one room at the back.

My first day at school was marked by a green banana, a bribe to get me through those portals of learning. We were dosed daily with a quart of milk and a tablespoon of cod liver oil in orange juice to bolster our puny bodies while a glaring teacher stood over us, defying us to spit or gag.

Five years later, my father's feet began their customary itch as parish life began to pall and faraway places beckoned. It was Africa that called, and this time there were five of us: two more daughters had joined the family.

The first eleven years of my life were packed tightly with a wealth of experiences. By the time I turned twelve, I had been to five schools. Ironically, it was Africa that brought the stability that I longed for – a truth that today, sixty years later, is risible.

Like many others who descended on to the Karoi plateau in the early 1960s, I was an impressionable and naive young woman, a bride of twenty-one, anxious and afraid of everything, for my upbringing had been narrower than that of most. Stuffed with church and clergy, compared to many of my contemporaries I was not socially adept and very much inclined to be prissy. My sisters, eight and ten years my junior, had an easier time, for they stood as one against the might and force of our parents, strong in argument and defiant to the end.

Missionaries are always, of course, hopelessly poor and overworked – it goes with the job. One is never off duty, so our only means of escape was to drive away from it, which in our case was from Cyrene Mission, famous at

that time for its artwork and crippled artists. Assisted by the era of cinema and film, Dad developed his own strategy of liberation. On most Saturdays he led us all to one of Bulawayo's cinemas, bought tickets for the back row, put his head back, and slept his way through the adverts, newsreels, coming attractions, and the main film.

His was meant to be a 'calling' rather than a career, and I believe it was. Having lived a life of comfort and some standing in Britain, we were now living a very different life of narrow means. However, my mother always taught alongside my father, and her salary paid for the extras – our 'creature comforts' – so it wasn't often that we felt underprivileged or were even aware of being so. Mum had a natural flair for home-making and created comfortable homes wherever we landed.

Although great emphasis was placed on God, of equal importance was education and learning. It was the be-all and end-all of life – so much so that my father used to return, marked and corrected, many of the letters that I wrote home during my college years. Looking back, it seems a rather high-handed thing to have done, but it was something that I fully accepted and found helpful.

Like most other Europeans, my higher education came at one of Rhodesia's most admirable government schools, Eveline High School in Bulawayo. It was one of many that were designed along the lines of the British public school, and while there I met my late husband, Andries Herbst, a student at the 'brother' school of Milton.

It was a meeting of two very diverse people from different cultures and backgrounds, but the relationship worked well. We met at a school dance, laid on for a touring Natal girls' hockey team in 1957. I had played for the Matabeleland side earlier that afternoon against the touring side, after which a social evening was organised by Townsend

School. The 1st XV – the rugby teams of Milton, Bulawayo Tech (now called Gifford High School after Phil Gifford's father, the founder) and Northlea – were invited to provide us with dance partners. For the two of us, it was, of course, a momentous occasion, for it was the start of a relationship that lasted twenty years.

Some vicissitudes later, with university and teachers' college firmly behind us, Andries and I married and, after one disastrous farming season in Gutu, joined the throng making their way to Karoi, where I lived for forty-five years. It was 1962, a year that afterwards always reminded me of the annual migration of wildebeest in the Masai Mara. It seemed that all roads led to Karoi in the early 1960s, where we were all staunchly ready to be exploited.

Karoi was good to us. It was a place of opportunity where, as long as one was diligent and hard-working, one could succeed. For a couple of years we ventured only far enough off the farm to meet our neighbours, for we were too busy toiling away to join any club or regular activity. Sixteen years after its inception, Karoi was already a thriving little community, with well-stocked shops and most other facilities.

From being impoverished we became comfortable – and then, I suppose, successful. We proudly bought a farm and ploughed much of our profits back into the soil in the time-honoured way. Our children were raised in the security and comfort of a privileged environment, cushioned from the ills of this world with all they needed. Then, slowly and inexorably, it all began to seep away, and the hard years began.

Civil war broke out, bringing its usual legacy of constant anxiety, which, in due course, turns to fear and then to grief, as men were maimed or died. The loss of people we loved, either in combat or in terror attacks,

in their daily civilian life, on farms or in road ambushes, became a daily dread. My beloved husband, Andries, at the age of 39, suffered a massive and fatal heart attack while on a PATU training course. For my family, life was never to be the same again.

But we were not unique. Others were suffering the same losses – other husbands, other fathers, sons and brothers gone. The journey of recovery is a long, slow process, but it is made easier by neighbours and friends, especially within a close-knit farming community like Karoi's.

An empty life had to be filled without disturbing the lives of my children, for the four of them were feeling as bereft as their mother. Gwen was already at Arundel school, but the youngest three – Sian, Andrea and Andrew – were still of junior-school age. My children were my saving grace, as was the bush war that raged around us – work at the casualty clearing station, catering at the forces' canteen, and being hauled in, as a Women's Institute member, to work at the library and take over as archivist. Then, in time, blessedly, a new marriage and another chapter began when I married Michael Lapham.

Karoi's history within the context of Rhodesia/Zimbabwe is punctuated by major struggles and conflicts. History reminds us that this is a common trend in any new country. The passage of my generation was destined to be a difficult ride, with many contentious issues arising along the way.

Any charm and distinction that existed in the opening up of Miami and, later, Karoi, came off the back of the mica fields, along with a handful of early settler farmers and miners who managed, from the second decade of the twentieth century, to eke out an existence on land that they cut out of the bush and hardened earth.

The experiences – mixed and varied, though perhaps a little less arduous and formidable – of those who followed are, however, just as worthy of recounting and remembering, for all pioneers have one thing in common – courage, resilience, and a stoical acceptance of all that they had chosen to face. Thus they gave their children a heritage to be proud of.

In the responses to my asking the few remaining 'originals' and their descendants to pass on their reminiscences, it is nostalgia that was the over-riding emotion, coupled with a terrible sadness that sees decades of progress and development go to waste. Not many would argue that they had an exclusive and privileged existence: it afforded many a chance to better themselves, but it was hard-earned. And now, after the stroke of a pen, the last bastions of a way of life are all but extinct.

I have attempted to put together for posterity a sequence of events, told by some of those early stalwarts who played an important role in the making of a close-knit community – those men, women and children who helped to shape its course and, in the fullness of time, made it one of the most desirable farming areas in the country.

Ultimately, what also developed along the way, sixty or more years after the curtain had been raised, was a situation that not even the most enlightened visionary could have predicted or foreseen, nor would hardly have believed.

All of us have had to approach a new cross-roads in life, have had to take another path towards the future. The young will survive, mainly because they have youth and vigour on their side – they are still in the midst of their best years, strengthened by the genes of their forefathers – and they will look back and be able to appreciate not only what their forefathers endured for their sakes in order to give them a better life but also that they come from 'good strong stuff'.

Wendy Herbst Lapham

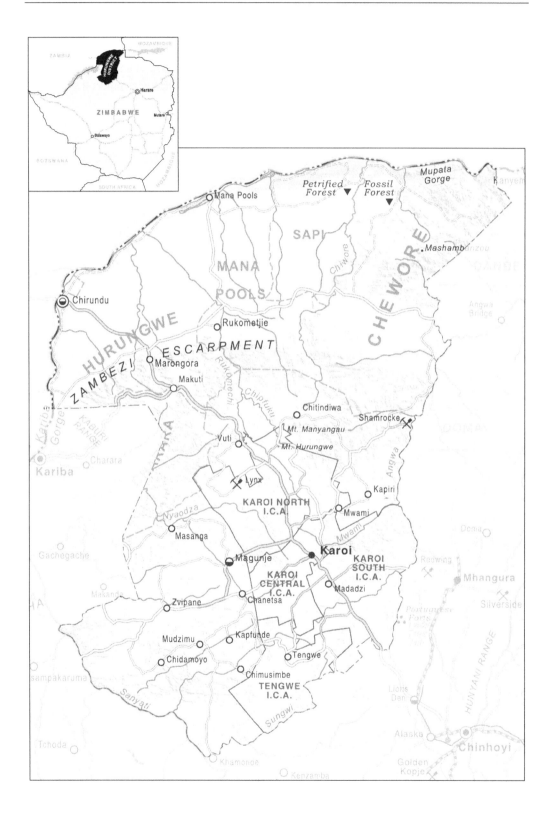

1. The Urungwe

There was a vast tract of land to the north of what we came to know as the Urungwe (now Hurungwe) that was as untouched and wild as they come, just waiting to be tamed, its modern boundaries loosely placed between the Umfuli (Mupfure) river to the west, the Angwa and Hunyani (Manyame) rivers to the south and east, and the mighty Zambezi escarpment to the north. Whatever the furthest boundaries of the 'legendary' land of Monomotapa might have been – it is certain that the Urungwe district fell within them.

A number of misnomers have been applied to the land of Monomotapa – 'legendary' being one, when it did in fact exist; 'kingdom' and 'empire' have also been used, though it was rather a confederacy of Karanga chiefs. Perhaps, suggests R. G. S. Douglas,[1] the earlier confusion refers not so much to Monomotapa as to the gold.

Arab sources of information had been rapidly transmitted through to Europe, the Portuguese in particular finding this news attractive, for they were experienced seafarers. After their adventures in Monomotapa's land, they realised that their hopes of finding huge mineral wealth were to be an illusion. What was the truth? The only lasting 'eldorado' that the Portuguese found was in Brazil, and even Rhodes realised years later that Mashonaland was not quite the great northern extension of the Witwatersrand that he had hoped for.

Sub-Saharan Africa was known to the Arabs as long ago as 500 BC, but we had to wait until the end of the fifteenth century AD for the enterprising Portuguese to give the world an approximate idea of the geographical shape of the continent of Africa.

Important landmarks were, of course, well known: Cape Bojador, rounded in 1434, Cape Blanco in 1441, Cape Verde in 1445; the discovery of the mouth of the Congo by Diego Cão in 1484, and of the Cape of Good Hope, rounded (but not seen) by Dias in 1487 and followed by Vasco da Gama in 1498.

From then on, there was only a vague outline of the 'Dark Continent', represented in books and atlases with most of its features falsely and rather ludicrously described. The interpretations seemed to be figments of wild imaginings – where mountains and rivers were so wildly out of place that, when the great French geographer, d'Anville, tried to make an intelligent assessment of them during the eighteenth century, he threw his hands up in horror and gave up. Then he made the very sensible move to obliterate everything on the map. He left the vast interior as a blank canvas on which to start again, leaving only the features for which there was clear evidence of existence.

And so it remained until Livingstone, a hundred years later, began his great and important exploration that gave the outside world a more accurate cartographic illustration of where landmarks and important features could be found.

The earliest inhabitants had been the Bushmen, or San people, who left their pictorial legacy on the sheltered walls of their rocky cave-dwellings, elevated to the tops of kopjes for safety against the hazards of the time and, more often than not, marauding warriors.

To the north of Karoi, obvious and isolated

---

[1] R.G.S. Douglas, 'Two early Portuguese in the Mutapa State', *Heritage of Zimbabwe* (1986), 6: 41–6.

amongst the flat pastures beneath, stand the stately dual peaks of Mount Manyangau and Mount Urungwe. Mount Manyangau is a sacred site, and it still bears the remains of old pottery. Legend has it that 'the gods' sent 'buffalo beans' to grow around it for protection, and that, if one were to venture to the top, one would find sparkling pools. Bob Pemberton, a one-time resident of the area, managed to mow a pathway which he climbed with only one leg, and during the summer months one would certainly find sparkling pools.

Mount Urungwe is the one with rock paintings at the top. Gradually the San people were driven out, and other peoples from the north and east began to infiltrate, taking their place. They came to be known as the Makaranga.

Because these peoples did not have a written language, historians of modern times have had to 'feel their way blindly' through oral histories and archaeological evidence in their endeavour to find out what happened in the region in those early years. The Urungwe area was very thinly populated for the primary reason that it was diabolically unhealthy, fever and malaria being rife. Life expectancy was short, and this state of affairs changed little until well into the twentieth century.

Early writings mention an Arab presence within the Lomagundi district in the fif-teenth century. (The name Lomagundi was taken from that of a local petty chief which has been written in several ways, including Magundi, Magondi, Magunda and Makonde.) Arab traders, operating from the eastern side of Lake Tanganyika, ventured up and down the Urungwe for many years before the Portuguese missionaries and explorers began their expeditions into the interior of Africa during the sixteenth and seventeenth centuries. These transient traders lived mostly towards the eastern side of the country, infusing their Arab blood with that of the local communities.

Arab trade routes can be traced on maps through the discoveries of copper crosses, 'Katanga crosses'. It is thought that these copper crosses and bars were fashioned in this way for easy handling in their trans-portation down to the sea. They became a common form of currency across Africa.

It was the plough that brought them to light in the Urungwe, when ex-servicemen tilled the soil and started a new chapter in the country's history. Down from Folliot farm, in the north, they emerged: on Mahuti, Ardingly, Sangalalo, Pitlochry, Hazelmere, Kilrea, San Michele, Chedza, Chumburukwe, Four Winds and Mshalla. Then the route of discoveries took a slight swing westerly from Lanlory, Welkom, Rocklands, Hesketh Park, Glenellen, Renroc, Longueil, Hazeldene and Loughry.

Greater caches were found in the vicinity of Chedzurgwe hill in Karoi (Scorpion farm), suggesting that it must have been an important centre long ago. A *n'anga* is said to have put a curse on the area, saying that anyone who ploughed the Chedzurgwe would die. Superstition kept the African

Katanga crosses.

people from Chedzurgwe for many years, but European farming development changed the landscape until the hill became little more than a mound on a rolling plain.

It is also said that, when the moon is full, jackals with human hands and feet could be seen there. Of the Chedzurgwe, Rita Leask Mills says that, owing to the very tall grasses and leaf mould, it was a very fertile hill with numerous antbear holes, so the moonlight could have revealed the creatures emerging.

As for the superstition: one of the first farmers who lived on Scorpion farm ignored it; he was constructing a silage pit, when the tractor fell back on top of him and killed him. Then Syd Jenkinson's war wounds in his leg reopened there and gave him so much pain that he and 'Bobbie' moved to Mazoe. My opinion is never to pooh-pooh a legend or 'voodoo'.

In 1514, the first European pioneer, António Fernandes, along with his 'entourage', traversed the unknown land between the coast and the middle Zambezi, which included the Urungwe.

Driven by reports of tremendous wealth – gold, silver and ivory – these swarthy, bearded Portuguese, dressed in strange, inappropriate apparel, unsuitable for the climes of Africa, struggled though the dense vegetation in uncomfortable heat, falling victim to unsuspected diseases and fevers as their party travelled steadily through a wilderness infested with unfamiliar flying creatures and wild animals. They made their way inland from the east coast of what today is Mozambique towards the north-west.

We can perhaps conjure up a picture of António Fernandes, a string of porters carrying in his wake stocks of muskets, cloth and beads to hand over to the chiefs as gifts. Although he was concerned principally with the wealth that it was reported could be

found in the land of Monomotapa, he may have had a more overwhelming and pressing need – to earn his freedom: for António Fernandes was a *degredado*, a political criminal who had been convicted in Portugal of some unknown offence.

Being sufficiently intelligent, he was offered a free pardon if he helped his country in the 'discovery' of southern Africa and the route to India. He was almost certainly the first white man to enter the 'kingdom of Monomotapa'. From 1514 to 1516 he traversed the uncharted land between the coast and the mid-Zambezi, collecting information for the king of Portugal.

An important account of his travels came to light as recently as 1939, discovered by Eric Axelson as it lay mouldering away on a shelf in the Lisbon archives. Hugh Tracey, who had a mutual interest in those earlier times with Axelson, met him by chance in Durban in 1939. Axelson gave Tracey his own translation of the Fernandes document.

Not only is it the first description of the land of Monomotapa by a European but it describes the country over a period of fifty years. This account of Fernandes's journey was written for him by his clerk, Gaspar Veloso, for Fernandes was illiterate and could neither read nor write. He walked through the area, noting its gold deposits in the year 1514, at about the same time that James IV of Scotland invaded England.

Hugh Tracey wrote in 1968:[2]

It is surprising that the Portuguese made no attempt to follow up his discovery for so many years. It may have been that his compatriots considered the word of António Fernandes, the *degredado*, unreliable. Had they followed his advice, Monomotapa would

---

[2] Hugh Tracey, 'Antonio Fernandes: Rhodesia's first pioneer', *Rhodesiana* (1968), 19: 1–26.

3

no doubt have been opened up much earlier.

About forty-four years after António Fernandes had completed his expedition in search of gold, earning the remission of his time as a convict, a Portuguese missionary entered the country in 1560 on a quest to convert the Makaranga to Christianity. He was Fr Gonçalo da Silveira, a nobleman by birth and a priest by vocation, and he was welcomed warmly by the Monomotapa at his residence – his *zimbabwe* – a great house of stone on the Musengezi river, some 160 miles from Tete, which is believed to be the oldest white settlement within the African interior.

Muslim traders were always around in great numbers, and although they felt no threat from the Portuguese in their hunt for gold, they jealously guarded their faith and spoke against the missionary, who was warned by the Makaranga that his life was in danger.

Silveira refused either to believe what he was told or to leave. Being a man of faith he decided to put his life in the hands of his Maker. However, on the night of 16 March 1561, he was strangled and his body thrown into the river. He was the first Christian martyr to die for his cause in southern Africa.

The Portuguese were never really success-ful in finding any significant goldfields to the east, owing perhaps to the fact that their primary settlements were to be found upon the Zambezi, where there was no gold. It could also be that the Arabs had depleted the primary lodes or, once again, they may have confused copper with gold.

The seventeenth century saw the power of the Monomotapa wane owing to in-fighting and rebellion so that the ruler of the day moved his *zimbabwe* close to the Portuguese fort and trading station of Masapa, which

is near Mount Darwin, not far from the Zambezi.

So the deeper interior bided its time and waited, unyielding and patient, for the appearance of the next batch of visitors to brave its virgin wilderness. For a further century the Urungwe remained hidden from the prying eyes of men who were in the business of opening up the new world to the old. Even the Makaranga, it seemed, tended to keep away, finding the place unhealthy and pestilential, and preferring to live along its edges, keeping to higher ground.

Other adventurers or hunters may have visited the Urungwe earlier, but the first trip that can be ascertained with some authority was made by two Afrikaners, Jan Viljoen and Petrus (Piet) Jacobs, and an Englishman, Henry Hartley, in 1865. 'Old Petrus Jacobs', the most experienced elephant hunter in South Africa, was part of a large hunting fraternity that hunted relentlessly up and down the country around that time.

George Woods was one of the last of the English professionals. He hunted in these parts in the company of veterans such as Hartley and sons, the Jennings family, and such men as William Finaughty.

Finaughty – a self-confessed harum-scarum, of 1820 Settler stock from Grahams-town in South Africa – was as renowned as Frederick Courtney Selous, who visited the area in 1864, twenty-six years before the arrival of the Pioneer Column. He can be said to have belonged to the Nimrod Club, of which Selous, Hartley and others were also members.

On one of his hunting trips his ivory spoils brought him in about $7,700. He stopped hunting when the elephants retreated into the tsetse-fly-infested country of the Urungwe, which necessitated going after them on foot. The rest of his days appear to have been spent in trading, freebooting and gambling.

Finaughty may well have preceded Selous into the Urungwe, but there is no evidence to substantiate this. We do know that Viljoen, Jacobs and Hartley had not travelled too far north of the Umfuli river, as the hunting rights given to them by Mzilikazi forbade them to travel beyond that boundary. These rights were greatly valued so were not abused. There were others, too, such as Carl Mauch, Edward Mohr, Phillips, J. Giffard (or Gifford; both spellings have been used), H. Byles, and, of particular interest to Karoi residents, Thomas Smith Leask, who was described as a 'hunter, trader and concessionaire'.[3]

Leask hailed from Stenness in the Orkneys, Scotland. He was the son of Robert Leask, a farmer, educated in the local school, and as a youth went to Glasgow to work in a warehouse. He sailed to South Africa in October 1861 and reached Durban on 9 January 1862, where he found work in Natal. He traded up country in the colony for his firm, and the following year became a partner with Millet, his employer.

He continued to trade in Basutoland for a further year from 1863 to 1864, by which time one surmises that the business had become insolvent, for after that he was described as 'a poor man, without assets and in debt'. However, he had a couple of good friends in Giffard and Phillips, who were already experienced hunters. They very soon persuaded him to join their elephant hunts in order to become solvent again. Giffard lent him a gun and Phillips some money.

In 1866, a combined party of thirteen, which included Leask, Finaughty, Mauch and Hartley, obtained the king's permission

to hunt in Mashonaland and, making their way up north, stopped en route to visit the missionaries at Inyati, sharing a meal with William Sykes, after which they crossed the Hunyani river. Never in the wildest of his dreams would it have crossed Thomas Leask's mind that some of his descendants would have ended up farming in those same parts fifty years in the future.

Rita Leask Mills has confirmed that Thomas was a member of the Karoi Leask family, but she cannot quite remember how. Working from the dates, he was too old to have been her father's brother, so in all probability he was her grandfather's brother, which would make him her great-uncle. She said that he was always considered to be the 'black sheep' of the family. However, it wasn't quite as bad as that.

Thomas Leask stopped hunting elephant in 1870, finding it distasteful after a while. He continued to wander around the southern parts of the continent, repairing firearms and trading. In 1872 he married Lucy Salmon, a school teacher. In time he became the largest merchant in the southern Transvaal and was a founder of modern Klerksdorp in South Africa. He returned home to the Orkneys in 1902, where he died in 1912.

It is not inconceivable that he might have entertained his family members, the youngsters especially, with tales of his African exploits, which would have enthralled and engrossed them. It was a popular pastime, especially during the winter months as they sat around a roaring fire. Unwittingly, he may have sown a subconscious seed of interest in the mind of his great-nephew, Robert Andrew Leask, who arrived in Miami in 1915 in answer to an advertisement that announced land for sale.

Another member of the hunting brotherhood was one Christiaan Herbst. A source in the Archives describes him thus:

---

[3] Edward Tabler, *Pioneers of Rhodesia* (C. Struik, 1966).

This Afrikaner had done several trips before 1871 from the Soutpansberg, northward to the Sabi River. In August he was at Lee's … the first white man to live in Rhodesia apart from the missionaries.

Herbst was an associate of Meyer, Henry Byles and Zietsman, who lived in their wagons and in a hut south of the Mangwe (Matabeleland) during the summer months when they were not hunting. That same year Byles came to Lee's place from a hunting trip to the Hunyani which he'd taken with K. Lee, Herbst and two Smidt brothers. They followed the Mangwe to its junction with the Simolwe and there they found the eldest Jennings, and his son George, and Potgieter camping there.

The history books mention many familiar Afrikaans names that had their origins in Germany and came into South Africa and Rhodesia via South West Africa (Namibia). Many of them, which include Herbst and Zietsman, are names familiar to us. Christiaan is a common name within the Herbst family, following the Afrikaner practice to name the first male child after his father. That the hunter Christiaan Herbst of the mid-1800s might also be part of the Karoi family is inconclusive, but it is interesting and is being investigated.

When Thomas Baines, the artist from Norfolk, first visited the Urungwe in 1869, his curiosity and enthusiasm galvanised him into a frantic need to get all he saw captured on to paper. He was the first artist to depict the Victoria Falls and was also an accurate cartographer.

He had been asked to join David Livingstone's 1859 expedition on contract to provide a pictorial record of their travels. However, he blotted his copybook by spending too much time painting portraits of the Portuguese, this being more lucrative, and was immediately relieved of his job. Once in Lomagundi, he set to with renewed enthusiasm and vigour, determined to commit to paper everything he saw as faithfully as he could for posterity. In this he was successful.

Accompanied by George Hartley, the two men advanced further beyond the Umfuli, coming across George Woods and his wife, who were the first white couple to be married in the country, the marriage having taken place at the Inyati mission. Thus it was that these three men rode to the northwest together, reaching the Hunyani river in 1869, which they followed up and down for several weeks.

Baines spent a year around Lomagundi. He described rivers and workings in the vicinity of what was later Raffingora and Mangula (Mhangura). While the others were examining the ancient alluvial gold works, Baines, in need of grain and provisions, rode to Chief Magondi's kraal, situated in the hills around the Mwami (Miami) and Magondi farms. Baines, helped by Magondi, drifted around the district, inspecting the quartz reef and old diggings. Magondi also showed him the ruin of a Portuguese house, the last remnants of that country's influence in central Africa.

Magondi's kraal was on the fringe of tsetse-fly country. The tsetse fly was a terrible curse – it was the bane of the hunter's life, not to mention the scourge of all who came within its wild precincts. Hunters, though, were more inclined to hang around longer, but experience taught them that when they followed dangerous game they were better off hunting on horseback during the winter months, the fly being more troublesome during the rains.

The early pioneers had by now found some

ingenious prophylactic remedies to ward off and overcome sleeping sickness. George Woods fed his horse with dead tsetse flies. Baines washed his horses with 'aqueous ammonium carbonate' and also sprinkled them with tar water.

The next important visitor was probably Frederick Courtney Selous, who, armed with a public school education from Rugby in the United Kingdom and aged nineteen years, arrived in Africa determined to become yet one more member of the hunting fraternity. A series of letters he wrote were donated to the National Archives by his nephew in 1952, which enlighten us still further as to his movements and activities.

He entered the Urungwe from the Zambezi side, following the river from the Victoria Falls, and reached the Kariba gorge in November 1877. He crossed from Matabeleland in May 1878 and reached Magondi's kraal in September of that year, where he bought grain. He hunted relentlessly up and down the Hunyani river, and it was said that he had as many as 400 hunters in his employ, during which time they all but decimated the area of much of its wildlife, rhinoceros in particular.

Of the people, he said: 'They seemed very industrious, cultivating great quantities of kaffir corn, mealies, groundnuts and a few sweet potatoes; they must have got any amount of vegetable food and lots of beer.' He also noticed cotton being woven.

Selous next entered the Urungwe in 1882 with the purpose of travelling north from the Hunyani to the Zambezi in order to map the route. After a few days of travelling he came into country which to him appeared desolate. It had obviously once been thickly populated. What had caused this desertion? No doubt the unhealthiness of the place and/or an invasion from the Matabele had driven the people from this rich and fertile area.

Early in September, Selous returned to Lomagundi suffering from malaria, which he nursed for several weeks and delayed his journey south. He again returned in 1883 and then for the last time in 1887. This was his last visit to Lomagundi before the occupation.

Selous also recorded that tobacco was being cultivated. There was no doubt that a primitive type of tobacco known botanically as *nicotiana rustica* was already being cultivated in Monomotapa at that time. The European pioneers would not have failed to notice widespread patches of it.

It is to Cortés that credit is given of introducing the seed of the tobacco plant into Europe in 1518. He gave these seeds to Emperor Charles V, who planted them in a Lisbon garden. So in all probability it was the Portuguese missionaries and military expeditions into the inland that brought the seed to Africa.

In 1889, the British South Africa Police built a fort near Mount Urungwe situated on the Chipfuku river, about 105 miles north-west of Fort Sinoia. It was reported to be an unhealthy place in general, bearable only during the dry, winter months, added to which communications were almost non-existent. As a result, police were recalled to Fort Sinoia for the wet season.

In 1890, after the Pioneer Column had disbanded, men dispersed in a great hurry to stake gold claims, believing that easy fortunes lay in wait for them. Numerous prospectors wandered around the Urungwe, which was rich in game. They were able to live off the land, carrying with them a pocket full of salt for flavouring. Salt was an expensive luxury because of its scarcity: at that time a sack of salt would have cost twelve pounds in Salisbury. This diet was supplemented by berries and wild mushrooms.

Almost without exception, these prospectors, as well as settlers on the land, found not gold but sickness, hunger and disillusionment. Nearly all of them caught malaria.

The true origins of the disease were unknown then. It was thought to be caused by bad air, together with a miasma arising from around swampy ground, and it was only at the close of the nineteenth century that the British scientist Sir Ronald Ross made the important discovery that malaria was transmitted by the anopheles mosquito; only then was there any attempt to introduce gradual preventive methods by destroying their breeding places, and to use quinine as an oral prophylactic.

No man in the bush alone could surely survive, and as the seasonal rains got under way, clothes rotted and footwear disintegrated. Men made their own rough sandals from antelope hide, and it is said that the habit of wearing shorts stems from when the lower parts of trouser legs were cut off to patch threadbare trouser seats.

In 1900 Kingsley Fairbridge, making his way up to the Urungwe, was warned by the Sinoia police that Urungwe was a 'death trap', adding that a camp had been built there for at least a year but had been abandoned because all the men who had done duty there had died. So much, then, for the first attempt at a settlement in the vicinity of Miami.

There is a map of the Mashonaland Mission from around 1890, drawn by Bishop G. W. H. Knight-Bruce, that shows the approximate positions of the villages that he and other mission workers of the Church of England had visited. It shows a narrow slice of the eastern edge of the Urungwe, and what is most notable is how very thinly populated this area was.

By 1902 the number of settlers countrywide was 15,000 men, most of whom were unattached. The BSA Company had spent millions, with no return, on expeditions into a land ravaged by pests and rebellion. The only achievements that could be recorded were the opening of the railway from Mafeking to Bulawayo in 1897 and from Beira to Salisbury in 1899.

2. Miami

Miami covers a huge area. The mica fields extend over 80 square kilometres and run for more than 190 kilometres from the northeast of what was to become known as Karoi, across the escarpment to Kanyemba on the banks of the Zambezi river, where the headwaters of the great Cabora Bassa dam rests today.

Modern mining came to these parts as long ago as 1896, when gold was discovered near the Angwa river, which was followed by the discovery of mica on the north-eastern plateau. Until 1917, prospecting and mining in the vicinity of Miami had been a disorganised, haphazard occupation. Then the first serious miners moved in by mule and ox-wagon, and the more affluent in T-Model Fords. Thirty years later the area was prolifically pock-marked with diggings made by the prospectors.

The small settlement of Miami can still be found on the map, and it takes its name from the river Mwami or Meyami close by (there are several ways of spelling it), although you would be hard-pressed to find much evidence of the place now. There is, however, a small pioneer cemetery, hidden from the road among some volunteer eucalyptus saplings and tall grasses. It was on a part of Kachichi farm, owned by Harvey Ferreira. Harvey discovered the place and made it a Rotary project in order to keep it in trim and in good order.

Miami sprang into life and importance as the result of the exploitation of its minerals. The mica was discovered in 1901, but workings and the exploitation of its commercial value didn't begin until some years later, between 1917 and 1919. Mica mining survived a number of setbacks over time, becoming very profitable at its peak. Between 1917 and 1925, eighty mica claims were registered. Production came to a virtual standstill during the slump of 1925/6, but thirteen years later it revived again, mainly because of its strategic value and importance to the war effort, with large exports making their way to the United Kingdom and America. It revived once again briefly in the 1950s, during which time smaller workings were encouraged by the Mines department, with offers of 80 per cent advances on mica from rail to broker in London.

The uses of mica are numerous and varied: it is used as insulation in a variety of commodities – elements in smoothing-irons and other electrical goods, for instance – as an additive in cloth-making and linens, and also in roofing, paints and wallpapers. It is used as a filler and as an additive in lubricants and greases, and also in tyres, and was used in moving-picture studios as snow. The potassium in mica is a valuable fertiliser. In many cases it replaced glass, as it did in aeroplane windscreens during the war, so it was a vital commodity at one time.

Mines such as Turning Point, Grand Parade, Catkin, Last Hope and D Troop all helped to open up the Miami area, which consisted of dozens of workshops, mostly open-cast, with miners grubbing out both mica and beryl. Grand Parade mine was once reputed to be the biggest mica mine in the world. It was opened in 1919 by Jacob (Jack) Goldberg (no relation to the Goldberg who owned the Sinoia Hotel), and produced ruby mica. He named the mine after the winner of the Grand National of that year.

At one time the total production value reached two million pounds sterling, although at present-day prices that figure

Lighting charges in a mica mine in the Miami area.

would be many times greater. Today the area is perhaps one of the most important in the country for pegmatite-derived gemstones, which include tin, beryl, tourmaline, topaz, quartz, wolfram and tantalite. Years later graphite and kyanite deposits were also found in the Miami area. Lynx mine, for instance, opened up after deposits were discovered in 1960 by geologist Geoff James, who lived on Mfuti hill in Karoi.

The mine was of vast proportions, and at its peak employed up to a thousand black workers. But the Great Depression brought with it many problems, and it was the owner of the Miami Hotel, Grant Trigg, who financed the mica producers as world buyers held back their payments.

In 1924 Jack Goldberg applied to the Ministry of Lands for 3,000 morgen on which to grow grain. He explained in a letter:

> I have found great difficulty during the past years in securing grain with which to feed the natives on the mine as well as the cattle.
>
> I feel the need to be independent of traders and farmers. I also intend, at a later date, to grow tobacco, and am in the process of making bricks with which to build a homestead and barns.

The firm of Maasdorp and Piers was the government's land surveyor and, in agreeing to Goldberg's request for land on which to grow maize, Maasdorp was sent up to the Urungwe to find something suitable. Maasdorp decided that the area of the Rukomechi/Rekometjie river (there are several ways of spelling it) would do quite well. He wrote:

> Most vleis can be ploughed, but in my opinion will not give a heavy 'mealie' crop. Also the only permanent water is from the river, which by the end of the season diminishes to standing pools. I'm having a rotten time in my surveying as the smoke [from bush fires] is so dense that there is no hope of connecting with trig beacons.

In the event, by 1925, Goldberg had selected a piece of land to the east of the Rukomechi which he called Grand Parade farm, using the same name as his mine. At the same time, three other pieces of land were purchased by Miami residents: G. G. Olivier registered his as Chigangas, which was situated on the very edge of the Miami settlement. D. G. Hartman registered his as Masterpiece, and this sat amid State Land to the north-east of the Miami. A third piece was bought by Captain Whitby, the supervisor for the Roads department; his land was called Pendennis. However, none of the three seems ever to have been farmed and, according to a survey map, one purchase was later cancelled.

Significantly, another large block of land around the Rukomechje (yet another spelling) was granted to Captain Boshoff, who farmed under the name of Miami Estates. In 1947 Miami Estates was sub-divided to make way for returned soldiers, and became Rekomitje A, Hill Top, Kent, Omega, and Grand Parade. Jack Goldberg had sold his farm to Captain Boshoff.

Another fairly large landowner came to the fore in the Urungwe at that time – Maurice Zimmerman, who is said to have changed his name to O. C. Rawson. (This was a common practice among immigrant Germans whose names made them suspects during wartime.) He struck a deal with the government, who wanted to exploit land he owned on the Great Dyke in order to develop chrome mines. Thus Maurice Zimmerman, alias O.C.Rawson, swapped his Darwendale land for land in Miami, though there is some confusion about exactly which area that covered.

In 1935, Jack Goldberg sold Grand Parade mine (not the farm) to Southern Cross Development (Pty) Ltd, one of several companies that included the London and Rhodesia Land and Mining Company, later known as Lonrho and owned by Tiny Rowland.

During this time, complaints came regularly from world buyers about the grading and handling of the mica – just as, in years to come, tobacco would be in the firing line, as buyers tried to control the prices.

Another prominent mining family in Miami besides Jack Goldberg's were the Deacons, who owned Turning Point, Trezona, Aqua and Ruby mines, all important in the area.

George Deacon married Isabella Ira Gilmour Rubidge, and they subsequently had two daughters, Henemoa Dixie and Maud Quinton Cavenagh, and a son, Portlock Gilmour. Isabella Rubidge Deacon had been a very beautiful woman, and had been presented at the English court. With her Rubidge hook nose and high cheekbones, she sometimes resembled a hex (a witch) and was called Wasabelle, a nickname she enjoyed.

The artist in her made her quite eccentric. She wore a picture hat at the dinner table because she couldn't stand the light in her eyes. One day she came across a dead sheep, and, thinking that the wool might be useful, she removed all the smelly bits, took off her bloomers, and put the remains inside

to carry back to the homestead. She lived to the good age of 92, saying that she just wanted 'Isabella' inscribed on her tombstone since she had had so many names that she couldn't be bothered to remember them all!

Isabella's son, Portlock Deacon, had initially farmed in Bindura on land he had named Trezona after a beautiful Greek girl he had been in love with. He must have still held a candle for this lost love, for the name accompanied him to Miami and was bestowed upon one of his mines. Portlock later married Hilda Barber, who gave birth to three daughters, Avril, Althea and Yoland. Avril subsequently married Hugh Chisnall; Yoland married John Nicholle; and Althea married Vic Dewdney, who became, for a short time, the first BSAP Member-in-Charge in Karoi 1947.

Remarriages seemed to happen quickly, perhaps in indecent haste, as widows or widowers were soon swept up to fill a gap, particularly when children found themselves orphaned. The Urungwe was not an area to be alone in, yet many women did become hardened and adept at coping on their own, learning how to handle a gun, and providing a living for their families.

George Deacon followed the rest of his compatriots into an early grave when, having stopped to rest on the road to Sinoia, he collapsed and died, though he had certainly seemed well enough before starting off on his journey, his daughter Avril said. Isabella then married Alex McCready, who worked for the Rhodesian Mica Producers Association in Miami, and she produced two more daughters, Viola and Idoni.

The name of Idoni Jackson, as Idoni had become by 1954, may be familiar to many an old-timer. She had already gained notoriety for many reasons, but one morning an unusual headline sprang out from the front page of the *Rhodesia Herald*.

> **Mrs Jackson 15 Years for Murder**
> *Mrs Idoni Rubidge Jackson,*
> *a European woman of 40 years,*
> *was found guilty in the High Court*
> *Salisbury yesterday of murdering*
> *her former neighbour,*
> *Harvey Patrick Argent Staunton,*
> *on the 24th February.*

It was, according to *The Rhodesian Herald*, the most sensational case ever brought to trial in Rhodesia and the longest heard in the High Court.

Judge Quenet and a jury of nine men returned from a summing up of the case, which lasted ten minutes, to consider if there were any extenuating circumstances. The jury thought that there were, owing to the state of mind of Mrs Jackson, who had stated that the prior relationship that had existed between herself and Mr Staunton had made her feel abandoned. Mrs Jackson's closing remark was that, in her opinion, Mr Staunton's behaviour had been quite out of character.

It was a strange remark coming from the perpetrator of a murder crime. Did she feel that this gave her a perfectly good reason for taking away a man's life?

Idoni Rubidge McCready was Isabella's fifth daughter. Her name lingers on in the minds of the Rubidge/Southey family as a 'skeleton in the cupboard', though not many families are without their scandals, of course. By the time she reached thirty, she was married to her sixth husband, having lived through the deaths of two of them and divorced the others. There was John Palmer, the father of her only child, Harry West, Joseph Moore, Noel Robertson, Patrick Gamble – who had once been married to her half-sister, Henemoa Dixie Deacon – and finally, Robert Jackson.

She set a record rivalling Dick Turpin's by riding around Rhodesia alone, a journey of one thousand miles. It is doubtful that she slept rough, for word has it that she used to put up at each and every police camp.

She started a dairy on a farm in Bindura called Memphis, and it was here that the trouble started. A youngster, newly returned from the war, took up residence on the neighbouring farm, Luxor. It would have taken a very strong man indeed to resist the seductive charms of this woman of the world. Harvey Staunton fell well and truly under the clutches of Idoni Jackson and an affair began. Almost inevitably, it turned sour as she demanded more and more from her young lover. Just what chance did the young fellow have? He enjoyed her as a mistress, but didn't want her as a wife. It was revealed in court by a Miss Pickett that, on the morning of his death, he had told her that he had placed a manager on Luxor and gone to the sanctuary of his parents' home.

It was what the French would call a *crime passionnel*, from which the Staunton family has never recovered. Idoni served her fifteen years in prison, subsequently to live on and accommodate four more husbands. For many an old-timer her infamy lives on.

As time went on, Isabella found herself widowed for the second time after Alex McCready too fell ill, soon joining the unending list of the dear departed. Her third husband was Donald Houghton-Brown, who ran Last Hope mine in Miami.

A number of letters filed at the National Archives dated 1936 confirm that the owner of Trezona, one Isabella Houghton-Brown, agreed to rent out her the house and grading sheds to the government for £4 a month as a mica depot. The lease was renewed in 1937 and then terminated, after a free lease by the Assistant Native Commissioner suggested that the clerk's office was empty and could be used instead.

This offer was taken up because, apart from being rent free, it was more central and saved 15/– per trip every time the railway lorry travelled to Trezona, and saved the producers a trip to Trezona. It was also conveniently adjacent to the telephone and telegraph. Thus the status quo remained until 1946 when the Clerk's Office was condemned and demolished. A cheque for £15 was forwarded from the Mines and Works Department in Salisbury to the Native Commissioner in Miami for the erection of a new Mica Inspector's quarters.

Isabella's granddaughters, Althea (Deacon) Dewdney and Avril (Deacon) Chisnall, recalled growing up in Miami during the 1930s. They remembered going out with their father, Portlock Gilmour Deacon, to look for reefs of mica. If boredom overcame them at such times, they would sit under the shade of a tree, a pair of scissors in hand, and cut out mica shapes and figures; this activity kept them entertained for hours on end.

The constant backdrop of nocturnal sounds frightened them as they lay in bed at night, particularly the roar of lions prowling around the settlement. Ditches were dug around the perimeter and filled with poison to keep these predators at bay. In the morning all the children rushed down to the ditch in excitement to see how many had died, only to be told off in no uncertain terms how foolhardy they had been. Horses, oxen and donkeys dropped dead by the score as they succumbed to the tsetse fly.

As a young lady, Althea Deacon met her husband, Vic Dewdney, in Miami, where he was stationed as a policeman. In 1946 he was sent to Karoi as the first Member-in-Charge and opened up the new police camp there, which consisted only of an asbestos office and two rondavels that were used as living quarters.

Althea used to visit him, putting up at the Karoi Hotel, which was no more than a couple of grass huts at the time. However Vic's tour of duty there was short-lived, for, by marrying before his first three years were complete, he was obliged to resign from the BSA Police, and the couple subsequently went farming.

Grand Parade farm, which Jack Goldberg had acquired in 1924/25, also became a popular 'holding ground' for cattle used by speculators when they drove their herds down from Tanganyika and other northern parts. On arriving at the banks of the Zambezi, they were able to ferry them across on pontoons, driving them on through the valley at night, when the tsetse fly was least lethal. They were ultimately held for distribution at Grand Parade.

Until the 1930s, rangers were given rifles to shoot tsetse carriers. It was a controversial issue, with a Mr Chorley in charge – controversial because game was decimated as a result. Subsequently other methods were tried and the Fly Chamber was erected at Vuti, so that vehicles passing through could enter and have their wheels sprayed. It should be remembered that, in the days of unsuitable transport, all cattle, whether a lone beast or in a herd, had to be driven by foot and protected at night from wild animals that could 'spook' or kill them. It was no easy task for the dedicated drovers.

The Miami settlement was never anything more than a hamlet, for neither time nor fortune was on its side. The rise and fall of mica demands dictated the ebb and flow of progress.

As well as Grant Trigg's hotel, the BSA Police and the Native Commissioner's camp, there was a hospital, a butchery, and a couple of stores – one owned by the Patels, now in Chinhoyi, and another by Arthur Levy, who years later owned Manica Cycles. (Levy is not, as some suppose, a relation of Isaac Levy, whose son Sam developed Borrowdale Village in Harare.) Despite its rather primitive appearance, Miami became the thriving business hub of the district – more important, perhaps, than it appeared.

During its zenith in the early 1930s, Miami also became important for a reason other than for its mica. Because it was on the main air route from England to the Cape, all planes had to fly over the district en route to Salisbury. A small meteorological station was manned by the Miami police, and in the rainy season, particularly when the weather conditions were poor, they had to send two-hourly meteorological reports to Salisbury, in code, through the Miami postal agency. Any passenger plane in trouble was instructed to circle the Native Department station in Miami and fire a Very light, and land if possible on the airstrip. If this occurred, the Native Commissioner at Miami then drove immediately to the aerodrome and gave what assistance he could.

However wild it may have been, and however remote and rough, Maureen Leask Grantham remembered only the grand times in Miami of the 1930s:

> Time was, there was a dance every month at the Miami Hotel, with full evening dress being the order of the evening. Em and Grant Trigg were the proprietors. Grant was much older than Em, his wife, and when he passed away, Em married Dick Shepherd, a twenty-year-old, who, it was said, was sent out to the colonies to escape the law after fatally shooting a policeman.
>
> The hotel bar was closed in 1930, after which time the booze had to be delivered by RMS from Sinoia.

The old-timers talked of a 'brothel' and the sharp-shooting ladies at the rifle range known as the Zambezi Barmaids. The shooting competitions that were held from time to time were keenly contested as there were many very good shots. As well as the Barmaids, ladies supplied the teas and lunches.

At night, 'tame bandits' (prisoners) provided electricity by the sweat of their brows as they peddled away on a stationary bicycle to generate light. There was very little crime during this time, but the few who came up against the law served their time in the local jail and were used as community labourers.

French Marie opened up the first butchery – her big bed (and even bigger wardrobe) tucked into the fork of one tree and the butchery in the shade of another.

She was used as a 'bouncer' when jollifications got out of hand at the hotel, sometimes using a device called a Cat o' Nine Tails if necessary. One night she bodily slung out a young bachelor named Fred Mulder when, after a night's carousing, he began to make a nuisance of himself.

The Deacon girls said they never knew whether French Marie was male or female, as she wore cropped hair, jodhpurs and jack-boots, which she liked to stride around in. They called her Mrs MaBroek (Mrs Trousers).

After a time, when she and her husband had become a little more affluent, they built a brick house that doubled up as an abattoir. It is said that they slept between the hanging carcasses, which probably explains why the poor man died of TB.

Bonny Laver (née Bonsor) was the first white child to be born in Miami, where her father was the compound manager at Grand Parade mine.

There was a Coloured prospector named MaGlass who was married to a white woman. When a resident asked what he did, 'Not much' was the reply. 'He just hung around.'

There was a visiting Bishop who wanted to play tennis but couldn't find 'takkies' big enough to fit his large feet, so he tied slippers on with bootlaces and got his game. There was also breakfast for a visiting tennis team, but the long-awaited boiled eggs never did appear. The cook had tried to boil ping-pong balls, which just became a soggy mess.

There was one party held on the occasion of Bonfire (Guy Fawkes) Night, to which the youth descended in droves from miles around, all of them ready for a party and in a festive mood. 'Mad' Perrem was one, and having imbibed a little more than was good for him, took on a dare to run through the fire – he very nearly became the 'Guy'!

The Native Commissioner also had to pay eight aerodrome groundsmen to see that the grass was kept short, that aardvark holes were filled in, and that demarcation beacons were painted white. There were two groundsmen for each airstrip: at Chirundu, 105 miles away; at Chipani, a distance of 55 miles; and at Vuti, 30 miles from the station.

This work was not as easy as it sounds. It took twelve hours for the Native Commissioner to drive the 105 miles from Miami to the Chirundu airstrip, as the track was over rugged country. No white lime was available with which to paint beacons, so mopane trees had to be chopped down and burned and the ash mixed with water to form a whitewash. On one occasion a huge baobab tree fell across the Chirundu runway, and it took two groundsmen three or four months to chop it up and remove it.

The Miami airstrip was situated on land which became Idlewood farm.

As well as looking after airstrips, Native Commissioners were also building and maintaining roads in an effort to open up the districts.

Native Commissioners came and went. The first arrived in 1922, with Assistant Native Commissioner B. G. Hassell in charge of the Miami post. His successor three years later was Jim Cullen. His wife, Colleen, described her time there:

> For six months, almost without exception, we saw no white visitors. It was the rainy season, and well we knew it, as all available baths were strategically placed about as we tried to cope with the floods from the thatched veranda.
>
> In 1926 our greatest moment was to be the visit of the Governor and his wife, Sir John and Lady Chancellor. We prepared as only the young and ignorant can, and borrowed silver plate and gorgeous tea cloths and many other things for the reception. Cakes were ordered from Pockets in Salisbury, along with many other delicacies.
>
> All this was but a week away when it happened – the house went up in flames after a piccanin lit our only system of illumination, the noble candle, in front of the bedroom window as a hurricane blew outside; net curtains reached the thatch.
>
> Within minutes the house, all the lovely furniture that Jim had made by hand and everything we owned had gone up in flames.
>
> How wonderful friends proved to be; such kind acts, still remembered now. Mr and Mrs Goldberg offered

15

their assistance and rearranged the reception, which I've no doubt was a great success.

On 1 April 1927, consternation and panic struck the community when Alex McCready, Isabella Deacon's second husband, sent a telegram to the Ministry of Health.

> From Mica to Eaton Eldorado:
>
> Consternation in Miami over removal of doctor [stop] trust you can intercede on our behalf [stop] considerable illness [stop] 35 children here now.

The total population of Miami at the time was 120 whites, 35 of them children, and 2,000 blacks.

In a letter backing it up, he wrote, on behalf of the Rhodesia Mica Producer's Association in Miami:

> The Sinoia doctor, owing to distance from Miami, with needs of his own within the district, cannot be considered to be available to Miami residents. Furthermore the distance is too great to move really sick people by car on our dreadful roads. More recently we have seen the death of one of our residents, who would not have died if a GMO had been available.
>
> The population here is greater than in any other centre where doctors and nurses and a hospital are available.
>
> Both black and white population is engaged in the hazardous occupation of mining.
>
> In the absence of a doctor many of our women and children leave the mica fields during the wet season.

Following this, a telegram was sent from Mr Moffat, Minister of Mines, to Bob Leggett, Minister of Roads:

> Please reconsider decision about Miami road. Urgently requested. Miami people only group of settlers in my constituency who are cut off from medical assistance during the wet season.

This was received in reply:

> Minister is unaware of condition. If as stated there are valid grounds for application for a good road and a resident doctor situation will be rectified.

A year earlier, Doctor Robertson had became the General Medical Officer (GMO) at Sinoia. A Dr du Rand had also done a two-month stint as a locum in Miami and refused to return after one rainy season, stating that living conditions were so bad and that the amount of professional work was very small anyway.

A petition was signed by the permanent residents in protest, which is of particular interest as it lists the names of Miami residents in 1927.

A new road was subsequently constructed from the main road to the Miami settlement in 1929. However, before this road was completed, Mr A. Alderman, Charles Olley, best known as a hunter, and Ray Crowther made a precarious trip to the Miami district:

> On our trip in 1929, the N.C. at Miami had built us a camp at the river's junction, and many were the nights the staff spent up trees to escape lion and elephants. It took us two days by car from Salisbury to reach this camp; we had seven days before the rains came, and then it took us seven days of hard work to get home again.

Also in that year, 1929, a police station was built, with Corporal J.L.W. Betts put in charge. In 1960, with more Crown land being cut up for young farmers, this building was incorporated into Fred Mitchell's farm, Kevlyn.

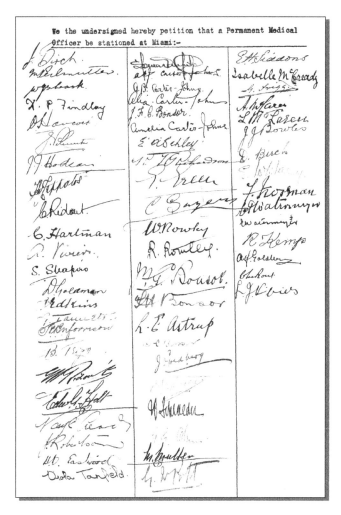

Roger Howman wrote this about his friend:

Corporal [Jack] Betts was one of the toughest characters in the BSA Police, whom Headquarters, in Salisbury, were undoubtedly thankful and relieved to assign to the remote station of Miami – and were just as reluctant to allow anywhere near 'civilisation', even for as short a period as a musketry course.

After his death, anecdotes about him abounded. He was a man with the strangest assortment of contrasting traits. He could play havoc in the mess, yet he had an intense love of flowers, which he insisted on conveying to everyone he met.

He delighted in the bush, in animals and in children, and he would keep these last enthralled for hours by his dramatic eloquence as he related his experiences to them.

The BSA Police was his whole life; he took pride in being a part of it, kept himself physically fit, yet what is described as a bottle of his 'dear enemy' could cancel it all out in a moment.

He delighted in writing official letters in exaggerated and flowery terms, sending a prisoner, for example, to 'The Palace of Justice'.

I once watched him prepare for a surprise inspection by an Assistant Commissioner. Having hidden all the horns normally adorning the quarters, whitewashed every stone, trimmed every flower bed, polished every door handle – not even a cup on the shelf was out of regimental alignment – he then calmly scattered a handful of dust behind the front door where it could readily be seen by the august visitor.

To my question, he replied, 'One must always have something wrong for the b— b— to find. Every dog likes to have a flea to scratch.'

Rita Leask Mills remembers one occasion when a pet monkey owned by Betts had to be shot after it had disappeared into the treetops with the jail-house keys.

For many years afterwards, Roger Howman kept in touch with his friend, and after he had died he found all the other tough guys rather tame compared to this man, who

17

Corporal Jack Betts standing in front of the Police Station, which also doubled as a Post Office, 1936.

could rhapsodise about his pansies as easily as about a buffalo bull.

The policeman's life was almost as isolated, lonely and monotonous as the prospector's in the 1920s. The policeman on horseback was quite alone, apart from his horse and local interpreter, and went on patrol for weeks at a time. Horses needed to be 'salted', still being prone to sleeping sickness from the tsetse fly. It was the same with oxen, so mules were often the preferred transportation.

One hundred miles from Miami was a police camp at Chirundu on the edge of the Zambezi river. It was the last outpost before crossing into Northern Rhodesia. The young police constable, along with his little entourage, patrolled the villages along the river and in the Reserves, where the local people lived their traditional lives and where large numbers of wild animals roamed free.

Murders and witchcraft took place, and British justice had to be seen to be done. When, after several weeks, the constable returned to 'civilisation', he often enjoyed the conviviality of a drink or two.

It was at about this time that the legend of 'suicide month' developed. The enervating heat of these northern areas, particularly in the Zambezi Valley before the rains broke after the month of October, regularly led men to their death. Whether from illness or acute loneliness, it took its toll on body and

mind. Life improved slightly with the advent of the first primitive radio sets, and still more when the farming districts filled up, for the Police were always accepted and welcomed as important members of the community.

Before the high-level bridges were constructed, the rains caused considerable trouble for everyone who travelled along the roads, particularly to Salisbury. The rivers would rise alarmingly and treacherously, and many were the times that folk became stranded on the wrong side of a swollen, raging river without sufficient food.

It was common practice to swap cars and food with those stuck on the opposite bank so that they could get on their way home or to town. Ropes and bath chairs were used to deposit people over to the required bank. In those days everyone could be trusted to return a borrowed vehicle.

During the Depression years in the 1930s, the dirt tracks that served as roads eventually gave way to welcome strips of tar in a plan devised by the Minister of Transport, Bob Leggett, so that unemployed men could work for food and pocket money. He was subsequently nicknamed Bob-a-day Leggett (a 'bob' was a shilling). The strips were a boon compared to the mud or sandy tracks.

Later still, when construction started on the building of the wide tar road, Captain Whitby, the Roads supervisor, told of a tragic accident that took place at that time. It concerned a chap called Angel King, who lived in Sinoia but whose job as supervisor of the road programme to the north required him to travel up to his job when necessary. One day he became the fatal victim of a horrifying accident when a boiler exploded, covering him in boiling tar. In his memory, the road along the power-lines became known as the King's View Road. This road eventually led to Tengwe when it opened up in 1961.

The Great North Road later became busy with railway trucks and army convoys, and the sensible driver always got off the strips. If you were bogged down, the last vehicle would pull you out. A new road was surveyed from the present Miami turn-off at Corner Store to meet another at Grand Parade farm. This made Chikangwe Halt a central point for a fast-developing farming area, which today is called Karoi.

One youngster, straight out of Britain and raw as they come at the age of eighteen, will never forget his first posting as a member of the BSA Police to Miami. Constable R.E. (Bob) Burrell, after three months of training in Salisbury, was sent to Miami in 1951, and to this day he has never recovered from the experience.

Still a teenager, a long way from his native Britain, the shock was overwhelming, particularly when he came up against the Member-in-Charge, Sergeant Graeme 'Jock' Gilmour, who was a hard nut to crack – a bachelor and dour workaholic who made sure that they all had a pretty boring time. Karoi was quite well established by then, with a Club and Hotel in use, but Gilmour was very strict about transport, so the men seldom got a chance to visit the Club.

The Miami police area included a large chunk of the Zambezi Valley including the future site of Lake Kariba. Bob made a couple of visits on duty and was shown the site of a landslide. He had a horse at Miami that wasn't good for much, as the Zambezi Valley was a tsetse-fly area where one could not take a horse.

He used to ride out occasionally in the early morning without much enthusiasm, as the horse fought every step of the way the further he got from the police camp. Sure enough, it wasn't long before an African constable was given the incredible task of walking the horse back to Salisbury, 200 kilometres away.

The police were required to contact HQ in Salisbury once a day, which they did with the aid of the furiously peddling prisoners on bikes. A fellow constable was 'Yank' Mercer, a genuine American, who probably saved his sanity. The District Commissioner at the time was Woods.

Bob's conviction for shooting an impala for the pot without a licence (though that's not the full story, which is told in his own autobiography), is one that illustrates just how naive he was at the time. In hindsight, his punishment turned out to be the kindest yet foisted on an unwitting criminal – a transfer to Beatrice, which, in comparison, was so much more civilized and afforded him an opportunity to play rugby as well.

Another incident that Bob remembers was when, after days of tremendous rains, a landslide occurred that embedded a makeshift camp in a sea of mud, killing several surveyors while they slept. He was sent to investigate, and the scene was eerie as he surveyed the aftermath. A bed-knob sticking out of the rubble brought the tragedy home to him as nothing else could.

Bob went on to become Senior Assistant Commissioner-in-Charge of the CID for the whole country. He retired in 1982.

An interesting situation arose during World War II, when the Miami community was asked to make contingency plans in the event of a possible invasion by Germany. In hindsight this might seem ludicrous – but the Germans weren't, after all, so far north of Rhodesia's borders, and a general scheme was put into place for the mobilisation of all Europeans in the defence of Miami.

Nameplates were removed from bridges and rivers, and a rallying point was decided on at Buffalo Downs. Instructions were sent to every resident telling them who would fetch them if such an event was to happen, and which vehicle would take them to a rendezvous.

A list of able-bodied males was drawn up from within the district: eight members of the Rifle Platoon (from World War I); four BSA Police, two from Miami and one each from Chirundu and Makuti; twenty-three other able-bodied males made up from local residents, fourteen of whom were members of the Roads department, employed on the Zambezi main road; nine women, five children, one Indian, and thirteen natives who were able-bodied, disciplined and armed.

A list of vehicles stated that Lieutenant B.G. Hassell, the Native Commissioner, owned a Ford V8; Whitby, a Ford V8 lorry, Bill Leask, a Hudson Terraplane, and so on. Eleven in all could be called upon if necessary.

From these lists we note that Messrs van Rensberg and Potgieter worked at Grand Parade farm, that Mr Hartman lived at Vuti, and that the missionaries from Magunje were as much part of the community as any of the others. Major and Mrs Walton, who were Canadians, were the Salvation Army missionaries at Magunje at the time – a lovely couple, it is said, who were transferred to Salisbury to open the Red Shield Hut, which served sumptuous breakfasts to the many young servicemen, especially airmen, who were training in the country during World War II.

By 1939 Grand Parade mine had changed hands yet again, having been bought by a gentleman called Gavin Paterson, whose introduction to Miami came about when he was asked to build a house for the Native Commissioner and a new Police Station, which doubled up as a Post Office.

Gavin was born in Glasgow, Scotland, and

brought up strictly in the 1890s as a member of the Plymouth Brethren. After school he became a cabinet-maker by trade, and then decided to seek his fortune by following the gold rush to America, but once he had observed how badly the immigrants entering the New World via Ellis Island were being treated by the officials, he immediately changed his mind.

Angry and disillusioned, he impetuously boarded the first ship out of American waters, totally ignorant of its destination, only to learn once he was safely on his way that he was bound for South Africa.

On arriving there, he listened to the talk around him and decided that the diamond diggings in Kimberley were as good a place as any to head for. Losing no time, he made his way up to those dry and dusty parts and noticed that, while all around him were digging for diamonds, the real need in the area was for water. Gavin Paterson became rich not by digging for diamonds but by becoming a 'water-carrier'.

Once his fortune was made, he bought a row of terraced houses in Scotland into which he installed his many relatives. The balance of his money he deposited safely in the bank, or so he thought: Wall Street tottered and crashed and many lost their livelihoods and entire savings. Nevertheless, Gavin was luckier than most, for he still had some investment in bricks and mortar.

After the Anglo-Boer War ended, Gavin returned to Kimberley, this time to discover that De Beers had 'tied up' all the diamonds, which put an end to any thought of enrichment by those means. However, he consoled himself with a new interest in the form of Joan Ball, whom he had met aboard ship. She was emigrating from Australia to South Africa with her family, and it was her father who started the tyre company Advanx. Janet Wiggins, grand-daughter of the founder, tells the story of how the name Advanx came about.

> It was supposed to be called the 'Advance Tyre Company'. However, the sign-writer got it wrong, and when this fact was pointed out, he realised he'd run out of space for the last two letters. Someone suggested that Mr Ball should write his initials, but Mr Ball was illiterate so he said, 'Write an X; that's how I usually sign my name.'

Joan duly married Gavin and, in the words of Cecil John Rhodes, they went North.

They raised three sons, Jim, Guy and Robert, all of whom joined them in the family business. Before moving to Miami, Gavin had made a living as a cabinet-maker in Salisbury, after which he was given a contract for house-building in Milton Park. As a carpenter, he was particularly in demand in the rebuilding of the Hudson Terraplane, which was flimsy and shattered easily.

Gavin liked the bush and bid for Grand Parade mine when it came up for sale. Thus the family moved en masse to the Urungwe in 1939. Jim had already opened up Camel mine, and was growing crops there. Robert had familiarised himself with the area, having done much prospecting previously.

Their move to Miami coincided with the start of World War II, and many men yearned to join up, but Robert had to exercise patience before he could contribute because of the importance of mica in the war effort. By now, the mica mine had reached a record output, with 50 per cent of that production coming from Grand Parade. Eventually he was released to join up in 1944.

Earlier, the government had sent Robert Paterson three Italian POWs (prisoners of war) to work on the mine. One of these was Giuseppi Tome. 'Tommy', as we knew him, was repatriated after the war and returned to live in Karoi, where he lived until he died many years later. After the war Tommy bought an old bus that he converted, with help from Ted Milton, into living quarters. It stood on a vacant piece of ground where, in the post-independence era, Charlie Slight started a business, subsequently bought by Ken and Lindy Griffiths.

The Zambezi Valley, almost on the doorstep of Grand Parade, was an ideal playground for the young Paterson brothers, who spent a great deal of time hunting and fishing there. One day, Guy Paterson shot an elephant, which dropped in its tracks. Thinking it was dead he approached too hastily and it reared up, fatally injuring him.

Others who worked at Grand Parade were Neuby Tatham, brother of Jack, and Neuby's son, Glen; the latter later became well known for his work within National Parks. Also at Grand Parade at that time were 'Friar' and Enid Tuck, who ran a store and a dairy.

A firm friend was Norman Stevenson, who owned a boat and later retired to live in Karoi with his daughter, Thea Cochrane. Robert Paterson, Neuby and Norman Stevenson used to spend a lot of free time visiting the Zambezi river, and they claim to be the only ones to have sailed upstream through the gorge. It was quite a feat, as the river was at its most fierce at that point.

Robert Paterson did all the prospecting for the mica using a trench digger, which incurred the wrath of many a local farmer who eventually came to settle there. In defence of the miner, it has to be pointed out that this method was the quickest and easiest way to open up the ground to find deposits. Mica comes in 'bubbles' that lie deep in the substrata, and apparently the correct term for a block of mica is a 'book'.

The mica was sold to the company of F.F.Chrestien, who had a holding ground at Buffalo Downs. The company was the buyer of all the mica extracted from the fields in

Miami. Resident inspectors checked all loads on rail to brokers in London.

One old-timer reported:

> We were important little people in the British Empire in those days and were visited by VIPs from all parts of the world. During the war, mica was a very important commodity.
>
> Our Air Ace, the late Ted Spencer, was once bogged down on the Miami strip and had to make a mad dash through the night over terrible roads by car to Lusaka to deliver mica to a mail plane leaving for London.

By 1958 mica mining was considered to be at its lowest level, and it became clear that the readily accessible mica had gone. Notwithstanding that, delays in payment by world buyers had worsened the situation by causing interest to wane. This would always be a bugbear of Rhodesian producers.

One of the early prospectors was Jack Fynn, who spent an inordinate amount of time roaming the area, criss-crossing the Urungwe in anticipation of riches.

Like countless others, he became a familiar sight during the early twentieth century – one of a breed of men easily recognisable by their habitual attire of the time – khaki trousers and shirts, the ubiquitous wide-brimmed hat, a belt from which hung a knife, a rifle over one shoulder and a bandolier across another. They would set out on their lonely trail, shunning society as they remained absent for weeks at a time.

Many of them were rough, down-and-out itinerants who travelled lightly and foot-slogged for miles, carrying everything they owned on their backs; the more fortunate possessed a mule or a horse. Even their belongings were meagre and basic – perhaps a tent, a pick-axe, a hammer and a shovel, plus some 'vitals'. Whether rich or poor, they

all had one thing in common – the overriding faith that drove them on in the hope that they would eventually find a 'lucky strike'.

Jack Fynn was known to people living in the Urungwe as recently as the 1960s. He was the grandfather of Tamsin Fynn, married to Ian Barker. He was typical of a free-spirited nonconformist. As a young boy he had shown early signs of being wild and unorthodox, happy only when unfettered by the constraints that ruled most of society at the time.

Jack Fynn attended St George's College in Salisbury and was often found hiding out in the wild parts of the Botanical Gardens. He married Hester Ferreira, the ninth child in a family of eleven siblings, when she was nineteen years old.

It was an irregular, disconnected kind of marriage, punctured with long breaks, that held together long enough to produce four sons, after which Hester returned to her father in Inyazura (Nyazura). She found work in Umtali (Mutare), where her boys went to school.

Before this, however, they had lived on various mines, including Shamrock, which Jack Fynn discovered. The family say that he never lost that 'let me out of here' look, an expression that was as conspicuous as it was desperate. One of his 'disappearing acts' took him to the Congo as a mercenary; at other times he would merely trek off somewhere to be alone.

Tamsin's mother, Sarah, married Kerry, the eldest of Jack's sons. He visited his father periodically in the Zambezi Valley, where Jack wandered for many years. On the whole, Jack had very little to do with his boys. However, at the start of the bush war, Jack and Kerry were involved with the forces, tracking as civilians for the SAS.

Rob Truscott, who befriended Jack in Karoi

during the years between 1967 and 1969, had this to say:

Jack Fynn was first introduced to me by Jannie Grobbelaar, who farmed at Manyangau on the edge of the Vuti block and the Zambezi escarpment. At that time I was farming close by at Myrlen, which I was leasing from Len Lundersted. I was 29 years of age and a family man. I don't know how Jannie and Jack became acquainted, but it's most likely that it would have been in one of the pubs in Karoi.

Although Jack did not take any alcohol when he stayed with us, I had the feeling he was 'drying out' from a previous era, which probably resulted in the estrangement of his wife and boys.

Even at a later date, his sons, when I met up with them, appeared to be uninterested in my association with their father. I did not meet Kerry Fynn, Tamsin's Dad, who I think was a helicopter pilot.

One day Jannie came over to explain that he was 'grubstaking' Jack, and suggested that I join him to split the cost in the expectation of reaping some of the rewards that Jack's prospecting ability might have turned up. Hopefully a bonanza!

For them, the advantage was that I owned a Mark II, short-wheelbase Land-Rover that I had bought from a policeman three years previously for £100. It never gave trouble and could negotiate just about any terrain, no matter how rough. Jannie and I also agreed to split the fuel bill.

Jack showed us the route from the base of Mount Manyangau down to the Escarpment, through the 'flygate' and on towards the headwaters of the Chitake river until we reached the Valley bed. It was a quick and accessible route and at times the track would disappear completely. Jack, however, was always able to get us back on to the correct ridge. Similarly, he showed us a way down to the Nyaodza valley though the Matsiga river. He really did know the Valley like the back of his hand.

Long before my association with him, and doubtless for some considerable period of time shortly after World War II, he had been prospecting within this area. He had done a lot of hunting as well. He had two Shangaan trackers armed with Martini-Henry rifles. They were very wise in bush lore and its animals.

Jack hunted for ivory in the Valley at a time when hunting was allowed. It was only later that controls were instigated. Years earlier, Jack had been an RSM in the Cape Corps, a unit made up of Cape Coloured servicemen, who then served in North Africa and Italy.

During this time the Dande people were still 'in situ' in the Zambezi Valley around the Chitake and Rukomechi rivers. He knew the chief and various headmen as well as the *n'angas* and spirit mediums. At the point when Jannie and I were ready to venture into the Valley with Jack, the Dande people had all been removed to the Mzarabani area at the eastern end, and likewise the two-toed tribe of the Chewore, who were equally well known to him.

Jack's two trackers were co-opted into the army to impart their knowledge of picking up spoor and imprints, but they were loath to give up their Martini-Henry rifles for the modern SLRs. The Shangaans used the same bush skill that they would use if they were surprised by elephants – clapping their hands, which usually made them give way.

Once, when walking though the bush looking for a copper claim he had pegged and allowed to lapse years earlier, Jack advised me to carry a stone a little larger than a golf ball to throw at rhino should we inadvertently run into them. Again it was advice passed on to him by his Shangaan companions. Rhinos abounded in the Chewore area at the time.

Jack also showed me evidence of an impala nursery, where a lone female will remain with several juveniles while the herd forages farther afield.

When walking in the bush, cross-grained across the Escarpment, Jack would urge: 'Do what the elephant do – walk on the contour.'

On occasions there were areas we could not negotiate with the Land-Rover and we had to carry our provisions for days up and down the steep stratum.

'Let's get going and do the loafing on the other side,' was Jack's wise suggestion. He must have been in his late fifties at the time, but his life of hard living had made him very fit and tough.

Sometimes he had to lodge with us on his return from the Valley, and it was during this time that Jack would relate animal stories to our three-year-old son,

enthralling him with hand signals used by the Bushmen to indicate the various types of wildlife. They are stories that my son, now forty-two years old, can still remember.

Jack was reticent about his hunting days but adamant that Clem Coetzee's claims that he had hidden ivory were unfounded. 'We never made a penny out of our prospecting sidelines,' he said.

Jack's claims were taken over by JCI but never mined. We found molybdenum at the top of the Escarpment, but prospecting ventures, even after serious surveys, were not taken up.

Speaking for myself, I felt enriched by all the adventure and all I had learned, and feel nostalgic for those days now, wishing I could have them back. They were free and easy and we were unafraid, even though the first of the insurgents of the coming liberation war had started to cross the Zambezi.

I lost contact with Jack Fynn at the end of 1969 when my lease had expired, forcing me to move on. The bush war was escalating furiously and the Valley was disturbed by military activity. Jannie Grobbelaar also left for Manicaland. Prospecting had become a dangerous occupation.

The last I heard was that Jack has succumbed to alcohol once more, but I have no verification of this.

There are several lonely graves dotted around Lomagundi. Many of them have been rendered inconspicuous and invisible over the passing decades, crude wooden crosses that once marked the last resting places of visiting travellers struck down by fever, or fatal meetings with men or wild beasts.

The harsh elements, too, have played their part in the final deed of obliteration, not to mention the myriad armies of busy white ants/termites that infest the bush, reducing everything in their path to dust and insignificance. Raised mounds have been trampled flat by animals and human feet over time, and more recently machinery has finished off the job as the land becomes another road or piece of virgin soil.

However, there is one cairn of stone at a spot close to the road between Buffalo Downs and Nyamanda farm, Karoi, built to commemorate the life of W.E.E. Scott.

Scott was born on 17 December 1873 and became a Native Commissioner in Lomagundi. He was killed by a buffalo while on duty on 17 September 1909. The cairn was erected by his friends and brother officers of the Native Department as a token of their esteem and affection for a faithful servant of the government, and a good man.

Among some volunteer sapling gum trees and tall elephant grasses, hidden now from view, is the once official Miami Cemetery. There are twelve noticeable graves, two with headstones now broken and semi-dismantled. A name, barely decipherable, etched on one stone is, tragically, in remembrance of a child, Gray Birch, who was born in 1922 and died in 1924, probably of malaria. The second, even less decipherable, is etched in Afrikaans and gives the date of birth as 1892 and the date of death as 1934. I think the name could be Snyder.

The Miami Pioneer Cemetery as it looked in 2007. L to R: Helen Winwood, Tawny Stidolph, John Winwood, Ian Gibson.

3. The Pioneer Farmers

Until around 1915, men had shown little interest in farming to the west of Miami, knowing it to be dangerously unhealthy because of the tsetse fly and mosquito. It would be an intrepid and courageous man who gave any thought at all to an agricultural career in a place of virtual self-destruction, where so many before had met their deaths from blackwater fever and sleeping sickness.

Nevertheless, there were such men. Some had survived the terrible ordeal of the Great War: they had overcome the horrors of the trenches, the discomfort of ankle-deep mud, where rats and lice took sanctuary on equal terms with humankind, deep below the surface; where, among the unhealthy detritus of daily existence, men itched and scratched and suffered putrid, running sores, and where the stink of rotting flesh and the smell of death constantly assaulted their nostrils.

Life expectancy at the front was measured in minutes and hours rather than in days and weeks. The foot soldiers were mere cannon fodder, used for the sake of expediency. The survivors probably felt pretty invincible, as well as immortal, so the peaceful and remote wilderness of central Africa beckoned temptingly.

There, away from the reminders of man's inhumanity to man, a tormented spirit might recover and find a panacea for all the ills of the world. Ironically, though, the Angel of Death, ever lustful, still loitered: millions more were to die in the safety of their beds, struck down by the flu pandemic of 1918.

One could perhaps understand the casual and stoical attitude to death and danger that was so lightly accepted by the early settlers, who were not easily deterred from their chosen path.

The first landowner in the Urungwe was William Harvey Brown, an American by birth, known also as 'Curio' Brown owing to his inquisitive nature as a botanist and zoologist.

Before coming to Rhodesia, he had been working in Freetown, Sierra Leone, on a research project, but had stepped into the breach after the leader of a team heading for the country fell ill. Cecil Rhodes gave him 24,000 acres of land for services he rendered in the collecting of flora and fauna of the country in 1892.

After spending some time on his research, he chose a large stretch of land in Miami that came to be known as Nassau. He acknowledged it 'as being the best piece of land I had come across in all my wanderings'. Nassau stretches for twelve miles along the present main road north of Karoi. Harvey Brown was also granted a farm south of Salisbury, which he subsequently named Kentucky, and this is the land on which the airport stands today. He was later to become one of Salisbury's mayors, and a street is named after him in the suburb of Milton Park in the capital.

Over subsequent years Curio Brown made a thorough study of every aspect of the country, including African law and customs, covering all the ethnic groups.

In his book, *On the South African Frontier*, written in 1899, he noted that gold was erratic in its occurrence and much of it low grade, but that there was coal and iron in abundance. He concluded that Rhodesia would be first and foremost a great mining country.

He also predicted that, in order to feed its people, it must be developed as an agricultural country and that it would eventually

Pioneers, 1905. William Harvey Brown is third from the right in the front row.

manufacture everything that can be made from its natural products.

Exactly when Harvey Brown took up residence in the Urungwe cannot be ascertained, but the land was certainly granted to him in the last years of the 1890s. He had hardly taken occupancy when he fell prey to the dreaded blackwater fever and died. He bequeathed his estate to his brother, who then took up residence himself, but he, too, died before long.

After Harvey Brown had died, his brother sold half of Nassau to a gentleman by the name of Robert Andrew Leask, who, having seen the land advertised, had arrived in Karoi in 1916.

Robert Leask was from the Orkney Islands, Scotland. He came to look over the land he was thinking of buying, liked what he saw and purchased 12,000 acres of Nassau. He then decided to remain. This piece of land he registered as Coldomo, after the home farm on the Orkneys.

For generations, the Leasks had been sea-faring men of the clipper era. Mr Leask senior, Robert's father, had reached great heights in his career as a naval man, which he seems to have neglected, given his rather ignominious death when the boom swung round and hit him. He had two other sons: Harold, who lost his life in the Great War, and William.

In Miami, Robert Leask ran cattle and generally lived the easy-going, carefree life of the early settler, when time mattered little and the veld abounded with game of every description. It was sadly inevitable that Robert Leask would also contract blackwater fever, and he died very shortly after taking up his new property. It seemed to be the lot of those pioneers. Robert Leask was a bachelor, and his estate was bequeathed to his brother William as the next of kin.

At the time of his brother's death, William Leask was in his third year as a prisoner of war in Germany, having been wounded at Mons. He had made two attempts at escaping and on the third succeeded, arriving in Holland a few days after Armistice. Upon hearing of his brother's death, and having the wanderlust of his marine forebears coursing through his veins, Bill Leask decided to travel to Rhodesia out of curiosity, expecting just to wind up his brother's affairs. He ended up staying.

He and his young bride, Mary Johnston Leask, née Drysdale, who had been a secretary in Glasgow before her marriage in 1919, decided upon reaching Sinoia by train that they would travel to Miami by ox-wagon, just for the fun of it – even though, by this time, they could have taken a taxi for the sum of twenty pounds.

The country appealed to the couple so much that Bill decided to give up his work as a marine engineer and settle on Coldomo. There they remained, subsequently producing three daughters to complete their family: Thelma, Maureen, who after the World War II married David Grantham, and Marguerite (Rita), who became Mrs Mills. Maureen remained in Karoi all her life, until her tragic death in 1994, when she was brutally murdered.

The rest of Nassau remained unoccupied until a Mr A.B. Roberts purchased it in 1940. He was an American, brought out to South Africa to teach others how to grow tobacco.

Years earlier, Willie Schultz had bought

William (Bill) Leask is in the middle.

land he called Good Hope in 1923 close to Coldomo, but he found the life a lonely existence and moved to Renfield farm near the Angwa river to be closer to his relatives in Sinoia.

Thus, when the area was opened up to mica mining, a mere handful of farmers occupied land in a bid to raise crops: Robert Leask on Coldomo, Willie Schultz on Good Hope, and Jack Goldberg on Grand Parade.

Other pieces of land occupied at around the same time were Rekomitje (Captain Whitby, the Roads supervisor), Chigangas (G.G. Olivier), and Masterpiece (D.G. Hartman). None of these was ever farmed, so these men must have bought 'on spec' or with the intention of farming them later.

Gradually more and more men became interested in making use of land in the remote areas of the Urungwe. Two brothers by the name of Le Roux settled on a piece of land that they named Karoi after the river close by. Carl Le Roux soon succumbed to malaria and, overcome with fever, urged his brother to dig his grave and send to Sinoia, fifty miles away, for his coffin. After Carl's death in 1928, the farm was abandoned.

Then in 1930 C.P. Robertson won first prize in the lottery, and with the proceeds he bought a farm (Buffalo Downs) on which he grew the first crop of Virginia tobacco in the area. Just before the Second World War, Des Evans, a former policeman, bought land next door to Buffalo Downs which he called Chelvern, and by the end of the 1930s, further interest was being shown in farming.

In general, farming life on the edge of Miami in 1920 was no fun. Mail came from Sinoia by 'runner'. Two 'boys' left Sinoia and were met halfway by two others from Miami. Briefs sent from Coldomo to Miami, which was the closest settlement and general centre of the district, were carried in the traditional way on a cleft stick. When eventually the Road Motor Service (RMS) started operating once a week from Sinoia, a 'boy' walked the fourteen miles to Miami and back again in one day, to collect the post. Bicycles were still an unheard-of luxury. All transport was done by wagon, including the carrying of huge boilers for the mine, which must have broken the back of many a trek ox.

The crops grown were maize, sorghum, groundnuts and sweet potatoes. Tobacco production was still some distance into the future, although it was already being grown south of the Angwa. In one year, maize was selling at five shillings a bag, landed at Sinoia. As this did not cover the cost of transport and the bag, Bill Leask burned his entire crop, which smouldered for weeks.

At the time, the local people in the Zambezi Valley were said to be starving because of crop failure, and although Bill Leask offered the crop to the Native Department, no transport could be organised. The people could have eaten all they could have carried on their heads; it was a walk that was quite often done in those days.

Bill eventually gained a market locally, supplying 'mealie meal' to the local mines, stores, Roads department gangs and the police. He also supplied the bricks to build the Miami police camp. Mary Leask ran poultry and made butter. She also supplied eggs to the Sinoia school and hospital, so that – apart from sugar, tea, flour, soap and salt – they were pretty much self-supporting.

Money was scarce in those early days, but as everyone was in the same position it was easy to 'keep up with the Joneses'. Every gallon of fuel used – when eventually one acquired a vehicle – came from Sinoia in two four-gallon tins packed in a box. These tins and boxes were used for every conceivable

purpose under the sun, and were sorely missed when 44-gallon drums came into being. Tsetse fly had to be coped with, and they could become a serious problem when all transport was ox-drawn and farming operations depended on the 'span'.

Lions took their toll of cattle, too, and for some reason were always more prevalent in December. One year, a pride of three lions killed a fully grown Shona steer and dragged it out over the top of a six-foot high, six-strand wire fence, also reinforced with thorn bush.

In the December of 1934, Bill Leask shot five lions that had killed two beasts and stampeded the herd out of the kraal. It was Christmas Eve and, upon hearing a beast being attacked, he used an old Dietz storm lamp to light his way to the kraal. Having shot two lions he returned to the house for more ammunition, shouting that 'the veld is alive with lions'. Off he went again, and they heard two more shots. Next morning, the four shots had accounted for five lions; one must have been directly behind another.

The five carcasses were loaded on to the back of a lorry and taken to the police camp in Miami to have the 'bandits' skin and bray them. The lone police trooper at the camp – Corporal Betts – having celebrated Christmas a little too forcefully, wondered if he was seeing double when he saw five lions. He took several snapshots, and for a while Peak's Store in Sinoia used two enlargements to advertise their ammunition.

Another year, Bill Leask tied the carcass of a beast killed by a lion to his own leg, and went to sleep at the foot of a tree, knowing that the lion would return but not touch him with all the beef around. That night he shot another lion.

However, he hated shooting anything at all, having great admiration for these creatures, but as the cattle were his livelihood they had to be protected. In those days, when one spoke of 'cattle', it also meant 'trek oxen', the sole means of pulling a plough and hauling. Leopards took over from where the lions left off, causing problems with poultry and calves.

With the construction of the Great North Road through Coldomo farm and the opening of the Otto Beit Bridge at Chirundu in 1939, the old way of life gradually gave way to 'civilisation', much to the sorrow of the Leasks – although it did make a difference having bridges over the rivers between Miami and Sinoia, plus a wide gravel road in place of the two rutted wheel tracks, and must have come as a tremendous relief to many who had to make the trip so often in real bone-shaking vehicles.

Motor vehicles were definitely more rugged at that time. Everyone had to be a 'bush mechanic'. Maureen remembers her Dad splinting a broken axle with poles and 'tambo' cut from the bush, and most engine ailments would be repaired with a piece of wire and some ingenuity. This quality in the early settlers was a necessity, for there were no garages or passing cars to call on for help. When you had a puncture, you didn't just change the wheel – there was probably no spare anyway – you sat down and stuck your own patch on, and in the days of 'split rims' it could be most trying.

There was one incident that Maureen and Rita were never allowed to live down. On their way home from school in the Chev-Tourer with celluloid windows that were only hooked on in rainy weather, they were forced to stop for their third puncture since leaving Sinoia. It happened just as they pulled out of the Miami drift after sundown, and Bill had to make a fire for light.

The girls had been aware of a hyena calling in the distance from the Chedzurgwe

and, doubtless remembering the curse of the witchdoctor, they began to feel nervous. The fire must have attracted the creature, and it prowled right up to the road and could be faintly seen in the moonlight. It gave an almighty howl – and anyone who has heard that eerie, sinister sound can imagine its effect on a pair of young girls.

With one accord, they leaped over the closed door and into the car – landing on the tools, which in those models were kept under the front seat, and were shame-faced to hear their father convulsed with laughter. While he was tightening the wheel nuts, he had been aware only of two pairs of legs disappearing over the side of the car.

Rita said they were always breaking down and often had to walk home, passing close by the Chedzurgwe hill. Because she was the youngest, Bill would carry her on his shoulders, and many were the times they just missed being 'assagaied' as they walked along the road, for anyone confronted by the pair would just see a double-headed apparition walking towards them.

Another great menace of those times were the locust swarms that darkened the skies and completely decimated a maize crop, despite every available human hammering on the good old petrol tins. (The most effective deterrent was spraying the hoppers with poison before sun-up while they were still on the ground.)

The few cars that travelled to Northern Rhodesia by this route had to cross the Zambezi by ferry – a flat-bottomed boat with dug-out canoes lashed to the sides and an outboard motor. There were no guardrails or other refinements.

The owner, Mr Vlahakis, locally called 'Jimmy the Greek', was known to every traveller who crossed the Zambezi on his ferry until he died in 1939. To avoid paying income tax – a penalty which, it seemed, was never likely to afflict him, as he was reported to have twenty-four children and about a hundred dependent grandchildren – he tried living on an island in the middle of the river. Flood waters nearly drowned him and drove him back to the bank.

In 1939 some of the aircraft carrying VIPs and the press to the opening of the bridge at Chirundu deliberately flew low over his stockaded kraal on the river bank, giving awed strangers a bird's-eye view of a distinctive man's home.

To cross the river, one would hail Jimmy from the river bank and then sit and wait as the ferry chugged slowly across, making allowances for the strong currents that kept sweeping it sideways. The local people gathered from all directions to watch the loading performance, and the event made a good topic of conversation for many a week.

The Otto Beit Bridge at Chirundu that spans the Zambezi river is one of the great bridges that the Beit Trustees financed in the development of Rhodesia's road system.

It was not an easy build. By the time it was opened by Lady Lilian Beit, widow of the baronet after whom it is named, in May 1939, 200 whites and 2,000 blacks had sweated in sub-human conditions of heat and torrential rains for three demanding years.

During that time the river rose to previously unrecorded heights, creating difficulties that drove the workers to the top of Chirundu hill for safety. At times the men could only work from 3.00 a.m. to 6.00 a.m. owing to the heat.

Rock foundation conditions differed on either side of the two banks. Steel girders shipped from Scotland were found to be warped after a rough crossing on the Bay of Biscay, and 800 miles of wire was used in manufacturing the suspension cables on the spot. Not one man lost his life, which

is an everlasting tribute to the contractors, Dorman Long.

Rita Leask attended the opening of the bridge. She remembers each of the ladies being given a snippet of the red-white-and-blue ribbon that Lady Beit cut.

Mr Rama senior – father of Shagan, Ambi and Lalloo – was one of the construction workers who were imported from India to work on the bridge. He stayed in the vicinity and began trading, and the Rama family became well-known and successful business people in the Urungwe.

Now and then there would be an occurrence that broke the dullness of farm life for a young girl. Rita remembers an occasion when the family heard something striking the roof of the homestead. They rushed outside and noticed a plane circling above. The pilot had thrown a disk with a written note inside alerting them to the fact that he was running short of fuel. The Coldomo roof was the only sign of habitation that he could see. He subsequently landed and Bill managed to find some aviation fuel for him.

Two years later, in 1941, Bill Leask tragically contracted blackwater fever and died. Mary Leask struggled on for another two years until tragedy struck again, when Thelma also fell ill and died, just before starting her nursing training in Salisbury.

One can only feel admiration for the Leasks and others like them of those times. Life threw all its adversities at them, yet with sheer fortitude and resilience they continued, never giving up. It is a quality that can be seen in all the early settlers.

Maureen married David Grantham, who was given land under the ex-servicemen's settlement scheme and went to live on Shawnigan. Mrs Leask kept Coldomo for a few more years, hoping that Rita would marry a farmer, but she was ambitious and took herself off to East Africa to follow her career, returning to Karoi only as a visitor.

Later, O.C. Rawson bought part of Coldomo and employed John de Lange to manage it for him.

Although Bill Leask and Jack Goldberg had experimented with growing tobacco during the 1930s, it was O.C. Rawson who made greatest inroads with Virginia tobacco – the quality of which led to the interest in, and introduction of that crop in the Karoi area.

In 1940, Allan Brooks ('AB') Roberts, bought the remainder of Nassau, but not without having first to endure the Depression of the 1930s. Prior to this he had been in Rustenburg, and it was there that he met his wife, Margaret Westerveld, a blonde Dutch girl who had emigrated from Holland with her family. AB first cast his eye on her at the local post office where she worked. After a period of courtship they married and made their way to Southern Rhodesia.

The Depression was well on its way and times were hard, as men lost their jobs and couldn't put food on the table for their families. AB was one of the lucky ones. He went to work for a farmer called Hastings in Marandellas.

Pearl McLaughlan (née Roberts), AB's daughter, recalled a period of farming in Rusape, and then a move to the Eastern Districts, where her parents opened a tea room known as the Melsetter Junction Tea Room. Pearl said they all had to 'get stuck in'.

The vacant part of William Harvey Brown's farm, Nassau, was still up for sale in Miami and AB wanted it. With his sights set on eventually buying the place, he started a trucking business, A.B. Roberts Transport, which later helped him to accumulate enough to buy it. Nevertheless he still had to call on his good friend Pat Fallon, the

well-known 'bookie', to put money into the venture with him.

In 1940 the Roberts family moved to Karoi, and with land at last to call their own, along with his knowledge of tobacco growing, AB started to farm.

Pearl's best friend as a youngster was Jocelyn de Beer, the daughter of one of the surveyors, Thomas de Beer, who was at the same school. The two of them would be allowed to tag along as he went about the task of dividing up land for resettlement, sleeping and living in tents and generally mucking about in the outdoors.

Coldomo, minus 3,000 acres, was eventually bought by AB's wife, Margaret, who renamed it Blockley. Thus 19,000 acres of the original 24,000 acres that had belonged to William Harvey Brown was now once more amalgamated into one unit again. It had been one vast tract of land, which for a long time nobody had looked at twice.

The remaining piece of Nassau, still known by that name, was bought in the late 1950s by a Mr Lubbe, who sub-divided it into several sections, and it changed hands over and over again during the next forty years. Names such as Paul Venter, Piet Nieuwoudt, Fritz Paulsen, Peter van Breda, Hugh Royston come to mind, all of whom owned part of Nassau at one time or another.

For many years William Leask and Jack Goldberg had reigned supreme in that vast corner of the Urungwe. The Leasks had paid a heavy price for their love of privacy and freedom – and for the privilege of being anonymous. Change was once again in the air, as ambitious plans for the area were about to unfold.

Miami had begun its sad decline as a centre of mica mining as world demand for the mineral diminished. But it was a slow and gradual process.

Throughout history miners have shown themselves to be breed apart. They are a philosophical lot, used to a transient existence. They understand the need to move on as the minerals they seek diminish in value or lodes peter out. Hardened prospectors continued to roam the Urungwe in their quest to seek a fortune for years to come.

The farmer, on the other hand, puts down roots, becomes one with his land. He is, in many ways, the more patient character, for he knows that success and progress don't happen overnight. He is content to watch and wait for results as he nurtures the soil. He understands that it is not enough just to 'take': he knows he must 'return in good measure' to be assured of gaining anything significant in the long term. The biblical adage that 'whoever sows sparingly will also reap sparingly, and whoever sows generously will also reap generously' holds as good today as it ever did.

Good land husbandry is the farmer's ultimate responsibility.

Desmond Evans, who lived on Chelvern, became a prominent figure in the district during both the Miami and then the Karoi years. His wife, Roz, in particular was known as a remarkable hostess. In the early days, the handful of farmers between Lion's Den and Coldomo were members of the Lomagundi West Farmers' Association, under the chairmanship of Des Evans.

Times were always hard then, and few farmers could afford a conventional holiday, so shooting trips to the Zambezi Valley were a substitute. The Mana Pools area had become a popular playground for local farmers and others. Des Evans and two friends had planned a trip to the Chewore river for three weeks in the 1920s, but as they owed so much money to local storekeepers they thought it polite and propitious to buy their provisions in Salisbury, travelling over the Mtoroshanga pass rather than having to pass the Dardagan store in Banket.

Only a hardy few knew Mana Pools in those days. Des had moved to Karoi from Sipolilo (Guruve), where he had farmed before buying Chelvern. He was never classified as a professional hunter, but he made trips to Mana Pools in 1927, 1928 and 1929, first with two companions and subsequently on his own. He wrote this piece on Mana:

> In 1927 I was lucky enough to get a lift to the top of the escarpment, or it would have been a case of using a bicycle or on flat feet.
>
> The carriers were given a four-day start, and then I was to meet up with them where the road ends on the Escarpment. We carried everything we needed, for there were no stores for replenishing supplies unless we trekked right through to the Zambezi and bought essentials at Feira, run by the African Lakes Corporation.
>
> After scrambling and sliding down the Escarpment, we followed a well-worn path that crossed the Dande and Angwa rivers, ending at Chapoto's kraal on the banks of the Zambezi. What a welcome sight after a long trek of about thirty miles from the Angwa through an area that was almost waterless at certain times of the year.
>
> At Chapoto's we got our canoes and paddlers for the trip up the river, in which the only obstacle was the Mupata Gorge. Even when the river was low it was a battle to get through, and by canoe it meant having to sleep a couple of nights in the gorge; with a boat and a good outboard motor it could have been done within a few hours.
>
> The gorge was not particularly interesting, but I always marvelled at the

number of klipspringers which bounded up what seemed to be the sheer walls of the gorge at an incredible speed. Baboons were in their thousands and naturally there were lots of leopards.

On getting though Mupata Gorge you strike the Chewore river, dry for most of the year, and with the country being very flat I preferred to walk rather than sit uncomfortably in a dug-out canoe.

After leaving the Chewore, the first pools to be found were known to the Africans as Mtawatawa, similar to the Mana Pools, which were about a day's trek away. All the pools were flooded by the Zambezi every year. When the waters receded, much sedimentation took place, and after the annual fires had swept through the area, the new green grass grew rapidly in this beautiful soil.

Game was everywhere. When I did my last trip to the pools in 1960 it was clear that elephant and buffalo had greatly increased in numbers, although rhino, of which I had once counted no fewer than twenty-seven in a morning, seemed to have dropped off. They had probably retired to the foothills to avoid being disturbed.

You were hardly out of sight of bushbuck in the early days, but their numbers have also dropped. Sometimes the elephant were so numerous we had to sleep on an island in the river.

Between Mtawatawa and Mana we once found a herd of more than 500 buffalo. With this great increase in numbers of the larger species, the veld was being 'bashed about', and the reed beds of the Zambezi are nowhere as big as they were thirty years before.

4. Preparing the Land

The team responsible, hunched up and visibly weary, sat around the table at the Ministry of Agriculture, the air pungent with the aromatic haze of hours of cigarette smoking. Their deliberations had just reached a conclusion.

For many months the men had debated back and forth in an effort to justify a decision to open up an area within the Urungwe to returning soldiers. These plans for Karoi, which was not even a name on the map as yet, was very nearly still-born (wrote Ben Fletcher in 1976), yet very few people realise it today. It was a scheme designed to bring about 'an explosion of tobacco' on to the world market.

The green light having been given, the Hon. Sir Patrick (Ben) Fletcher, Southern Rhodesia's minister responsible for land settlement, swiftly bought the meeting to a decisive close, his inner apprehension hidden, for he still wasn't convinced that the resettlement scheme should be allowed to go ahead. He would have to speak to the Prime Minister once more to allay his fears.

A world war had just come to an end, and there were austerity measures in place as each country started to rebuild. Shortages were felt everywhere. Ben Fletcher suddenly felt weighed down with the responsibility of it all, but having been given the go-ahead, it was now left in his hands to see that the scheme got off the ground. Burdened with doubts, he took his predicament to the Prime Minister, Sir Godfrey Huggins, and together they debated the issues once more.

Absolutely everything seemed to advise against the scheme. Within the Ministry of Agriculture, maize was selling at 13/6 a bag; Rhodesian best beef was 47/– per 100 lb (cold dressed weight), rising to 51/6 in the off season; common sense argued that no one was going to gamble on growing tobacco.

The outlook for that crop didn't seem rosy, for South Africa had warned the Rhodesians of its intention of withdrawing the Union's quota. The United States had enormous stocks still on hand, and the UK was hopelessly involved with the American dollar, added to which Miami was 150 miles from the Salisbury markets along strip roads.

To cap it all, there was an alarming report of tsetse fly encroachment. Although they had taken drastic steps with native cattle to prevent an invasion, the fly was a rather frightening phenomenon, for, apart from its menace to livestock, it had caused several cases of sleeping sickness in the valley. In 1912, following about forty deaths, 300–400 Africans had had to be relocated from the Kamamgwe area.

So it was no wonder that Ben Fletcher was apprehensive and reluctant to try and settle ex-servicemen, who, along with their new young brides drawn from all four corners of the globe, were to be enticed into an undeveloped and unhealthy environment.

There had been no need to emphasise that the British government had its own problems to sort out with the United States. It wouldn't want to be bothered with fighting multimillion-dollar tobacco tycoons who would surely bring pressure to bear on the UK industry on Rhodesia's behalf.

Rhodesia's UK grades were obviously going to be faced with drastic cuts anyway. And all this was at a time when the settlement scheme was designed to 'explode' the production of tobacco for a worldwide market.

However, Sir Godfrey Huggins backed him. Together they had proposed, firstly, to declare a shooting war on the tsetse fly, and secondly, to gamble on tobacco:

> Ben, go and see Smuts about the Union quotas but the UK is a very different problem. However, we shall hammer away at them. Our young chaps are tough and can take it, but whatever happens we will have to keep them going.
>
> The wives are a different kettle of fish. Those from the cities of Europe will have a hell of a time, so make sure you have a Government Medical Officer out there from the beginning.

In 1945 Rhodesia was still a poor man's country, with very little money in circulation and little to spend it on. But there was plenty of land, and professional surveyors were required to ply their skills before settlers could move on to farms.

Alex Fry was one of a number of surveyors with the firm Maasdorp and Piers, who completed the surveying of land in Karoi after World War II ended. He wrote:

> One of the interesting facts, which applied to the land in Rhodesia, was Rhodes's foresight in regard to the opening up of a survey office immediately after the arrival of the Pioneers in the country. Professional land surveying began soon after, with the surveyors following the taking up of land and putting into place beacons in order to register for land title.[1]

These surveyors did a magnificent job in carrying out their work without modern transport as they walked great distances with teams of assistants who carried their equipment and food supplies on their heads. They also carried a number of farm instructions with them in a trunk and simply moved from one farm to the next.

The scheme for ex-servicemen in Karoi required a massive amount of survey work, which started in 1943 with several different surveyors working around the area. Maasdorp and Piers had been the first service providers to the government, followed by Vernon Mills in the early 1940s and Alex Fry after the war.

Land Settlement Board executives Les Hill and Fred Jameson had charged Frank Cilliers with cutting up the land around the area close to the Chikangwe Halt in the Miami area. The first five farms were completed in 1945 and taken up by their occupants in 1946. These first farms were deliberately well spread out in all directions in order to establish someone in each area or block. It worked like this:

One made an application, went before a committee, and was either approved or turned down. If successful, one received a choice of two or three pieces of land. Mr Tindale was the government representative, and he lived in a rondavel around which the settlement was later to develop. Mr Landman took the successful applicants around to make their choice, after which the government found and drilled for water. Farms were not taken up until water was found.

Then one was left to get on with it alone, though a strict eye was kept on all the new settlers. An added requirement from each applicant was that if they had had no experience of farming they would have to work on an established farm for at least two years as a form of apprenticeship.

When the war ended Alex Fry was charged with completing the task of surveying in Karoi:

---

[1] Alex Fry's words come from an early draft of his book, *How I Won the War: Personal Accounts of World War II* (Durban: Just Done Productions, 2007).

I was faced with the huge problem of cutting my way through the bush. I took on a section of twenty-two farms, while Pat Green, one of my partners, tackled an equal number further north.

In view of the heavy bush and the low, rolling hills, I decided to traverse down the proposed boundaries, many of which were rivers, and these had to be surveyed by following the banks – or in the river bed where possible, preferably when they were dry.

I met a young doctor who had qualified at Cape Town university, and he persuaded me to stop taking malaria prophylactics in the belief that, if I did catch malaria, he would be able to diagnose it with certainty. (Many doctors today still advise this.) I foolishly accepted his advice, to my cost.

On my way up to Karoi I had spent a night with friends in Mangula and soon realised that I wasn't going to have much sleep with the 'mozzies' running riot around me and having the feast of their lives, and with no net to protect me. Ten days later, when camping on Peter Gibson's farm Nyangoma, the dreaded disease took hold of me.

Pat Gibson took me to the doctor, who confirmed my ailment. Pat, being a nursing sister, was able to give me the quinine injections and nurse me back to health.

I met many farmers in the district, one being Doug Fox, who owned a beautiful black Labrador that never left his side. I was also rapidly becoming knowledgeable about the important aspects of tobacco production, especially about the curing of it, in those tall barns that had begun to dot the skyline.

Occasionally I would be asked to watch over the curing while the farmers were in town. This entailed examining temperatures on the thermometers hanging just inside the doors and I would call on the men to stoke the furnaces.

I loved the smell of curing tobacco, especially when the green leaves were hanging from the *matepes* in tiers that reached the roof. I found the tobacco industry very interesting and admired those who were leaders in their field.

A close friend, Blair Ewing, had this to say in his book entitled *The Charmed Life*:

'Without doubt, growing tobacco is one of the most challenging and difficult forms of agriculture, because there are so many decisions needed; each one requires a skill and judgement. And if only one or two of those are wrong then you have a disaster instead of a success story.

'Flue-cured tobacco, you see, is not just an agricultural crop; there are very substantial elements of manufacturing involved before you sell the leaf, which comes after processing it, grading it and packing it in a factory-type situation.

'Curing the leaf is a skilled and exhaustive activity because it involves the grower in checking each barn at least twice a night, and in so doing he has to make a decision whether to increase or decrease temperatures, or to reduce humidity or ventilation.'

One night, I returned to camp, and as I put my head to the pillow I heard the pounding of hooves so loud that it could have been thunder. I pulled my blanket over my head until the sound faded away.

Next morning I examined the spoor and discovered that a large herd of sable antelope had stampeded past my tent and in so doing had trodden in places between the guy ropes. The herd had been grazing along a stream and had been frightened by bush fires. Wild animals, though, never caused me any concern.

Very often the surveyors themselves named the farms that they mapped out. Sometimes these pieces of land were renamed by the new settler out of personal sentiment, but in most cases the names stuck. Alex himself named two or three farms for various interesting reasons.

The Fry family had its roots in Cape Town, but Grandfather Fry had been adventurous enough to travel up to Rhodesia with the Pioneer Column in 1890 and was given the right to a farm of 3,000 acres, which he never took up. In 1896 he sold it to the Meikle family for seventy-five pounds, a goodly sum in those days.

The Fry family were also rugby lovers to the point of obsession. Alex and his brothers all played whenever they were free to do so. At the time that Alex was surveying the open spaces of Karoi south, two of his brothers were selected to play in a Springbok side about to face a visiting touring team from abroad. This was in the early 1950s.

The 'Boks' played two tests and won both games, having had two Fry brothers playing for them. Alex was so elated by those wins that he consequently named the farm he was surveying in their honour. This was Springbok Heights subsequently settled on by a Mr Pretorius.

Another farm he christened was Janetville, named after his girlfriend, who eventually became his wife. Janetville later became incorporated with Nascot, also named by Alex, where Charles and Sue Stewart settled.

The completion of much of the first land surveys opened the way for occupancy, which came under the supervision of the Department of Irrigation, in 1943. The supervisors then were Messrs Odendaal, Blanckenberg and Browne, and the task ahead was as vast an undertaking as it had been for the surveyors; and it was virtually impossible to please everyone concerned.

Water, of course, was paramount, for without it nothing could get off the ground. Government was committed to furnishing an assured water supply on each farm, and, if the survey did not find subterranean water supplies on certain farms, there also had to be an investigation into the possibility of setting down a storage scheme.

On each blueprint, divisions had been made up so that surface water could be found on each individual holding, and where there was no prospect of a borehole water supply being developed successfully, alternative means had to be sought.

So began the drilling of numerous boreholes, which, of course, in many cases, dictated where future homesteads would be built. Many a future visitor must have wondered why a farmhouse was situated on the least attractive area of a farm. That was the reason: all development – be it a homestead, barn, shed or compound – had to have a reliable water supply close at hand.

The Land Settlement Board agreed that it was highly desirable that a complete programme of protection for each farm should be drawn up and committed to paper so that all works and the subsequent opening up of new land would fall within the general scheme of things, and to ensure that all long-term plans were adhered to.

Early into the scheme, representatives of the Rhodesian National Farmers' Union (RNFU) had written to say that they considered that the Department of Water was oblivious to many of the major problems confronting the settlers in Karoi, who were not being given adequate attention. Reacting to this criticism, Mr J.M. Caldicott and the Hon. John Parker, in charge of Land Settlement, went to investigate, accompanied by Captain James.

They reported that they had spoken to a considerable proportion of settlers on their farms, had observed and been impressed by what had already been accomplished, and noted also that the labour situation was better than they had anticipated. It later emerged that this was not quite the true picture and that labour was short. It may have been adequate for a small beginning, but, as time went on and farms developed with larger crops going into the ground, the shortage of labour became an enormous problem. Conversely, in general the first settlers spoke appreciatively of the Land Settlement Board and its officials.

However, some matters did need attention. Water supplies were inadequate – and in one case unhealthy, as one young lad had gone down with typhoid. Roads were good but had been built without drainage, which made them troublesome in the rainy season.

A sort of co-operative ploughing scheme was put into place so that those without adequate machinery or oxen to plough with could have lands prepared for them. This perk was paid for by the farmer and docked from his loan account. A letter in the National Archives mentions that W. Soames and E.R. Thomson had used up their current loans and so had to pay fifteen pounds from their own pockets.

As already stated, it was impossible to please everyone, and many people had different ideas of what they were entitled to. Some of the correspondence illustrates the differences. For instance, the area around the Mani/Mlichi was considered to be wet, so the government was not prepared to provide free boreholes.

Hugh Ormerod wrote to the Land Settlement Board:

> Mlichi is now a mere trickle. A supply of domestic water is extremely difficult and I am not able to find a suitable seedbed site as nearly all the land on Mlichi is old 'kaffir land'.
>
> Regarding dips, the nearest is nine miles away, on Mr Robertson's farm, Buffalo Downs, which entails a two-day trek, and with labour in short supply it is out of the question.

To which the Department commented:

> There is little or no substance in Mr Ormerod's letter. His complaints about water are purely frivolous.
>
> Mr de Beer, our senior inspector, went over the adjoining land a week ago, during which time he examined the Mlichi river very closely and he is satisfied not only from this inspection but from previous knowledge that this stream is perennial.
>
> The settlers on this block should therefore make their own arrangements for the development of luxury supplies of water, and then only if their own funds permit.

However, a further report noted that 'Mr Ormerod was a married man, whose wife appeared to be an excellent type. She would go a long way in helping him to become established.' Another comment stated that, on Mlichi, the tree stumping was more satisfactory because the trees were healthier.

More correspondence to the Director of Irrigation, Mr J.E. White, stated that visits to Messrs Oosthuizen, Moore and Fischer in 1946, and to Mr Glover on K20, Musuku, by Major Palmer, reported that the Glovers were not the stereotype but older. Mrs Glover was anxious to do poultry on a large scale.

Mr Syd Jenkinson, after another visit, had

been reported to have had his fair share of veld fires and was contemplating marriage; he was cheerful and gave the general impression that he would succeed.

Of Mr Thomson, on Nyarenda, the general impression given was that he was not a good organiser. Mr Heywood, a Land Inspector who had visited him with Major Palmer, looked at the stumping carried out by bulldozer: it had not been well done, nor had the land been properly cleared. The stumping had broken trees off at the roots so that there was considerable work still to be done in removing them.

Dan and Bessie Oosthuizen were well pleased with their farm and had been fortunate enough to purchase a span of oxen; at that date they had stumped out forty acres. Mr Oosthuizen planned to grow twenty acres of Turkish and thirty acres of Virginia.

Sonny Shakespeare, who had recently arrived, was down in the dumps as his wife had refused to join him on the farm, but his labour position was adequate – thirty in all. Potgieter, Clift and Lund complained about heavy transport costs and the absence of a Government Medical Officer.

So, from these snippets of correspondence, we get an inkling of the problems that arose and how differently each settler reacted to them as the area was opened up. A close paternal eye was kept on everyone. Settlers had to be seen to be diligent, progressive and ready to meet their challenges half way.

The new residents at the Chikangwe Halt settlement were supplied with water from two good boreholes found in the vicinity of Tindale's Hill, opposite New Forest Farm where Robert Harry Townsend lived in two mud huts.

Harry's official title was Resident Supervisor for the Irrigation Department. He had been persuaded out of retirement to super-

vise the water supply between Lion's Den and Chirundu, being responsible for the maintenance of pumps and boreholes that would ensure that all the residents were supplied with water at all times.

Harry's son, Andy, with the same qualification from the department, took over the job in 1957.

Several companies drilled boreholes – one being the firm Bennett and Webb, who drilled boreholes on several farms in the district, including one for Mary and Dennis England on Mshalla farm in 1947.

Natalie Stotter (née Bennett) must have shaken her head in wonder when she looked back on how her life had turned out: years later, she married Donovan, the nephew of Mary England, and subsequently became the mistress of Mshalla, where the borehole put down by her father eventually enabled her to create a beautiful garden, winning her many awards.

There were three Bennett brothers: Johnny, Geoff and George. All three farmed in Karoi at one time. Ironically, Johnny Bennett, once a staunch RF supporter, was the father of Natalie, Cynthia (Pybus) and, more significantly, Roy Bennett, the well-known farmer turned MDC politician.

Jack Sealy was the first to open an engineering business in Karoi. It was called Modern Engineering, but, said Hazel Townsend, the Sealy workshop was limited. This led Andy to open up in opposition, and despite difficult times over the next decades Karoi Engineering survived. From its inception they specialised in borehole maintenance and repairs.

In this, they were assisted by an endearing little man called Tom Wilson, a long-standing family friend, who one day pitched up on their doorstep in need of comfort, and never left. Tom became a familiar sight on farms as he worked on these lifelines. He was an avid reader who was constantly at pains to improve his knowledge. Being a follower of Mrs Malaprop, his vocabulary could be a little peculiar: he spoke of sculpture instead of culprit or of subscription instead of prescription!

Over the years, Andy's wife, Hazel, has kept books for storekeepers such as Kostelac and Downey, Maureen and David Grantham and Brian Rhodes, all of whom had trading businesses in the village at one time.

Whitehead and Jack, another reputable firm, set up shop in the industrial sites as specialists in borehole drilling.

5. Making a Town

In 1947, true to his word, Sir Godfrey Huggins made sure that a Government Medical Officer (GMO) was appointed and installed in Miami, and he visited the area on a regular basis to keep an eye on the fledgling community.

'Pat was not the first doctor to take up residence at the Chikangwe Halt as was generally thought', said Edna Taylor, the wife of the new GMO, Dr Philip Anthony Taylor, known from his initials as Pat.

Peter and Muriel Henson were there first, but not for long, and it was through them that we heard of this place, a job advertised as being in Miami.

The main centre then was Miami. That's where the Magistrate was, the Police, the main African Clinic and the Native Department.

Each piece of land was given a number preceded by a K. K15 was set down as the area for the proposed African Township, although the name Karoi had not been thought of at that stage.

To start with, pieces of land were taken up around the area known as Chikangwe, which was no more than a halt for the railway lorry. There, the RMS off-loaded provisions ordered by phone and sent from Sinoia fifty miles away for the handful of farmers in the area as well as the mining community.

There was nothing but an ordinary turn-off from the main, very bumpy, gravel road of the time, just two houses 100 yards apart, one for the Doctor the other for the Government Representative, who was Mr Tindale. We were the whole of Karoi – just the two families; there was nothing else.

Our house was built about fifty yards from the turn-off to the right and the Tindales were further down on the left. They were a remarkable family – a united family and very good neighbours.

Our house consisted of two rondavels, joined together by a veranda at the front and a kitchen and bathroom at the back. Adjacent to that, a few yards away, was a rectangular building of Kimberley brick, properly roofed, and between these two was another room which served as a surgery. [These two buildings were in the vicinity of where the 'tip' is now – opposite the present-day high school.]

African surgery hours were officially at set times in both morning and evening, but in reality these hours were ignored and a steady stream continued all day and night.

Naturally we had no electricity, so we used pressure lamps, candles and sometimes torches. Water came to us in a cart, filled from a borehole close by for the cold-water tank, which served the bathroom, kitchen and a 'pull and push' loo. A bathroom was quite a luxury in those days, and there was a hot-water tank with a fire underneath – the legendary 'Rhodesian boiler'. However, we were allowed only five inches of water to bathe in.

Borehole water delivered by ox-cart.

Rhodesian boiler filled by buckets.

The road from Salisbury was reasonable up to Sinoia, but thereafter … forty-odd miles of strip road, then miles and miles of corrugations – a nightmare returning from Salisbury in the late afternoon with clouds of dust swirling in one's wake and the blinding sun hampering one's vision. Very dangerous.

Pat wrote a letter to the Public Health Department, dated 25 September 1947, to complain about the state of the house and outbuildings. He reported that the thatched roof was 'in a rotten condition' and that borers had made the supporting timber completely unsafe. Although he liked the house, he objected to paying any rent until it was repaired.

A reply from the Director of Public Works, written on 13 November 1947, indicated that 'only the most urgently required maintenance work' would be put in hand, although it had been recommended that 'an

---

C O P Y

Government Medical Officer,
Karoi,
via Sinoia.

Public Health Department,   25th September.
P.O. Box 587,
Salisbury.

Rental : G.M.O.s House : Karoi

I entered into occupation of the house on Friday
September the 12th 1947.

At the moment there are many repairs needing to be
done to the house and out-buildings, and I wrote to the Public
Works Department about these as soon as I arrived here, but as
yet have had no reply.

The roof is in a rotten condition, and needs urgent
re-thatching before the rains start here. But before this can
be done, new supporting timber will have to be erected as borers
have made it completely unsafe. There is no wire-netting in
any of the windows. The clinic roof pours a continual stream
of borer dust onto all the equipment and drugs, both my own and
Government property, and the door lets in clouds of dust and
won't lock properly. White ants in the door beams of the house
have made locking of many of the doors impossible. There is no
accommodation for the car when the rains start. These are but
a few of the most important renovations needed.

While I like the house, and it is excellently situated,
and will be really quite reasonable to live in when the repairs
have been done, I fail to see why I should pay any rent until
then. Our furniture and linen is being slowly ruined, and will
be completely so, if the rains get ahead of the P.W.D., and the
mosquitos appear every time a window or door is opened.

Perhaps a note from you to P.W.D., on the extreme
urgency of the roof repairs might help things along.

P.A. Taylor,
G.M.O. Karoi.

No. T.312/2577

PUBLIC WORKS DEPARTMENT,
P.O. BOX 365, SALISBURY.

13th November, 1947

A312|1092|6
18 NOV 1947

The Secretary,
Department of Mines and Public Works

KAROI : GOVERNMENT MEDICAL OFFICER'S HOUSE

      With reference to your minute No. A.312/1092/5
dated 4th November, 1947, this building is of a typical farm type of
construction and owing to the presence of white ants and borers
in all the timbers it will not be possible to maintain it in a
habitable condition for very long without virtually re-building it.
It has been recommended to the Medical Director that if permanent
quarters are required for a Government Medical Officer an entirely
new building should urgently be considered.

      In the meantime only the most urgently required
maintenance work will be put in hand, such as renewal of ant eaten
timbers and provision of a metal flashing to the roof. The cost of
such maintenance work does not alter the rental valuation of the
building.

      I would mention however for the information of the
Accountant, Division of Mines and Public Works that the valuation
previously given has had to be reconsidered as it had been assumed
when the building was first inspected that it would be put into good
condition and maintained in the same way as other Government
Buildings. A fair valuation, based on 1939 figures, is now given
as £400, and rents based on this figure will of course be retrospective
from the date of occupation.

      Correspondence is returned herewith as requested.

DIRECTOR OF PUBLIC WORKS

JRM/IVW

6

entirely new building should urgently be considered'. A 'fair valuation' of the building, on which the rents would be based, was given as £400.

In 1952 Pat Taylor built a two-roomed surgery at his own expense, which included a WC. This was at the top of Harris Street, between two plots later purchased by Chiefie Maidment. This building was eventually sold and converted into a residence. Ronnie Saint, who owned Karoi Butchery in partnership with Bert Hacking, lived there until he built a more upmarket place on the Crescent. So did Bruce Humpage, when he set up John and Bruce Motors. Harris Street was the first street in what one could then have called the suburbs, where the first residences began to mushroom. It was named after the first child to be born in Karoi.

The new surgery was used by all patients, both black and white, including the police and others who were entitled to free government treatment, in addition to private patients. The Secretary for Health supported a request for a free supply of water.

Later the Ministry of Health sanctioned the building of a new house for the GMO in the area behind where the Gwen Scrase Hall was soon to be built. This was Chiefie Maidment's first government contract: an isolated building on an open patch of ground some 100 yards or so from the hospital. Pat and Edna were the first occupants. These days it is literally caged in behind a security fence within the hospital compound.

Pat's job as the local GMO certainly had its interesting moments. His responsibilities far outweighed his doctoring duties. For instance, the RMS lorry would sometimes be delayed, and in exceptionally hot weather, orders were left at the Halt and forgotten – meat causing a real health issue. On one occasion Pat was called to the Halt to bury Sonny Shakespeare's meat order, the stench of which was unbearable, and as the doctor he had been called to dispose of it.

In 1953, plans to build a dam were put in place, which originally included the flooding of the local cemetery. Pat had to explain why it would not be a good idea to do this. Work did start on the dam in 1953 but was halted six months later when funds ran out.

The planning of a dam had been instigated by reports of unsanitary water supplies, about which Mr Palmer (Karoi Township Management Board) wrote saying he would be grateful if steps could be taken to alleviate the situation as it had become critical. To start with, all water supplies came from two good boreholes, and although these were constantly maintained and overhauled, they were only just adequate for the first few residents.

Stands were in demand, thirty-three having been purchased by 1953, and although not all had residents on them, this supply was not sufficient. From the two permanent residents in 1947 (Messrs Taylor and Tindale), the number of consumers had risen to twenty-four by 1953.

One evening, said Edna, an old man was wheeled up to the surgery in a wheelbarrow with his foot hanging off – the result of a

The first house built at Chikangwe Halt, Miami, later Karoi, with surgery for the Government Medical Officer, 1947.

The GMO's house after a storm.

The first surgery takes place.

accident on a cart. Pat stitched him up and he recovered well. On another occasion a patient took an overdose of something lethal. Pat was away and not due back for some time, so Edna had to take over and she spent the night making him drink copious pints of salt water to make him vomit. He stayed in their spare room and by morning the mattress was sodden with perspiration. He was in a very bad way, but he did recover.

Before long the small settlement showed signs of growth. For a small community, Edna recalled, they had an inordinate number of interesting characters: a potential murderess and a few polygamists, as well as a good deal of wife-swapping as marriages broke down and partnerships changed. War brings about many casualties, not all of them the walking wounded or mentally scarred. Men returned to their wives after five or six years apart and both found that they no longer had anything in common.

The most interesting twist in a marriage arose [wrote Edna] when a young man, Maynard Featherby, arrived from England with his mother, Kitty, after the war. He found work as a farm manager with a Mr Clatworthy in Marandellas. It wasn't long before Mrs Clatworthy, whose name was Joan, began to cast her eyes towards Maynard Featherby in an unbecoming manner. To cut a long story short, the couple absconded, descending on relatives in Karoi, where Joan had relatives in the Mitchells.

The cuckolded Mr Clatworthy then turned to Kitty Featherby, who by that time had become his ex-wife's mother-in-law, and, probably in a fit of pique, married her. Thus Joan's former husband became her father-in-law – and if you're up to it, you can work out the rest of this complicated relationship!

Pat was often in trouble with the Central Mechanical Equipment Department (CMED), because they thought he treated his government car badly. But he travelled such difficult roads that he had no choice but to drive in first gear much of the time, sometimes through deep mud, in an effort to reach his patients.

The surgery had trainee orderlies, and it happened once that one of them committed a misdemeanour by injecting a patient with the wrong *muti*. The case came up in Miami before the magistrate, John Hamilton, and the prosecutor was John Pestell. Pat was speaking on behalf of the appellant, and he managed rather skilfully to get

in all his gripes against the government medical department – how difficult it was to work with so little support, equipment, supplies, etc. This apart, the defendant was ultimately given a number of lashes – and he then had the temerity to ask Pat for painkillers. We thought that very amusing!

Occasionally Pat doubled up as the local veterinarian. He had operated on our own dog when it had suffered a hernia. Then the Tindales' turkeys were attacked just before Christmas, and Pat was called to stitch them up. He was heard to mutter, 'All those years of studying medicine, and here I am stitching up turkeys!'

Edna remembers the disastrous occasions when two homesteads burned down on local farms. Fires were a fairly common occurrence in those days. The bush was thick and thatched roofing was inevitably vulnerable during the searingly hot and dry months. Shortages of both labour and mechanical aids made it difficult to create efficient fire barriers around the developing nucleus of the farms.

The first to go up in flames was the house on Grippos, lived in by newly-weds Gerry and Gwen Marillier. Because they had not been married long, it was filled with wedding gifts – all of which perished in a matter of moments. Gwen and Gerry lost everything. Any ideas of family planning that the newlyweds might have had went up in a plume of smoke when 144 tins of condoms, kept in a cupboard with an arsenal of ammunition, exploded in the fire. The roof had been made of thatching-grass and the floors were covered in malthoid, both very inflammable substances. They rebuilt their homestead on the opposite side of the road and started again.

Stuart and Nan Maclaurin's thatched

house on Naba farm also caught alight, but on that occasion the casualties were not nearly as significant – just Stuart's mundane cattle records, but obviously very important to him.

One of the first couples to take up their land on the ex-servicemen's scheme were Mary and Dennis England. One morning in February 1946, some months after they had made their choice of a farm, Mary England woke up to hear her husband calling to her:

'OK, let's go. Pack your things – we're off.'

She was astounded. 'But how can we? We only have a boss-boy, a driver and a handful of piccanins!' And that was the full complement of their labour force.

Mary's father, Mr Dodd of Trelawney, had given them a span of oxen, and other good folk an old plough and various other bits of machinery, tools and vehicles. Materials were all in short supply following the war, and until a pump and engine could become available they had to make do with filling drums of water from the vlei.

These shortages stemmed from years of war, and also left the country without sufficient chemicals and fertilizers. It was ten years or more before the situation improved. Both groups – the farmers who had continued to farm throughout those war years, as well as the new settlers – tried to make do, although it was a constant battle.

Fertilizers and chemicals had always depended on imports from Britain. Alternatives had to be found, and many are the stories of how this was achieved. Some took the obvious route, using compost and manure to enrich the soil, but it was recorded that others used the extreme method of paying locals to collect bones from the veld at 3*d.* a gallon-tin full. When new supplies did trickle through, there was delight in discovering new, improved chemicals that controlled the ravages of fungi, which flourish in hot, wet seasons.

So the Englands built a house of thatching grass, and camped in that for ten months until they could make bricks and start building something more solid. The first tobacco crop went into the ground in 1947. They also built three barns for curing, though one of their greatest problems was finding labour. The indigenous people in the area were not keen to work on farms.

Dennis named his farm Mshalla, meaning 'God Go with You', from an old Syrian saying that he had picked up in the Middle East when he was buying wheat from the Arabs for the 8th Army. Sadly, Dennis didn't have long to enjoy his new farm, for he died in 1951; Mary later married his brother, Peter.

This was the general pattern then, during those early post-War years: A farmer's property was about twenty times as large as his ability to finance its development. He began by living under mud and thatch, then, as time went by, under brick and iron, which he built and supervised himself. He added a room or two every now and again.

Most of his sticks of furniture were shabby but comfortable. In his kitchen, his office, and even in the bedrooms, his cupboards, chests and shelves were often made out of the wooden boxes used by the petrol companies for packing the paraffin tins that supplied the fuel for refrigeration and lamps.

Bath water was heated in an old 40-gallon oil drum above a wood-burning furnace lit by a domestic servant and which supplied copious amounts of hot water. Wood was there for the asking and lasted many years, both for the stove and for the old 'Rhodesian boiler'.

The privy – which went by the more crudely named 'long drop' or PK ('piccanini kia') – would be either too small or too large,

The Moment of the Rose

but it was as far away as was sensible from the homestead, built with discarded farm bricks and shut off from 'society' either by sackcloth or with a wooden door haphazardly nailed together and hung from a couple of rusty creaking hinges. Many's the time that the inaccurately named 'privy' led a fellow to break out into song to ensure that his bodily functions were private and undisturbed.

Those, too, were the days when a farmer looked the part. He was recognised by his distinctive khakis, his sweat-soaked shirt and trousers, and rough-looking homemade veldskoens – though it was, of course, his deeply suntanned craggy complexion that gave him away, identifying him as an outdoor man.

His wife had an equally heavy load: despite the polishing and sweeping being done by the 'houseboy', she was just as industrious. She sewed and upholstered, nursed, and dispensed *muti*. She tended to the chickens and produced a bounteous garden. She made butter and cheese. She drove the truck, fetching and carrying. She taught her children to read and write. She often ran a farm store. She baked bread and made preserves. She played tennis and danced, and above all she contributed enthusiastically to the development of her community.

The children ran freely, bare-footed and half naked around the farm, wandering at will – gun or fishing rod at hand. They collected pets – from bush babies and chameleons to duikers that they fed from an old rubber teat on a whisky bottle. Tortoises came and went. They gathered and ate at random the wild fruits from the bush – mazhanje and mahobohobo – and sat around their harvests, naked as the day they were born, while indelible juices dribbled down their dirty faces.

They kept company, in an unconsciously imperiously manner, with their black counterparts, feeling at home in the veld and absorbing all around them. Many a youngster was fluent in the Shona tongue, which he would ashamedly cast aside when sent off to boarding school.

Each farm was an almost self-contained settlement and both sets of inhabitants, black and white, rarely left it. Self-sufficiency was the order of the day, for the nearest store and butchery was probably miles away. This was illustrated by a story that Mary England recollected:

Mr Tindale, the government representative, wore a number of official and unofficial hats. Officially, he was the 'pound master', which meant that he was legally allowed to retain and lock up in an enclosure any stray animals that happened to be wandering around. Unofficially, he kept a couple of dairy cows and provided the residents with milk. Moreover, Mr Tindale kept boxer dogs and feeding them was a problem.

One day, during the course of a conversation that Mary had with Nan Maclaurin, she happened to mentioned this, implying that, if anything at all died on the farm, the late whatever-it-was would be gratefully received by Mrs Tindale for her dogs.

Not long after this conversation one of Mary's sheep died of unknown causes, so she cut a leg off the carcass and hastened to Mrs Tindale, who took one look at the leg of mutton and promptly declared, 'That's not going to the dogs – we'll eat it!'

Over the following months the Karoi district filled up with its full complement of ex-servicemen – immigrants flowed into Rhodesia tempted by the opportunity of a new life and escape from war-torn Britain and Europe.

Nevertheless, whatever the anticipated vision had been for an 'explosion of tobacco on to the world market', the young wives of Karoi raised a storm of their own as, one by one, twenty-six out of thirty-three new resident brides lost no time in becoming pregnant. It could be said that nature was trying to make up for the loss of life.

Doctor Pat Taylor, busier than he'd ever anticipated, had no time now to operate on any more turkeys. Those new young ladies-in-waiting well remember turning up on his surgery steps thinking how thoughtful their doctor was. The new surgery had a swivel window but no curtains – gallantly Doctor Pat draped his white coat over the aperture, pegging it in place with a pair of forceps, in an effort to give his patients some privacy.

The first trading store belonged to Alec Atkinson. He had traded in Miami but transferred his business, Northern Stores, to Karoi. It was David Grantham, one of the first ex-servicemen farmers, who built him a house a little way up from the Farmers' Co-op. Ely Elefteriades was his business partner. At that time it was the only trading store between Sinoia and Chirundu.

The Farmers' Co-op arrived in 1947, invited by government to assist in the establishment of retail outlets, and they undertook to provide a simple depot in Karoi. Materials being short, they transferred to Karoi a shed at Mapunga Siding near Bindura that had been unused for several years. When it was dismantled it was discovered to be riddled with termites that had destroyed many of the timbers; however, it was reconstructed and was ready for use by the time they needed it.

This trading store became of immediate value to the new farmers. In 1948 it housed a postal agency on behalf of the Post Office, which was discontinued in 1952 when it was found to be unprofitable. The first manager was Sandy Fraser, and the postal agency was run by Maureen Leask, who by now had become Mrs David Grantham, David having come to Karoi on the ex-servicemen's scheme.

Foly Wesson was Sandy Fraser's successor as manager for many years, until Bert Hacking became a director of the Farmers' Co-op for many years later still. He had Foly removed to Salisbury but not for promotion: he installed him in the Maitland Bottle Store – a particularly malicious gesture which ultimately destroyed him, said his friends.

Geoff Lockett was a 'remittance man' – mad as a March Hare, they said – who had bought a portion of Sonny Shakespeare's Caversham farm and registered it as Romford. He had fought with the Chindits in Burma, which may have accounted for his eccentricity. Geoff's light fingers kept the whole of the Farmers' Co-op staff on tenterhooks as he pilfered away to his heart's content. Someone was always instructed to keep tabs on what he took and bill him for it later. The age of the supermarket had not yet arrived.

Next to arrive and set up a business was Arthur 'Chiefie' Maidment. In November 1947, two Royal Navy destroyers made their way down from Britain to the Simonstown docks of the South African cape. They were to be handed over to the South African government, and aboard one was Chief Petty Officer Maidment – newly pensioned off after twenty-two years of service and now a volunteer who had agreed to accompany these vessels on their journey. His own destination was Southern Rhodesia, and by this action he managed to procure for himself and his family paid passages into Africa. He had trained as a cabinet-maker in an earlier life and was now keen to start afresh.

His first job was to build a dwelling for his family who would arrive later. He would then start a business, for there were many options in a settlement that had nothing. The family consisted of Rose, Chiefie's wife;

June, his eldest daughter, married to Peter Veck; Audrey, who soon married Francis Heron, an original settler who lived on New Forest, K14; Jill, who was still at school; and, bringing up the rear, young Billy.

The original Maidment house stands right next to the Farmers' Co-op, and for a long time the windows were unglazed because glass was unobtainable in post-war Rhodesia. One night Rose took a terrible fright when she awoke to find a head looming over her, only to discover it was another of Mr Tindale's itinerant cows from the pound.

The commercial enterprise of 'Maidments' began more or less by accident, along with a great deal of providential circumstance. Chiefie had become a builder and had all the necessary tools at his finger tips. He was surrounded, though, by new settler farmers, all of them busy building and developing farms. They were constantly borrowing from him and forgetting to return tools and various other things, so Chiefie decided that this was the first gap in the market and took advantage of it.

He applied for a trader's licence, built a shed at his builder's yard, and invited his daughter Jill to run a hardware shop for him. Jill, hating being at boarding school anyway, jumped at the chance to leave. From there Maidments took off.

In 1950, June and her husband Peter arrived from the UK to help run an ever-expanding business. Peter took over the hardware from Jill. He very quickly became an asset, for he was artistic and creative and knew instinctively what would sell. Peter's sense of humour was also a big draw. One would enter the premises feeling depressed and leave not only cheerful but loaded down with purchases one didn't actually need. June took over the books and tucked herself away in a little office corner.

Next, Ronnie Thornton arrived in Rhodesia from Newcastle to join the BSA Police. He was posted to Karoi in 1955 and became Chiefie's drinking partner. It was a novel way of courting the girl – court the father first.

Ronnie did get Jill in the end, and they went on to become the first couple to be married in the newly built Gwen Scrase Community Hall. The Register of Marriages states that Jill Patricia Maidment, 19, shop assistant, and Ronald Thornton, 23, brick-layer, were married by the Revd Norman Clayton, Rector of Lomagundi, in 1956.

Needless to say, Maidments had long out-grown the shed at the bottom of the builders' yard, and in its place went up a row of 'boutiques', all with large glass frontages just like proper shops; a mini-emporium had evolved. In one, Rose and Jill started their haberdashery and drapery department, and Ronnie had become an ex-policeman who was helping Chiefie to build Karoi.

Peter's hardware shop was filled to over-flowing, like an Aladdin's Cave with every-thing one could imagine from the mundane to the luxurious. This was the place where a young Keith Simpson, spying a lavatory bowl on display in the window, promptly climbed up and utilised it.

Here, each year at the eleventh hour on Christmas Eve, an out-of-breath Stuart Maclaurin would dash in with a stocking to fill for Nan, his wife. In it he would stuff all sorts of trinkets and dainty luxuries: jewellery, flimsy lingerie, Avon cosmetics – anything, in fact, that would fit.

On one occasion, Brian Rhodes's first wife strolled in with a baby elephant. It had been orphaned and wouldn't let her out of its sight. Not to be outdone, Alan Bunnett rode through the threshold on a horse because he said he couldn't get near the counter.

But the *pièce de résistance* came one morning when Mrs A. B. Roberts, now in the winter of her life, confused and not quite 'with it', strolled into Rose's haberdashery to purchase some knickers. Still in her nightdress, enhanced by a hat, gloves and pearls, and entrusting her handbag to her chauffeur, she tried them on 'in situ'.

Truth to tell, it was that kind of shop, and the 'Maidment family' were those kind of people – tolerant of individualism and usually managing to see the humour in most things. They were never interested in extracting the last penny out of anyone – no mark-ups on old stock – and they held the old-fashioned view that the customer was always right. In that shop of theirs they notched up a tale or two – and they had seen everything over the fifty-odd years they were in Karoi.

For a brief time Chiefie Maidment was the only builder in town, but early in the 1950s opposition came in the form of the Whitely brothers. At that stage John Hall had started to build the 'hotel'. He began by erecting a couple of rondavels where overnighters could stay if they wished.

Traditionally, in any new town, the church went up first; in Karoi it was a bar. Harold and Clarissa Whitely, new arrivals on the African continent, were travelling to Northern Rhodesia with the idea of looking for something to invest in. The hot, tedious travel over great distances along corrugated, undeveloped country tracks persuaded them to stop and refresh themselves at the first little 'dorp' out of Sinoia. That bar has caused many others to remain in this place of potential riches, people who never did continue on their intended onward journey.

Jimmy Upton recalled the moment that Harold Whitely strolled into the bar and announced that he was looking for something to invest in. 'Eyes shot up from all directions', he said. 'In anticipation and delight, I was

wondering if he would be interested in my bakery.' But it was John Hall who won the day. Grabbing his opportunity, he offered to sell his 'hotel', and the rest, of course, is history.

Harold subsequently sent for his brother, George, his wife, Edith, and their four children, who were still living in England. They arrived in 1955, and from then on the hotel took off at a gallop. The row of brick-built bedrooms at the back were the first to go up.

Following this, they built the main body of the hotel: a stylish foyer and reception area, a dining-room, kitchen and a second bar – a ladies' cocktail bar – as well as another row of bedrooms running parallel to the main north road, which completed the quadrangle at the back, later to become the venue for a drive-in cinema, and, off the side veranda, a dance floor.

Between them, the Whitely and Maidment families built much of Karoi.

George Whitely's daughter, Madelaine, met her husband, Peter Depinho, in Karoi. He was a road surveyor who was contracted out to the company Field Engineers, who were building the road twenty kilometres either side of Karoi.

When they became engaged, Madelaine's parents invited the whole district to a celebration at the hotel. Everyone had a wonderful time – except the happy couple, who were stuck behind a raging Pote river that had risen up in flood.

Madelaine remembers Jock Rutherford, who used to pitch up each night on his horse and ride straight to the bar.

Two cottages were built on the property. George, Edith and family lived in one, and Sandy Fraser, the manager of the Farmers' Co-op, moved into the other. The Whitelys had the brickfields, which subsequently came up for tender that was advertised in

51

the *Gazette*, and the Maidments then applied for and got the tender for the quarry.

The brickfields operated first on an area that was subsequently flooded by the Karoi dam, then moved closer to Halstead farm. Rob Watson was a bachelor when he settled on Halstead as a returned soldier, but he wasn't one for long. Eve stepped in and became Mrs Watson.

Once the Whitelys had finished building the hotel, they employed Phillip and Heidi (née Scala) Aldridge to manage it for them. From the beginning it did well. Heidi Aldridge and her sister Ingrid, both blessed with above average looks, drew admirers like bees to a honey-pot, and the residents watched with interest as the bachelors lined up for Ingrid's hand. She eventually settled on Robert Early, a policeman stationed at Makuti, who subsequently wrote a best-selling novel, *A Time of Madness*, published by Graham Publishing in 1977.

The hotel's deputy managers were John and Enid Hargreaves. They and their only child died in a plane crash when they were travelling home on leave to the UK, probably the Central African Airways crash near Benghazi in 1958. That flight was also full of young Rhodesian scholars going on a students' tour of Europe and Britain. Still at school at the time, I had known a few of the passengers who lost their lives; I also knew one of those who survived.

The first baker in town was Jimmy Upton, and it has to be said that he was a very reluctant one. By his own admission he had been happier in the Navy, where his brain was in no danger of being damaged or extended as he just followed orders. After being demobbed, he had no idea what path he should choose – everything he tried just didn't feel right.

He had tried following in his father's foot-steps as a journalist, and had quite liked the idea of a career in forestry, but when the war ended it was the older men who were given priority entrance into colleges.

Complicating things still further, his girl-friend, Val, had taken herself off to Rhodesia, fed up with his prevarications and the lack of a marriage offer. It took young Jimmy three months to decide that she was worth pursuing, and within three days of landing in Salisbury they were married. But civilian life still held no prospects and he drifted from one job to another. He would leave a job just in time to avoid being sacked.

Eventually fate led him to a bakery in Salisbury, which in turn led to an encounter with a friend who suggested that he should move to Karoi, where there was an opening in that field. Despite his vehement protests that his knowledge about such things was limited, the friend offered to set the business up for him and show him the ropes.

So began the baking of bread in Karoi. Jimmy approached the millers, who extended him thirty days' credit; he was confident that he would be able to sell a considerable number of loaves in that time. It seemed that Jimmy Upton was on his way at last.

In those days, residents were thin on the ground in Karoi town. One of Jimmy's favourites was a man called Basil Wilson, who ran a so-called garage, and Jimmy recalled a very funny moment when D.D.Tate strolled in one morning and said, 'Gentlemen, allow me to introduce myself. I am Major Tate.' Basil replied, equally politely, 'How do you do, Sir. I am Squadron Leader Wilson, and this gentleman here beside me is Captain Palmer.' All of this showed that the pomp and order of the war still lingered like a bad smell, not having dissipated at all. Sadly, Basil and his wife were both killed in a car accident between Karoi and Kariba some months later.

Major Shalto Barnes, who lived on Chiwuwa, to the extreme north of Karoi, showed similar signs of officious snobbery. He seemed to do little more than spend his time at the Club, and he was a stickler for rules – as long as they did not apply to him. He saw to it that the owners and the assistants did not mix. Should a stranger enter the Club and order a drink, Barnes would call out 'Is this man a member?' to the embarrassment of all present. Peter Richards didn't think he was much of a farmer either, because when he leased Chiwuwa in the 1960s, he found the place derelict.

Jimmy recalls Ian Palmer as a very witty fellow with a wonderful sense of humour. He once arrived at a Club party dressed as a Commissar, holding an umbrella, although it was not the rainy season, and he would speak only French.

Jimmy Upton wasn't really satisfied with his life as a baker, but one day a chap called John Vernon strolled into the bakery for a chat. He said that he was at a loose end and had time on his hands, having just been fired by Harry Wells on Montesuma. He looked around and declared, 'You know, I'd love to run a little business like this.' Jimmy gaped at him in amazement and replied, 'You can't be serious. But if you are, it's all yours, mate.' And almost in the blink of an eye, the bakery changed hands.

Not long after this, Jimmy met Harry Wells, who offered him Vernon's job. 'Within a week of working on Montesuma, I knew I'd found my niche – and an almighty relief it was, too. It was Harry Wells who sorted me out, and I never looked back', said Jimmy. After five years with Harry Wells, Jimmy bought Broad Acres, owned by Ernie Went, in partnership with Alec Cummings, and when that partnership was amicably dissolved, he bought Chiltington from Susie Simpson, who had married Peter Adams.

By far the greatest character in the Karoi of those days was the aforementioned Jock Rutherford on Chedza farm. Despite being regarded as having 'gone bush' because he lived with a local black woman, he continued to drink at the pub.

Each night, as the bar prepared to close, people would wait for the inevitable rap on the window, followed shortly by a woman's voice calling, 'Jocko... Jocko... Time to go home.' He would stagger to his horse, someone would give him a lift up, wallop the horse on its backside, and it would take off, hell for leather, straight for home – meaning just that. Ignoring the roads, the horse lurched over dongas, vleis and rocks in a cross-country gallop before finally depositing his master in a heap beside his hut.

One day, the residents were surprised to find that Jock had a visitor from Scotland. It was his sister, who had arrived to check up on her brother. They were equally surprised to find that she was a cultured and educated lady – 'very up-market', was Jimmy's description. She must have bought him a car, because after she had left, he started travelling around in one.

Kees and Maartjie Bakker arrived in Karoi in 1955 to take over a property that then consisted of a wall with arches in it, behind which were broken tractors and a small office.

Until then it had belonged to a Doctor Portman, who was in partnership with a farmer, whose name Maartjie has forgotten, and someone else called Mitchell. It was very run down, but with Kees as manager, and his brother Hans as a partner, plus help from Shell, the place was gradually transformed into the establishment that came to be known as Karoi Motors.

However, the very first garage was started by Lionel Searle, whose partner was Giuseppi Tome. 'Tommy', as we knew him, had returned from Italy after the war, having had a taste of rural Rhodesia as a prisoner of war in Miami. He had worked for Rob Paterson on Grand Parade mine.

The garage he ran for Lionel was next to the stand on which the Fraser Building was eventually built. Expansion kept pace with farming developments as each piece of land was taken up.

Stuart Maclaurin was an early cattle breeder and one of the first to take up land in Karoi. Here remembered:

> When one spoke of cattle it meant 'trek oxen'. They were our sole means of propulsion on the farm. They ploughed our land, ridged our tobacco, and hauled our sleighs back to the barns with the golden dollar. No wonder, as we cursed our so-called drivers, we built up a respect and love for these animals that pulled us out of the mire.
>
> There were a few generous helpers already well established in the district – like Mrs Des Evans, Mrs A.B. Roberts, Mr and Mrs C.P. Robertson on Buffalo Downs, and Mrs Bill Leask on Coldomo – who had a few motley cows tied up in the kraal at night for milking the next day and who helped out when babies were born.
>
> In our fledgling village, Bill Tindale had a back-door cow, and any one of them would have helped out when Karoi's first babies, Jocelyn Harris and Humphrey Tate, first saw the light of day.
>
> I soon acquired a few cows myself, but the 'breeding boom' didn't really start until 1946/47 when the government decided to dispose of its tsetse test herd in the Urungwe Reserve. Then you could apply for cows at the fair price of

two pounds ten shillings a head, and what's more, the cows were in calf.

> I was lucky in my application and got seven head, while Sam Barrett-Hamilton and Noel Bichard got only six. Sid Jenkinson got a Grade Sussex bull and Sam a Grade Hereford.
>
> In 1947 at least 200 native cows came from the Cold Storage Commission priced at four pounds ten shillings. My own purchases were inspired by Guy du Barry, whose theme was, 'You can't go wrong – buy a cow and buy a bull. They produce a calf every year and only eat grass.' He was, in fairness, the first to admit that it wasn't quite as easy as all that. I also learned the difference between a short or a bogey truckload.
>
> Bill Tindale was very proud when he off-loaded, by way of his anthill ramp, Karoi's first pedigreed bull, the Hereford Penrose Union – or 'Moaning Maurice', as Nan promptly called him.
>
> Peter Gibson restored order among the heretics to the government's anti-exotic policy by demonstrating how well the Afrikander did under extensive conditions of 'free range' from the Angwa to Lion's Den.
>
> Charles Murray, the director of CONEX, in an inspiring speech in Karoi designed to overcome the national milk shortage, at least found a convert in David Grantham, Snr. To Dave, the very word 'orthodox' was quite enough to set off some ingenuous chain reaction.
>
> Thus, to cross a Jersey bull with a native cow was a real challenge. Not only would it aid his country, but prove his own ideas and practice to be true.
>
> In 1949 Dan Oosthuizen told me that he had acquired from Gwelo a dozen Grade South Devon cows at two pounds ten shillings – six for himself and six

for me. What could I say but 'thank you very much', but to Nan I laid bare my thoughts: 'Two pounds ten shillings for a cow – for one single cow!'

Times change, don't they.

In the early days our cattle died of poverty, but never under that name. 'Veld poisoning' was the best description, as certainly their sole means of nutrition was veld grass.

Barbed wire was virtually unobtainable until some ex-POW wire was unearthed from Gwelo. This wire can still be seen to-day – rusty, but unmistakable, with the barbs only inches apart. This was in 1976.

Finally, let us not forget the young mother's friend, the old milk cow. She went by many colours, from black to white to red. She went under many names, from Blossom to 'that damn old bitch'. But most assuredly she was responsible for many a strapping young lad in Karoi.

A Cow's Lament

Though I've just given birth to a heifer,
And of pride and of milk I am full,
It is sad to relate, that my actual state
Was not brought about by the bull.

I have never been naughty – I swear it,
In spite of the calf I have borne.
By Freddie Ford's book I am 'virgo intacta'
And I've not had a bull by the horn.

How dreary the farmyard and meadow,
The cowshed seems gloomy and grey,
For the one bit of fun in the year's dreary run
Has by science been taken away.

I know that the farmer's in business
Where all of us pull our full weight.
But I'd pull and I'd pull for a nicely built bull
For this phoney arrangement I hate.

It must not be thought that I'm jealous,
There are things that a cow shouldn't say
But these rotten upstarts who handle my parts
Still get it the old-fashioned way.

Author unknown.

6. The Ex-servicemen Arrive

Life in an earlier Miami had been taken at a leisurely pace, where creature comforts were few and far between and the only modern convenience was one telephone shared among many.

It was the 'City of the North', they said. Hardly a city, not even a town or a village. Perhaps a hamlet. But in truth it was the last place of so-called civilisation before the descent into the Zambezi Valley to the bridge over the Zambezi at Chirundu into Northern Rhodesia.

The Miami settlement had never ever been much more than a scant collection of roughly built dwellings, very often belying the good breeding behind those doors. Residents occupied themselves in a languid fashion, for time mattered little.

And so, finally, men cast aside their army, navy or air-force uniforms after five years away and descended on the plains to join the handful of farmers who had hitherto enjoyed the Urungwe as their private preserve and domain.

It must have been an exciting time. Here was reward for loyalty to the Crown, an opportunity that held some expectation. And they came from all walks of life – the high and low, rich and poor, educated and bewildered – and among them were the natural leaders, the layabouts, the schemers, the mavericks and undesirables. They all had one thing in common – they had to learn a lot about growing tobacco.

The ex-servicemen's scheme was offered primarily to Rhodesians, although it did embrace men from Britain and South Africa who had fought with the Commonwealth. A handful broke through the net, acquiring farms by default: they had never worn a uniform or fired a rifle in their lives.

One started to notice new tracks to the left and right of the main road to the north. Nameplates went up, precariously tacked to the tops of posts or simply nailed to a tree, announcing to the world, and anyone else who happened to pass by, that someone lived at the end of that rutted road.

Most incongruous of all, and certainly puzzling to the stranger, was a little hut at the entrance. This was for the protection of supplies that were dropped off by the RMS. Susie Simpson never did get used to the way her weekly meat order, wrapped up in sacking, was flung out of an RMS truck on to the ground, somewhere in the region of the entrance to their road.

In places, the pecking order of the forces continued, as erstwhile officers found it difficult to forget that the war was behind them and that they were in 'civvy street' again. The hierarchy of the British forces clung adamantly to their titles, as vehemently as they did to their handlebar moustaches, their plummy accents and fly-away khaki shorts.

Signposts informed passers-by that Major D. D. Tate lived at Kyogle, that Colonel Stuart Maclaurin was at Naba and Captain Nesbitt at Spring farm. The clipped upper-class accent of the arrogant British gentleman mingled with the harsh guttural speech of the Afrikaner and the more gentle rounded vowels of the Rhodesian-born.

Gerald Marillier, newly demobbed from the navy, decided he would not be outdone and facetiously tacked up his own sign, which announced that Ordinary Seaman G. V. Marillier lived there. Gradually, for the most part anyway, the officiousness faded away, particularly when it was obvious that no one was impressed.

A story is told of two officers, one of whom was employed by the other. However, their ranks were now reversed, with the Colonel working for the Sergeant Major. So as not to appear too forward or precocious, the manager would make his way to the *munda* (fields) in the early morning on a separate path from that of his 'boss', even going as far as sitting under a different tree to eat his lunchtime sandwiches, although the two could have had a perfectly good conversation together, so close were their trees.

This ridiculous snobbishness seems utterly ludicrous now, but was perhaps quite understandable then, when society still had a distinct and acceptable etiquette that seemed to work.

Progress was hampered by shortages of materials and machinery, and tasks took twice as long to accomplish. Oxen were used for ploughing, and sometimes even native labour was used to pull a small plough. The purchase of a tractor took precedence over a car. One family managed to procure a tractor that pulled a plough and a trailer by day and became a social conveyance at weekends. The whole family would perch precariously

on any available space as it travelled to the Club on a Saturday night!

Impatient air-force pilots, anxious to get home, rashly volunteered to fly Lancasters back to Africa but never made it, for these vehicles were past their best and in disrepair.

Some, like Peter Adams, were selected to fly troops back to South Africa, but Peter was impatient to return to his medical studies and did not relish the task. However, there were no flies on Peter – he complained that, because his feet were so big (size thirteen) and the aircraft pedals so close together, he had had to take off his shoes and fly barefooted, which he thought was dangerous. That really alarmed the authorities and he was released from duty.

Back into civilian life again, aeroplanes were the cheapest mode of transport and easily obtainable: many second-hand planes were available after the war, and they were cheaper than cars. (The Belvedere airport in Salisbury was used then, an area that later became 'the Indian quarter'.)

This led to many Karoi residents being

Ploughing without cattle.

keen to get their flying licences. It was useful for getting from A to B, as the roads at the time were awful. Gwen Marillier recalled that a trip to Salisbury could take anything from three to five hours, but it was only an hour in a little Piper and even less in the bigger Stinson Voyager.

In 1950 a flying club was formed and a runway was built on Paul Pearson's farm, Tarquinia (not to be confused with Mafalo, where Jim Pierson was), which was an excellent strip because of his own keen interest in flying. The two instructors were Paul himself and David Grantham, and the first pupils were Connie Pearson and Maureen Grantham, their wives.

In 1951 the flying club held an 'Air Rally and Ball', with the BSA Police band in attendance. 'The band was a great attraction and our hearts were young and gay,' wrote one of the ladies.

Other keen members followed swiftly. Apart from Gwen and Gerry Marillier, there were David and Vyvyan Cockburn, Sam Marnie, Guy du Barry, Fred Mulder and Alex Atkinson. Both Bill Gain and Bert Hacking could already fly, but they joined just for the fun of it.

Gwen was also Club Secretary for four years, but when Gerry was killed after their private plane crashed with him at the controls, she understandably didn't have the heart to continue.

The first five ex-servicemen to take up their land, either a little before or after 1947, were David Grantham on Shawnigan, Jack O'Hea on Longueil, Ernie Went on Broad Acres, Peter Groenewald on Lancaster, and John Blanckenberg on Maora.

Arriving hard on their heels were Dennis England to Mshalla, Stuart Maclaurin to Naba, Peter Fisher to Leconfield, Billy Postlethwayt to Coniston, Jimmy Oxenham

to Nyamanda, Sid Scolnik to Jenya, Sam Barrett-Hamilton to Chisapi, and Guy du Barry to Buttevant.

From then, others followed in quick succession.

As the years rolled by, the Urungwe underwent a gradual metamorphosis. By 1945/47, the determination of human endeavour had begun to pave the way for the ex-servicemen's scheme. The area lost its tedious pattern of uniformity and became more interesting as the agricultural revolution got under way.

A variety of sounds rent the air as more and more activity took place, and the hitherto sleeping veld listened as men swung their axes against wood, and the echoing sounds reverberated across vleis and ridges. Here and there could be heard the distant rhythmic chug of a diesel engine, as it steadily pumped water up from rivers and pools.

At the roadside, the few weary travellers sat up, agreeably alerted by a sudden flash of russet through the trees, as farm-made bricks progressed from kiln to tobacco barn in an exciting process that would lead to tobacco curing.

Little by little, the bush took on a new aspect. Open spaces revealed what had remained hidden for so long, and the soil was turned by the plough in preparation, ready now to prove its worth.

It was back-breaking work, that chopping down of trees and stumping out of roots. The precious commodity of wood was removed and stowed away to be used in innumerable ways – as timber for building sheds, barns, and eventually homesteads, and as fuel for curing tobacco, heating water and cooking meals; not a stick was wasted.

Farmers gazed in satisfaction as this metamorphosis took shape. Ploughing with oxen could be frustrating, but it was a peaceful occupation – the slow, perambulating bovine creatures straining to pull and turn the virgin soil, the shrill whistling and shouts of the boys in the background, driving on their team, beasts of burden who would never know that their importance would soon become obsolete. It was a million miles away from the noises of war.

Homesteads were initially of secondary importance. The women coped as best they could with near primitive conditions. Crops took priority, for loans had to be met. A dearth of glass left windows unglazed for months, and a mix of lime and sand took the place of cement.

Paddy Barrett-Hamilton was only four when he arrived on the edge of the Magunje Reserve in 1946 to live with his parents, Sam and Dot, on Chisapi. The journey from Sinoia, where they had overnighted with Sam's brother Frank, had taken three hours on bad roads.

The Barrett-Hamiltons had their origins in Ireland and left because of the increased activity of Sinn Fein, who had started to burn down houses and pitchfork people. They were one of the first to take up residence in this far-flung, remote area, as a result of Sam losing an eye and being invalided out of the war early. On the 3,300 acres allotted to them, they experienced a few narrow escapes and turning points over the years, but survive they did.

Like everyone else, they first lived in a thatched hut. Two separate huts were built at the same time, one for Granny Maud and another for Sir Godfrey Huggins. This was always known as the PM's hut. 'Huggie' used to visit Karoi regularly and always stayed with Dot and Sam.

Training plough-oxen was always a problem, and especially frustrating if they were cultivating maize. The beasts were more interested in eating the soft green growth around them than being led on. Brian McKay said he used to fix wire netting like a muzzle over their mouths.

The arrival of a brand-new paraffin refrigerator to replace the meat safe was a day to remember. They were cumbersome and erratic but they did keep supplies cold. Meat safes weren't nearly as efficient and their legs had to stand in tins of methylated spirits to prevent ants from crawling up to the perishables above. Water was constantly dripped down in an attempt to keep the temperature cool.

Dot and Sam were the epitome of kindness and gentility, always good-humoured and friendly. All the children loved to visit Dot because of her sweetie drawer. There was always a toffee or barley sugar to suck on.

Dot and Granny Maud paid me a neighbourly visit one day when we were on Marshlands. They arrived looking so smart with their hats and gloves that I nearly fainted from nerves, but they were so chatty and cheerful, and they didn't turn a hair as they chewed their way through my mushy biscuits. Why on earth had I been so fearful?!

Somewhere along the line Sam was forced to sell off part of Chisapi to recoup some losses caused by his brother-in-law, who had overspent. Noel Blazey bought a piece, which he called Red Leaf, and Bert Hacking another called Bonnyvale.

Further north of Chisapi was an enormous piece of land called Peverell Place, owned by Bill Rayburn, whom some considered to be lazy and something of a 'veranda farmer'.

Hats, gloves and stockings were still considered the proper dress code, even in the middle of the tropics of Africa, and Mrs Rayburn never ventured off the farm without them. She quite fancied herself as the doyenne of Karoi society and dished out advice willy-nilly to all the new young wives, especially if they were new immigrants from Britain.

In fact, the acknowledged matriarch of the time was Mrs Des Evans. She set the benchmark and handed out good advice to all the new young wives – how to survive in the bush with all the post-war shortages and how to budget and make do.

Bill Rayburn very quickly lost Peverell Place, being forced to sell off his vast acreage. He sold to Frikkie Herselman, brother of Tommy and Sienie Strydom. Frikkie very astutely sub-divided it into seven pieces, keeping one for himself and selling off the rest. Bert Hacking bought three.

Fred Bishop, father of Arthur had reached Bulawayo via Natal in the late 1880s. He had been what was called a 'Rhodes Runner', whose jobs entailed mapping out easy routes up to the British South African Protectorate (Rhodesia) through Bechuanaland (Botswana), routes where good supplies of water could be found for travellers and their beasts, along a path which held no insurmountable obstacles. In other words they were 'forerunners', especially needed when the Pioneer Column made its way up through the Tuli block and onward to Salisbury in 1890.

As a reward for his services, Rhodes gave Fred Bishop a gold watch. A well-known Rhodes Runner employed for this service was, of course, Courtney Selous, the formidable elephant hunter, who undoubtedly knew many of the routes like the back of his hand. Selous travelled up with the Pioneer Column in 1890 as a guide.

When it was Arthur's turn to do something 'for king and country' at the start of the Second World War, he joined the South African Armoured Corps, which became ceded to the Scottish Argyll and Sutherland Highlanders, and for this dubious honour he had to wear a kilt. At some stage along the line he gave it away, generously handing it over so that a corpse could be buried in it. Arthur's war took him up to Italy, which he reached by driving a Sherman tank from Cape Town to Cairo. He was also present at the fall of Monte Cassino.

After the war, Arthur travelled up from Bulawayo to Karoi, twice, on both occasions on a motorbike to look for land. He cast his eye around and chose K67. Unfortunately, he wasn't the only contender, so the matter was settled in the time-honoured way by drawing names out of a hat. Arthur won the draw and called his selection Zebra Downs.

When he moved up to begin farming, his father gave him the traditional strong door, and a strong Ndebele youngster called Vunzai, who stayed with him on the farm until the day he died.

It's a pity that doors can't speak, for no doubt it could tell a story or two. That first night on the farm there was such an infestation of lion that they had to sleep up in the trees. Arthur hauled his door up and lay on it through the night. Vunzai climbed into another tree, tying himself tightly to it where he slept soundly without fear of falling out. Needless to say it wasn't long before they built a mud hut.

Arthur met his future wife, Sylvia Johnson, a teacher, when she visited a friend, Mary Duffin, in Karoi. Sylvia had been a WAF, stationed in Singapore during the war. Her first teaching post in Rhodesia was in Macheke, where she met Joan Ham. They became firm friends.

Macheke was in the middle of nowhere, a place from which one could escape only if one was lucky enough to have a car; but neither of them had wheels of any sort.

In desperation, one day they walked to the railway line in front of the school and stopped an approaching train. In those days one could run alongside a train, keeping up with it quite easily for a mile or two until it managed to stop. The driver would allow them to sit in the guard's van. It was all highly illegal of course, but it was a way of being liberated for an hour or so.

Sylvia married Arthur, and from there Joan met Hastings McFadjean and the two of them married. Joan and Sylvia taught for many years in Karoi.

Arthur was 'a soft touch', said Sylvia, a man who helped many a new settler to get started. He became involved in mining tantalite, walking the length and breadth of the valley to and from Kariba with a black man who had fought with the King's African Rifles as his companion.

Sylvia remembers snippets of information about life down the Buffalo Downs road. In spite of all the years of teaching, she still found time to raise six children of her own.

She remembers a woman who lived alone in a substantial stone house on Granite farm. She had once been a practising doctor and for some reason had become a recluse. She had no transport and would emerge from her home only to walk to Peter and Pat Gibson's house to use the phone, but since Peter's death her name has been lost to us. She was thought to be mad, but Dr Pat Taylor refused to have her certified, saying that she was as sane as most – and adding that she was just eccentric.

Another neighbour was Peter Moore, who farmed Garahanga farm. He left farming to become the paymaster for Rupert Fothergill, who was involved with 'The Ark' project that moved wildlife caught on the islands that sprang up as the waters rose when Kariba dam was formed. These animals had to be rescued and were carried to the safety of the mainland.

On the corner of King's View road – 'up the power lines', as everyone said – lived the Kinds. They arrived from Chakari after the war and settled on Milverton, which they named after the farm they had left behind in Chakari, subsequently purchased by Ben Lubbe's father. Bob Kind suffered a heart attack while playing tennis, and his family buried him in the Zambezi Valley, beneath a baobab tree.

Mrs Carpenter, alias 'Carpie', was a formidable character who lived on a farm along the King's View road. She had a reputation for instilling obedience and fear into all around her. Dennis Prince used to be her neighbour when she farmed along those power lines. He woke up one morning, upset to find that all her cattle were in his maize.

'Hey, Carpie,' he complained. 'Your cattle are in my maize.'

'Well, move them,' she replied.

However, when Carpie moved into the village, she took in a generation of children too young to enter the boarding hostel, and taught them impeccable manners.

In 1947 Dennis was the youngest working adult among all those who arrived to farm in Karoi. He had just left school and was sixteen years old. His half-brother, Sonny Shakespeare, just back from the war, invited him to tag along and help him on his newly acquired land, Caversham.

Dennis had hoped that the war would last long enough for him to enlist. It clearly didn't, and he remembers the disappointments felt by his contemporaries – who had already joined up, were trained, and had even been issued with kit, only to find that the war had ended. Nevertheless, they had become eligible to take up farms. Eric Pope was one, and Bert Hacking was another.

Dennis, eighty-two when I spoke to him, looked back on those days with nostalgia. He chuckled when he remembered them and was very amused to realise that he himself had joined the elite vintage group of octogenarians.

Dennis had two other brothers – Bob and Clive. A little after Dennis arrived in Karoi, word revealed that Mrs Leask was looking for a manager to run her farm. This brought Bob Prince into the district. He supervised the building of barns on Coldomo so that tobacco could be grown there. Mary Leask, who had been widowed in 1941, had had high hopes that Rita would marry a farmer, but Rita was a career girl and left Karoi to train as a secretary. She subsequently joined the diplomatic corps and worked in East Africa.

Meanwhile, Sonny had sub-divided Caversham and sold a portion to Geoff Lockett. This was registered as Romford, and Clive Prince at the age of eighteen went to work for him in 1949.

He moved around the district, working for Stuart Maclaurin and Harry Wells, and finally on Chitonga in Tengwe for his stepfather, Harry Berenfeld. Daisy May, mother of Sonny, Bob, Dennis and Clive, was a Russian Jewess who, having survived both her first two husbands, Mr Shakespeare and Mr Prince, then married Harry Berenfeld.

The new settlers were working hard but also playing hard. Poker schools popped up around the district, with Sam Barrett-Hamilton, Peter Fisher, Lionel Searle and Peter Gibson forming one of them.

Peter Fisher endeared himself to everyone because he had a bad stutter, an affliction that didn't help in the game of poker. His stutter would become more and more pronounced with each splendid hand he was dealt – which was, of course, a dead giveaway and the cards would be thrown in. As the most junior member in the group, Dennis was used as the 'minder': it was his job to see that his peers arrived home safely.

There were many unmarried men around, bachelors who cast envious eyes at the married men, all of them turning a lustful eye and harbouring lecherous thoughts as they flirted through nights at the Club, longing for the moment when they, too, might have a partner beside them. Any unattached woman who happened to pitch up didn't have long to wait before she was snapped up into matrimony.

While they waited patiently for their love lives to improve, the bachelors devised their own means of amusement by drawing up a 'list of approval', rating the wives in the district. Paddy du Barry, having divorced Lionel Searle and subsequently married Guy, topped the list as number K1. Nan Maclaurin was K2 and Gwen Marillier K3, and so the list grew under the watchful eye of young bloods.

Dennis Prince spoke of 'French Marie', the first and only butcher in the area. She drove round the farms, trying to sell meat to anyone brave enough to sample it.

Robbie and Mary Purchase also lived along the King's View road. Robbie had a few strange habits, which may have been a legacy from his fighting days. He kept sticks of dynamite in his shed, and from time to time he would be overcome with a compulsion to make a loud noise. Mary would remonstrate with him: 'No, not now, dear. The children are sleeping.' But he would become agitated and cry out, 'No, it's got to be now. I have to do it now.' He once kept a crocodile in the bath and a python in the shed to keep rats away.

There is still a farm called Wester Moy, Muir-of-Ord, in Ross-shire Scotland, owned by a Chisholm – it was here that Alexander (Sandy) Chisholm was born in 1915, the second son of seven siblings. The Chisholms were staunch Catholics; that never changed.

Sandy arrived in Rhodesia in 1936, tempted by Cecil Gair, who had grown up alongside him on a nearby estate. Sandy's war began with training in Gwelo with the Rhodesian African Rifles. He served time in East Africa, as a Sergeant. He held the army shot-putt record for a number of years, which led his daughter, Cathy Oldreive, married to Brian, to remark dryly that clearly all those years of tossing the caber back home had not been in vain.

Sandy married Catherine Madge Patrick, who was born in Bloemfontein in 1918. Her father, Hubert Patrick, was of South African settler stock, and her mother, Alma Ann de Scally, had her roots in Ireland. Great-grandfather Scally was a typical wild anti-British 'Paddy', who made his way to South Africa to fight with the Boers against the British. He was, of course, neither the first nor the last to take up that stance.

When Sandy decided to apply for a farm in Karoi, his first choice was land that was coveted by Zak Olivier. They drew lots and the land now known as Moy became Sandy's.

Sandy and Cathy Chisholm.

The usual pioneering lifestyle followed; pole'n'daga huts, Dover stove in a cooking hut, and a long drop.

An iron tub stood in a tent, and ablutions were forbidden after dark because the tent would turn into a 'shadow theatre', with entertainment for all, as bodies became silhouetted against the light of a tilley lamp. Tilley lamps were disliked: they hissed, and the children seemed to spend their lives pumping them up.

There were only a couple of telephones in the whole district. One was one on Vuka farm that belonged to Trevor Harvey. Trevor used to trundle over with emergency messages on his bicycle – usually with news of births, deaths and the dates of the next Farmers' Association meeting.

The first summer of the 1947/48 season was memorable, as the rains fell in unrelenting deluges, day after day. It was impossible

The Chisholms' pole'n'daga house.

Oxen used for transport.

The river in flood.

Tying matepes.

Storing tobacco in bulk.

to keep anything dry. The Staceys had built a house down by the Ricoco river, and after one particularly heavy storm they were flooded out and had to move in with the Chisholms, whose own huts were also leaking furiously.

Moira Stacey was a tiny baby, so she was put into a Moses basket in a wardrobe to keep dry. Granny Patrick lost her false teeth in the mud and took herself off to bed in a huff, but then had to sit upright under an umbrella all night because of the heavy leaking. It was the first season for most of them and it was pretty memorable.

The Native Commissioner's office was still in Miami, so Sandy would have to take new labourers there periodically for their new 'situpas' (passes), which the workers were obliged to carry. The children loved to go along and play on the mine dumps.

There was still nothing in Karoi except grass huts at Chikangwe Halt, where the RMS dropped the mail bag plus supplies from Sinoia for the farmers who lived along the Chumburukwe road. The RMS travelled up to the Leask Halt, where Corner Store is.

Everyone loved mail day because all the farmers north of the Halt would gather there to wait for the lorry to arrive. In no time it would evolve into a social occasion, with lots of chit-chat and kids playing around during the wait. Mums would complain about spoiled goods and Dads would take no notice, open another beer and 'talk shop'. After one 'road party', Cathy got really fed-up when she saw all that was left of the margarine was a big greasy spot in the box.

Cathy said that there was always a Club, and Sandy, a cricket enthusiast, played for Karoi. So did Trevor Harvey next door. For a few seasons the cricketers used a coir mat that usually lay in the passage in the Chisholm home. Cathy said it kept the snakes away, and maybe it did. Each Sunday the mat was carefully rolled up and loaded into the back of the station wagon and used as a wicket.

Ian Chisholm's birth came rather prematurely and he was born on the farm. Roland Whitaker, who had taken over from Pat Taylor as GMO, arrived with his wife Margaret to help with the delivery. Ian was the first white baby to have been born actually in Karoi, but Bonny Laver claims that distinction, though it is likely that her birth was registered in Sinoia. When Sandy went over to the Miami office to register Ian's birth, he was informed that they didn't have the relevant forms as they had never been needed.

Cathy junior was very jealous when her brother, Hamish, and Moira Stacey went off to Mrs MacDonald's school, which was held in the Gwen Scrase Hall in 1958. She was just one year too old, and like all good Catholics, she was shipped off to the Salisbury convent.

There had been no improvement in the roads even by the 1950s. Strips of tar continued through Maryland, Darwendale and Sinoia from Salisbury, and then a very dangerous piece of road as far as Lion's Den. Beyond that it was dirt and potholes. Salisbury and home seemed so very far away on

those occasions, and the Karoi people didn't make the trek too often.

The wheel of the car came off the Chisholm car on one occasion as they drove from town. 'Oh,' Cathy senior exclaimed, 'I wonder where that came from?' An almighty crash gave them the answer as the axle hit the ground. No one was hurt – one could not drive very fast on those roads.

Cathy kept a massive kitchen garden and was able to supply the Italian engineers and workers with vegetables and poultry when the Kariba dam was being built in the late 1950s. The Kariba project brought along with it the advantages of a wonderful new tarred road, which also helped to open up the district.

The Chisholms felt themselves fortunate in having the Staceys as neighbours on Templecombe farm. Amy Stacey and Cathy Chisholm were sisters, and the cousins were great company for each other especially during school holidays.

One Saturday afternoon they were playing tennis when a kudu bull broke through the wire mesh, followed closely by a lion. This illustrates just how wild it still was at that time and how dense the bush. Clearing for *munda*s (farm lands) was hard work, and Cathy remembers a rhino chasing one of the labourers who had wandered down to the river for water.

Other neighbours were Charlie and Pearl McLaughlan. Pearl's parents were Mr and Mrs A. B. Roberts, who had bought the remainder of Nassau in 1940. Charlie was an enthusiastic hunter who always had biltong, and the Chisholm kids loved to visit him.

In 1971 Mrs Amy Stacey, widow of Dave, the first farmer to be killed by guerrillas in the bush war, wrote the following poem, taken from 'The Good Old Days', published in the Silver Jubilee issue of the *Karoi Chronicle*.

Karoi was very famous,
    in those far-off early days,
We almost broke the record
    for 'the crop that never failed'.
We also grew tobacco,
    and a little bit of maize,
And we made a little money –
    if we didn't have the hail.
We came up here quite penniless,
    'Where angels fear to tread',
But we didn't eat 'mazhanjes' –
    we baked our own white bread.
And then we progressed, yearly,
    and got more civilised,
With engines, ploughs and tractors,
    we slowly mechanised:
The LSB were happy,
    and a little bit surprised.
We had fought so many battles,
    But we'd actually survived.

Peter Stafford Gibson was born on Berea farm, Nyabira. It was his humorous claim that he had lived in six different countries without ever having crossed a border. This is how he figured it worked:

In 1922, the year that Peter Gibson was born, the country was governed not by the Crown but by officials of a commercial undertaking known as the British South Africa Company. Later in that year the electorate were asked to make a choice in a referendum, and in 1923 it became the self-governing British colony of Southern Rhodesia.

Then in 1953 Southern Rhodesia became part of the Federation of Rhodesia and Nyasaland. The Federation was dissolved in 1963, and the country reverted to being Southern Rhodesia once more.

Following the Unilateral Declaration of Independence in 1965, the country was known as Rhodesia until 1979, when for a few short months it became Zimbabwe-

Peter and Pat Gibson.

Rhodesia, under Prime Minister Bishop Abel Muzorewa.

The Lancaster House agreement at the end of that year meant that the country was briefly Southern Rhodesia once more under the Governorship of Lord Soames, until internationally recognised independence in 1980 and the final appellation of Zimbabwe.

John O. Gibson, Peter's father, died young, as so many did in those days. Two pewter mugs give testimony to his success as a cattle breeder. One inscription reads: 'Rhodesian Agricultural and Horticultural Society to John Gibson for Best Devon Bull 1919', an award presented to him in an official capacity by his friend and neighbour in Nyabira, Mr Glanfield.

Fashions change over time, and beer tankards seemed to be the choice of award for expertise in many fields in those days, in much the same way as the next generation were presented with silver cups. These accolades obviously meant little to the recipients, for as fast as they were presented they were sold for beer money.

John Gibson married an Australian, the daughter of an Anglican clergyman from Adelaide. Her name was Eileen Stafford-Needham, whom, it was thought, John had met in Britain. Three sons were born to them, Peter was their second.

He started his education at Ruzawi in 1928 and then went on to Prince Edward School, where he attained the ultimate achievement of becoming Head Boy in 1939. He played for the 1st XV rugby side under E. J. 'Jeeves' Hougaard, who went on to become the headmaster of Churchill High School. He also played first-team cricket, but it was tennis, in fact, that was his great passion and it was through this game that he met Pat, his wife.

After school, Peter became a cadet in the Native Affairs department (later renamed Internal Affairs). His first posting sent him to Goromonzi, where he was assigned an 'askari', or messenger, to work with him.

The two men made a pact with each other: each evening they would practise their mother tongues, Shona and English, for an hour – thus each became proficient in both languages. This diligence, dedication and motivation would account for Peter's later successes in life.

When war broke out Peter joined up, becoming the first non-commissioned officer in the Rhodesian African Rifles. Their first training camp was situated among the gum trees along the Borrowdale Road in Salisbury, where the racecourse stands today, and the first route march was a vigorous stepping out to Marandellas and back.

The war saw him being sent down to Cape Town and drafted into the 51st Cape Town City Highlanders and, as part of the Fifth Army, he was sent to Egypt and across to Italy. Bilharzia, a disease then not as easily cured as it is today, put him in hospital for six months and out of the war.

He returned to Rhodesia and found a job on a farm in Banket. He stayed one season and, on collecting his bonus, discovered that he had been short-changed. After tackling his erstwhile boss about the discrepancy, he was told, 'every time you asked me a question, I deducted money as a consultation fee'. That is how it was then.

Following this he applied to the Land Settlement Board for a farm in Karoi. Peter's choice of the surveyed farms was Longueil, which he lost to Jack O'Hea. He accepted his second choice, Nyangoma, which was named after the nearby river and in Shona means the noise of a drum, a sound it probably makes when in full flood.

Peter married Patricia Elizabeth Pilcher in 1949. She was born in Kenya where her father, Captain J. T. Pilcher, grew coffee. Captain Pilcher had initially been a member of the British Royal Marines and was the first, although retired, to be called up in World War II, subsequently to be made head of security at the Durban docks. It is thought that he met his wife, Catherine Rudland, known as Bobby, in Durban.

Clearly it was love at first sight, for, having decided that they would dispense with a lengthy courtship, the couple eloped and set sail for Mombasa; the trip aboard ship sufficed as a honeymoon after the captain had performed a marriage ceremony.

Catherine's father, Thomas Wilburn Rudland, was the last surviving Pioneer in Rhodesia. He had joined the Pioneer Column in 1890 and travelled up to Bulawayo. Born in London, he had emigrated first to the New World but returned disillusioned, not only with America but with his errant wife, who had gone off with someone else. Thomas then decided to follow the herd to South Africa.

The lure could have been diamonds or just a wish to start afresh, but some family members say that he never bothered to divorce his wife – 'which would make us, his progeny, bastards, and him a bigamist,' says his great-grandson, Ian Gibson, with glee. However, other family members rise up in indignation and vehemently deny this. The truth evades us, but it makes a good story.

Pat left Kenya with her parents and brother, Roy, in the 1930s. The Pilchers leased Grasslands farm outside Marandellas, which was eventually to become the Grasslands Research Station. There they ran a dairy, supplying milk to the town and Ruzawi School.

Later they moved to Blarney farm, where the Red Fox now stands, supplying milk three times a day to the town centre. The habit of dairying never left Pat, and she used to supply Ted's Butchery with farm-made butter and cream for many years.

Pat's education led her first to Lilfordia (founded in 1902) and then on to Girls High in Salisbury, where she was awarded a Beit scholarship to train as a nurse, although her first choice of career had been veterinary science.

At the bottom of the Buffalo Downs road on Ruwanzi Ranch lived ex-serviceman, 'Bez' Bezuitenhout. His face was badly disfigured, so he lived a reclusive kind of life, where Arthur Bishop and Peter Gibson kept a kindly eye on him.

His story is intricately linked to that of Alex Fry, who surveyed many of the farms in Karoi and was mentioned in an earlier chapter. Peter Gibson became an important connection between the two. Alex tells the story:

> Shortly after the war ended, the day came when I was told to supervise the removal of all the live ammunition from the SSB tanks. We had parked at the Monza race track on the outskirts of Milan. That same day Major Poultney asked me to turn out for the SSB rugby team.
>
> I informed him that I had been put in charge of a duty to remove the ammunition from the tanks for delivery to the central ammo dump in town. He asked

me to try and find a Lance Corporal to take over from me.

I was reluctant to do this and discussed it with one of my friends, Bez Bezuitenhout. His immediate response was that he would do anything for rugby and I must play. He would do the unloading for me.

I don't remember the rugby match, but I will never forget the reports of that fateful morning in the tank park. The men were loading the shells. Bez and another soldier, John Munro, were packing the ammunition into cases, their task nearly over. Bez caught a damaged shell and when he bent down to pack it away, it split open and a cloud of phosphorus exploded in his face.

Munro shouted 'run for your life' and fell to the ground, but Bez didn't follow and Munro realised he'd been blinded by the fumes. John took immediate action and jumped back on to the truck, throwing Bez down on to the ground, dragging him away from the inferno just as the truck blew up with a loud explosion. John was burned, but not to the same extent as Bez, who was screaming from pain. It was an extraordinarily brave deed.

Bez was in a terrible state. He was screaming with pain as the phosphorus continued to burn his body. His colleagues did their best for him as they raced him to hospital. The doctors and nurses attended to him immediately and did what they could, but his life hung by a thread.

I feared for his life, and couldn't get over the dreadful feeling that he should not have been there in the first place. I was asked to visit him and was warned that he was not a pretty sight, as the burned areas had to be left open.

My immediate reaction was to run away, horrified by what I saw. There was nothing left of his face. The nose had gone completely and there were no lips, eyebrows, eyelashes or ears.

I greeted him and did my best to get him to talk, but he remained silent; frankly, I was at a loss for words. I did not stay long as I didn't feel capable of succeeding where the hospital had failed. It was the most shattering experience of my life.

After four years of studying for a degree in Land Surveying at the University of Cape Town, I left for Rhodesia and joined the firm of Maasdorp, Piers and Hopely. In 1951 I was surveying a block of farms in Karoi and had camped on a farm belonging to Peter Gibson.

One day he stopped me as I was driving to work to tell me that a cattle inspector had arrived who was badly disfigured about the face. I asked Peter if his name was Bezuitenhout, and he said that it was and related the story.

Peter asked me to join him for a few drinks that evening, and he would ask Bez to come so that I could meet him again. Frankly, I was unhappy about the idea but Peter was sure that the two of us should meet.

That evening, I arrived at the Gibsons' house and we sat on the veranda having a beer. A short while later, a government truck drew up and I went down the steps to meet Bez. I had last seen him in hospital in Milan, Italy.

Bez put out his hand and I was aware that most of his fingers were missing. It was an emotional moment as he seemed very pleased to see me, and this broke down any barriers that might have existed between us. Over a few beers he told me his story.

He had spent six years in hospital, having one graft after another. The doctors could do only one graft at a time because of the extent of the area of his body burnt by the phosphorus.

He willingly spoke of his facial rebuild. It was remarkable how well his lips, nose, eyebrows, cheeks and ears had been recreated from his body.

One day a nurse told him the doctors were just using him as a guinea pig and that if he wanted to lead a normal life he should just walk out of hospital.

It was advice he took, but he returned every year for further skin grafts until they were satisfied there was nothing more they could do.

The next day, Peter suggested that I go down to the cattle dip and watch Bez at work. I went and was immediately impressed with his strength. A well-built calf escaped from the race and Bez ran across the pen and grabbed it by one leg, bent it double, and led it to the dip where he forced it to join the queue.

He managed all this with his damaged hands and I complimented him on his achievement. He was pleased that I had seen the action.

I never saw Bez again, but that interlude, engineered by Peter Gibson, and meeting up with him again had somehow put my mind at rest.

Happily, some time later Bez moved down to the Midlands. There he regained some semblance of normality when he fell in love with a neighbour's wife, whom he subsequently married. It's a story with a happy ending.

Jimmy Pierson farmed on Mwala ('a shallow-rooted tree') and because he was a brilliant shottist, he built a rifle range. Paul Pearson, who was often confused with Jimmy Pierson,

69

farmed on Tarquinia and was a keen flier. He not only started the flying club but flew the *Sunday Herald* from Salisbury to Lusaka each week.

When Paul left to live in Kenya, Tarquinia was sub-divided. Willie Nel bought Buffalo Downs in the early 1960s, and also 'the high part' of Aerodrome farm, as it was nick-named, and to that he added Nicotiana.

Geoff Holland, farmed on Mafalo; it was the last farm along the Buffalo Downs road before crossing the Angwa river. He had once thought of running a bus service to Umboe/Mangula along the shortcut, but gave up the idea because the timing was wrong as politics intervened and the bush war started.

Many farmers are given apt nicknames by their labourers, who are quick to grab on to a glaring physical trait, habit or mannerism – even a piece of clothing. In Geoff's case it was easy, for he was never without his favourite piece of headgear, which had the old copper pennies – holes in the middle of them – sewn around the brim. He was known as Boss MaPenny.

In 1962 Geoff sub-divided Mafalo and sold two portions: one to Gigi Falzoi, who had just arrived in the country from Eritrea, then a province of Ethiopia, the other to Rupert Hawley, who registered it as Tollington.

Allwyn (Bob) Lewis A. P. Thomas farmed Nyamahamba and Zakanaka. His wife, until 1954, was Barbara Kathleen Ayers, who was a brilliant pianist and taught music in both Salisbury and Bulawayo. Bob, of Welsh descent, was born in Ceylon, where his father was a diplomat. He was partially raised in Australia before migrating to Rhodesia before the Second World War.

Before selling to Willie Nel in the early 1960s, he leased out his farms to various people, one of whom was Anthony Hardy, who was with Scanlen and Holderness attor-

neys in Salisbury. One of Bob's daughters, Diana, married Hans Hansen. The two of them lived in Kariba for a short time.

Both were aboard the Viscount Hunyani when it crashed in 1978. They not only survived the crash but the subsequent attack as well, and Hans wrote about their experience in a book entitled *The Deafening Silence*.

Lionel G. Searle, DFC, was born in Peddie, South Africa, close to East London in the Cape. He came to Rhodesia with his parents and brother. The two Searle boys attended St George's College in Salisbury and he was barely out of school when war broke out. Like many other Rhodesian youngsters, he itched to join up and do his patriotic duty.

After returning home, having been awarded the Distinguished Flying Cross for night work from Malta on the invasion of Sicily, he was discharged in September 1945. He applied to the Land Settlement Board for land in Karoi as an ex-serviceman, and moved there with Paddy, his first wife.

All applicants were required to have two years of farming experience, so Lionel did a year at Gwebi and a year with the Lamb Brothers before being allocated a farm.

He arrived on his piece of virgin land with a 'buck sail', which he threw over a tree branch for protection, a chest of drawers and a Great Dane. Help came in the form of Simon Gasangarari, a local Shona lad, who remained with him until he stopped farming. That first night a herd of sable stampeded past their camp – close enough to stir up the embers of the fire. Simon exclaimed, 'We have disturbed the sable. We should call this farm Pangwarati, which means "home of the sable".'

In 1951, retired Brigadier Mike Wearing, his wife, Sylvia, and daughter Elizabeth (Liz) arrived from Britain. Mike had hoped to mine mica in Miami but he had left it too late

– the mica was petering out. He managed to find work with Lionel on Pangwarati.

After Paddy left, Lionel married Liz Wearing and they moved to Wajetsi, a neighbouring farm that had remained vacant. Today, Liz remembers Karoi being populated with wonderful characters who were remarkable people.

In those days, barn fires were a common occurrence, the Searles experiencing one themselves. Within hours it had been extinguished with the help of neighbours. The next morning those same neighbours turned up with replacements: Arthur Bishop arrived with a couple of doors, Doug Fox with some flues, and Cecil Gair with sheets of roofing. That was what living among farmers was like, she said.

Ex-serviceman Arnold Miller de Haan was the first Hollander to farm in Karoi. He called his new property Pompey, a name given to Portsmouth in England after it had been razed to the ground during the wartime bombing. Arnold had a special affinity with Portsmouth because it was where he met his wife, Jackie.

They visited Britain every year, where they had a lovely home and a Bentley car. Arnold came from an affluent family that owned a Rembrandt painting that he couldn't afford to insure.

From the time the country was opened up, there was a breed of men known as 'remittance men', and a few were among Karoi's ex-servicemen. They were men who were sent to the colonies over the centuries, and Africa received its fair share. In general, they were members of the wealthy upper classes who had blotted their copybooks and were paid a sum of money to stay away. Many of them made good, but for some it was too late.

The old-timers said that W.B. 'Bill' Soames slotted into this category. After the war he managed to acquire prize land along Maclaurin Road, which was called Sherwood Forest on the first survey map. It is probable that this was a name given by the surveyor, because we knew the farm as Rufaro.

Bill Soames is remembered as a charming drunk, whose addiction to the bottle afforded him little time for farming. He was also rumoured to be a relative of Lord Christopher Soames, who married Winston Churchill's daughter, Mary. Christopher Soames was the last colonial Governor, appointed to steer the country through the transition from Rhodesia to independent Zimbabwe.

The distinctive Soames eyes are a very pronounced family feature: Anne Soames, who married Billy Postlethwayt after Eileen died, has those eyes. As a farmer, Bill Soames made no progress at all, and within a year the farm had been taken away and given to Paul Philip.

When Paul arrived on Rufaro, little if anything at all had been achieved. His first season was 1948/49. It was a difficult one because after the first rains in mid-November no more fell until 1 January, though the crop was saved by later rains.

Paul grew thirty-two acres of tobacco and cured it in three barns, which he had managed to build as the crop grew, but there were no sheds, so all the tobacco had to be baled immediately and stored elsewhere. Ultimately, things improved, and for the next twenty years he farmed successfully.

Paul built a nice house and then looked for a wife. 'I was the lucky one,' said Maureen:

> John New had bought Hunter's Lodge from Frank Lucas in the interim. Colin and Honor Duff managed the place for him, and it was from their house that I met Paul.
>
> The Club was a very lively place then

71

and a great meeting place after shopping on a Friday ... this was the brick building which replaced the pole'n'daga original. It was big enough for us to play badminton inside, but it was cricket that was the first sport played seriously.

Frank Lucas was a neighbour on Hunter's Lodge. He was a real character and drove an ancient vintage Rolls-Royce.

Bertram Cecil William Hacking does not quite qualify as an original settler. He has been recorded as a farmer, businessman, director of companies and active public worker, who was the first chairman of the North West Development Association.

When he was elected President of the Association of Rural Councils, he had been a member of the Karoi Road Council and the Rural Council for twenty-five years. In 1975 he was awarded the order of the Legion of Merit for his many years of public service.

His interests were varied, but his main concerns were for agriculture. However, that said, his contributions were singularly unimpressive, though were recognised by his appointment in the early 1970s as Chairman of the Farmers' Co-op in Salisbury, a position he kept for many years before being unseated in a boardroom 'putsch'.

The first Hackings moved to Rhodesia in 1909 and, after serving in the First World War, Cecil Rhodes Hacking went farming tobacco in Norton with his two brothers.

Bert was born in Cape Town on 10 April 1926. After schooling in Umtali, he was employed by the Rhodesian Treasury and then, at eighteen, he joined the air force to train as a pilot. He missed the war, but somehow managed to acquire two pieces of land on the ex-servicemen's scheme after an injury to his ankle ended his rugby-playing career.

In 1952 he started a butchery in partner-

ship with Ronnie Saint. This was to absorb the cattle from the Reserves and to feed the new population at Kariba when the building of the dam commenced.

Jimmy Oxenham and his wife, Kay, were the first occupants of Nyamanda farm, where, apart from growing tobacco, Jimmy bred racehorses. They sold the place to Fred Mulder who, with his wife, Mary, were known to be a very industrious couple.

There was not much that was not produced on their farm. Fred had worked for A.B.Roberts in Miami. He had often felt the sting of French Marie's whip, and had run around in a T-Model Ford which he had had to thatch when the roof started to leak. Nor was he averse to walking through the bush on a Saturday to play tenniquoits with the Leask girls on Coldomo.

Fred was such a devoted father to Mary's children, Barrie and Mary Anne, that they never realised that he was not their natural father. Mary Lou made history and broke a record when she was born several weeks prematurely. She survived, only by the dedicated nursing of Sr Vicky Fox and Sr Fran Reid (Fran Fraser) at the Sinoia Maternity Hospital. Mary Lou was the smallest premature baby ever to have survived at that time.

Captain Hector Stanley 'Zook' Nesbitt was the first owner of Spring farm bordering the Mvagasi river. He was the nephew of Randolph Cosby Nesbitt of Mazoe Patrol fame.

On the opposite side of the river, Mike Reynolds, son-in-law of Zook, built the Twin River Inn, known originally as the Golden Parakeet. Mike Reynolds's daughter, Merle, married Dennis Armstrong, who farmed on Pumula. He was Sandhurst-trained, and was awarded the coveted Sword of Honour. (Tom Simpson, son of Maurice and Eve, Good Hope farm, was another Sandhurst boy who distinguished himself by winning the same award, years later.) He rose to command the SAS as a lieutenant colonel, and was also a talented polo player.

Seven or eight years on, by 1954, some of the original owners had begun to realise that happiness for them had nothing whatever to do with farming, and they began to offload their properties. They sold to younger men waiting in the wings, men who knew, from working for others, that there was money to be made. One of them was Mark Gaisford, who bought Leconfield from Peter Fisher in 1954. He remained there for close on fifty years.

Mark was born in Quetta, India (now Pakistan), where his father, Sir Philip Gaisford, was the 'Resident' or Governor of Mysore. His title was conferred on him in recognition of this service. Sir Philip retired at partition and migrated to Southern Rhodesia.

As members of a staunch Catholic family, Mark and his younger brother had been sent to the well-known Catholic public school of Downside in Somerset. The third brother escaped this long-distance education and attended St George's in Salisbury. Both Mark's younger brothers became Jesuit priests. Father Dominic Gaisford subsequently became the Abbot of Worth Abbey in Sussex. When Mark left Downside he joined the Irish Guards and managed to squeeze in a few months of war service. He was present at Arnhem in Holland, the story of which is told in the film, *A Bridge Too Far*. He then returned to Rhodesia, bought Leconfield, and married Denise Cullinan in 1955.

The name Cullinan has, over the years, become pretty much a household name. It entered the annals of history in 1905 with the discovery of the world's largest diamond, which came to be known as the Cullinan Diamond.

Denise's Cullinan Gaisford's grandfather, Thomas Major Cullinan, came of humble origins. The family lived in the eastern highlands of the Cape, where he had worked as a builder, although all his life he had been an inveterate prospector. He married Annie Harding and they produced ten children. Denise says she's not likely to forget her Grandmother Annie, for she was a real tartar and very forbidding.

In 1903, shortly after Tom had begun to dig prospecting pits at the mine, he promised his wife that one day he would bring her 'the biggest diamond in the world'. She had laughed and had soon forgotten the promise. Two years later that promise was fulfilled.

Tom Cullinan had always suspected that there were one or more large diamond pipes present on Elandsfontein Farm near Pretoria, but the Prinsloo family who owned the farm stubbornly refused to sell.

Four years passed before Thomas Cullinan's dream was realised, and it came as the result of the Anglo-Boer War, which changed the fate of both the Prinsloo and Cullinan families. The first were forced to sell, having fallen on hard times, and Elandsfontein became the property of Thomas Cullinan after a promise of part payment in gold sovereigns.

The Cullinan Diamond emerged to the light of day at 5.00 p.m. on 26 January 1905. The surface manager, Frederick Wells, was led by a black worker to one side wall of the infant mine who pointed to a bright object caught in the sun's rays and embedded in yellow ground some nine metres below the surface. Wells investigated and dug the object out with his penknife and pulled out an enormous diamond weighing 3.106 carats.

Because of its size and quality, it was sent to Holland to be cut and polished by the best diamond-cutter there, Joseph Asscher in Amsterdam. It produced nine major gems.

Two were retained for the British Crown Jewels, subsequently set into the Sceptre and Crown.

In 1910 a knighthood was conferred on Thomas Major Cullinan in recognition of his services, both as a member of the Legislative Assembly of the Transvaal, and as Chairman of the Premier Diamond Mine. He had come a long way from being a builder.

Sir Thomas was also granted a concession of land at Matepatepa in Rhodesia by Cecil Rhodes, which is named Ruia Ranch. Hence, Denise Gaisford came to be born in Southern Rhodesia. Denise has a replica set of all nine major gemstones cut from the Cullinan.

After the first momentous discovery, the Premier Syndicate was formed and shares divided among the subscribers. Two of them were A. Mackie Niven and Sir Percy Fitzpatrick, the author of the children's classic, *Jock of The Bushveld*, both good friends of Thomas Cullinan. Both Niven and Fitzpatrick were imprisoned for their part in the Jameson Raid.

Their two families became linked by marriage and from this union came Rose Niven, who married Peter van Breda. Peter and Rose lived in Karoi for many years.

Brian McKay was another youngster who took advantage of a farm that came up for sale in the mid 1950s. He – like Mark Gaisford, Harold Herud and Harry Wells – bought a farm from the original settlers not long after the area was opened up. He bought Pitlochry from Ian Laing, who had decided that he just didn't have the temperament for farming.

Brian arrived in Southern Rhodesia from Queenstown, where he was born and brought up. After leaving school he had joined a firm of solicitors. Most people could have pictured him holding forth in court, for he had a wicked dry humour and a lively eloquent mind. But Brian was used to the outdoor life on a farm and decided to follow an alternative direction.

He was visiting friends in Bulawayo when heard that the north was the place to be, where farmers were making money hand over fist in the production of the golden weed.

He heard of an opening with George Hackwill at Lion's Den and went there first; then he went to work for Vic Tucker in Karoi on Sapi Valley. Vic later swapped Sapi Valley for Waterfalls on the edge of Salisbury, which belonged to Dolan Hampson.

Brian McKay leased Pitlochry for a season before buying it from Ian Laing. He then bought neighbouring Strathyre from Alec Watson, who used to top his tobacco with a *panga* (a grass-slasher). Alec was once working on a roof, and his wife sent him not only his breakfast but his lunch as well – a big hint that she didn't want to see him again until the roof was repaired!

Brian also bought Vermont when Flossie Hoskyns left there. Brian was known to his friends as 'California', because he once made a very unwise purchase of a horse that turned out to be too wild to handle.

If you happen to be travelling around the roads of Miami, you might, even now, catch a glimpse of the bizarre Pitlochry Ambulance trundling along. It is a true Brian McKay device, a quaint conversion of an ox-drawn trailer designed to carry the Pitlochry sick to the clinic in Miami … as fast as possible!

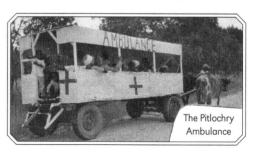

The Pitlochry Ambulance

In 1959 Brian married his long-time love, Beth Scott, whom he met while still at school.

Not counting the long-standing Leask family of Coldomo farm, only four farms were still in the hands of the original owners at the time of the farm invasions in 2000. In an African context, this is quite a distinctive achievement. They were: Chisapi, owned by Paddy Barrett-Hamilton, son of Sam; Zebra Downs, owned by Chris Bishop, son of Arthur; Nyangoma, owned by Ian Gibson, son of Peter; and Mahuti owned by Derek Olivier, though Derek says he cannot really be counted as he has since learned that he was not Zak's son. Nevertheless, he was born and brought up on Mahuti as Zack's son and continued to farm there until it was taken from him.

There was also the Ormerod family who were on Mlichi farm. George Ormerod, son of Hugh, was still living there and owned the farm but was not farming it himself.

Donovan Stotter could also be included. Although he was not an England, he was Mary's nephew and stood to inherit Mshalla. Furthermore, but for a tragic car accident in which David Grantham junior lost his life, and subsequently the appalling murder of his mother, Maureen Grantham, no doubt there would also still have been a Grantham in residence on Shawnigan.

The Southey (or Sowthey) family can trace its roots back to the sixteenth century, to one Thomas Sowthey, born about 1550.

Fortune-seekers were then exploring the trackless highways – traders, smugglers and adventurers of every description were sailing from the shores of Britain at about the same time that Drake and Raleigh were setting off. But Sowthey was not quite so courageous and stayed put to become a 'clothier'. Drake,

Raleigh and Sowthey were born within a few years of each other and, indeed, but a few miles apart in Devon.

Three hundred years passed. Then, in 1820, the history books bring to light another Thomas Sowthey, whose son, George Sowthey, married to Joan Baker, had, at the age of forty-three, taken his wife and brood of five sons and two daughters to the Cape Colony in the Kennersley Castle. They were, of course, part of the 1820 settlers.

The youngest boy, named Cannon, died on the voyage out, but the fourth son, Richard, then twelve, was destined to become one of the most distinguished of the settlers. He was appointed Lieutenant Governor of the province of Griqualand West in 1873, and was knighted in 1891, becoming Sir Richard Sowthey. He was Beth (Scott) McKay's grandfather.

Apart from Beth McKay, what had this illustrious gentleman to do with the Urungwe? Depending on how one views history, perhaps not much. But we do find that many of his descendants have lived in the Miami–Karoi–Tengwe district over the years, having married into other well-known pioneering families over the decades.

Another branch of George Sowthey's family trekked up to Rhodesia in 1897. They were brothers Charles and George Southey (the spelling had changed) who, along with their father, Robert Southey, and a brother-in-law, Glynne Peacocke, began the long, slow journey northwards towards the Limpopo river. Other members of the family followed, and as a consequence Rhodesia was inundated with Southeys and their off-shoots. A dynasty began.

In the late 1890s the Fynns were to marry into the Southey family when Melvyn Dick Fynn married Louisa Southey. Starting in Miami from the 1920s we find that the prospector and adventurer Jack Fynn, the maverick grandfather of Tamsin Barker, was a descendant. Isabella Rubidge, who married George Deacon, was another, as were their son, Portlock Gilmour Deacon, and daughters Althea (Dewdney), Avril (Chisnall) and Yoland Nicholle. Other names such as Peacocke, Gilmour and Morkel are all interlinked by marriage.

Gwen Marillier was a Southey – her grandfather was Charles Southey, brother of Sir Robert who trekked up to Rhodesia in 1897. Other Southeys who lived in Karoi were Richard (Dick) Southey,

Gwen Marillier
(née Southey).

married to Janet. They opened the first tea-room called As You Like It and then bought the bakery. The loaves he produced were flippantly called 'Dicks Bricks'.

Ray Hill, married to Pippin, who lived on Hillandale farm in Miami, was another descendant. One of their three sons, Anthony, survived the first Viscount crash and the subsequent shooting by terrorists. Fay Cumming, married to Guy Lilford who farmed Dixie, was a descendant by marriage. Douglas Hoets, married to Janet, farmed in Tengwe and was another. So was Margaret Southey, married to Dave Ward, a Karoi policeman in the 1970s. She was killed in Mount Darwin when the vehicle they were travelling in hit a land mine. Dr Ivor Briggs, who was the GMO in charge of the TB clinic in Miami, was married to Ruby Fussell, another Southey descendant.

One of the first subdivisions within the framework of the ex-servicemen's scheme had to do with Chiltington farm.

Margie Herud's father, Glen Simpson, used to work for Arthur Bishop. In fact, he was best man at Arthur's wedding when he married Sylvia Johnson. Then Gwen Marillier became a widow after Gerry, her husband, crashed his aircraft and left her with a farm to run. Glen subsequently went to manage Grippos for her.

Glen had married Ann (Susie) Harkins, who came out from Scotland to teach in Rhodesia. She was a fashion-conscious city girl, and the wilds of Africa came as a great culture shock to her. Some months later Glen was diagnosed with cancer, and one of his immediate concerns was that he might die, leaving his family unprovided for.

Everyone had a good word to say of Glen – indeed, he must have been a very strong character because he kept his sense of humour despite what he was facing. On one occasion, the Club held a fancy-dress party and Glen tied his foot into a shoe box and went as 'One Foot in the Grave'.

Gwen was equally concerned, and decided to give a piece of Grippos to Susie in lieu of a bonus. She then applied to the council for a piece of municipal land, which, incredibly, they agreed to. So Chiltington was created as a farm for Susie Simpson either to lease out or to run with a manager, thus providing her with an income. She subsequently employed Dennis Hook. Margie Herud wrote:

> There were happy times followed by difficult ones after Dad's death. Maggie James, who was Harry Wells's mistress, came to live with us, and so did Granny Emily, Dad's Mum. Both had a wonderful zest for life which lifted the atmosphere somewhat so it wasn't as gloomy as it could have been.

Susie had advertised Glen's job on Grippos as having become vacant, and a man called Anthony Mortimer applied. It was Maggie James who phoned to give him the news that he was to join the merry little throng of people who bolstered one another up in that neck of Karoi.

Gwen had lost Gerry, Susie had lost Glen, Tony was getting over a broken marriage, and Maggie James was hoping for some permanent relationship with Harry Wells. It was a brief time of madness, especially when Susie married a man called Ryan, which lasted only long enough for Alistair to be born; after that, Ryan was summarily dismissed, apparently not before time. Peter Adams arrived on the scene, fancying his chances with Susie. So, for a while, life was one big muddle.

Anthony Mortimer was a first-class fellow, but he had one great weakness. Dot Barrett-Hamilton used to say, 'We did warn her, but too late; she married him.' He was a good grower, however, after his training in Banket, but a reluctant one. His love in life was music, the arts and sports.

Ant was the youngest of three boys born to the Reverend and Mrs Mortimer, who resided in Christchurch, New Zealand, where his father was the archdeacon of the cathedral there. It was Archdeacon Mortimer who was responsible for the installation of the Rose Window that graced the transept wall.

As I write, Christchurch has been the victim of a terrible earthquake, with the cathedral being one of its chief sufferers. I was glad to see that, although little of the cathedral had survived, the Rose Window had.[1]

The Revd Mortimer died of TB when Anthony was a very small boy, so his mother, a former ballerina, returned to Britain. There she established a school of the arts, which thrived and became the prestigious school of ballet in Camberley known as Elmhurst. Over the years the school has turned out some notable dancers and actresses, including the prima ballerina Beryl Grey and the actress Jenny Agutter.

Anthony was fortunate to find that he possessed a fine boy-soprano singing voice. He was subsequently 'discovered' and was, until his voice broke, contracted out to the recording company His Master's Voice. The money from this put him through Lancing College, one of Britain's elite public schools, where he completed his education. In the world of today, Tony would have been a child celebrity, as was Aled Jones years later.

Tony was a natural in all games, once having boxed for his school; he played a very decent game of golf and played cricket. He listened avidly to all the cricket commentaries on the radio.

A very private person, he often took himself off to one of the islands off the east coast, or to Mozambique or the Seychelles to snorkel and photograph sea life. This was usually when Gwen started turning the house upside down with her many renovations.

After an early distinguished life full of classical music, Africa and tobacco growing, the age of seventeen must have come as a rude shock, for it was the usual story of the cultured classes being unable to decide what career a third son should follow within a family that had once been courtiers to the King of Spain.

During the Second World War he was lucky enough to be sent to Italy, where the world of opera never faltered, even for a world war, and he was able to attend many

[1] Sadly, after this was written, a subsequent tremor caused what remained of the Rose Window to collapse completely.

concerts in between waiting to fight the Germans.

For forty years 'the Morts' were good and reliable neighbours of ours, and those years were full of the sort of humour that only two families can share. I remember the day when Simon casually leaned on his rifle, which was resting on his foot after a hunting foray into the bush, and somehow, without any finger action, managed to shoot off his big toe.

That wasn't funny, of course.

But there was another occasion when he was giving Tony a lift to town and it began to rain. The windscreen wipers of his old jalopy were no use at all.

'Really, Si,' said Tony, 'you should be more responsible. Don't you ever drive in the rain?'

'Never,' said Simon. 'I usually wait for it to stop.'

'OK, so what do you do when a bird shits on your windscreen?'

'Well,' said Simon, 'I never take her out again.'

7. Communicating with the Urungwe

Land is worth nothing of itself:
it is the work that men put into it
that makes it valuable.

It took a couple of years to find a new name for the Chikangwe Halt in Miami. Finally the townspeople named it after the nearby river – Karoi, a derivative of the Shona word *muroyi* and meaning 'little witch'.

Despite what some may think, she is the benevolent kind. Over the years she has survived many assassination attempts, both on her legendary character and her symbolic figurehead, by various simple-minded religious extremists and by passing military personnel as target practice. But that came many years later.

Not long after the christening of Karoi, the Rural Council held a competition, asking residents to submit designs for a suitable logo for the town. Artist Elizabeth 'Liz' Searle's imagination was stirred sufficiently to enter and she won the prize with her illustration of a witch in full flight on her broomstick.

This was duly adopted as Karoi's official emblem, and for many years 'she' confronted travellers and residents alike: an embossed emblem affixed to wide concrete posts that heralded the entrance to the town.

There was, and still is, a certain amount of humour attached to the witch, for she provided the male section of our community

with the perfect tool to fall back on when, in frustration, they were able to imply that many a 'stroppy female' was the original and ultimate version of the Karoi witch.

In general, however, our community was an example of all that was good – in the way that it pulled together under adversity, when neighbour looked after neighbour, nursed them when ill, provided for them during periods of difficulty, and comforted them when they grieved. In all seriousness, our witch was more akin to an angel than to anything malevolent.

Honor Duff, however, came up with an alternative reason for using the name Karoi. She says it could have stemmed from the huge prevalence of witchweed (*Striga*) in the area. Honor and Colin Duff ran Hunter's Lodge for John New not long after Karoi opened up. She said that the place was 'full of the pesky stuff'. It took years to eradicate with the help and advice of the investigative and wonderful pest-management fellows, and finally 'she' – the witchweed – was destroyed.

You enter the rolling countryside of the Karoi district from the south shortly after crossing the Angwa river on the main road from Harare to Chirundu or Kariba. The farming area lies on the watershed of two river systems at an altitude of over 4,000 feet, and the rains generally provide a reasonable reserve – enough for seedbeds and stock-watering at the end of the dry season.

From the Angwa river the road rises all the way up to a plateau on which the Miami/Karoi settlements developed. Only the insensible would not notice the long and tedious climb – ever upward and on.

When the first visitors to the area roamed up and down those parts, they would have observed the same undulating landscape – a panoramic view of mile upon mile of unrelieved woodland and savannah that seems to press down threateningly upon man and beast in a suffocating swathe of vegetation, when only the bright, verdant colours of summer could gladden the eye after the winter's dry and brittle sepia hues.

The colonial visitors of the nineteenth century had penetrated the interior, leaving hardly a trace, for most had made their way by foot or on horseback, and not in great numbers; the choice of passage would have made little difference.

Later, as the century closed, the first prospectors, who wandered around, and the first farmers, who began to settle, beat a fairly consistent track, which became erratic and undetermined only when they had to deviate if their passage became mired in mud or hampered by thick sand, depending on drought or flood.

A two-rutted trail scoured the earth and wound through heavily wooded bush, where trees grew at above-average height, giving testimony to satisfactory rainfall, and where the grasses grew thick and tall, hiding a variety of creatures within. Not much of the beautiful lush vegetation had changed over the centuries.

The year 1929 saw massive alterations as the modern world infiltrated – the tide of civilisation could no longer be held back. Powerful equipment moved in to disturb this once peaceful part of Rhodesia. The tranquillity and solitude that had always been a feature of this vast area was lost.

Now, huge pieces of machinery lumbered forward like prehistoric monsters in a concerted effort to carve out a wider, smoother and straighter road, which came to be known as the Great North Road. The main reason for this road was to facilitate the building of the Otto Beit Bridge, which was completed in 1939.

Communication by telephone, according to one source, began when the Miami Post Office opened in 1928. Another source gives a date in 1924 for the opening of the post office, which can be verified from a copy of an 'acknowledgement of receipt' for a registered letter, stamped with the name Miami and dated 1924. A railway extension from Sinoia to Lion's Den and Zawi began that same year.

Throughout the years of the Depression, strips of tar had been laid down, and low-lying bridges had been built by gangs of poverty-stricken farmers, who were soon joined by an ever-growing number of unemployed civilians. Only after the Second World War was the road covered in a full bandage of tar, when Kariba Dam went under construction.

When Cecil Rhodes's Pioneer Column had entered the country in July 1890, the great tracts of land to the north were known only to a few, so any idea of developing those regions was initially dismissed. That changed after further exploration showed that there was greater potential on the western side of the country, thanks to the fertile Zambezi Valley that extended right up to the lands of the Barotse (Lozi). There was nothing worth reporting about north-east Mashonaland.

Early communications with the outside world had been through the elephant hunters, traders and adventurers, who made

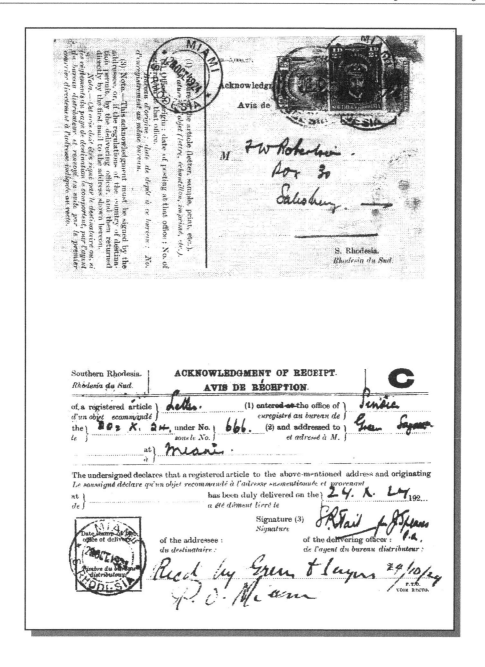

their way up from the south at frequent intervals. These early 'postal services' were quite unofficial, at least from Gubuluwayo (Bulawayo) in Matabeleland, where postal facilities existed only after 1888. Further south in Bechuanaland (Botswana), post offices were controlled by the Cape Colony Postal Administration.

Rhodes's dream of a Cape to Cairo railway with an accompanying telegraph was a boldly ambitious one. The Royal Charter establishing the BSA Company made specific provision for the extension of the telegraph system, and in 1898 the first subscriber to the African Trans-Continental Telegraph Company was Sir Abe Bailey, who sent

Rhodes a cheque for £10,000. In discussing the construction, Sir Abe wrote, 'We used to talk about the elephants knocking down poles, or the danger of white ants attacking them if they were made of wood.'

A feasibility study was drawn up in London, with the cost of a line from Khartoum to Pretoria, a distance of 4,000 miles, being £400,000, to which had been added the cost of two lake steamers and other miscellaneous items amounting to £100,000.

Although the scheme was generally received enthusiastically, some felt differently – including experienced explorers of the African continent such as Sir Samuel Baker, Sir John Kirk and Sir Henry Morton Stanley. Baker, who had travelled a lot in the upper Nile region, predicted that the wire would be stolen by natives for the purpose of firearms. He also laid stress on the unhealthiness of the country and advocated that the line should take its course along the east coast of Africa.

As the debate and wrangling continued, a submarine cable reached Zanzibar in 1879 and was extended to Durban. A second, along the west coast, was laid in 1889 and terminated in Port Nolloth, north of Cape Town.

Meanwhile, running parallel with the occupation of Mashonaland, plans for the construction of the railway and telegraph system were put into place. The extension of the telegraph system from Vryburg in the Cape Colony to Salisbury was considered to be part of the responsibility of the BSA Company, although it became necessary for Rhodes to finance it from his own purse. Rhodes appointed Sir James Sievewright to organise the construction of the railway line and telegraph, and work progressed quickly under his supervision.

The telegraph reached Salisbury on 16 February 1892 and extended to Mazoe.

Relevant to the Urungwe was that this first telegraph line continued north-east from Mazoe in a gentle arc towards Tete, running through Mount Darwin. From there it was understood that it could easily be extended to the Miami river area.

However, war, in the form of the Shona uprising, intervened; disease followed, with both black and white workers dying like flies, and thirty years were to pass before a telephone line linked Miami and Salisbury.

Years later, a connection cropped up between the Cam and Motor Gold Mine in Chakari and the Urungwe telegraph lines. The mine itself was pegged by Leander Starr Jameson and is as old as the colonial history.

Its eventual link with Karoi was due to the mine's massive consumption of wood for its boilers that private contractors cut from the surrounding forests and delivered to the site. Forty thousand cords of wood consequently denuded the area around Suri Suri and Chakari, and to ease the transport problem a light railway was laid down in 1914 to facilitate deliveries.

Although the company was permitted by law to cut wood on unalienated land, there was an immediate outcry from the small-workers in the area. Their grievances were considered moral and legitimate and they received a sympathetic hearing. As a result a compromise was arrived at and the company altered its railway route to a point ten miles east of Chakari.

R.C. Smith wrote:

> In later years, when the railway lines were recovered from some of the disused mines, they were sold to the Posts and Telegraph department for use as telephone poles at a time when steel poles were difficult to obtain due to the 1939/45 post-war shortages of steel and coal.
>
> The poles were erected in the Karoi

District which was then being opened up to tobacco farming.[1]

The new telegraph lines went from Sinoia to Zawi and up through Nyangoma farm (Peter Gibson), from there to Miami and Pitlochry farm (Ian Laing). It continued north-westerly, travelling through the old Customs and Immigration Post – where the European farming area came to an end at Chiwuwa farm (Shalto Barnes) – and beyond to Makuti, Chirundu and Northern Rhodesia. Brian McKay, who bought Pitlochry from Ian Laing, says that at one time he had the Chirundu Hotel and the Sugar Estates on his party-line.

As well as the telephone installed at Miami in 1928, Peter Gibson mentioned a telephone nailed to a msasa tree at Buffalo Downs, which could possibly have been put there temporarily for the mica-holding grounds which were also there, now known Madadzi, though nicknamed Nel's Spruit. It had been bought by Willie Nel's step-father, Werrie Rademeyer, who installed many of his family members on it.

Subsequently a branch line was extended to Chikangwe Halt (Karoi) from Miami. The story goes that quarrels and fights often broke out among the residents who queued up to use the phone, situated in the area behind Karoi Butchery.

One old-timer said that the only sure way of reaching the mica fields, particularly in the rainy season, was by the Road Motor Service (RMS), which started in 1928. If you travelled by car along the bush track you took your 'scoff box' and said a prayer or two.

The country owes a great deal more to this service than is generally appreciated. Apart from conveying mail, hardware and occasional passengers, perishables such as eggs and meat were also transported to and from the various farm halts. But one of its greatest feats must surely have been the transportation of steel girders and components for the construction of the Otto Beit Bridge by the firm of Dorman Long at Chirundu.

During the wet season, the heavy loads invariably caused the lorries' axles to sink into the mud when crossing vleis, and it took many hours of manpower – supplied by the farmers, road-gangs and others – to enable them to negotiate corduroy-like stretches, a nightmare for the drivers one would imagine.

One can empathise with signs such as 'Hell's Gate' (accredited to them), which remained for a considerable time at the top of the escarpment, taking into account their speed and the time it took to negotiate the hills lining the Zambezi Valley in the mid-summer temperatures.

After 1929, this amazing service was a godsend for the Leask family and others in isolation on their farms and on mines in and around the Miami settlement. Not only did these drivers transport their varied and much-needed cargoes to inaccessible places, they also acted as Good Samaritans when the rivers were in full spate, unable to be crossed. The old-timers can't praise them enough – they were the salt of the earth.

Peter Richards has fond memories of one of them:

> Tom Powfrey used to drive the RMS Flyer. This vehicle was not one of the traditional large lorries but a five-ton Thames Trader 4D, which was faster and very much more nimble than the bigger vehicles used.
>
> Every morning, Monday to Friday, Tom would load his truck in Sinoia with the bulk mail for Karoi and Chirundu, along with any supplies and replace-

---

[1] 'The Africa trans-continental telegraph line', *Rhodesiana* (1975) 33: 1–18.

ment parts ordered from Sinoia by the farmers who were fortunate enough to live close to his route, and by the traders in the Karoi village.

He would set forth for Karoi, where his first stop would be the RMS depot, at which some of his cargo would be redistributed.

Next he would call at Ronnie Saint's butchery and the Farmers' Co-op in order to collect farmers' orders for delivery to points north of Karoi.

His last call was the post office, where he collected the bulk mail on the long haul to Chirundu, stopping at each halt for which he had goods or mail.

After deliveries to the last farm, Waterloo, where Eileen and Frank Dalkin lived at that time, his next stop would be the Vuti Fly Camp, followed by Makuti and finally Chirundu, where he inevitably had a lot of cargo to deliver to the Sugar Estates.

He also had supplies for the hotel, the police camp and the Posts and Tele-communications engineers stationed there.

We lived on Chiwuwa at the time, and Tom was our lifeline. Journeys to Karoi and further afield were rare for us, with most of our daily needs coming to us on the Flyer. Groceries, meat and veggies, medicines, rations for labour, spare parts and much more were brought almost to our doorstep.

We shared a mail bag with the Dalkins and the Lessings, so the mail was dropped off at the Lessings' store, where Chris or Ems would sort its contents into three piles.

Tom's schedule was tight, and while one may not have been able to set one's watch by his arrival, it was always within thirty minutes of the expected

time. Many were the times when I would drive to the main road and sit under a large erythrina tree at the halt, waiting to hear the sound of Tom's truck grinding up the long hill from the Lessings' store, after which it would pick up speed again as it breasted the rise and then pull up at our halt a few minutes later.

A smiling Tom would be behind the wheel, his black assistant sitting beside him, and while the latter opened up the back door to offload our supplies, Tom would find time for a few words before setting off again.

He was a quietly spoken man of average build and a ready smile. He was not a scandalmonger, but he certainly knew all about the folks and developments along the route. Once our stuff had been offloaded, Tom would set off again on the longest section of his journey.

If on some occasions we were not at the Halt to collect our consignment, he would leave them under a tree alongside the road to await collection. Nothing was ever stolen.

Once he had reached Chirundu and offloaded the last of his freight, Tom would turn his lorry around and begin the long haul back to Sinoia, calling once more at the Karoi Post Office to collect the outgoing mail.

How he managed to keep up with such a gruelling schedule I could never understand, but keep it up he did, year after year. He was in many ways our window to the outside world, and I for one will always remember him with gratitude and affection.

When we left Chiwuwa and moved to Angola, Tom was still driving the Flyer. I met up with him several years later at Lion's Den, where he was RMS Driver-in-Charge and pretty much office-bound. He told me that he missed his driving days on the Flyer – a service that has since been discontinued.

Karoi residents may remember other RMS drivers who drove up and down that route.

Brian Rhodes started his working life as one until he became a businessman in Karoi.

Tony Hesselton studied for and gained a degree in agriculture in his spare time, but he never stopped driving because the pay was more lucrative.

The gentle, smiling Eddie Pringle hit a landmine driving out to Shamrock mine during the time of the bush war in the 1970s. He survived.

8. Organizing the Community

A number of farmers' associations had been formed since 1892, but it was not until 1905 that these associations combined to form the Rhodesian Agricultural Union.

The earliest farmers in the Karoi area were members of the Lomagundi Farmers' Association, which stretched from Lion's Den to Mrs Leask's farm, Coldomo, established as a district organisation of the Rhodesian National Farmers' Union (RNFU), which was formed by the merger of the Rhodesian Agricultural Union with the Matabeleland Farmers' Association.

After 1946, with the opening up of the district to returning servicemen, the farming fraternity expanded rapidly and they decided it was necessary to form a separate branch of their own.

The association's inaugural meeting was held early in 1946 on the veranda of the 'K' Block supervisor's house, situated at the time on the hill opposite Francis Heron's farm, New Forest. Desmond Evans was the obvious choice for chairman, as he had already been chairman of the Lomagundi Farmers' Association.

A survey of the new association's initial activities shows that the men and women of that far-flung settlement had a sense of humour as well as a spirited resilience to adversity. The minute book reports that Stuart Maclaurin (on Naba) had not yet learned to keep his mouth shut, so he was made Honorary Secretary and was left with the task of drawing up a constitution and getting the organisation under way.

At that time the district was still known as Miami, so it was initially named the Miami Farmers' Association. Once the transfer from Miami to the new town of Karoi had been completed, it became known as the Karoi Farmers' Association and meetings were held once a month, in either a farmer's home or tobacco shed.

One of the first speakers was the Minister of Agriculture, Ben (later Sir Patrick) Fletcher, who was accompanied by his wife. As the only telephone in the area was situated at Miami, thirty miles away, the news was passed around by a 'runner' on a second-hand bicycle.

After Des Evans, there was a memorable spell under the chairmanship of David Grantham of Shawnigan. Then followed D.D. Tate of Kyogle, who put in much work and, like Dan Oosthuizen of Avalon, was known at times to have an awful lot to say!

When Karoi was assigned its own Rhodesia Tobacco Association area, A.B. Roberts of Nassau became its first representative. The RTA, subsequently the ZTA, was a body to which all registered growers were obliged to belong and to which they paid a levy on crops sold. It was designed to look after matters pertaining only to tobacco.

An additional function was to provide comprehensive, accurate information, in advance, to buyers about a range of aspects of the world tobacco situation, current trends and market requirements. The task of the RNFU (subsequently known as the Commercial Farmers' Union), on the other hand, was to look after all aspects of crop farming under one umbrella. It was as a result of acrimony between the two bodies that the RTA had been formed in 1928.

A.B. Roberts's first task was to cool the heads of the other districts, who wanted to march on Salisbury with guns blazing to repeal Sir Edgar Whitehead's infamous tobacco-tax law. Karoi, being the biggest ex-servicemen's settlement area, was presumably meant to lead the fray. As one farmer later put it, 'the others felt that we had let them down badly by being too damned reasonable'.

The colony had awoken on Friday, 18 March 1949 to read headlines in the *Rhodesia Herald* to the effect that a 20 per cent tax would be levied on all Southern Rhodesia's flue-cured tobacco that was exported during the coming sales:

> The government have decided that the general rate of development must be maintained, and after long and careful consideration as to the best means of raising the additional funds (£1.5 million) with the least injury to the country's economy, we will impose an export duty on tobacco.

In the long run, the burden would no doubt have landed on the shoulders of the growers and, based on the 1948 figures, the average return would drop by 6*d.* to 26*d.* per pound. It was clear also that it would fall mainly on the men who were opening up farms and still working on a small scale.

Both the Prime Minister, Lord Malvern, and Sir Edgar Whitehead, themselves farmers but not tobacco growers, must have felt confident that the tax would be acceptable, but within a short time they found that their proposals were condemned, not just by growers but buyers and merchants alike.

The RTA had the difficult task of trying to convince the government that they should withdraw from it in such a way that they could retain their honour, for the threats to postpone sales would bring the economy to a halt, as almost everyone depended directly or indirectly on the inflow of cash from tobacco.

Government then decided to reduce the tax to 15 per cent, and that a board would be set up to award relief to growers in proven cases of hardship. This offer was rejected, but before the quarrel could lead to a political crisis, the RTA suggested that a tax be replaced by a levy in the form of an interest-free loan to be used against future calls for income tax. This saved the day, but the resentment continued for some time. Nowadays, it all seems to have been a great deal of fuss about nothing.

Peter Newhook of Tavoy followed Stuart Maclaurin as the RNFU representative, to be followed in turn by Dan Oosthuizen, who, because of his long spell in office, became almost an institution at their congresses. Others who played an important part were Ernie Went, Dennis England, Zook Nesbitt, Mike Reynolds, Syd Jenkinson and Noel Bichard.

A memorable meeting was held in 1948 at Jimmy Oxenham's home to put forward the plight of drought-stricken farmers. The whole of the Land Settlement Board had turned up in force, and Maud Field was on her feet, urging the farmers not to despair, when suddenly, with an almighty clap of thunder, the heavens opened to herald one of the best farming seasons to date.

One old stalwart recalls:

> Great days they were. We were a power in the land.
>
> It is surprising that none of us became famous in Rhodesia – perhaps it was merely the great distance from Salisbury, but more probably due to the lost years at war.
>
> The gap was just too much to bridge in adjusting to new conditions.'

A pole'n'daga hut had been built in 1946 as a clubhouse, and this was used as the venue for many of the monthly meetings.

One old-timer remembered that the men held their meetings in the morning and then looked after the children so that the wives could enjoy their WI meetings – after which there was a good party for all. Mrs E. Bailey, who was secretary for many years, mentions that membership totalled 240 in 1973, and it is likely that many farmers came to meetings regularly despite not having paid their annual subs.

The conservation movement in Rhodesia started in the commercial farming sector. There is a difference of opinion as to when and where the first Intensive Conservation Areas (ICAs) were formed, but the date can be narrowed down to around 1943/44, following the establishment of the Natural Resources Board in 1941, and places like Umgusa, Marodzi and Tsungwezi can produce documentary evidence of this.

Regulations such as the Water Ordinance and the Herbage Preservation Ordinance had existed since at least 1913, and indicated concern about uncontrolled veld fires, streambank protection and the indiscriminate cutting of firewood. In 1927 the Water Act was passed which proscribed cultivation in water courses.

This in turn led to the Rhodesian Agriculture Union requesting that district committees should be set up. This was agreed in 1936 and funds were made available for loans to meet the cost of contour ridging and green manuring.

On 1 October 1941, the Natural Resources Act was passed, which set up the Natural Resources Board. The country was divided into small Intensive Conservation Areas, with local committees of interested people ensuring that local resources were looked after properly.

The years between 1943 and 1949 saw the gazetting of about ninety ICAs. The Department and Conservation and Extension (CONEX), an advisory service for the Natural Resources Board, was also formed at the time.

The records show that in 1948 the white settlers of Urungwe formed their own ICA. There were three areas: North Karoi, Karoi Central and South Karoi. In 1950 these ICAs obtained grants from the government to build dams on fifty European farms.

CONEX expanded rapidly. More subsidies were offered for earth-moving equipment and ICAs were given the authority to place 'restrictive orders' on deviant farmers who didn't toe the line as regards good land management. These were rare and not lightly placed, but 'Swifty' Rautenbach in North Karoi was one I remember who couldn't escape a restraining order.

Many farmers served their district one way or another by sitting on various committees, whether it was the RNFU, RTA, Farmers' Association, ICA or Road Council. It was a path to achieving greater things. Peter Walsh, for example, served for many years on the Road Council under the chairmanship of Bert Hacking.

Many men and women served on the voluntary committees that made up the conservation movement, and each farmer took his turn. There were social evenings, sporting competitions, ploughing contests, guest speakers, grower of the year awards, shooting contests, each ICA area competing against the other.

In fact, most farmers did their stint on the ICA, and Pat Bashford, Jimmy Flight and Ian Fraser are names that come to mind as former ICA chairmen.

Because of Jack Wilson's enthusiasm for competition, we hosted the annual national ploughing championships twice that I can remember, which led to Jack himself, Dusty Laver and others becoming judges.

One year it was held on Montesuma and another at Broad Acres, and it was during the latter event that one of the lady spectators, seeking a PK in Karel Kirstein's home, encountered his fully grown leopard that was roaming around. It was sent to Marongora soon after and released there. The lady recovered.

Months earlier, that endearing bundle of delight had jumped on to my infant daughter when we were visiting Jose and Theo Venter who worked there. No harm was done, but it must never be forgotten that these animals are wild and erratic!

Some years later the Act was updated to reduce the annual recurrence of uncontrolled fires that ravaged many thousands of acres of valuable grazing each year. It was impossible to assess the loss in monetary terms – nor was it only grazing that was lost, but hay as well, with damage to posts and fencing, buildings, and even crops.

The most effective means of bush control was by the judicious use of fire itself, called back-burning. Each year around June, farmers were obliged to make firebreaks along their northern and eastern bound-aries. These had to be at least thirty feet wide, fifty if possible. No one risked leaving their boundaries vulnerable to the vagaries of human error or strong winds, especially if an exceptionally good maize crop stood to be lost.

From time to time, aircraft would take to the skies, hired from various local farmers, for the purpose of enabling committee members to get a bird's-eye view of the situation on the ground. From that perspective they could observe the condition of each and every farm – badly eroded lands, streambank culti-vation, desertification and mismanagement stood plainly out.

But it took a very strong stomach indeed to put up with the acrobatics of a small plane to the end of its gyrations, much of it deliberately and cunningly exaggerated by a devilish pilot, which left many a man suffer-ing the indignity of losing his last meal into

his shirt, and feeling as if he was about to lose his very soul. He would alight at the end, pale, enfeebled and as limp as a wet rag. For some, it was not the best part of the job!

Not many Karoi-ites realise it today, but the first unofficial planners of Karoi were the ladies of the Karoi Women's Institute, whose original members were made up of the wives of the first ex-servicemen. Not for nothing had the WI earned the nickname 'Petticoat Government'. From them came the blueprint of what was deemed necessary for the fledgling community.

It was at a farmers' meeting held on 30 March 1947 that the new settler wives decided that they should start a branch of the Women's Institute. The ladies felt that they had much to contribute to the district – and they had their own ideas as to what was needed.

While the men were kept abreast of their world through the Farmers' Association, it was only right that the ladies should have an opportunity to play their more feminine role in what should happen in their new world. One cynic was jokingly heard to say, 'Oh Lord, deliver me from women's assassinations.' Little did our jester know how much the women were to accomplish over subsequent years.

At the inaugural meeting, Mrs Tom Williamson, National Honorary Organiser of the National Federation of Women's Institutes of Rhodesia, gave a talk about the Women's Institute, a self-governing body organised to enable women to take an active part in the life and development of their community. Originally founded in Canada in 1897, the WI had been set up in the UK during the First World War to encourage women to become involved in growing and preserving food.

The first minute book records that in 1947 Mrs R. P. Evans was elected as the first chairwoman; she had lived in Karoi on Chelvern for a good few years already. Other attendees were Mrs Harris, Mrs du Barry, Mrs Oxenham, Mrs Glover, Mrs Grantham, Mrs Maclaurin, Mrs England, Mrs Tate, Mrs Jenkinson and Mrs Barrett-Hamilton. The minutes were inscribed in long-hand, in delightfully correct and formal terms, and all the ladies were referred to as Mrs So-and-so – not a Christian name in sight!

As yet there was no planned layout for the town, hardly any infrastructure, and certainly no money, but a planning committee was formed to draw up a list of priorities. Top of the list was the need for a school, a library, and a request for more telephones in the district.

Meanwhile, the women began by doing what they do best – organising, scheming, arranging, designing, bossing and proposing. Added to this, they petitioned, pressed, and fought government for the priorities that headed their list. It was a state of affairs that lasted many years.

As new occupiers took up their blocks of land, their wives were invited to attend a meeting to ascertain if they would like to join – it was a very brave woman who declined! However, most found the opportunity to socialize and meet other ladies of the community an attraction.

Said one member: 'Really, to begin with, everyone was so busy starting new homes on virgin farms that not a great deal was accomplished in those first few years, although it wasn't from lack of trying.'

However, they did manage to get a baby clinic going by September 1947, with Mrs Kate Boardman as the nursing sister in attendance; she was Hugh Ormerod's sister, Kay (Kirsten) Ormerod's sister-in-law.

Mrs Boardman and Doctor Taylor were

kept frantically busy as Karoi proceeded to break one of the highest birth-rate records, pro rata, among populations in the world. This is quite true: the population explosion had begun, even if the tobacco explosion hadn't quite got under way! But it wasn't until November 1949 that the first paid District Nurse was officially appointed.

In the Christmas of that year, the WI organised the first Christmas Tree Party in Major Tate's grading shed, and they continued to do this until 1960, by which time the district had grown so large that affairs became unwieldy and the Club took over. It was the highlight of the year for the children, who talked about it *ad nauseum* until the next Christmas arrived.

Getting a school and a library built was proving more difficult, but these remained a top priority. Many letters of application to different ministries were posted from around March 1947, but it would be seven years before there was a hint that the Ministry of Education had even heard of their application. No doubt there were times when those long-suffering civil servants and various Permanent Secretaries began to wish they had never heard of Karoi or of the Women's Institute!

If one is allowed to feel a touch of sympathy at all for those in government it would be because of the sheer size and weight of national requests at a time of austerity as the world recovered from a devastating war: everyone wanted something, but all had to wait their turn.

By October 1946, the pole'n'daga clubhouse had been built; a cupboard inside held the beginnings of a library. Fund-raising continued to be the order of the day: international and national projects were included in this list of 'needs', which must have been an irritation when domestic needs seemed so much more pressing.

One example of this was in 1948, when, out of all the funds raised countrywide, a portion was sent to the children of Great Ormond Street Hospital, London. This was all very worthy, of course, and showed just how patriotic Rhodesians were towards their mother country at that time.

In 1949 the WI asked the Revd Mr Spenser if he would arrange for a church service to be held every three months at someone's home. This was at Mrs Boardman's request and was mainly for the children of the Sunday morning tennis players. She didn't want their offspring becoming 'godless'.

The Catholics, with Fr Zincan presiding, were already holding services, and it was indeed a memorable Sunday when, at one of these home services, a beaming Cookie would rush into the room each time the bell rang, thinking he had been summoned to make the tea.

To begin with, meetings were held at farmhouses close to the main road, particularly during the rainy season when the roads further inland became muddy and impassable. When the rains became particularly heavy from time to time, as they had in 1947, meetings were suspended; there were also petrol shortages then. By 1955 they could be held at the newly built brick clubhouse.

Mrs Barber from Salisbury was a guest speaker at one meeting. She spoke of a project about to be launched for 'unmarried mothers' – which was the start of the St Clare's Homes. If only they could have seen ahead to modern times they could have saved themselves a lot of trouble.

When the community hall, later known as the Gwen Scrase Hall, was built in 1953, the WI loaned the Anglican building fund £200, interest free, on the understanding that they could have the use of one room in it for a library. Pop Mitchell from the Club erected wall shelves so that at last the library really

could expand. By now the WI had accumulated £600 from their catering drive.

Pressure continued for a local school to be built, and finally government suggested that this could be solved by opening up one or two farm schools around the district. This scheme had already been experimented with several years earlier in other remote districts such as Melsetter and Chipinga, but hadn't worked out very well.

The same suggestion prompted a very indignant and scathing response from the committee, who informed the ministry that, as the farms were so widely scattered, several such schools would be necessary. Added to this, as well as the classrooms, the teacher would need accommodation. Clearly, the ministry didn't have a clue.

Then came a second and more sensible suggestion from the government, that of tutoring by correspondence. This was most acceptable, and was taken up by many farming families. It was to continue up to 1980 through the School on the Air and correspondence lessons.

For this method of education to work, it was necessary to have an efficient mailing system to back it up. Today, it would not work, but at that time it gave many a farming child a good early grounding, despite all the tears it caused on occasions, along with disrupted tutoring.

With the WI having helped towards the cost of the toilets at the Gwen Scrase Hall, the first hurdle was overcome when the Karoi school opened in January 1954 with a government-paid teacher. She was Mrs Greta MacDonald, and she kept this post until the first government primary school opened two years later, where she continued to teach for many years. When a second hostel was eventually built, they named it Greta MacDonald House.

In 1958 the first nursery school opened,

The Nursery School, 1959.

Joan Newhook, and tree planting along the streets to beautify the town also began.

By 1962 the WI had started to build a permanent library building, and with the help of the whole district – members paid double subs one year – and a State Lottery grant they moved into a smart new building in November 1963 with everything (building, stand and furnishings) having been completely paid for.

In October 1965 the WI launched another fund-raising campaign, this time for an ambulance. It received such a good response that within months one had been purchased and was run by a small committee under the Rural Council.

Over the years, the ladies of the Women's Institute have always rallied round when needed. They fed Belgian refugees when they poured down from the Congo in 1960. They raised funds for numerous charities, as well as for our own local needs. They continued to work diligently all year round for the benefit of the community, and had plenty of fun doing so.

Some readers will have heard of, or perhaps even seen, the National Tapestry, made up of embroidered panels that depicted

sponsored again by the WI, and was run by Mrs Natalie Herud. The tennis pavilion at the Club was used for this – it was a boon for working mothers and ran for five years.

The African Homecraft Club started in 1959 under the guidance of Mrs Maureen Philip in the Chikangwe township. This, too, continued for many years, with the involvement of Mrs Margaret Fussell, a highly skilled cook, knitter and seamstress, giving it a tremendous boost in 1973.

The women met once or twice a week and were taught dress-making, needlework, knitting and simple cooking, and they received relevant lectures from the mobile Land-Rover managed by the National Federation of Women's Institutes and run by competent African women lecturers/demonstrators.

The first Flower Show was held in February 1960 under the able organisation of

An early flower show.
Joan Newhook (1st Prize Winner), Mary England (Chairman), and the judge (unknown).

various historical aspects of Rhodesian life. It was created by Women's Institutes around the country as a memorial to the Pioneer Women, and once completed it toured the country for the nation to see. It was then hung in the Rhodesian Parliament. After independence it was sent to the Bulawayo Museum, where it hangs ignominiously out of sight.

The first panel on the Tapestry was embroidered by the Karoi Women's Institute and depicts a map of Africa, 'The Unknown Continent', at 611 BC.

The Tapestry was reproduced in a book with text by Oliver Ransford, *Rhodesian Tapestry: A History in Needlework* (Bulawayo: Books of Rhodesia, 1971).

9. Harry Wells

After the war had ended, the value of Southern Rhodesian tobacco exports exceeded, for the first time, the value of gold shipped overseas and reached the figure of £6.5 million; in 1948 it realised £11 million.

The increase in production came mainly from the new growers, who had gained experience as managers and assistants a little before and also after the war. The lifting of war restrictions had enabled them to set up on their own.

Land values shot up sharply and many of the old farmers made what were, by Rhodesian standards, fortunes. Credit facilities were also limitless, and it was possible to set oneself up as a tobacco farmer with relatively little capital.

Merchants in Salisbury willingly granted credit against a future crop, their security being the stop-order that the farmer signed, authorizing the auction floors to make payments to his creditors from the receipts of each sale.

However, this said, the average farmer was never out of debt. Before the proceeds from the sale of one crop had cancelled his liability, he was already borrowing for the next. Today it is no different. The demands on the farmer's resources were as unavoidable as those on his time. The title deeds that made him the rightful owner of the farm also made him the custodian of the soil and gave him the incentive to master the land to his own end.

The first farmers had taken up their land and started from scratch, cutting out a field from the virgin bush. Before he could plant, a farmer had to clear away the trees and scrub. He had to ensure a water supply by drilling boreholes or creating dams and weirs. He hacked roads through thickly wooded, undulating veld, bridged rivers and drained vleis.

He had to build some sort of shelter for himself and workers. Every brick was burnt on the farm, and the timbers came largely from the trees he chopped down. The houses, the curing barns, the machinery and grading sheds, the store-rooms and outbuildings were all constructed by the farmer with the help of his labourers.

All this was necessary before even a small crop could be planted. It was not an overnight achievement but a constant, ongoing battle over a period of time. As time went by, there was crop rotation to think of, cultivated pastures to put under grass, modern methods to keep abreast of, paddocks to fence – the litany was continuous, and as each year passed, the tobacco income had to stretch further and further.

The farmer learns to wear many hats: he develops skills he never knew he had. A jack of all trades he may be, but some he does master with experience. In his time he will have had to turn his hand to quantity surveying, become a technological and mathematical whizz-kid, a builder, a mechanical engineer, a plumber and an electrician. But above all, he must be blessed with phenomenal patience.

Patience, though, was not Harry Wells's forte. He hit the Urungwe in the early 1950s like a tidal wave. His unbounded energy and modern ideas soon put the Karoi district on the map, as he steadily became successful and rich.

His story is memorable today as an example of 'poor boy makes good'. It is one of a youngster who dragged himself up by the bootstraps by dint of hard work, audacity and acumen. One wonders what the outcome might have been had he not been born into gruelling poverty. Would it have been the same? It was said that he had set himself a target of making four million pounds a year. Whether or not he did is not for us to know.

Harry Wells wrote:[1]

> My mother was one of eight children, born on the outskirts of London where her parents worked in various laundries. Her father was a brutal bastard, constantly belting his wife and children; my mother, being illegitimate, received the worst of it.
>
> Home was a crowded mews, where the smell of horse urine permeated through the floorboards. The man she married, my father, James Wells, was an out-of-work plasterer, a layabout without any 'guts'.
>
> I was born in 1926. Phyllis, my sister, was four years older. We lived in one room on the top of a crumbling tenement block. There was a large double bed in which we all slept, head to toe, and in the middle of the floor was a black box with most of our worldly possessions fitting inside it. It was covered in newspaper and served as a dining table. I still have that box to this day.
>
> Our main diet was burnt or stale loaves – they were the cheapest – and when they became too stale we crumbled them up into milk or water for breakfast. Supper was more of the same with perhaps some dripping or jam, depending on how solvent we were at the time.
>
> One of my earliest memories is of sitting on the step outside, cracking fleas with expertise between my fingernails. Water came from a standpipe outside and, like the coal, had to be carried by bucket up five flights of stairs.
>
> The stock market crashed in 1929 putting millions out of work, and my father took to disappearing for six months at a time and my mother had to cope on her own.
>
> Our clothes were worn thin and my socks had so many holes in them they could be put on in ten different ways, all of which made me a prime target for teasing at school. I had to become tough, learning to defend myself.
>
> Hunger was ever present, and there were times when we stole what we could to eat. I swore to myself then that one day I would become rich.

Out of necessity and the desire to help his mother, Harry took a part-time job with the local grocer. He started by running errands, sweeping floors, filling the shelves and weighing out dried fruit which came in large boxes. He cut fifty-six-pound slabs of butter into half-pound pats, and so well did he work that he was promoted to serving behind the counter.

For a brief time he became the leader of a gang of delinquents, often narrowly avoiding trouble, but time was a luxury he could not afford and he watched his mates playing while he worked. His life was so full of chores – school, work, duties at the Catholic Church on Sundays – that all this probably saved him from falling into a life of crime.

At the age of eleven he surprised everyone by winning a scholarship to the grammar school, but he continued to start his day at 4.00 a.m. in order to deliver newspapers. However, James Wells complained about being woken so early, and Harry, infuriated by this, exploded in anger, chased him up the

---

[1] The words of Harry Wells were narrated to his daughter, Alex Sheppard, who allowed me to use them in this book.

stairs kicking and punching, and shouted that he would kill him. James Wells packed his bags and never lived with the family again. As a result they became better off.

On leaving school Harry decided to train as a toolmaker, raising his age by a year as one had to be sixteen to apply. He graduated with high marks and was sent to the Isle of Wight to work on aircraft. It was while he was there that he had a conversation with a young RAF man in uniform who told him stories of bombing raids and close brushes with death.

'I was convinced,' said Harry,

that joining up would be far more exciting and glamorous than the routine factory work I was currently doing. Besides, a uniform and the 'brevi' (half-wing badge) gave one an instant advantage with the girls, not to mention a higher wage.

However, I was only seventeen. One needed to be aged eighteen and a half to join up, so I had a problem, and I said as much to a friend at the factory who was several years older and had been turned down on medical grounds the first time.

We decided to swap identities if he was called up again – he would take up my reserved occupation status as a skilled toolmaker and I would use twenty-two-year-old Henry Bulmer's identity card instead. Shortly after, I did have to report for a selection course, aptitude tests and a medical. I made sure I botched the Morse code, not wanting to be a wireless operator, and managed to reach the last stage when I was called in for an interview.

'There's just one more thing we would like to ask you, Mr Bulmer,' they said. 'According to a past medical, one of your legs is shorter than the other and you have a squint in one eye. Can you

explain your remarkable recovery?' I was completely tongue-tied.

They told me to go off for an hour and think about it. I returned, giving them a potted version, including the fact that I'd stolen the identity card. I could see they were amused but were trying hard not to show it. I was told that I would be accepted for aircrew training, but only in a year's time.

As I left the room I heard one chap remark to another that I would either go far or have a short life.

Harry was twenty-two at the close of the war and he very quickly became disillusioned and frustrated by the limited opportunities available to youngsters in post-war Britain, with wages measured by age rather than by skill.

He scoured the papers for adverts and noticed one calling for recruits to train on the gold mines in South Africa, with assisted passages by boat. This he pursued, and he attended night school to learn more about geology and maths.

However, he very quickly realised that this was going to get him nowhere fast. Fate played a hand when he picked up a newspaper describing the fortunes being made by tobacco farmers in Rhodesia.

He found work in Macheke as a manager for Moore-Gordon through the kindness of Maurice Hawkes. He also married his girlfriend from England after she had pitched up without warning, imagining that theirs was a relationship far more serious than it really was. As neither had the money for her return fare, Harry had no alternative but to marry her. At that time, a spinster could not enter the country without having a deposit of £1,500 in the bank.

After two other jobs that turned sour, plus a partnership with Doctor Gordon that worked well, he was able to lease his own farm. By 1953 he had saved £30,000, enough to buy his own farm. He heard that Montesuma in Karoi was for sale – three thousand acres owned by Aubrey Lewen – and it was going lock, stock and barrel for £14,500, the terms of payment being half down.

Aubrey Lewen had grown 100 acres of tobacco but I wanted more and planned to expand as quickly as possible, so at the same time I leased Kyogle from D.D.Tate, a little chap with a bristly moustache, a pukka English accent, and a pair of cavalry breeches that he still wore from his days in the Indian army.

He was an alcoholic, which I knew for a fact having discovered dozens of empty whisky bottles stashed away in the thatch of the sorting shed where his wife couldn't find them.

There I grew 70 acres, with a manager to oversee it. I asked Jimmy Corbet, a neighbour from Marandellas, to come up and help me manage Montesuma, and although he had more experience he agreed to take orders. He was also better at dealing with labour than I was.

In five years my life-style had changed dramatically. From a freezing rat-ridden hut I was now installed in a house of which I could be proud. Altogether, I was growing 275 acres in my first season in Karoi and everyone thought I was mad. Before I had arrived, A.B.Roberts, who had been farming for twenty years, had grown the largest crop.

The way I did it caused much comment, not all complimentary. Some time during the first year I remember a conversation with a farmer's wife. She was attractive and we were flirting a little on the dance floor. She said,

'Everyone thinks you will either make a million or go bust.'

Meanwhile on Montesuma I was stumping out another 60 acres of land, and then I decided at the last minute that a 40-acre piece that should have remained fallow would also be planted because I had an excess of seedlings. Luckily this was just prior to the rains. Putting all four tractors in at once, I completed planting everything in 48 hours.

Although I had taken over all Aubrey Lewen's labour, there weren't enough men to run a crop of that size. Labour shortage was a major problem, as Karoi was really the end of the line before hitting the Zambezi river. I resorted to using 'blackbirders', a term given to men who recruited blacks from Northern Rhodesia.

These men would arrive wearing little more than a sack, looking emaciated and malnourished, and they were reluctant to be on any farm at all. Precautions had to be taken to stop them jumping off the trucks, and guards were employed at the compound to make sure they didn't leave. I used to build up their physiques by giving them extra rations and ease their workload until they were stronger.

There wasn't a job on the farm that I couldn't do myself except for tying hands of tobacco, which needed the nimble fingers of the women. I was not a farmer but a time-and-motion-study man. I timed exactly how long it took me to do certain jobs, and would then gauge how much work each worker could do and how long the whole operation would take. I paid attention to detail, and this was one of the main reasons why I was a success at farming.

By 1955 there were 42 barns on Montesuma. Harry Wells developed the down-draught system that cured tobacco quicker. Noticing how quickly he was using up wood, he started to plant gum trees – a hundred acres at a time, which would then be coppiced for barn poles within five years and provide curing wood within fifteen.

He was staggering his crop and had developed the dry-planting system that enabled him to plant a crop with rains. Instead of applying water to plants individually with cans, manufacturers developed 450-gallon tankers that were towed behind tractors and dispensed water through nine hoses with a labourer directing the hose on to the plants.

He also planted at night, when the soil was cool. Power produced by a generator on the back of a trailer gave light, its rays bouncing off bent aluminium sheets effectively. Work began at 3.00 p.m. and by sunrise was done.

Needing more water, he bought another thousand acres off Jack Hay on Ceres next door because it had an excellent dam site. Then he bought Ungwa owned by Ronnie Callon:

> He was an idle bugger who spent all his time in the Karoi Hotel, drinking and reading paperbacks. He was an ex-naval officer who kept a log of the weather as if he was still on board ship.
>
> Although he'd had a farm for ten years he hadn't developed it. He had built the barns in the vlei because it was the only place where there were no trees to clear, and he cultivated a few fields around them.
>
> His house was a hovel, the bed a wooden frame covered in skins, and next to it was an old sardine tin full of cigarette butts. I needed to put my hat on before wandering inside to keep off the fleas.

> Billy Postlethwayt also had his eye on the place, so to make sure I got it I offered Callon £10,000 pounds. Immediately after signing the agreement he asked me for a thousand. When I asked why, he said: 'I'm going to the Argentine and I'll need it for the fare. But actually, come to think about it, better make it two thousand – my trip will cost a thousand and my booze bill will be a little more than that.'

Harry then began to run stores. His first was on Montesuma, which he hastened to enlarge after hearing that Peter Groenewald, next door on Lancaster, was planning to open one as well. His stores became an enterprise in their own right. He employed Paul Downey to run them, and they did well. A chain was set up called Karoi Trading Company, and within three years they had reached twenty. He later sold out to Paul.

He built a magnificent workshop, enormous and well equipped, but it took a while to find a decent workshop mechanic. Eventually he came across Bill Speldevinde, who was a marvel:

> I used to buy my ration meat from the local butcher, which invariably was terrible quality and stank. Once it was so bad that I took it back and dumped the whole bloody lot there. [The only butchery at that time was Hesketh Park butchery.]
>
> I had many managers over the years and they could count on intensive training while they were with me. To their credit, most of them left after a year or two to set up on their own. If they were still around in their third year, I fired them as a matter of course as I considered that they had insufficient ambition.
>
> The best manager I ever had was

Jimmy Upton, who came in my second year at Montesuma. At first appearance he didn't have a lot to recommend him. He was a small guy, rather overweight and didn't look as if he could do an honest day's work. He had been running the Karoi Bakery with his glamorous wife Val, whose presence behind the counter probably accounted for the steady stream of customers.

Jimmy admitted later that he probably wouldn't have taken the job if he had known what he was in for. He told a story from when he had just started at Montesuma:

> We were in the lands, I was under the trailer, making some repairs, and Harry was giving orders. Three of the gang were causing trouble so Harry lashed out at them and all three fell unconscious around the trailer. I, crouching underneath, saw them fall one by one and thought I wouldn't be lasting long at that rate.

Jimmy worked so well that I offered him a partnership on a lease on Wingate. I didn't want to go to the effort of building so I bought Nyodza, a tiny five hundred acres next door that had barns on it.

I had three Jimmys working for me at one time and the initials of their surnames put together formed UTC, which was appropriate because they were also the initials of a business called United Tobacco Companies.

Jimmy Thompson came up from Marandellas having heard how well Jimmy Corbet had done. However, he didn't last too long and I got rid of him. I pulled out my 'boss-boy' and put him on the third section and he did a splendid job. Naturally, by this time I had acquired a reputation for having a short fuse and for being a hard taskmaster.

At the Club one year, they put on a few skits for a Christmas show. The curtain went up and there lying on a bed in dim light, was 'Flossie' Hoskyns, a long, bespectacled fellow. A black man dashes in through the door and helps himself to a few cigarettes off the dressing table in passing. Puts them in his pocket and then wakes the boss.

Hoskyns sleepily lifts his head saying, 'What's the problem?'

'Lo tractor ena fili.'

Hoskyns mutters, 'Ziko indaba,' rolls over and goes back to sleep.

A little while later the Cookie dashes back in.

'The tractor is on fire.'

Flossie says again, 'Ziko indaba, Ziko indaba,' turns over once more, and Cookie goes out taking another handful of cigarettes.

After a few moments he is back.

'Lo ma barns, ena kunna motta.'

But Hoskyns just pulls the covers over his head mumbling, 'Ziko indaba, Ziko indaba.'

Again the black man dashes in, really agitated by this time and says, 'Lo Boss Welass, ena buyili.' [Boss Wells is coming.]

With that, Flossie leaps out of bed and runs off the stage. Everyone in the audience is roaring with laughter and I'm sitting there, arms akimbo saying 'What's funny about that?' – which people found even funnier.

I was told of another episode when two white boys were having a fight outside the butchery. The fisticuffs were followed by a slanging match that went something like this:

'You're nothing but a bastard.'

'You're a white pig.'

'You're a shit.'

And then came the final blow:

'And you're Harry Wells!'

However, I did not go undefended. There was an occasion when, at the Karoi Club, Jimmy Upton and two other managers were talking to a visitor from Northern Rhodesia, also a tobacco farmer. After asking them who they worked for they told him.

'Ah, Harry Wells,' the man said. 'I've heard about that bugger. He really makes a man sweat blood and pays them nothing.'

The chap was obviously expecting them to agree, but instead they stood up and punched him on the nose. I can't have been that bad after all!

As 1957 drew to a close, Harry was fairly pleased with the quality of his life. He had learned to play polo, which brought along with it a great social life. He had an absent wife, a good mistress, and Montesuma was a burgeoning enterprise.

Harry counts 1957 as the highlight of his career. He called it his 'Banner Year'. By this time tobacco growing was clashing with an increased interest in the commercial side of agriculture. True to character, he had focused on producing the weed and succeeded, but he saw flaws in the marketing and transportation side of the industry. Karoi, he thought, was not being represented effectively so he stood for election and became a member of the Rhodesia Tobacco Association.

As well as being a prestigious body that looked after the interests of tobacco farmers, the RTA was also known to be a breeding ground for many a politician: P.K. van der Byl became a junior member in the government. Carol Heurtley was to become president of the RTA and also a senator. Winston

Field was not only a past president but went on to become Prime Minister of Southern Rhodesia from 1962 to 1964. He was the grandfather of Shane, married to Jonathan Wells, who farmed on Basella farm in Karoi.

The year 1957 was also the year in which Harry experimented as a grower by planting a third crop. The planting of a second crop had worked well, so he tried a third crop in February. Other farmers thought he was pushing the limit.

As a result of this, he was interviewed by the *Rhodesian Tobacco Journal*, who wrote that he had become the biggest tobacco grower in the world. This, in turn, was picked up by the *Sunday Mail*, who mentioned his humble beginnings and subsequent success, giving Harry a chance to pay tribute to Dr Roberts and the part that his work in tobacco research and pest control had played in his success.

The third crop did work well for a couple of years, but it matured slowly and was therefore reaped late. Because of this, the cycle of aphids wasn't broken – which subsequently flattened the crop. Not being able to identify the cause, he had someone from Kutsaga Research Station come out to investigate.

Initially they called it 'Wells' Disease', but he objected to that and they changed it to the 'Karoi Virus', which was also objected to. Eventually they labelled it 'Curly' or 'Bushy Top', and restrictions were put on the length of time a crop could stay in the ground. It still remains a problem.

Harry Wells became prominent in tobacco circles. Within a short time he became a director of Tobacco Sales Floor, an auction floor set up in 1958 in competition with Tobacco Auctions Limited and Tobacco Producers' Floor as an outlet through which tobacco could be sold.

10. The Polo Set and Sport

The Karoi Club was the local watering hole, and as the community was such a small one at that time – stuck out in the sticks, miles from anywhere – it was a place where all the farmers gathered at the weekend.

It was run by a man who was called 'Ted the Head', simply because he had been the hangman for the whole of southern Africa. The authorities used to fly him to any spot where his services were needed, all expenses paid plus five pounds a head.

Ted relished having an audience, which soon gathered as he described the intricacies of his trade – the importance of the length of the rope in relation to the body weight: if the rope was too long, the force of the fall would not only break the spine but pull the head right off! On one occasion he had been sent to Northern Rhodesia to hang a couple of people and at the last minute they were reprieved. He sent a telegram to the Club which read, 'No noose is good noose.'

'Polo all started from the Hunt Club,' said my friend and neighbour, Gwen Mortimer, who was always known as Mrs Mort, even after she had married Peter Adams. And even he called her that.

> We had a pack of hounds kennelled by Frank Lucas on Hunter's Lodge. We used to hunt for pigs on Sunday mornings, dressed in pink jackets and even using horns. We ended up with a hunt breakfast and it was all great fun.
>
> Eventually we gave it up when the dogs got thinner and thinner – despite all the meat we had delivered to feed them with. Then we discovered that Frank was giving it all to his staff as rations. He wasn't very popular after that, I can tell you.

But one person we all admired was Harry Wells. He had never been near a horse in his life before, but he decided to play polo. He bought some horses, learned to ride, and eventually played a very reasonable game.

One evening, Harry Wells, sitting at the bar with a few of the players, had begun to pull their legs:

'You blokes don't really get any exercise – all you do is sit on a horse, wave a twig around, and gallop up and down yelling at each other. I can't understand what you get out of it.'

'If you think it's so bloody easy why don't you do it?' said one. Harry had never been on a horse before, but it didn't look too difficult.

'If I give you a horse, will you try it out?' said another.

'Well, if you put a saddle on a bloody crocodile, I'll ride it!' said Harry.

And the deal was on.

He borrowed some boots and a pair of ancient cavalry breeches from one of his managers, and then sauntered down to the polo ground. The whole team looked on as he was given a leg up onto a horse owned by Guy du Barry that was about to be sold. No one else was willing to let a complete beginner loose on a pony they valued.

Harry continues the story himself:

> I was shown how to hold the reins and the stick, and the fundamentals were explained something like this:
>
> 'This is the front of the horse and this is the back, and when you wave the stick don't try to hit the ball with the sharp end but with the flat.'

Everyone drew back to a safe distance and, with an air of great bravado, he took an almighty swipe at the ball. It rocketed half-way up the field.

I dug my heels into the unsuspecting horse and flew after it. I hit the ball again and found that I had a terrific eye.

When it was time to put on the brake, I leaned back, pulled the bit up in its mouth till it almost reached its ears and hauled it on to its haunches. The first time I accomplished this manoeuvre, the horse reared with the sudden impact of steel grating on its teeth, and when I kept my seat I was convinced that I was a born natural.

I had taken on the challenge for a laugh, but it gave me a taste for the game which I persevered with.

There were various instructors, but Rory Fraser was the best. He was an excellent horseman but, being down on his luck and short of cash, his tack was always tied up with string. However, he was a real gentleman and always ready to give Harry Wells a few pointers on badly needed etiquette.

Says Harry:

It was recommended that I pay a visit to Bruce Reid – The Saddler in Salisbury – where I could buy equipment. As I was a learner, he suggested that I get a large comfortable saddle, something akin to an armchair.

I bought one, along with stirrups, leathers, bridles, nosebands – the list got longer and longer: curry combs, martingales and tail bandages, then a polo helmet, knee guards, stick, whip and practice balls. I thought he was never going to stop. I was becoming convinced that Reid, taking me for a sucker, was intent on selling me everything in his damn shop.

When he said, 'Of course your pony will need boots', I had had enough.

'This is the f*****g end,' I said. 'I've got all this equipment and taken your word for it, but I've never seen a pony wearing bloody boots, so will you stop pulling my pisser and give me my bill.'

Reid patiently explained that the boots didn't go over the hoof but around the fetlocks. After that I was under no illusion that polo was a cheap sport.

The Polo Club was started when Dennis Armstrong, a South African military type, came to Karoi. His wife, Merle, was quite a character, with a very colourful use of language: she could be heard over the sound of galloping hooves shouting instructions from the grandstand.

Dennis was the captain and the driving force behind the polo team – a terrible loser, they said, but good on strategy. He was a very high-handicap player, as was his assistant 'Junior' Steyl. They were both 6 handicap, and most A-Division players in the country at the time were 4. With two such very good players in the district, it seemed a waste not to have a team.

David and Vyvyan Cockburn, Gerry Marillier, Ian Laing, Brian McKay (and later both his sons), Peter Fisher, Humphrey Tate and his father Major D.D. Tate, Rory Fraser and Guy du Barry all played. Gwen Marillier was very relieved when extra people came because she used to have to play to make up the numbers for two sides when they practised.

The polo team had initially practised on D.D. Tate's farm. In about 1952 the Polo Club managed to acquire a piece of land adjoining the Karoi Club, whose sports section was well equipped with a golf course with sand greens, tennis courts and a cricket ground. The polo ground was renowned in Rhodesia for having such a slope towards the far corners that not only the ball but even the players could disappear from the view of the spectators.

One morning, Sam Marnie arrived on the grounds by plane in great style, but he was soon brought down to earth when he was mounted on a one-eyed animal. He took his first shot and was soon planted on the ground. Unfortunately, his foot was caught in the stirrup iron and the horse took to the maize land that bordered the polo field. The going was heavy and this one-eyed monster pulled up before they reached the mahobo-hobo trees. Sam, a newly-wed, was forbidden to continue the dangerous game ever after.

The Polo Club closed in 1958 and opened again for polocrosse, a much less expensive game that can be played with one or two horses each: A-Division polo players need at least five or six.

Only the McKays went on playing polo, which they did from Banket Club, and the Armstrongs left Karoi. In the early 1960s, others who joined and excelled were Basil Kerns, Jackie Waddle, Frank Anson, Alec Cummins, Andrew Robb, and the Johnsons – father and sons.

There were eight or nine in the Polo Club, and Harry describes them fittingly:

> David Cockburn was short, slight and a complete and utter drunkard. I've never known a man of his stature to have such a capacity for booze. Ten or twelve beers in a night were nothing and he would arrive at polo on a Sunday morning having already emptied a couple of bottles.
>
> He had been a jockey and was an excellent rider. He was always poverty-stricken, the profits soon spent, even if he'd had a good crop. I told him that one day he would make a fortune. He asked me how that might be, and I replied: 'When you return all your empty bottles and get the deposits back!'

Ian Laing played with us for a year. He was a Scot, five foot ten high and five foot wide. He was a terrific back in the team, as he was very strong. This also came in handy if there was trouble in the bar. He had quite a temper and had reputedly threatened to throw his barn boys in the furnace if he found the temperatures too low; consequently, he had a little bit of a labour problem.

Laing farmed Pitlochry, a farm that Brian McKay bought off him. Brian subsequently joined our polo team. He was a cocky little bugger. He had a very good crop after his first year, and I remember him standing at the bar saying: 'I've just bought a new gun, a new car and some new horses – there's nothing to farming at all, it's too easy!' He became the biggest tobacco grower in Karoi, with a large portfolio of investments.

Guy du Barry (Guy de Bary) was one of the older members of the team – a middle-aged Belgian – middle-aged in comparison to the rest of the 'young bloods'. He, too, was short, and he spoke with a pukka English accent. He was a bit prissy but very courteous.

He had a well-appointed, gracious house and a string of good horses, but his pride and joy was a Mark V Jaguar. He was so fond of his Jaguar that he ordered a special air filter from England that was suitable for desert conditions as the roads were so dusty that he feared his engine would be ruined. The filter eventually arrived – it was enormous, measuring three foot across and two foot deep. Du Barry lifted up the bonnet of his car and had no idea how he was going to fit it in.

He rang the manufacturers in England – which took a lot of doing in those days – and asked them, in a very aggrieved fashion, how he was supposed to fit it in. They said he would have to cut a hole in the bonnet and stick it in front of the windscreen.

Du Barry nearly blew his top. The very idea of cutting a hole in the beautiful shiny bonnet was anathema to him. But the ultimate irony was that his temper got the better of him once again and, much to everyone's amusement, he kicked the bodywork of his car, making a great big hole himself.

Guy du Barry was one of the original thirteen occupants in Karoi. He farmed Buttevant along the Chanetsa road. He really was a complex character, was known to be impotent, and had a violent temper that didn't seem to abate until he had let off steam by firing a few shots with his pistol.

Guy was chairman of the Polo Club for many years. His (maternal) grandfather, F. Andrea, presented the first polo trophy to Bulawayo in 1904 – the solid silver Andrea Cup. His uncle, S. A. G. Andrea, played in Bulawayo before 1914.

Guy's wife exchanged him for one of his managers, but without rancour he backed them to go farming in Raffingora. Then, when Lionel and Paddy Searle divorced, Guy married Paddy, but it was a short-lived marriage which left him resorting to a mail-order system to find a wife.

The story goes that he saw a photograph of a model in an English magazine that really struck his imagination. He wrote to her and, after a period of correspondence and an exchange of photographs, he sent her a ticket to join him with a view to proposing marriage. The trouble was that the photos that Guy sent of himself were not current but twenty-five years old.

The Karoi polo team (left to right): Rory Fraser, Dennis Armstrong, Harry Wells, Brian McKay.
Taken at the John Browning Memorial Grounds, winter 1957.

However, he duly arrived at the airport to meet her and, on coming face to face with a gentleman hardly in his prime she said: 'How nice of you to collect me, Mr du Barry, I was expecting your son.' Travelling back to Karoi he confessed to his duplicity, which she seemed to take well.

The time inevitably came when he gave in to his sexual proclivities. Taking fright, Mary phoned the hotel for help. It was Giuseppi Tome, our returned Italian prisoner of war, who answered her distress call – all to his advantage, for she stayed and eventually married him.

If Guy was not good marriage material, he was a good polo player. His antics were usually the butt of much amusement and mockery but were taken in good part. Brian McKay recalls a very amusing incident when the team were playing in Salisbury one weekend. The street end of the field had been closed off with wooden panels. Guy came galloping at a fiendish rate down the field, unaware of the new partitioning ahead, and was ignominiously tossed over it and deposited into North Avenue.

Shaken, but unhurt, Guy picked himself up and made his way to the public entrance, where they refused to let him in because he didn't have a ticket and his story seemed to be so far-fetched. He was eventually let in when a team member went to investigate his long absence.

'The first match I played with this motley crew', said Harry Wells,

> was rather a non-event, even though we went on to win for our section. A record number of teams had been entered for the tournament so there was a tight schedule.
>
> Our team was in the D Division – the lowest of the low – and we were not only cut down to two-chukka matches but

made to play in the early hours of the morning. It was so early that there were no spectators, except for the grooms. However, we won our division.

Afterwards, at a ball held at the Grand Hotel, Rory Fraser gave a speech that began: 'When the sun was creeping over the horizon and the mist was still lying on the ground, we, of the two-chukka division, came shivering out on our ponies to play to an audience of grooms.' It brought the house down.

I had gone to the ball on my own as Eileen was in England. Rory invited me to join their party. There were several glamorous girls, two of whom were Denny Gaisford and April Piercy, and altogether it was a superb evening. I was always grateful to Rory for giving me an entrée.

The facilities at the Karoi Club were very basic. Matches were watched from seats of hay bales at the side of the ground, and one couldn't see the action at the bottom end as it sloped downwards. The lack of grass also meant that the horses were virtually obscured by an incredible cloud of dust.

The players decided to club together to improve things. They divided the ground up, each taking charge of a portion to plant with couch grass ready for the rains. They held a gymkhana to raise funds to build a grandstand, and, as Harry had the largest labour force, he managed much of the building and roofing himself.

We had toilets dug which were nothing more sophisticated than a 'long drop'. A farm labourer had cut up a few boards as seats, but the edges weren't smooth and a bit rough on one's backside.

Major Tate came over to join the conversation. 'You know, old boy, what we need for the toilet is sandpaper.'

Deadpan, I answered: 'Well, that may be all right for you, Major, but I prefer toilet paper myself.'

Jack Waddle was a relative latecomer to Karoi but was original enough in his own right for more than just a passing glance. He was probably one of the last great adventurers – a self-confessed hunter/poacher during the 1940s and 1950s, who would have fitted better into the nineteenth century, alongside other early elephant hunters. He was, if you like, Rhodesia's equivalent of Crocodile Dundee, a description which would no doubt have amused him no end.

He grew up on Ledbury farm in Bindura and became a 'bushman' from the day he was born, soaking up the environment around him like a sponge. This later spurred him on to venture out and explore those more distant parts of his beloved Africa, which he did on foot. In time, he came to have a phenomenal knowledge of the flora and fauna and of local customs, for which he became widely respected.

As a person, he came across as a shy, taciturn kind of character who preferred the tranquillity and privacy of the bush to the hustle and bustle of city life. Catherine, his daughter, said of him that he fostered in her a deep love for the African outdoors. He walked from Rhodesia to Dar es Salaam in Tanganyika, and Catherine, having travelled that route many times by car in more recent times, can appreciate the enormity of that feat.

According to his family, the reason for these travels must have been entirely illegal, for he was cagey and secretive about his movements and never involved any of them in any way. However, he did once mention being incarcerated in a jail in Mozambique by the Portuguese for ivory poaching. Luckily he was released after some kind intervention by the Lasobsky family of Salisbury, who paid his bail.

The fruition of one of these trips was his acquisition in Lusaka of a brand-new Jaguar, the gratification of which was short-lived as he promptly drove it into the Kafue river.

Despite the audacity of his very wild and private escapades, there was a fairly respectable side to Jackie Waddle. He was a notable and talented national polo player. He once laughingly insisted that he could catch the opposition out with the ambidexterity of a sneaky little left-handed flick under the horse's tail.

During his youthful farm-apprentice days he talked of robbing the ponies of their blankets after the owners had long retired for the night to their hotels. Then he would sleep in the stables to save money. It was during those days that he cultivated the habit of opening a bottle of whisky: throwing away the cap, he would say nonchalantly that it wouldn't be needed again. It was just as well that the horse knew its way home!

While on a visit to the UK he stayed at China House and joined in a shooting party as the guest of 'Sonny', Duke of Marlborough, at Blenheim Palace. There he attended a ball at which Princess Margaret was to be guest of honour. For this occasion it was necessary for him to wear a borrowed dinner jacket. The family said it was probably the first and only time in his life that he ever wore one.

His journey back home to Rhodesia was taken overland, south from Europe and down through war-torn, strife-stricken North Africa, during the 1950s on his honeymoon. This journey ended in tragedy when the Land-Rover in which he and his new wife were travelling hit a land mine. His wife was fatally injured, though he survived with a shot in the leg, but he spent many months recovering in a French military hospital before returning home.

He acquired a Tiger Moth in lieu of a debt owed him and enjoyed observing the farm from the air.

A close friend of Jack's, Ian Nysschens, first met him when Jack walked towards him one evening in the Zambezi Valley with the brilliant and spectacular light of the setting sun behind him. He had a toothbrush in his shirt pocket and only the bare necessities in the camp. They were two of a kind, living life in much the same way and shared a common interest.

Ian recalled affectionately the many times when Jackie and his friend Jock MacDonald exploited him during his years as a game ranger:

> They got me under some pretext to take them down to the Zambezi Valley towards the gorge. They only had a motorcycle and loaded it into the back of my Land-Rover. I off-loaded them and continued on to Lusaka.
>
> They in turn went poaching elephant in my territory, unknown to me. I had signed them into the Valley, which meant that, technically, they weren't there. Of course, they informed me of this later with amusement, but I didn't care: we were all the same type of men.

Jackie met Judy, his second wife, soon after he returned from France. They moved to Karoi in 1960.

A clubhouse that provides many sporting facilities – like the library that provides books – plays an important role within a rural community far from anywhere. The first clubhouse, a humble pole'n'daga hut, was built in 1946/47, and Sir John Kennedy was invited to open it with great ceremony.

Later, in 1952, a more substantial shed-like building was erected in brick to take its place. Edna Taylor, the doctor's wife, says she remembers ordering the roofing. The

Sir John Kennedy opens the first pole'n'daga clubhouse.

managers of the Club were 'Mum' and Pop Mitchell, the well-respected parents of Paul and Ken. This (penultimate) new Club was big enough to play badminton in – Maureen Philip said that she and Paul played there twice weekly. Paul said that cricket was the first outdoor sport to get going there, and he was correct.

Miami had done rather well during the preceding years to provide sporting facilities for its far-flung population. John Impey – who first farmed a piece of Pitlochry and then bought Crown land called Toro (later named Chisanji) in 1954 – promoted a six-hole golf course there. By 1958 the last transfer of officialdom had been completed and all concentration was then focused on Karoi.

A golf course very quickly followed the cricket pitch. Sonny Shakespeare played excellent golf, and so did George Neaves, who had once been a Manicaland champion.

Names that crop up as notable tennis players are Dennis Prince and Charlie McLaughlan, who won the men's doubles a few times, as did Des Evans and Sonny Shakespeare. Of the originals, the 'tennis greats' were Sadie Potter, Sue and Charles Stewart, Pat and Peter Gibson, and Bess and Dan Oosthuizen.

Mark Gaisford was acknowledged to be an excellent all-rounder. Like Flossie Hoskyns, he was a sporting natural who seemed to

The Karoi Cricket XI, 1957.

win everything with ease. However, it had been noticed that on occasions at various club championships, Mark's expertise would diminish after the lunch session.

On one occasion Mark travelled down to the lowveld with the golfers and decided for once to drive down by car instead of going on the chartered flight. After a resoundingly successful weekend, everyone, including Mark, hopped on to the plane for the return flight home.

On landing at Salisbury, a very puzzled Mark wondered why Denny wasn't waiting to pick him up. Eventually after finding a lift home he demanded to know why he'd been forgotten. 'But where's your car? You drove down,' Denny reminded him.

The name John Impey later became associated more with cricket, when he became a patron of the sport. By employing keen young cricketers as assistants on his farm, they were at liberty to take time off for team training and national tours abroad. Brian Oldreive, Kevin Curran, Geoff Edwards and Robin Brown were just four of them.

After Flossie Hoskyns sold his farm, he took on the job of groundsman for the cricket section. On one auspicious occasion, Karoi hosted a two-day match between Mashonaland and the 'Goofie' Lawrence XI, and he was justifiably proud when Goofie praised the pitch, saying that it was good enough for a five-day test match.

Some of the teams at different times included Dennis Prince and Keith Harvey, Flossie Hoskyns, Noel Blazey, Rod Cawood, Arnold Bathurst, Charles Postlethwayt, Rob Hay, Dave Chadwick, Tony McKay, 'Potty' Potgieter, Frank Donnelly, Roy Robinson, Neville Quail, Buddy Donaldson, Alan Bunnett, Steve Jacobson, Dave Lazelle, Brian Oldreive, Geoff Edwards and Honk Hyde. Audrey Bryson was the scorer.

A small swimming pool was built by the council at some stage along the line, and it went through several stages of neglect and revival. Chris Wilkinson was the last 'caretaker' – it was his forte and he kept it sparkling clean. Then came a bowling green, a rugby field and a squash court.

The rugby section of the Club came to the fore as the boom years started in the early 1960s, with enough young men to make up at least three teams, who played rugby enthusiastically at league level.

Lorrie Lemmer, Mike Bailey, George Donald and Dick Bylo all coached at one time or another until call-ups intervened. Those who played in the 1960s and 1970s were Mike Bailey, Mike van der Merwe, Eynon Deere, John Sealy, Neville Quail, Andries Herbst, Honk Hyde, Ian MacMillan, Ed Weigall, Dave Chadwick, Nick Haasbroek, Gerald Smith, John Moore, Piet Nieuwoudt, the Nel brothers, Willie and Hans, and Tony McKay.

Chartered flights to South Africa to watch international tests were not only tremendous fun and excitement but an eye-opener into the antics of men on the loose.

Rhodesia, if you remember, was at one time a sporting province of South Africa, and many Rhodesians earned their Springbok colours. One such chartered tour, organised by Thomas Cook in conjunction with the Rhodesian Rugby Board, took many enthusiasts and their wives to Johannesburg to watch the Lions *v.* Springboks tests in 1974.

Our landing at Jan Smuts airport had coincided with several other flights, and clearance through Customs and Immigration was slow. Having already begun their celebrations prior to the on-flight breakfast, Piet Bosch and Porky du Preez were well on their way to 'paradise', and they decided to climb high up on to a parapet that overlooked the queuing passengers down below.

With only the luck of the inebriated devil, they proceeded to serenade the entire hall – and they weren't half bad either. When the police eventually arrived, they had a terrible

job trying to persuade them down to ground level and they never did get to watch that test match. Needless to say that episode was very funny and entertaining. It's hard to imagine how it would go down nowadays.

One night, as a group of us were walking through the centre of Pretoria after dining out, Neville Quail looked around ingenuously and remarked, 'Who's this guy Kroeg? He must be very rich. He owns all the bars in town.'

The third and present clubhouse was built in 1972/73. For some reason it never did capture the atmosphere and warmth of the old one. More money than sense was spent on it over the years, all to no avail. No amount of altering was ever able to improve its impractical design. It eventually became a white elephant, and politics did the rest. Its doors are now closed and firmly locked.

Those of our community who put us on the sporting map were:

Marietta van Heerden, daughter of Hennie and Joan, who was selected for the Rhodesian Olympic team in the shot-put discipline.

Andrew Ferreira, son of Ethne and Harvey, who was awarded his Rhodesian colours for table tennis at the age of fourteen. He then went on to play rugby for our country. He was equally talented at tennis, and won club and provincial championships.

Ian MacMillan, Barry White and his sons, David and Ian, who were well-known national motorcycle scrambling enthusiasts.

Brian Oldreive played hockey as well as cricket for Rhodesia, and Robin Brown, cricket.

Roy Bennett played polo for Rhodesia.

11. Research

Karoi was opened up as a tobacco area at a time when the demand for Miami's mica was coming to an end. The first crop-growers in Miami had concentrated on maize, sorghum and beans, although some, such as the pioneers of the area like William (Bill) Leask, Jacob (Jack) Goldberg, O.C. Rawson and C.P. Robertson on Buffalo Downs, had already experimented in the 1930s with both Turkish, air-cured, and Virginia, flue-cured. All these, and A.B. Roberts in the 1940s, paved the way for the introduction of the crop into the area.

The tobacco industry was to become the economic backbone of the country, but it could not be called an overnight success, even though, by and large, when ex-servicemen began to take up their land north of the Angwa river in 1947, many of the industry's teething problems had been resolved. It was by no means the end of troubled times.

As early as 1902, Earl Grey, a director of the BSA Company, under whose protection the country was ruled, had concerned himself earnestly with identifying a crop that would attract permanent immigrants to Rhodesia and provide them with a livelihood. He felt that there had to be a strong magnet, a trump card with which to tempt new settlers.

Initially it had been gold, and then it was thought that land might entice people to live here – this was certainly the motivation behind the arrival of many, including the Afrikaners who trekked up from the south at the instigation of Cecil John Rhodes himself.

But by far the biggest problem that occupied Earl Grey's mind was what the new pioneer settler was to do with his land once he arrived. It was a question that he had discussed with a young man called George Odlum, who, forty years later when he had retired, explained in a letter from England how he had had a hand in getting the industry started. George Odlum was an American missionary with a wide knowledge of crop-growing. He told how cotton and other fibrous and oil crops, even rubber, were considered but rejected because of the vast areas of sandveld and granite that made up most of Southern Rhodesia.

Clements and Harben, in *Leaf of Gold*, relate how the Earl had asked him a short question, the answer to which decided the country's future.

'Well, what about tobacco, then?'

'I confess', said Odlum, 'that I was stumped. I was aware that the tobacco plant would grow in just about any country, but places where leaf of merit resulted were not common. I also knew the difficulty of introducing even a leaf of good quality into established markets.

'To cut a long story short,' continued Odlum, 'Earl Grey said to me, "Go to America for a year and study the industry and then decide."

'So I went to America and followed the industry in every aspect, field market and factory', he said.

'I had letters of backing from the Earl which induced many in high positions to part with their information and opinions and in later years some of those gentlemen said that they regretted having done so, and as late as 1932 I was refused information or entrance into a factory.'

Odlum returned and, based on what he had gleaned in America, the British South Africa Company intensified its efforts to stimulate tobacco production.

Therefore the year 1903 could be recognised as the foundation of the tobacco industry.

From the early days, professionals in the government provided advisory services to tobacco growers, though their most valuable work lay in developing varieties of tobacco most suitable for growing in Rhodesia.

The foremost men were H.W.Taylor, an American who was appointed Chief Tobacco Officer in 1918, and D.D.Brown, who succeeded him in 1925 and nurtured the industry for a further twenty-five years.

From 1948, their chief role was to teach newcomers about the tobacco industry – how to grow the crop from start to finish. However, because these advisory officers were thin on the ground, the RTA improvised an extension service of its own. To start with, retired growers or those qualified in other ways were recruited to pass on elementary advice to novices.

The experimental farm K.34 was opened in Miami in 1948/49, with H.P.Pearse in charge. When its future was in jeopardy for financial reasons at the break-up of the Federation in 1963, the chairman of the ICA, Thomas (Pat) Bashford, wrote to the Department of Research and Specialist Services, saying that it had become not only a great institution in the full sense of the word but that it had been of great benefit to the farming industry; closing it would have a detrimental effect on the whole area. His appeal fell on deaf ears, and the farm was later sold to Syd Baxter, a local farmer.

Karoi was particularly fortunate in the staff of its Department of Conservation and Extension (CONEX). In 1960 Roger Barclay-Smith was appointed to Karoi. He became a particular friend of the Flight family, Veronica and Jimmy.

Roger, whom many will remember, was a Cambridge graduate responsible for opening up the Vuti settlement, which is situated geographically north of the last two farms that were surveyed for ex-servicemen, appropriately named Chiwuwa and Omega. Vuti was opened up for black farmers, and Roger, who had a special interest in getting it off to a good start, went up there to live. Later he moved to Nyasaland/Malawi and grew Burley tobacco.

He never married, and when he died in 2008 he left a substantial legacy of $2 million to his old college, Caius (pronounced 'keys') at Cambridge.

> On leaving Caius he headed straight for Africa – a powerful instinct which influenced him all his life.
>
> In 1959, he went to Rhodesia where he worked until 1975, when he joined the Food and Agriculture Organisation of the United Nations, based in Rome.
>
> He continued to work in Africa, partly in Swaziland but mainly in Malawi. In 1984, he started farming on the personally owned estates of Dr Hastings Banda, the President of Malawi, and remained there for eleven years.
>
> He retired in 1995, but remained in Malawi living in Dedza, 'a mountain paradise', until his death in August 2008.[1]

When Andrew Flight was born, Roger was asked to be his godfather and, interestingly enough, Andrew Flight now finds himself growing tobacco on those same farms that Roger once did.

Another CONEX officer who made a small but interesting contribution was Peter Whittle. Approximately five miles north of

---

[1] James Howell, 'The Legacy of Roger Barclay-Smith', <http://www.gonvilleandcaius.org/Document.Doc?id=178>.

Karoi, there is a turn to the left opposite a store that belonged to Chinyerere farm, once part of Coldomo, previously part of Nassau. The store survived many unexpected events one way or another – nocturnal drivers from the Magunje road who failed to take the turn in time, break-ins before and during the war – until it became more trouble than it was worth, and the owner, Hugh Royston, knocked it down. However, for a period in Karoi's history it was a useful landmark: 'Turn left at the store and you'll find yourself on the Magunje road,' one said in answer to a request for directions.

Before turning, however, the really observant traveller would notice, on the immediate left, a fenced-off arboretum of indigenous trees. One day during the 1970s, Peter stopped to admire the abundance of *Erythrina abyssinica* (the 'lucky-bean' or 'coral tree') that grew around there.

As June drifted into July, that corner would become a profusion of bright red hues, not easily overlooked by travellers, for their vivid colours stood out starkly against the clear blue sky of that time of the year. In a good year it was a wonderful sight, yet none of them was planted deliberately. It must have been a favourite place for cattle, and over years they munched their way through fallen seeds, distributing them as nature intended, only for them to germinate again.

But that wasn't all. Peter noticed a variety of other wild species, more than was usual in one small spot. So, with the farmer's permission, he fenced off this little gem of nature, set up a preservation sign that announced that it was a government conservation site, and labelled all the trees; Hugh Royston kept the grass cut. Few locals were aware of this. Hopefully, the trees are still there, but I doubt that the fencing is.

Peter Stidolph was also a CONEX officer who discovered that, since he had been dishing out advice for others, he might as well put his knowledge to good use on his own behalf, and he joined the tobacco farming fraternity. He became very successful.

Jerry Stocks was another who, after attending university, was sent first to the Trelawney Research Station and then to Karoi and Tengwe as an Extension Officer. He was Tengwe's first appointee. Later Jerry joined the staff of Kutsaga, where he remained until he retired.

Youngsters drew on the knowledge of the 'old hands' who lived in the district. In almost every farm block there is someone who will always respond to the call of a colleague or neighbour, and this was very much the case in Karoi. These mentors gain nothing, except perhaps satisfaction.

Among the men who entered the industry in the post-war years, there is hardly one who does not have the most vivid memory of a 'godfather' who saw him through the frightening and unnerving first crop. Andries Herbst, my late husband, had Neville Royston to call on, having known him in Gutu where he, too, had been a CONEX officer before becoming a farmer in Karoi. Thirty years later, my son, Andrew (Melek) Herbst, was fortunate enough to have Phil Gifford and Sven Johnsen advising him, and to both of these gentlemen we are deeply indebted.

Rothmans, in the pursuit of excellence, initiated a 'Tobacco Grower of the Year' competition. Early winners from Karoi were David Chadwick, who farmed on Manyangau, in 1974, and Donovan Stotter, who farmed on Mshalla, who won twice – in 1980 and 1985 – one of only two growers ever to have done so.

In 1987, Fred Mitchell of Kevlyn farm won, and during the 1990s there were John Impey and Peter Walsh from Tengwe, and Richard Black, Geoff Kockett and Rob Howes.

12. Schooling in Karoi

It was a red-letter day when, in January 1954, Mrs Greta MacDonald became the first teacher of a small school that would teach up to Standard 2 in the Gwen Scrase Hall. It opened with seven little boys and one rather apprehensive teacher.

Mrs MacDonald sent me her reminiscences in 1980, just before she died.

> Wilson was waiting at the door, offering his services as caretaker-cum-messenger, and right faithfully he served me for two years. The boys were Patrick Armstrong, Hamish Chisholm, Robin Hay, John MacDonald, George Ormerod, Mike Rowe and Ricky Wadley.
>
> These seven were soon joined by Ian Kind, John Watson, Trevor James and, at last, some little girls: Judy James, Ruth Stewart, Erina Grobbelaar, Theresia Serfontein, Carol Wesson, Elise Oosthuizen, and Moira and Diana Stacey.
>
> The ministry had already sent a case of equipment, and the unpacking of it helped to calm my nerves and I began to feel more interested and confident. It was amazing how we all settled down in that – to us, huge – hall. I was not kindergarten-trained but I had intelligent children and we all soon fell into a routine and I began to enjoy teaching again.
>
> The mothers were marvellous, bringing in their children each morning from farms – there was no village to speak of in those days. So what were they to do with themselves while they waited? Karoi was too small to offer any morning jobs. Those who lived near Karoi did the double trip and returned mid-day. Others played golf or visited friends to pass the time. None of this was ideal.
>
> I gave a lift to the children who lived north of Karoi, and a bit later D.D. and Jan Tate started a boarding hostel for boys at Kyogle farm (where they lived), which was a tremendous help. Soon after, John and I joined them; Jan very nicely consented to have me as well.
>
> I found the short trip on narrow tar marvellous after eleven miles on the North Road with its shocking deviations, for they were preparing to tar the road to Kariba and we churned up dust in winter and mud in summer.
>
> One or two highlights stand out vividly. One was the day when a new piano was delivered from the ministry. Previously, we had walked up to the Club where Pop and Mum Mitchell kindly allowed us to use the piano for singing and games – great fun! There were always scones and cakes for us afterwards from Mum, the soul of generosity.
>
> It was wonderful to have our own piano, but not so wonderful was the day when the man from the ministry returned to tune it and found a family of mice in a gorgeous warm nest of felt when he removed the front! He was furious with me for my neglect, and I was well and truly slated.
>
> Living so far from Salisbury we became a law unto ourselves, arriving at our own solutions to overcome the difficulties that arose from time to time. I once went down with an attack of laryngitis and could only whisper, so Natalie Rowe, Michael's mum, volunteered to teach if I looked after her

young daughter, still in a pushchair. So I had a pleasant morning pushing the baby around Karoi – which didn't take long in those days! And Natalie said afterwards that she had thoroughly enjoyed her morning's teaching.

On another occasion, I had arranged to close the school early so that a funeral service could be held there, and who should turn up but Dr Rogers, the Chief Inspector of Schools, so I had to tell him of our arrangements. He was a good sport and took it all in good part: he left by 10.30 and I closed the school at 11.00 as arranged – not without a sigh of relief.

As time went on it became more and more apparent that the number of children would never rise above the twenty-three then in the school because of the distance from Karoi of many of the farms and the difficulties of transport. So in 1955 the ministry decided to build a new school and a hostel for the boys and girls on an excellent site opposite the police camp.

We watched it grow, course by course, and when it was finished we actually moved in for a term, the last of 1955. Friends helped us to move desks, blackboards and the rest of the equipment into an empty classroom. Thus the ministry saved themselves a term's rent to the church authorities.

So it was that, in January 1956, Karoi Junior School opened its doors and went from strength to strength, continuing to educate the children of the district until 1981. And an excellent place of learning it was, too – though it had taken seven long years of constant petitioning by the Women's Institute to get the Ministry of Education to agree to the building of a school in Karoi.

In 1973, a long overdue suggestion was acted on when the girls' hostel was named the Greta MacDonald Hostel. Still full of beans and verve when she retired, she went to live in one of the Jubilee Cottages.

Then, one day in 1980, she drove herself and three of her friends to Salisbury. On the way she had an accident, killing herself and two of her friends. It was thought that she had either fallen asleep at the wheel or suffered a stroke.

Mike Rowe, whose mum filled in on occasions for Greta and was one of her first pupils, recalls very little except that he was always in trouble and was constantly being told to 'shut up'!

Greta had a difficult job trying to teach a composite class of pupils of different ages and levels of learning. The only activity that they all did together was music, which they did standing around the piano. Later, when Mike met her as an adult living back in Karoi, he realised how competent she must have been to keep the class in order and to teach them as much as she did.

Teresia Bosch, née Serfontein and the winner of the Victrix Ludorum for athletics in 1959, remembered that Mrs MacDonald did handstands with them in KG1 and the older girls stole their tuck as payment for watching their tree acrobats.

They trekked all the way to the club for a swim, which at that age seemed a very long way. Joan Newhook taught them ballet and put on super shiny shoes. Marietta Skilton took singing, and Karoi sports teams always did well and won all their games.

Patricia (Tish) Duguid, née Marillier, offered her memories:

> Perhaps I should explain my title before launching into somewhat hazy recollections of one of my earliest school days. The recycling specialists would

certainly approve – I was one of the original 1956 KG1 pupils when Karoi Junior School opened its doors.

I spent the usual seven years there, a further five at senior school, and returned, this time on the other side of the desk, as a student teacher in 1968.

It was almost like having been in a weird time-machine. The head, Pat Taylor, and two of the teachers were the same: Greta MacDonald and Daisy Hook. It seemed almost disrespectful to be in the same staffroom.

More ironic still was the fact that my first classroom as a pupil became my first as a student teacher and then later my first as a fully fledged teacher. How I enjoyed teaching there, possibly because I'd known my Standard Three pupils as babies and possibly because I felt so much at home.

However, the school to which I returned as a teacher bore little resemblance to the one I had left in 1962. Originally there had been the four core classrooms, ending in the two offices and toilet block. To these were soon added a further two classrooms, a book-room and staffroom, and a second toilet block to the north end. This addition was still not quite sufficient for all the Standards to have their own classroom, so Standards Four and Five were composite.

Before the two new infants' classes were added, I recall Mrs MacDonald teaching us in the prep-room of the hostel. We performed a play, *Peter Rabbit*, in the adjoining courtyard, which doubled up as a hall because we also held Christmas-carol concerts there. Joan Ham, later Mrs McFadjean, was most adept at transforming the mundane courtyard into a festive area

with dozens of stained-glass windows.

The early arrival of a teacher named John Laughlin played a great part in the school, and it wasn't long before most of us became athletics-mad, with Karoi School excelling at most of the Lomagundi, and even the Mashonaland, sports meetings. As usual, parents were ever generous in their support and helped in transporting us from sports field to sports field and providing all the necessary equipment.

Karoi was always a 'community school' in the true sense of the word. Parents always played a supportive role, and without their help in cash, in kind and in time, I doubt if the school could have enjoyed the facilities that it had. Mr Tiens Vorster, for instance, donated the athletics field. He was in charge of vast earth-moving equipment and concerned with bush-clearing during the building of Kariba.

Extramural lessons were offered by local people who were talented in various fields: ballet-dancing, music, singing, and even French lessons. The school badge was designed by Joan Newhook, one of the mothers, and she and others were responsible for the original choice of uniform, a grey-and-white check with red trimmings.

At this juncture it might be pertinent to note that the red trimmings often included more than our belts and hatbands, as more often than not most of the Standard Threes upwards suffered skinned elbows and knees from a dangerous games called Open Gates, which, for some reason known only to juvenile minds, had to be played on the tarmac around the flagstaff.

Severely grazed cases were sent to the hostel to be treated by Mrs Booysen, who firmly applied liberal quantities of iodine. It was a treatment guaranteed to stop one from participating! We also indulged in other, more genteel, 'evergreens' like hopscotch and marbles, which we played on the dusty pathway to the hostel.

Religion played a greater part in our lives than it does today. Every day began with Assembly. The piano was wheeled out on to the veranda; we stood on the lawn below to sing one of our pianist's limited repertoire.

At the risk of sounding distinctly school-marmish, I think that the discipline was quite a lot stricter, too. No doubt the younger pupils would protest and argue my point. My brother and his friend – those legendary accomplices-in-crime, Buster Marillier and David Grantham – actually competed to see how many loose braids they could pull off the office chair over which they had to bend while being caned. It was fairly threadbare by the time they left!

All in all, our junior-school days were happy, and most of us seemed to hold our own in the various senior schools we later attended.

Greta MacDonald, Daisy Hook, Sylvia Bishop, and the Headmaster, Pat Taylor became entrenched in the school: their teaching careers spanned almost the entire pre-independence years of the school's history. Pat Taylor retired just before independence and went to live in South Africa. Daisy Hook also left, and Sylvia Bishop retired to her farm, Zebra Downs, until she and Chris, her son, were 'invaded'.

As dedicated teachers they played an enormous part in preparing our children for the wider world, and for this we are grateful. Sylvia, of course, knows far too much about

Sylvia Bishop.

us all, having taught two generations and, in many cases, being well acquainted with the third. However, she has been discreet to the end. She tells only one story about a time when it became obvious that a mother was doing a child's homework for him. Eventually, having marked the work, Sylvia wrote at the bottom, in exasperation, 'Well done, Mum!'

Ray Townsend remembered Dennis Sanderson coaching the Karoi Junior School rugby team when he was there. The boys had such respect for him because he was partially crippled from polio; running about on the pitch wasn't easy for him, but he was so enthusiastic that they appreciated all his efforts.

Many past pupils and parents have often wondered what the GVM Cups stood for, both in name and merit, over the years. These cups were presented to best senior boy and girl at the end of their junior school career in recognition of their work and sporting achievements. They were deemed the most prestigious accolade attained by a school-leaver and were held in high esteem.

The initials GVM stand for Gerald Victor Marillier, the husband of Gwen (née Southey) Marillier, well known and more familiar to us as 'Mrs Mort'. Gerald Marillier was the father of Gerald Jr (Buster) and Patricia. After his death, Gwen married

Anthony Mortimer, father of Simon and Sarah, and years later, after Tony's death, married a family friend and former Karoi farmer, Peter Adams.

Gerald Victor Marillier farmed in Karoi from October 1946 until January 1955, when he was killed in a flying accident. His father, G. E. Marillier, who also farmed in Karoi, presented the cups to the school in his memory and asked that they be awarded to the Standard Five (Grade 7) girl and boy who had best combined academic work and sport during their junior school career. Mr Marillier senior felt very strongly that many

children got through their school days doing as little work as possible because they were important members of the school sports team, while others excelled in exams, only giving time to studying and not making any contribution to sport or any other school activity.

When Pat Taylor retired as headmaster in 1973 – he had been there since its inception – Alec Morris was appointed in his place, but he didn't stay too long. Richard Emmett then arrived, and he and Keith Brown served alternately as acting headmasters until Keith's position eventually became

Achievers of the GVM Trophy

Year	Boys	Girls
1956	David van Wyk	Isobel Bekker
1957	R. Hill	Julia McDairmid
1958	Keith Maxwell	W. Williamson
1959	Richard McDairmid	Joan Neilsen
1960	Richard Sheppard	Ruth Stewart
1961	Brian McDairmid	Jennifer Potter
1962	Alan Brnjac	Gillian Potter
1963	John Neilsen	Sharon Prince
1964	T. Lebron	Cheryl Spargo
1965	S. Esterhuizen	Denise Humpage
1966	G. Jahme	S. Wesson
1967	Michael Brnjac	Diana Duguid
1968	M. Sanderson	Sandra Loney
1969	K. Ackerman	Jennifer Thornton
1970	Ainsly Sanderson	Jean Dabbs
1971	Brett McClachlan	Beverley Roebuck
1972	Ralph Spargo	Barbara Wilcox
1973	J. Visagie	Cindy Postlethwayt
1974	H. Cronje	Leana Visagie
1975	R Ferguson	Gwendolyn Herbst
1976	not presented	
1977	Andre Minaar	Sian Herbst
1977	Mark Letcher	
1978	Ian MacLagan	Cheryl Duvenage
1979	Stephen Gauche	Nichola Quail
1980	Chris Watson	Andrea Herbst
1981	Ewan MacMillan	Cindy Johnsen

Keith Brown

permanent. He was the last white head-master of Karoi Junior School.

During the late 1970s, the school became a community school. In essence, that meant that it was semi-private. A board of governors was elected, and the hostels, in particular, were run as a private enterprise.

At independence in 1980 the school lost that status as the newly elected Zimbabwean government expressed its disapproval of the concept. It passed a bill abolishing the system, and thereafter all community schools returned to being government-controlled. A highly indignant white population prepared to build a private school and made plans to move to another venue. Unfortunately, those who instigated the idea failed to take into account how this move would appear to those in authority at the ministry, as the whole school – staff and pupils – were preparing to move en masse. This was not a lesson in diplomacy, and it lacked finesse and discretion.

The entrepreneurs of Karoi, with the generous backing of the Karoi farming and commercial community, acquired Rydings farm, just out of town, and, with the help of a clever architect, proceeded to transform the barns and sheds into a uniquely original establishment, all done in double-quick time so that no teaching time should be lost.

The year 1981 will be remembered for

many reasons, not least for the difficulties and frustrations that lay ahead, as the government became obdurate and intransi-gent as regards the education system. The new Rydings School did not get permission to open as scheduled.

There followed many meetings with the Ministry of Education, and the road between Harare and Karoi became worn-out with use and red-hot with frayed tempers. The pro-spective headmaster, Humphrey Tate – born in Karoi, the son of D.D. and Jan Tate of Kyogle farm – along with the governors and trustees, travelled up and down the Great North Road ad nauseam, spending hours in discussion.

It was a deeply disturbing and depressing time for the district, and it was many months after it had been ready that the school was finally given the go-ahead to open. The government made one stipulation before the green light was given: Karoi School's former staff and pupils were asked to return to their former venue for one more term to show no ill-will. This was agreed to, and finally, in 1982, Rydings School opened its doors for the business of education.

Over the years, the change of staff at Karoi Junior School had been phenomenal. Fledgling teachers, most of them young ladies fresh out of college, were sent up to 'the sticks' to begin their teaching careers, only to find that Karoi wasn't such a bad place after all, for a multitude of bachelors were queuing up to sweep them off their feet, straight to the altar. The majority were farmers, but some were policemen, others members of the Internal Affairs department, or teaching colleagues, along with a few exceptional individuals like the butcher, Anthony Saint.

Two of the first were Joan Ham, who married local farmer Hastings McFadjean, and Sylvia Johnson, who married another local farmer, Arthur Bishop. Joan and Sylvia had arrived in Rhodesia almost immediately after the war. They discovered Karoi when they visited Mary Purchase, herself a teacher, who had married Robbie, a local farmer. While waiting for the school to open, Joan Ham did a spell in Kariba, where she taught for eighteen months.

Others teachers who married locally were: Rae Campbell, who married Tony Hunt (farmer); Paddy Barrett-Hamilton (farmer) and Sylvia Hess (teacher), both bought up in Karoi; Peter Stidolph (CONEX) met Tawny Keatly (teacher); Tish Marillier married Keith Duguid (geologist), both were local kids; Args Mauvis (teacher) met James Watt (farmer); Anthony Wells (farmer) met Dawn Brunette (teacher); Anthony Saint (butcher) was luckier the second time around when he married Sheryll Marchesson (teacher); Ed Flight (farmer) met Suzey Moore (teacher); Ian Scott-Roger and Karen Rosettenstein were both members of the teaching staff; Lindy Laver (teacher) married Ken Griffiths, both were brought up in Karoi; Anne Purchase (teacher) met Rory Duffin (farmer). Sandra Coast (teacher), Karoi-bred, met Des Hill (postal engineer), and after Sandra's tragic and untimely death, he married Tengwe-born-and-bred Lydia Johnson (teacher); Margaret Simpson (teacher), born in Karoi, married Chris Herud (farmer); Joy Macnaught (teacher) married farmer Tiens Moolman; Ian Gibson (farmer) met Moraig Scorgie (teacher).

Pictures from the last years of Karoi Junior School.

13. 'Tiny' Rowland

Roland Fuhrhop, alias 'Tiny' Rowland, was born on 27 November 1917 in Simla, India. His father was German and his mother Dutch-English. Before emigrating to Rhodesia he had 'helped' Jews to move their possessions – furniture, art works, jewellery and money – from Germany to Britain, but despite this he was always to remain a suspicious and dubious character within the minds not only of the British government but of many others as well.

After the war ended, Tiny earned his living by selling off war-surplus goods in London. He moved to Rhodesia in 1948, and during this period spent time in the Karoi area, on and off. He became a familiar sight at the Twin River Inn, built by Mike Reynolds, with whom he had a partnership in Shamrock mine.

In 1969 copper prices were rising appreciably and frantic development ensued, with Shamrock experiencing a time of great remunerative benefits. The mine was never targeted during the bush war owing to Rowland's sympathies with and generous funding of the nationalist campaign. He had many interests in Rhodesia/Zimbabwe and was perhaps best known, years on, as the chief executive of Lonrho, a company that he developed but from which he was eventually ousted.

'Not many men in public life have so successfully covered their activities in secrecy, nor provoked such controversy and mystery', wrote Tom Bower in Rowland's biography.[1] He had been educated in Germany and Britain, then joined the British army and was imprisoned and discharged

by them. Sent with his mother to the Isle of Man for the duration of the war, he was left embittered for the rest of his life – mostly on behalf of his mother, whom he loved dearly.

He admitted having to leave Britain after problems blew up with the Inland Revenue, but returned to London in 1961 from Rhodesia to develop the London and Rhodesian Mining and Land Company (Lonrho) into a huge global commercial empire that employed 100,000 people. He took over *The Observer* newspaper in 1983.

When Lonrho decided to close Shamrock, Tiny Rowland went to the government and said that the ground on which the mine had been built would make an ideal training ground for the troops. Would they be interested in buying it?

The government said they would wait until it was abandoned, for they had had him under surveillance for a long time and knew that he was funding the nationalists. (Most of us had already worked that out because Shamrock had never been attacked during the bush war.)

Then one day the government contacted Brian McKay: Would he be interested in dismantling the mine buildings? How long would it take him should he be interested?

[1] Tom Bower, *Tiny Rowland: A Rebel Tycoon* (London: Heinemann, 1993).

He would be allowed to take everything but the roofing, which they wanted. He put the offer to Jim Barker, and the two of them began to demolish everything there.

It was a wonderful set-up – 'as mines are', said Brian. There were sixty houses and more, in pristine condition for blacks and whites, all standing abandoned – a clinic, school, clubhouse, and every facility one could wish for. They took away piping, tons of scrap metal and steel, and mounds of other materials, all of which became very useful on their farms.

Tiny Rowland was saluted as a genius by many, as they watched him amass great wealth. He was ultimately considered to be a millionaire, a merchant adventurer, political intriguer and accomplished power-broker who was welcomed by presidents and prime ministers throughout Africa, Asia, America and Europe.

Yet later, amid a startling series of allegations, his own empire began to rock beneath him as he struggled to clear his name. Rowland was investigated by government agencies more often than any other businessman. He died in 1998, not long after he had lost his position in Lonrho.

14. The Karoi Dutch

It wasn't only the British who grabbed at the opportunity of a new life in Rhodesia after the Second World War – the Dutch poured in as well, anxious to put war-torn Europe behind them. Several made valuable and indelible contributions within the boundaries of Karoi.

Father Zincan, a Jesuit, was the first Catholic priest to be established in the parish of Karoi. For many years he was a familiar figure around the town and on farms as he went about his work.

Arnold Miller de Haan was the first Hollander to farm in Karoi when he settled on Pompey farm to the west. Wendy Miller de Haan wrote:

> We arrived in Karoi in 1947. Dad was an ex-serviceman who was allocated a farm which my parents named Pompey, a name given to Portsmouth in England by the British after it was razed to the ground during the war. It was where they had met.
>
> Pompey in Karoi, Africa, was just *bundu* [bush] when we arrived, so while a mud *pondokkie* [shack] was being constructed and crops were being planted, my mother and sisters lived with Gwen and Richard Scrase on Shambatungwe farm.
>
> Dad slept in a truck on Pompey. Our first house was the standard building of the time, with a veranda and outside PK – a long-drop where we sat on a wooden box and used newspaper as toilet paper.
>
> Little snippets of memories are of the houseboy filling the water jug from the rain that poured through the roof, and having to walk over planks from one room to another because the floor was one big muddy puddle – clearly it was a good rainy season!
>
> The kitchen was outside, separated from the rest of the house, and despite those conditions both the cook and houseboy were always immaculately dressed in white uniforms.
>
> There was a meat safe, its legs standing in open tins filled with methylated spirits that kept ants and other creepy-crawlies from getting to our food.
>
> I remember sacks of water hanging in trees, snakes in the thatched roof, and our pet monkey running along the tops of the walls and throwing things at us. The most exciting event of all was finding a leopard sitting under the shade of the coffee table on the veranda! We also found buffalo grazing among the *mombes*.

Kees and Hans Bakker became prominent citizens of Karoi when they took over an old garage that developed into Karoi Motors, and it was they who were responsible for bringing many Hollanders into the district.

Kees and Maartje, his wife, left Holland in 1953 to take up work as a mechanic with Mr Ewing, a well-known tobacco grower in Banket, where he stayed for two seasons. He was soon joined by his bachelor brother, Hans, who had still been living in Holland. He took over the administration side of the business while Kees continued to manage the workshop. The business went from strength to strength, with Kees continuing to draw more and more of his compatriots from Holland.

In 1957 Siem Timmer and his wife Ri

arrived. He later managed Checkers Motors, built on a plot next to Maidments. Siem then branched out on his own.

Next to arrive was another bachelor, Wim Potemans. He came in 1958, independently, having no connection with the Bakkers, and took on the job of Workshop Manager. Another bachelor, Dick Heynes, joined him in the same year as Spares Manager.

Dick recalled having to drive new tractors out from Salisbury, 130 miles away. In those days, the new road over the Dyke had not been completed, so it was a case of travelling on the old strip-road through Maryland, which could be very precarious.

Hans Bakker eventually married Marge, a petite, fine-boned Scots girl who was working as a secretary at Consolidated Motors. She is remembered for being very fashionable, wearing spindly high-heeled winkle-pickers and wearing her hair in a high bee-hive: one would avoid sitting behind her at shows. George Kennedy, as luck would have it, had no choice on one occasion and Marge noticed he was bobbing about quite a lot behind her. 'Are you all right, George? Can you see?' 'Oh, don't worry, Marge,' he said. 'It'll be all right once you've taken your hat off.'

Wim married Frieda who was a mail-order bride. Dick left for South Africa and married there.

Lydia and Gerard Stroobach became great friends of Kees and Maartje Bakker's. Kees and Maartje were always ready to help Gerry when necessary – 'perhaps the loan of a tractor or something,' said Lydia. 'Holland has changed a lot over the decades. I have been away fifty-five years but my heart is still in Africa.'

Gerry and Lydia started off in Karoi working for Wessel Rautenbach. They were hard times. After a little curing competition that Gerry won, Wessel offered him a higher salary if he would stay on.

However, neighbour Arnold Miller de Haan, had already offered them a partnership on Pompey. They had a very happy time growing tobacco for Arnold, who used to complain that since Gerry had been there he had had to pay super-tax because they had made an enormous profit. The boom was well on its way.

After Pompey, the Stroobachs bought Hill Top farm, situated on the main road to Kariba. 'We had some wonderful, and scary, years after the war started,' said Lydia.

> We grew flowers for seed for export to Holland, and what a marvellous sight they were. It was a beautiful time, and when our 300 acres of flowers were in bloom – all sorts of colours, but set far apart because of the cross-pollination – we had scores of people turning up to admire the sight. Sometimes on a Sunday Gerard would put hay-filled sacks on a trailer for people to sit on, and our faithful old driver would give them a tour around the farm.
>
> We then moved to George, South Africa, and had happy years there. This was after a period of growing flower seed in Chile. Back to Hill Top: our neighbour, Schalk Engelbrecht, a nice man, was not happy with us when we decided to give our labourers an annual two-week holiday with pay. We had been on holiday in Holland and seen the new liberal attitudes among workers there, where gangs built roads with bricks by hand, who were telling each other 'not to work so hard' as they 'still had a life ahead of them'. That made Gerry realise how good our workers were.
>
> We loved Karoi and its people. Our best friends were Kees and Maartje Bakker and Karel and Liesje Romkes, who worked for Piet Groot.

Community service was the middle name of Ko and Dini Voorn, who arrived in Karoi in 1959 in answer to an advertisement placed in a Dutch newspaper. It was offering employment for mechanics in Karoi, Rhodesia. Ko applied, was interviewed by Hans Bakker and accepted. Ko then had five days in which to persuade his girlfriend, Dini, to marry him and brave the wilds of Africa.

Setting sail from Amsterdam on a cargo boat they fell into conversation with a compatriot called Cor Moerbek and discovered that he, too, was bound for Karoi. It was a fourteen-day trip, with the boat stopping off in Lisbon and Las Palmas before docking at Cape Town, where they had their first breathtaking sight of Table Mountain. They entrained for Rhodesia, disappointed to find that they had to share a cabin with Cor Moerbek. Some honeymoon!

Being of the tough and outdoor variety of Hollander, they revelled in the South African sun and settled down to sleep with the windows wide open. Next morning they were covered in black soot, for the trains were still driven by steam in those days. It was indeed a 'dark' introduction to Africa!

The living quarters being built for them on Mufuti Hill on the Crescent were not yet ready, so for three months they lived in John New's house behind the Karoi Butchery, followed by another move to de Lange's house, next door to Selous the chemist. Although it was February and the rainy season, they found Karoi hot and dusty; it was a drought year.

Disillusioned with his employer, Ko took a break from Karoi in 1962 and accepted a job at the Eastern Highlands Tea Estates in the Vumba. He resigned three days later owing to boredom. He was immediately taken on by Pusey and Payne in Umtali, removing his furniture over several trips after work until the entire household was transferred. They were happy in Umtali but were enticed back by the Bakkers who came up with a better offer.

Their house on Mufuti Hill was a semi-detached one, with Wim and Frieda Potemans on one side and the Voorns on the other. Ko recalled a very embarrassing moment when he climbed up onto the roof to rescue a toy that his son Anton had thrown up there. Being a large man, once up there Ko very quickly realised that the tiles were not going to carry his weight for long. The thought was hardly in his mind when, with a crash, he disappeared through them and the ceiling, only to fall into the bath with Frieda Potemans, who had until then being enjoying her ablutions below.

Once in Karoi again, the Voorns threw themselves into all aspects of community life. In whatever way – through the church, by running the Sunday school, the Women's Association, as a lay preacher, counselling, or helping Myra Kennedy and Dr Chris Lewis to run the Casualty Clearing Centre – one could always count on Dini.

Ko enjoyed being a Mason, a Rotarian and his PATU work during the bush war. He and Dini joined the Dramatic Society, and let's not forget the contribution of both Ko and Dick Heynes in running the drive-in cinema. In 1970, Ko went into partnership with Geoff Bennett, Pete Burgess (known as the one-armed bandit) and Giuseppe Tome (the one-time Italian POW in Miami) in Sable Motors.

Piet Groot and his wife, Nitsa, farmed on a sub-division of Chedza called Trianda. Before coming to farm in Rhodesia, Piet had spent a lot of time drifting around the Far East – in the Dutch East Indies, Sumatra, Java, Indonesia – and even taught geography in Hong Kong for a while.

Strangely he was always more comfortable with his second language than with that of his motherland. Piet met Nitsa when she was visiting her sister, Rebecca Khan. Every now and again, Nitsa would take herself off to her Greece for a necessary injection of her home culture, returning more Greek than the Greeks – bronzed, rejuvenated and relaxed.

In complete contrast to his friend Willem Komen, Piet was taciturn and shy, muttering quietly through his pipe. Willem was large, jovial and loud, with a hearty demeanour – very difficult to overlook. Piet became a very successful Brahmin breeder, and during the 1980s managed to acquire many of the sub-divisions around him.

It was Piet who had encouraged his friend Willem Komen to leave Holland and come to Rhodesia. Both men came from large, traditional Catholic families, thirteen and fourteen strong. Piet used to say that he would never recognise his older siblings even if he bumped into them in the street. They were out of the home long before he was born, fleeing the nest and emigrating to various parts of the world. One or two entered the Church and took holy orders as priests or nuns.

Back in Holland, Willem had been a driver in the Dutch army during his younger days and was constantly in trouble because his truck, he said, with tongue in cheek, insisted on stopping whenever it saw a pretty girl. Rhodesia was his saving grace, for it brought him great happiness – as a successful farmer on Tavoy farm and in his marriage to Astrid McKay (née Johnson). He described himself as being a 'lapsed Catholic' as his presence in church was rare, but the Catholic Fathers knew him to be very generous, as was shown when the Catholics and Anglicans were raising funds for the new church they were building together.

At that time the committee came up with the idea that they would ask each farmer

to grow one acre of maize 'pro Deo', for God. It wasn't long before Father Thamm approached Willem, who proclaimed very vociferously that there should be no distinction between God's acre of maize and his own. To be on the safe side, he would give a percentage of the entire crop just to ensure that God blessed it all.

The Fathers were put into a quandary one day when Willem claimed a fine bell that lay mouldering away in the priory grounds to be his. Bells were dear to Willem's heart, for he had been a bell-ringer at his local church as a boy. Using his particular brand of humour on Father Christian, Willem told him that the bell had been one that had hung in the belfry of that church in Holland. As it could not be known whether he was telling the truth, Willem got his bell and set it up on Tavoy to call and dismiss his workers.

Herman van Durren spent some time in Karoi and then married an English girl from Rusape and started a garage business called Dutch Motors in nearby Macheke. Until 2009 his son was still running the place.

Appei Snaater worked for Felicity and Richard Sims on Jenya farm. He subsequently married Sue Heurtley.

Bernard and Anneke Houttern took over from the Snaaters when they left Jenya.

Karel and Liesje Romkes worked for Piet Groot.

Jaap and Mep Moelman worked for Guy du Barry.

Fred and Geesha Reus worked at Buffalo Downs, and it was said by their compatriots that they were full of 'airs and graces'.

Kees and Erica Radermaker farmed in Tengwe. It is believed that she was a member of the Dutch royal family.

Theo and Bep Harbing worked for Peter Groenewald on Lancaster and lived in the cottage on Amore farm, owned then by Phil and Margaret Gifford. After Theo died, Bep married Louis Botha of Voorspoed farm in Melsetter. During the bush war the couple hit a landmine on the farm road which fatally injured Bep, but Louis survived.

Then there was Jan and Eus Matern. Jan was an agronomist who worked for CONEX and later for the Windmill Fertilizer Company. Jacque Bouvey took his place at CONEX.

Leo de Boer was an assistant at Leconfield farm, working for Mark and Denny Gaisford. During his time in Karoi he courted Margaret Fussell's sister, whom he married but subsequently divorced. Village residents well remember that arduous courting, suffering frequent disturbed nights when Leo started up his noisy DKW in the early hours to drive back to the farm. The sound of the engine could be followed all the way to the Buffalo Downs turn-off.

Jan and Tina Koppenol farmed in Karoi for many years. Initially, Jan worked for Bert Hacking, but later leased land from Piet Groot and then bought a farm on the edge of Tengwe called Vuna. Jan had been a policeman during World War II, and was present at Arnhem ('a bridge too far') during the liberation of Holland. He and Mark Gaisford met on the bridge and reminisced about the incident forty years later.

Jan retired from farming when he began to have bronchial trouble, caused by tobacco dust or chemicals. He had had a lung removed after an injury during the war and now the remaining lung was being affected. After moving to Salisbury he took up his former hobby of painting, his particular forte being reproducing old Dutch masters skilfully and faithfully. He copied them so superbly that he could have made a good living as an international forger. In this he had certainly missed his vocation in life!

Bill Speldevinde, his English wife, Cathleen, and her mother lived on Montesuma farm owned by Harry Wells, where Bill was the farm mechanic. They were murdered there in 1966.

Bill and Dorrie Renson lived on several farms in Karoi. They were a happy, gregarious couple who never seemed to progress.

There was for a short while a butcher called Dykstra, who ran a business on Broad Acres farm. And last, but not least, a relative latecomer to Karoi was Joachim van der Sluis.

15. Karoi in the 1960s

Towards the close of the 1950s, tobacco prices slumped in many districts. Growers, alarmed and disappointed with the low prices that didn't cover their costs, began to worry about a future that no longer seemed as secure as it had once been.

Many bankruptcies followed the season of 1961/62 in particular, after which a number of farmers sought alternative means of making a living. It was the old Rhodesian story once again. This situation affected areas such as Marandellas, Rusape and Inyazura, as well as more southerly regions such as Gutu, where almost overnight many of the younger people moved away. The old cry was heard once again: 'Go north, my boy.' They left the land to their peers for cattle farming.

Within the more established farming areas, tobacco had been grown successfully for years, but all this changed when the leaf they produced was noticeably inferior to that grown in Karoi. The world market had shown itself to be fickle and capricious once again, but now no one could blame them – they saw the quality of tobacco which was being produced in the north. At long last, Karoi was coming into its own. How long the industry had waited for this moment.

The cooler, shorter reaping season that prevailed in the south could not compete with the better climes of Karoi. Ripening slows down the longer the leaf stays on the plant, and its quality diminishes. In the north, the reaping season was more intensive and of shorter duration, resulting in a better quality leaf. Weights continued to be good from the other districts, but it was the quality that excited the traders.

From the Rusape area came the Flights, the Phillips, the Ferreiras, the Cawoods and the Mitchells. The Gutu Nels descended thick and fast, as did the Roystons, Herbsts, Moolmans, Bezuitenhouts and Esterhuizens. It could almost be likened to the animal migration of wildebeest in the Masai Mara!

At the same time, others were honing in on the Miami plateau from other points of the compass. From Northern Rhodesia they poured in: large, extended families like the Watts and Kirsteins with their sons, daughters, in-laws, and assistant managers. Roy Watt (senior) and Karel Kirstein bought Broad Acres in partnership from Jimmy Upton and Alec Cummings. Richard (Dick) Bylo bought Four Winds from John New. Brothers Ben and Hannes van Zyl, Pat and Cornelius Niemandt and sister Lettie, who was married to Piet Strydom, Theo Venter, the Kendall-Smiths and Phillip Gifford, their son-in-law, married to Margaret, Una and Dudley McKenzie – all feared the worst, anticipating a change of policy as that country sped towards majority rule and independence.

At the same time, cattle ranchers in Matabeleland experienced their worst drought in a century and were forced to relocate northwards so that the cattle industry could survive. Peter van Breda arrived fresh from that catastrophe.

The result of all this for Karoi was a boom of great proportions, which left a shortage of land, jobs, housing, and places at the local primary school. At the school, building started on an additional block of classrooms and a second hostel. Five years later the size of every school class had doubled, so every grade from KG1 to Standard Five had two streams. The newest school entrants either stayed in their former schools as boarders, or attended Sinoia primary school, or boarded privately in the Karoi village with Mrs 'Carpie' Carpenter and Vicky James on the Crescent.

That period – roughly from 1958 until 1965 – could be described as the most idyllic period in Karoi's history. The future looked rosy, and Harold Macmillan's dire warnings of 'winds of change' were by and large scoffed at. Looking back, many had entered throughout the preceding years and left like ships in the night, causing hardly a ripple; but there were also those who had stayed and slowly prospered, and it was into this community that the aforementioned newcomers flocked.

It had taken time for Karoi to reach its full potential, and many an old-timer had his private theory as to why it had taken so long. To begin with, it took time to sift the human wheat from the chaff – it was said that 'there were an awful lot of bums around' – and the initial mix of itinerants, mavericks and bone-idle drunkards were eventually weeded out. Others discovered that they had no feel at all for farming. The remainder probably felt that it was just too remote and uncivilised for the likes of them.

Each original settler had taken his piece of land gratefully, together with his two-thousand-odd pounds to see him on his way, but there were the inevitable abusers of the system. One fellow had taken his loan and immediately gone on the holiday of a life-time. Another said: 'We weren't experienced enough in tobacco growing – it is not an easy crop to grow and most of the time we learned as we went along, for one has to learn that no two crops are alike and no two seasons the same.'

Perhaps it had needed a 'tornado' in the form of Harry Wells to show the way: his practices did have a motivating effect. In his ambition to make a fortune in as short a time as possible, he experimented,

sometimes failed, and often resorted to some hair-brained scheme, but mostly he won the day. Fortunately, however, there were also those who just loved the life of a landowner in the bush that they loved, with its wide open spaces and a feeling of freedom. They were the majority and, as the tide turned, Karoi expanded.

Employment rose as men learned that tobacco flourished with marvellous success in the Urungwe, attributed to its warmer climate, rare frosts and reliable rain. And so the explosion of the 'golden weed' on to the world market began in earnest.

The tobacco floors in Salisbury – there were three of them by 1960: Tobacco Sales Floor, Tobacco Auctions Limited and Tobacco Producers' Floor – advertised the success of the north, with growers from depressed areas gaping in wonder as row after row of sharp-edged parcels, tightly pressed quality leaf, fetched prices hitherto only dreamed of. The fan club was inflamed with renewed vigour and rushed north, alight once again with enthusiasm after the disillusionment of seasons of depressed prices.

A 'gold rush with a difference' brought along that second wave of eager young agriculturalists. They came with the same enthusiasm but without the shortages and difficulties that their predecessors suffered. Their entry was by car on a good tarred road to face a small, but established, well-run village that was beginning to see signs of prosperity. These men also arrived with fresh-faced brides as helpmates, and perhaps they, too, had to rough it a little, but in comparison it was all so much easier.

Ever the optimist, the tobacco farmer has within his make-up the instinct of an inveterate gambler. His hard-earned money, once it is in his hand, disappears faster than ever, back into the earth, swallowed up and devoured by land preparation, fertilizers, pesticides and labour costs. Then he awaits, optimistically, the vagaries of the elements – hail, which he can insure against, flood, or drought, and disease.

There will always be something not to his liking. There are interferences he has never dreamed of, all of which can make or break him. Yet he accepts his chosen path, for it is the love that he has for his farm and for the soil he is trying to master that helps him to forgive what is thrown at him. Farming is a great leveller, for just at the point when the farmer promotes himself to one step from God, Nature steps in and plays one more little joke, bringing along another disaster to wrestle with, knocking him down to size once more.

In general, the farmer's habits are dictated by the climate and/or whatever occupation is on hand at a given time. He makes an early start: at 5.00 a.m. he can be seen taking advantage of the cool, fresh, morning hours. His lunch break is two hours long, so as to avoid the worst of the heat, and by then he deserves a good rest, for he has already had a full day in comparison to the city slicker.

The lunch-time break is sacred, disturbed only by exceptional circumstances – veld fires, planting rains, and difficult births could perhaps be categorized as such, for they do not choose their times by the clock. The farmer is on duty twenty-four hours a day. He must be ready to plant tobacco on Christmas Day, or fight a fire at 4.00 a.m. on a Sunday, just when he has planned to lie in.

Men flocked into the area despite this – and despite stories of dishonesty and impromptu sackings. For instance, a seventeen-year-old assistant, Anthony Mortimer, who arrived in Rhodesia before World War II, was not paid at all: his mother did the paying – she paid an established grower in Banket to take him on as an apprentice grower.

Peter Gibson had money docked from his bonus each time he asked for advice. And long is the list of men who were cunningly fired just before the end of the season. Yet, in 1960, men poured into Karoi, happy to be exploited just to get a foot in through the door.

In 1961, the government opened up more Crown land to the south-west called Tengwe. Another block was opened up north-west of Maora, and yet another in Miami, while a good many of the original ex-servicemen saw the sense in sub-dividing portions of their farms, offering them up for building leases. Thus it all began again – the building of barns and sheds, the clearing of virgin land for growing crops, the drilling for water, the fumigating of seed-beds.

The most coveted farms in Karoi were on the so-called Golden Mile, which, it was said, embraced all the farms on either side of the Chanetsa road as far as Derepat, at which point the longest mile in geography turns right to pass Montesuma, Ceres and Coniston, and eventually hits the Chumburukwe road. There the traveller would turn right, opposite George Potter's Nyamabidzi, and right again along Maclaurin Road, past Naba, Four Winds and Avalon, and back on to the Chanetsa road – a full circle. In truth, to a competent agriculturalist, there was not too much difference between any of them.

Cecil John Rhodes's Rhodesia, a British colony, had had a constant flow of early settlers travelling up and down the worn thoroughfare between the Union of South Africa and Bechuanaland. Most of these pioneers naturally had their roots in Britain, either directly or via South Africa. Nowadays, after sharing residence of a country for over a hundred and twenty years, the great divide between the Afrikaner and

British, born out of war and animosity, has by and large disappeared; it is the older generations who keep a candle of resentment aflame. Though it still lurks in a few, and for different reasons, it remains in dark recesses, where it belongs these days.

Time, a good education and a shared bond thinned the wedge so that, as Rhodesians, they began to feel at one with each other. Strong Afrikaner blood mingled with its British counterpart in so-called mixed marriages. In Karoi it stemmed mainly from the descendents of the Gazaland trekkers, who had had a longer time to get used to integration.

One such family was the Moolmans – Betty Moolman was a Martin. It was her grandfather, Martinus Martin, who had led a group of settlers on the second trek into Gazaland in their covered wagons, pulled by oxen, in 1893. The Herbsts and Bothas were others, as were the van Hysteens. Annetjie van Hysteen, who became Mrs Willie Nel, told a story about her grandmother, who picked up a black baby on the trek. Perhaps it had been deliberately abandoned, inadvertently dropped or mislaid on the route, but she picked it up and adopted it, calling him Optel.

By the 1960s Karoi's population had become not only cosmopolitan but heterogeneous. The classic character of the original type of 'Rhodesian' – either upper middle-class English sons or land-hungry 1890 Afrikaners, whose chief aim was to get as far away as they could from the 'English' – had changed. Rhodesians had become an amalgam of both – and of many others.

All had reason to be proud of their ancestry, as well as of the contribution they made to their new country. There were substantial minority groups from Italy (returned Italian prisoners of war), Holland, Germany, France, Greece and Poland, and among them were many of Jewish extraction. The Scolniks and Jacobsons, whose families had escaped the early pogroms, had established themselves as part of the new nation, and the country became the richer for it.

One Saturday evening saw an interesting clutch of residents seated around a dinner table in Karoi: From Holland, there was Tina and Jan Koppenol, and Piet Groot with Nitsa, his Greek-born wife; Edith and Wilfred Matthes, were Germans; I, Welsh, was there with my husband Andries, a third-generation Rhodesian/Afrikaner; there were Ted and Ewa Kordonski from Poland; and Franca Spiegnese – a spicy, 'Heinz 57' variety of mixed blood from Denmark, China, Russia and Italy – and her American–Italian husband, Charlie. More varied than the League of Nations and as far away from Brussels as you could get!

While the Second World War remained fresh in people's minds, it bonded Britain's colonials; sixteen years later, although British patriotism remained strong, the Rhodesians had gradually built a nation with its own identity, and their feelings towards Britain were as weak as a third cup of tea.

Most of those who were educated in Rhodesia attended schools designed along the lines of the British public-school system, but, as time went by, politics reared up, widening the estrangement between the two countries. Yet we continued to stand to attention while we sang the British national anthem at every public gathering. We marked the King's and Queen's official birthdays with ceremonies and parades each year.

We used the pound as currency, the silver 'tickey', a word apparently derived from Malayan, for the threepenny bit, and a copper penny with a hole in the middle, all of which bought goods directly from the 'mother country'.

Wars seldom make sense: they destroy more than they build. They have been instrumental in dividing families and tearing nations apart. But the Second World War had brought people from many countries together. A new nation was evolving out of a common bond. Rhodesians were becoming identifiable as a separate nation.

Such, then, was the atmosphere that prevailed around Karoi in the 1960s.

The youngsters took stock of their surroundings, for some had never driven north of the capital Salisbury before. Some had intended just to pass through, but Mike van der Merwe, footloose and fancy free and on his way to the copper mines in Northern Rhodesia, never could pass a pub, and he got no further north than the Karoi Club. There, fortuitously, he met Morris Bell, who took him home and offered him a job.

That was Mike van der Merwe sorted. After one year with Morris, another with Willie Smyth, and a third with George Neaves, he was well on his way to success. He ended up with New Haven, a sub-division of Gremlin, Buttevant from Guy du Barry, Four Winds from Dick Bylo (that farm came with the landlady), and Coniston, acquired after Billy Postlethwayt died.

Charlie and Franca Spiegnese were honeymooners, travelling through Africa from America, where they resided permanently. Karoi was supposed to be a one-night stop, but they became embroiled with a few of the locals, and enjoyed themselves so much that they stayed. They bought a piece of Mrs Leask's Coldomo, plus another, owned by Paul Rawson, called Asuahi Valley.

Paul 'Porky' Rawson was a pilot. He never farmed but employed others to farm for him. He married Shane Palmer's mother after his first wife died in a flying accident. Shane Palmer married Alan Bunnett.

Donovan Stotter, nephew of Mary England, could almost be called a local lad, for he was born in Sinoia – on the doorstep, so to speak. He, too, went from strength to strength. Don did his pre-college year working for Rupert Hawley, and went on to Gwebi Agricultural College. He took a gap year and then spent three years in Europe, travelling and working.

One job involved driving a tourist bus around Italy, even though he had no experience or knowledge of the language. 'They drive on the "wrong" side of the road,' he said, 'but it was much easier in those days; only two rules applied: no parking in a shop or on top of another vehicle – anything else was permissible.'

After Europe, Don returned to Karoi and worked for Basil Kerns; then he felt ready to take over Mshalla from the Englands. He went on to win the prestigious Tobacco Grower of the Year award. He won it twice, in fact, one of only two men to have done so.

The newcomers observed the affluence and prosperity around them, much of it revealed in shiny conveyances: the Mercedes was the status symbol for many years, a badge of affluence and success. Others chose differently.

The Rautenbach brothers preferred flashier modes of transport – long, sleek American limousines, adorned with tail fins and canvas tops that rolled back at the touch of a button. It was all too obvious that money flowed, but so too did the booze, and it was the main cause of a man's downfall. Brian McKay said, 'We made a lot of money – and we spent it.'

Karoi was different from similar towns because there was more money. It also had its complement of colourful characters – flamboyant dressers like Peter Veck, John

New and Dick Bylo. As a rule, farmers do 'scrub up well', but they are inclined to be conservative in their attire and short on words. Nevertheless, ply them with a pint or two and they are transformed into positive Lotharios.

There were colourful, Wild West cowboy types like Eynon Deere and Sam Marnie and, to a point, Brian McKay. There were rough diamonds, such as Wessel and Gert Rautenbach and Rufus Snyman, all of whom could be perfect gentlemen when so inclined. Peter Adams was a real character, who married several times. Two of his latter-day wives were Susie Simpson and then Gwen Mortimer. There were a few hillbillies like George Purchase and Ronnie Callon. There were also a few big personalities among the women, and Fran Fraser was certainly one.

Eccentrics were two a penny, but Francis and Peter Pilcher were different. They never did finish their double-storeyed house on Laughing Hills. Until the farm invasions they had reached their bedroom by way of a ramp – and beware if you happened to open the front door and step out: you would have broken your neck! Admittedly, we were all a little odd – farmers are more so than others and several of us have had our moments of notoriety.

Imposters were two a penny. One man who arrived in the midst of Karoi one day pronounced himself to be Lord Howe: no doubt his Rolls-Royce and baby grand are still bouncing away on the high seas, despite his declaring that they were on their way to Karoi by cargo boat to join him. To be fair, he was a brilliant pianist who used to entertain us for hours at the Club or in the Hotel's cocktail bar.

Commander Mike Blake had never been a Commander, and the Rolls-Royce that he insisted was his actually belonged to his wife, Mary, who had inherited it from her father who had once been a Governor of St Helena. As for the remittance men, by the 1960s they had become as extinct as the dodo.

We saw social etiquette relax along with dress codes, although hats were still worn to church – always a fashion that has been difficult to relinquish. We got away with it because of the sun. Rhodesians were always more restrained and conservative on the whole; by choice, they had a certain pride in remaining aloof from the rest of mankind in a kind of reverse snobbishness.

Moral discipline took its time and rarely were we bothered by drug-taking. The 'pill' invited sexual freedom, but again Rhodesians took their time in embracing any advantage that came with it as they distanced themselves from Western pop bands who screamed yelled and revelled in 1960s Beatlemania, flower-power, mods and rockers, and shocking 'love-ins'.

A typical role-model remained Sir Edmund Hilary, who had reached the peak of Mount Everest on the day of Queen Elizabeth II's coronation. But, gradually, gloves, hats, stiff petticoats, seamed stockings and suspender belts were relegated to old trunks in a clobbertorium, and the stiff upper lip was loosened, ever so slightly.

'Throw away your bra and live!' was the call of women's lib movements in the 1960s. That was all very well for some with flat chests but, contrary to popular belief, it was actually the brassiere that liberated the weaker sex: how else could they have 'rocked and rolled' with such gay abandon throughout the night without being bound up?!

As all these changes came to pass, it wasn't difficult to shock the prudes. Now and again a juicy piece would find its way into the classroom, and a child would write their 'daily news': 'We had fun last Saturday night. We saw all the Mummies and Daddies swimming without any clothes on.'

In 1968, Council records show that town residents paid fifty cents per thousand gallons for water. Monthly charges for electricity were between $6 per month for urban dwellers, and $30 for those on farms; commercial businesses paid $8 per month for single phase and $20 for three phase.

Land was rated at two cents in the dollar and improvements at nine cents. Rural rates were levied per one thousand acres, or part thereof, at $50 up to 4,000 acres, after which a decreasing scale was applied. Urban commercial and industrial land was readily available at a cost, on average, of $4 per acre. Tobacco lands expanded from 600 acres at the start, to peak at 28,000 acres in 1963/64.

Signs of prosperity could now be recognised throughout the area in the form of well-laid-out properties, numerous dams and fenced paddocks, not to mention the many beautiful and impressive homesteads and gardens.

The total population of the Urungwe district, as provided by the 1969 census, was 118,310. Of that number 1,418 were whites on farms and surrounding areas, the rest residing in the town of Karoi. Approximately two-fifths of the 116,380 blacks in the district were employed on farms and mines, along with their dependants; the balance was to be found in the adjacent Tribal Trust Lands.

The children of those vintage years remember how they were left to sleep in station wagons while their parents partied the night away. For those still 'below the salt' and not yet ready for a Mercedes, a Peugeot station wagon became the ideal mode of transport: there was no way round it if you were the social type.

One would almost have thought that the French designed them specially for the young Rhodesian family man, who seemed to produce babies in litters like rabbits. Colleen and Rod Cawood somehow managed to make do with a little blue Volkswagen Beetle, squeezing their three little boys in at different angles for a night of sleep. The eldest, Craig, was primed to say to passers-by: 'My-name-is-Craig-Cawood-I-am-four-years-old-and-my-mummy-is-Colleen-and-my-Daddys-name-is-Rodney-please-call-them-and-tell-them-that-Gary-and-Mark-are-crying.'

Farm kids grew up wild and free, wandering barefoot and in safety within the wide open spaces that were afforded to all rural folk. Alongside them were their black counterparts, from whom they picked up scraps of Shona and who picked up some English in return.

They learned at an early age to drive tractors, use a gun safely, and fish with a piece of string attached to a stick. They camped overnight and were early recipients of malaria and bilharzia. During the rains they were left to splash in puddles and play in the mud.

They adopted many a wild creature found in the 'mundas' and veld around them – duikers, bats and *nagapies* (bushbabies). They raided mazhanje trees and sat like miniature witches in a coven around their harvested cauldron – naked as the day they were born (to save staining their clothing), greedily scoffing the wild, fleshy fruits with undisguised pleasure, the juice dribbling all over their chubby cheeks.

Structurally, the little town of Karoi was beginning to take on some sort of shape: the streets and roads, though still rough and gravelled, were tree-lined and the sidewalks paved.

At the approach to the town, a residential suburb mushroomed, built on elevated ground that looked down on to the dam. It was called the Crescent and had tarred roads that wound up and around to join the original streets. Some were named after the 'founding fathers' – Burt Street, Fred Jameson Avenue, the main road running out to farms New Forest and Chumburukwe, Harris Street, Palmer, Church and Mfuti Hill.

On the highest point, looking very much out of place, was one of the very first home-steads, built by a Mr Selous, the first chemist to open up in town. As modern houses sprang up around it, this standard, roughly built colonial home, square-shaped with a wide veranda on all sides, began to look more and more out of place.

Eventually it was bought by the Rural Council for David and Edith Beattie. Dave was in charge of the roads and kept them well maintained and graded. Years later the Rural Council levied the farmers so that each main arterial road could be tarred, piece by piece, ten kilometres at a time. When the Beatties left, Axel McDonald took over that job and bought the house for his retirement.

By 1962, electricity had only just arrived. The townspeople were the first recipients, and it took several more years to reach the furthest outlying farms.

Since the establishment of the first store in 1948, commerce had kept pace with the farming development on which it relied. The Farmers' Co-op was still run along old-fashioned lines, where each customer stood at the counter with a shopping list and was served individually. Friday was recognised as the main shopping day and shoppers queued.

The American-style supermarket was soon to revolutionize trading forever, but not quite yet. At one end, the store sold hardware; at the other, groceries and fresh produce. A long counter ran the full length of the shop, behind which, sitting on high stools, were white shop assistants, puffing away languidly on cigarettes: Margaret Fussell, Lyn Wesson and Pat Pickard. They called out the requirements from lists that were handed over the counter, and black assistants scurried back and forth like ferrets as they fetched and carried, while all about them, on both sides of the counter, customers gossiped and chatted, catching up with the latest news.

Behind them were the shelves, groaning with a vast array of imported goods – every-thing was imported. Luxury items lined the counter within tempting and easy reach. If you stood there long enough, psychology kicked in and you were seduced into buying something you hadn't planned to – tit-bits that stretched or broke the monthly budget and found their way into the mundane weekly supply of sugar, coffee, tea, candles and paraffin: Cadbury's chocolate biscuits, boxes of Milk Tray, tins of Quality Street, tinned salmon, Sobranie cigarettes and cigars. There was an alarming array of choice whiskies.

Long, fat cartons of Star, holding small packets of ten unfiltered cigarettes for one penny, were affordable even by the poorest, and they lasted for weeks. We bought tins of lightweight, dried vegetables when fresh veggies were unobtainable: beans, peas, carrots, and sprigs of cauliflower – all had to be soaked before they were cooked.

A new Farmers' Co-op had been con-structed in 1956, and although the early years had proved unprofitable, the building of the Kariba dam and the installation of a grinding mill created business for the Co-op. The fear that trade would decline once Kariba had been completed was proved unfounded, and as the area developed so did the store's annual turnover.

In 1964 a warehouse in the industrial sites was built for the storage of heavy and bulk items. This building was named the J. S. Brown Building in recognition of all that Mr Brown had done for the Farmer's Co-op. He was the General Manager at the time the project was initiated. By the time it was fully developed, the shop consisted of ladies', gents' and children's outfitters, a grocery outlet, and a well-stocked hardware department, as well as a limited supply of fertilizers, grain bags and animal feeds. It was Karoi's major retailer for many years.

In 1955 Foly Wesson succeeded Sandy Fraser as manager of the Farmers' Co-op. By now Sandy Fraser had become the 'leader of the opposition', along with Maidments, after building Fraser's Building, down a slip-road that came to be named Rose Way.

Mrs Russell opened a café there for a couple of years during the 1970s. Mouths water even now at the thought of those delicious pies and Chelsea buns, the aromas of which wafted across the street, inviting the world to spend money and put on weight. She used to urge all her 'little darlings' to help themselves from behind the counter, spurring them on to an early life of crime as they repeatedly pilfered goods from other stores, encouraged by Mrs Russell. Confused, my son thought he could just help himself to things without paying – and what determined arguments ensued: 'No, Mum, you're wrong – we don't have to pay. Mrs Russell said so!'

Some years later, Ray Townsend remembered, after Betsy Wiggill had taken back her premises to run a restaurant herself, there was an altercation between Betsy and a man who went in there to buy bread. She charged him first for the bread, and then for the wrapping. The customer argued vigorously, repeatedly saying that he didn't want the wrapping and would not pay. Betsy, incensed, eventually lost her temper and yelled, 'Listen here, I cover the bread to stop the flies shitting on it, so you're jolly well going to have it and pay for it.' Such was the

hard business mind of our Betsy. She was legendary for short-changing the kids.

We new arrivals listened in on conversations, anxious to discover who the 'hierarchy' were and what they looked like. It was worth the wait in the queue. It came as a bit of a surprise to see Anne Postlethwayt step out of her Jaguar wearing ankle socks with high heels. And how fascinating it was to hear every sentence end in a clipped 'what, what?', with a couple of elbow nudges, just to make sure that one understood.

The Groenewalds were known to have lofty ideas. Mrs Peter Groenewald (Sylvia) – over-blonde and over-dressed but definitely glamorous and eye-catching – looked decidedly out of place as she shopped in Karoi on a Friday afternoon. It was said that their rambling homestead on Lancaster had one or two rather eccentric features. One bathroom had two bath tubs and the walls covered in mirrors; no doubt Freud would have had a ball analysing that one. The floors looked like chequer boards, in black and white tiles, reminiscent of a Masonic Lodge. One old-timer remembers several pieces of sculpture dotted around the place that gave the appearance of a Roman villa.

Then there was fragile-looking Nan Maclaurin, mini-skirted and looking as if she could do with a good, wholesome meal. Beautifully bronzed, she kept her tan by bathing once a week in permanganate of potash – according to Forest Whenman, whose stepfather, Frank Lucas, once owned Hunter's Lodge farm, making them neighbours with the Maclaurins. Nan had been on the stage in London and fascinated the youngsters by painting 'beauty spots' on her face, like Margaret Lockwood, in the Hollywood style of the day.

Nan and Kitty Featherby both used long cigarette holders, which they waved around constantly at head height in a supposedly sophisticated manner reminiscent of the social upper classes. By then, neither of them had quite retained the attractiveness of their earlier days, though their charm and fading beauty was still apparent.

Kitty, in particular, floated around holding court, gesticulating and conversing with all who would listen, her conversation dispersed with double entendres, for which she was well known. One year, she stopped to inspect an arrangement of anthuriums at a local flower show and, after a lengthy study of them, she boomed out, 'You know, girls, these remind me of my husband; they should be re-titled 'Good morning, darling!'

Mark and Elizabeth Foster had a tribe of six. Thrifty Elizabeth budgeted by making them knickers out of linen flour-bags, which, once depleted, could be washed and bleached – truly commendable. Every so often, one would catch a glimpse of the faded word 'Gloria' emblazoned across a pair of buttocks!

One feature of those 'good old days' was that it was possible to survive and grow a crop from start to finish without having to pay out any cash at all for months on end. For that we have trade and industry to thank, for they extended credit for an entire season.

In 1962 Ko Voorn and Dick Heynes, both of whom worked for the Bakkers at Karoi Motors, made a phenomenal contribution to Karoi entertainment when they elected to run the drive-in cinema in the quadrangle behind the Karoi Hotel.

It was the most popular form of relaxation on a Saturday night in the small town because it embraced the whole family. To this day it heads the list of what is best remembered. For 12/6 one could buy a cine-dinner ticket, which covered the cost of an excellent three-course meal and included the movie afterwards. It was so popular that one

had to book in advance. Babies slept safely in the backs of station wagons and cars, while their parents enjoyed a good meal. Older kids munched away on chips and sweets and ran around raucously with their friends. Presiding over the dining-room and everything else was the proprietor, Bernard Hill. It was into that very dining-room that Gerald Turner strolled and boomed out, 'So, Andries, I see you're here with your incubator.'

Dick and Ko operated two Bell and Howell, 60-mm projectors, which showed films to three rows of people in chairs at the front and 35 vehicles parked at the back. Half-way through, Ko would announce, in his broad Dutch accent, that 'drinks and snakes' would be available during the interval. The two Hollanders made all the repairs to the speakers and serviced the projectors. It was indeed a wonderful service, greatly enjoyed by the community.

Mr James senior was an eminent Rhodesian ornithologist. Geoff himself, was a geologist and prospector, and it was he who discovered the Lynx graphite mine north of Karoi. Ronnie James, his brother, made a name for himself in the world of horticulture. He used to present his own gardening programmes for the Rhodesian (and later Zimbabwe) Broadcasting Corporation, and also designed the layout of the Salisbury Gardens.

Tom Smith was the first postmaster. Des Brooking came later and remained in that position for many years. Roy Bromley – who was married to Angela Shepherd, daughter of Dick and Em Shepherd, one-time proprietor of the hotel in Miami – followed him until independence. Rena Bennett and Winnie Smith ran the counters. Rena, Johnny Bennett's second wife, was the mother of Roy Bennett and Cynthia Pybus, and step-mother of Nat Stotter, married to Donovan. Telephonists were Monica Royston, Dot Lemmer, Toets Myhill, Mavis Snyman and Janine Maidment.

Kathy Quail told me that, in 1965, Neville was the manager for Willie Smyth of Shola Park on Inverness farm:

> This was before we were married.[1] Willie's son, Peter, also worked there. Both Pete and Neville had been in the same intake at Gwebi, so these two very naughty bachelors shared the same house, and the same cook, whose name was Love.
>
> We were still on a party phone lines at the time, and during the course of her work, Mavis Snyman overheard Neville shouting, 'Love, fetch me a pencil.' Shocked, she broadcast the news that Pete and Neville had a woman living with them.

More and more garages sprang up, and before long there was one on every corner. Joining Sable Motors, the first, and Karoi Motors, the second, there followed the BP garage across the road, John and Bruce Motors, belonging to Bruce Humpage and next to Maidments. Checkers Motors was built by Kees Bakker and managed for him by Siem Timmer. Later still, Siem built his own garage opposite and called it T&T Motors.

Among the cosmopolitan mix of people who arrived in Karoi were Tadeusz ('Ted') and Ewa Kordonski. Ted ran a butchery, the second to be opened for business, from the late 1960s until his retirement. As their names suggest, they were Polish.

Ewa was fresh out of Poland when she arrived, speaking shyly and carefully, but her broken English very quickly became fluent. In those days she looked very much the Polish housewife with her gathered skirts and head scarves in the traditional Polish style. Long used to frugal living, Ewa walked everywhere pushing a pram, an extension of herself as she bustled along the roads purposefully, with half her brood in the pram and the other half in tow, clutching her skirts.

The Kordonskis' first home was the little house set back from the road down among the trees – next door but one to the original As You Like It café that Dick and Janet Southey ran.

Ted's story is a sad but courageous one. His family were taken by the Soviets on 10 February 1940, together with hundreds of others who were the very first Poles to be transported to Siberia at the start of the Second World War.

This was in the depth of winter, in freezing-cold temperatures, at two o'clock in the morning. They were given fifteen minutes to dress and pack a few belongings. The family comprised the parents and seven children. The eldest son had already died before the war from a riding accident; the two youngest were girls of pre-school age.

In Siberia they were put into camps, where conditions were diabolically unhealthy and uncomfortable, where there was an acute shortage of food and heating, and where the inmates soon fell prey to sickness in many forms. Cholera and typhoid were the most prevalent, and Ted and his sisters all caught both diseases but miraculously recovered.

Mr Kordonski senior and Ted's oldest surviving brother were both taken away to fight and were never heard of again – not even that they had died. It was as if they had never lived at all.

Many readers will know that, soon afterwards, the Soviets changed sides, swapping their allegiance from Germany to Britain

---

[1] Kathy's father was Dolan Hampson, who farmed Sapi Valley.

and the Allies. As part of a deal struck by Prime Minister Winston Churchill, several Poles were released from the Siberian camps and transferred to various camps throughout the Commonwealth. One was in South Africa at Oudtshoorn, and another in Marandellas, Rhodesia, called Digglefold.

Not all of the children were eligible, however: there was an age restriction of between twelve and eighteen. Ted's two older brothers were in that age bracket, but Ted himself was still only eleven. The older boys were trucked to ports, where they embarked on boats that took them to their destinations. But Ted Kordonski refused to be left behind.

He decided to set off on his own in pursuit of the convoy of trucks that carried his brothers to freedom. He walked, ran and cadged lifts. Inadequately and poorly dressed, and without money for food, he stole loaves of bread along the way. It was a journey of many days that tired him to the point of exhaustion until he collapsed and could go no further.

It was an experience that even seventy-odd years later he could not talk about. To do so was to evoke the terror, the complete wretchedness, the pangs of hunger and feelings of utter loneliness and isolation that beset him so far away from what was left of his family. It was a brave and courageous feat by an eleven-year-old boy who collapsed in the Ukrainian snows and very nearly died.

But some higher being was watching over Ted Kordonski that day. A local peasant found him, and guessing, probably from the language he spoke, where he was heading, put him on his donkey and took him back to his humble home, where he nurtured him back to strength and alerted the authorities about his safety.

Probably because of his determination, Ted was allowed to join the other compatriots and left for South Africa alongside them.

He never forgot the kindness of those extra-ordinary Soviet people. They were so very poor, he said, but were still prepared to share their meagre supplies with others.

Once at the camp in Oudtshoorn, the young Polish lads continued with their education, taught by Polish teachers who had elected to travel and care for them. At the close of war, many of the Poles remained in South Africa, mainly because Poland had then come under communist rule. Of the three Kordonski brothers who arrived in Oudtshoorn, one more was to die before the end of the war when he accidentally electrocuted himself. Ted and his one surviving brother remained in South Africa.

Ted learned cabinet-making at school, a hobby he always enjoyed and at which he was very talented, but it was the gold mines that called when it was time to leave. Later he made his way to Rhodesia, where he tried a variety of occupations. For a while he even managed a nightclub, but ended up learning the butchering trade in partnership with a fellow Pole in Hatfield, Salisbury.

Some years later, Ted decided that, at thirty years of age, it was time to visit his mother and sister who had returned to Poland; perhaps, if he was lucky enough, he would find himself a Polish bride. In a second-hand car, he and a friend travelled through Europe and finally reached their homeland. It was on this trip that he met eighteen-year-old Ewa, who was about to enter university.

Within three weeks they had fallen in love and decided to marry, but many obstacles still had to be overcome before there could be a happy ending. For a start, there was no freedom of religion, and the marriage had to be performed in secret by an 'underground' priest.

Bureaucracy was overwhelmingly difficult when it came to applying for a passport and obtaining permission to leave the country. Everyone was a suspected spy. It was a long and tedious process. Ted had no option but to return to Africa and his job. After several months of waiting, Ewa finally received her passport and was able to leave for Rhodesia and her new life.

Ted, with Ewa at his side, made a success of the business they began together in Karoi. He became the 'biltong king' of southern Africa, and became famous the length and breadth of the continent, with orders coming from as far away as Cape Town – and from Munich, Germany, added his friend Wilfred Matthes of Lynx mine.

Wilfred and Alex van Leenhoff remember a trip to the Valley when they shot a hippo and Ted helped them to cut it up. That beast kept them busy for hours and hours, and in the end gave them over 2,000 kg of biltong.

I remember him buying two enormous bulls from a local farmer. He cut out the four fillets, which were well over a metre long, and hung them up to cure. I bought one for my son-in-law's birthday and flew down to Bulawayo with it. It was impossible to wrap up, so I walked off the plane with it over my shoulder, rather as if I was carrying a rifle. He had a hard time believing it was just a stick of biltong!

16. The Churches

God and the Gospel still seemed to reign supreme, as church buildings made the fastest inroads in the town.

The Gwen Scrase Hall continued to be in full use during the first half of the 1960s, with Anglicans, Methodists and Presbyterians all using it on different Sundays of the month. Farmers' meetings were frequently held there, as were productions of the Karoi Dramatic Society.

For a long time the Catholics had a tiny church on a piece of land on the corner of – what else? – Church Street.

For some inexplicable reason, the town planners had decreed that all denominations should build their houses of worship not quite in clusters but certainly in one long row. Fortunately, the congregations were small enough, and the plots big enough, not to have to compete in hymn singing. Perhaps they thought that it would help the Good Lord if all the 'sinners' were kept together – easier to keep an eye on them if they were all in close proximity. Whatever the reason, it was a stupid one.

Years later, in the late 1970s, when an off-shoot of the American-style Baptists, the Assemblies of God – often referred to as the 'happy clappers' – arrived in town, they kept away from 'Holy Row' and used the old hall on the hill, on the lower boundary of Kyogle. There the congregation could clap to their hearts' content. They even had a tantalising view of the Twin River Inn; in fact, it was so well positioned that anyone who wished, could free-wheel down the track, across the tar road and straight into the pub. After all, weren't they all saved?

Their first pastor was a man called Tim Salmon. 'What's all this about tinned salmon?' I can still hear Pat Wells say! Until

then, our religious practices had been pretty traditional and conservative. Evangelism had become the 'in thing' and fashionable, and the evangelist had to have clean good looks and charm, the gift of the gab, and come armed with a crash course in theology from an American bible school.

Pastor Salmon was replaced by Pastor McCabe, and then came the doyenne of them all, the exasperating Antoinette Dick, and her husband Ron. Soon after their arrival, my son came home from school one day mightily impressed with what a new boy had said to him in class. He told him that his father had met Jesus in jail. 'Well,' said Andrew, 'my father has never been to jail, but I know he's with Jesus somewhere.' Claude Ainsley, known as Cloud Nine, was the last to leave.

The Assembly congregation caused a lot of unnecessary trouble within the community from time to time and much of it appeared to stem from Antoinette Dick. Sadly, Lyn and Alan Coast's daughter Sandra, married to Des Hill, was dying of cancer. The couple were still young and had two small sons, and as if that wasn't tragic enough, it was awful to watch a beloved daughter slowly fade away. Dick and a few other zealots wrote letters to the Coast family, intimating that Sandra's illness was caused by a brass Buddha, which happened to adorn their mantelpiece. Apparently it was 'anti-Christian'.

I thought that this act, as well as lacking delicacy and infringing on the privacy of a grieving family, was unbelievably malicious and cruel. The community was up in arms, and in the end the retired Anglican Bishop of Ireland, who happened to be staying in Karoi, got together with John Millns, the

Methodist minister, and the two put a stop to it. These people also did their utmost to try and do away with the symbol of the Karoi witch.

In 1961 the Dutch Reformed Church built an all-purpose church/hall, situated half a kilometre down from the A-framed Methodist church built by Quentin Smith in 1963. In the late 1970s the Church of Christ went up. That left an unfilled gap between them and the Dutch Reformed Hall and Rectory, and the Masons built a Lodge there.

Tradition has always dictated that one of the first things the Afrikaner builds after he has settled anywhere is a church. Members of Karoi's Dutch Reformed Church were no exception. They probably accounted for at least fifty per cent of all Karoi's practising Christians in 1961.

Not only are they a God-fearing people they are also very community-minded, and they gave generously of their time and money over the years. Every year the Dutch Reformed Church fetes were awaited with anticipation, for the men and their wives were very industrious, spending weeks prior to this important event baking *beskuit,* and traditional delicacies such as *koeksisters,*

The Church of Christ being built.

melktert and the lightest of sponge cakes. They made jam, marmalade and *konfyt,* and cut up *mombes,* all donated by parishioners, into thousands of strips of biltong and hundreds of yards of boerewors. One year, the men made five tons of it and sold the lot, for there's nothing as tasty and succulent than a piece of homemade farmer's sausage.

It was the money raised by the fete that paid the wages of their dominee. An affluent area could demand the best of them. It must have crossed the minds of many a poverty-stricken Anglican or Methodist clergyman that he'd chosen the wrong denomination to follow.

The Revd Jacobs was the first pastor to live in the Rectory.

Karoi's Anglican congregation of the 1960s was also a large and faithful flock. Certainly they rallied round more attentively than they did later. There were enough members to form a strong church choir, which was led by Marietta Skilton and a few others with useful strong voices. Marietta's sister, Elizabeth Foster, played the piano or harmonium, whichever was preferred.

Not until Holy Trinity Church was built a decade later did they acquire a proper organ, which showed all too soon that it was 'possessed'. At one funeral, for which Kay Simpson was the organist, it emitted a banshee wail in the middle of the service, scaring the life out of the congregation who thought that the corpse had resurrected – an embarrassing moment for poor Kay!

In the old days, June Norman always took charge of the Easter hamper that was raffled for church funds, and Dennis did his bit when it came to auctioning the contributions at the harvest festival, showing that he had several hidden strings to his bow, not the least of which was his humour. It was the custom to hold harvest festivals on different farms each year, bales of hay being set up to sit on in an evocation of a typical rural scene of yore. It certainly added to the atmosphere.

One year it was held on Musha Wedu, home of Neville and Daphne Royston. Unfortunately, they had no piano to accompany the hymn singing, so Elizabeth gallantly offered to play her squash-box. All was going well as we began to sing the well-known harvest hymn 'We Plough the Fields and Scatter', but it was clear halfway along that something was wrong.

Elizabeth, in a fit of fevered haste, was way ahead of the rest of us, and when she came to the final chord, she turned around with a look of triumph and achievement – only to see the rest of us, puce in the face, battling on bravely, with three verses still to go and trying to stifle hysterical laughter. That was a harvest festival the Anglicans will never forget!

Once the organ was installed in the new church, Cecily Saywood took over the organ-playing, and from time to time I relieved her. But my playing was fit only for funerals.

The Anglicans had to wait until 1975 before they could start building their own church. Long before there was peace in Ireland, they did the unthinkable by negotiating a partnership with the Catholics, who owned land but were poor. Devout Catholics, such as Mrs A.B. Roberts and other well-heeled faithful, generously donated money towards interior features such as the ornate railings by the font.

Meanwhile, to raise the necessary funds, the two denominations held a monthly 'cake stall' on the pavement outside the Farmers' Co-op, with their permission of course, and for three years this continued until Holy Trinity had enough to start building. The building was supervised in the main by George Kennedy, aided by Andries Herbst and Neville Royston, between call-ups.

Holy Trinity Church.

The Garden of Remembrance.

George considered it an honour to take on this task, saying that it wasn't everyone who had the privilege of building a church in his lifetime.

Francis Pilcher and Moira Saywood provided flower arrangements year after year. Some very fine altar cloths were crocheted by Mrs 'Dickie' Southey, Gwen Mortimer's mother.

The Jesuit Fathers Zincan and Thamm were the priests-in-charge of the Urungwe Catholic circuit for many years.

German-born Fr Thamm had, as a young acolyte, been passionate about Russia and had even learned the language in readiness to fight the battle against communism. However, his superiors deemed otherwise, saying that it was not a good time to be sent to Russia and instead sent him to Africa.

Other incumbents were Fr von Walter, who left during the bush-war years to do a stint at St Albert's Mission Hospital in Mount Darwin; Fr Grainger; Fr Eaton, an Australian of nervous disposition, who returned home as soon as he could; and Fr Christian, who succeeded him and was then posted to Chinhoyi.

The Catholic Fathers were a decent lot, human enough to enjoy a glass of something and a good hearty meal. They lived in the priory, a modest house one street away from the church. Trouble came once when their neighbour kept some scruffy hens, among which was a threadbare cockerel that persisted in crowing loudly at 4.00 a.m. every day only a few metres from the windows of their bedroom wing. The Fathers put up with this stoically, though the early awakenings made them irritable.

One day, one of the Fathers casually asked Charlie Slight if he owned a pellet gun. Charlie said yes, his son Khurt had one. One day not long after this, just as the sun was rising, a discreet *crack!* was heard – nothing

for anyone to worry about, just a car back-firing, perhaps.

The Fathers began their day with a loud hymn of praise and an enthusiastic recitation of prayers for the dead. I would have so loved to have been a fly on the wall when the time came for confession!

Over the years, Anglican souls were well tended by the Reverends Clayton, Kirk, Williams, Furlong and Haaroff. Hugh Williams and Pat, his wife, gave, without exception, an enormous amount of time and effort to the spiritual health of our congregation. Hugh's bizarre bray – it cannot be called a laugh – will long be remembered, both with affection and amusement.

Whether Anglican, Catholic or Methodist, the clergy were kept phenomenally busy within the vast Diocese of Urungwe, for it covered all the communal areas from Kariba down to Banket, and almost as far as Gokwe and Umboe from east to west. The Anglican incumbents all lived in Sinoia. There had been a very short period when an Anglican priest lived in Carpie's (Mrs Carpenter's) house on the Crescent after she died, but it had proved to be too expensive to keep two priests and two households in the Diocese.

Not long after he left us, the Revd Andrew Furlong, who became the Dean of Clonmacnoise, Ireland, hit the headlines in Britain in 2001. He had published a number of articles on his church website challenging traditional doctrine and making statements that Jesus was not the Son of God. He refused to resign and change his beliefs, and was therefore charged with heresy. He very nearly became the first ordained priest in 100 years to be tried for this crime, but he resigned the day before his trial.

Andrew Furlong was perhaps another of those round pegs in a square hole. He fitted in socially and was well liked. He was athletic and played all sports well, which helped him to get to know his congregation – it even boosted the numbers in church for a while. It took him three years to learn Shona and to become proficient enough to preach in that tongue, so his dedication was evident.

Somewhere along the line, however, his doctrinal thinking changed. With hindsight, it is evident why we found his sermons so unconvincing and dull. The poor man did not believe in what he was preaching – the doubts had begun. If only he had had the courage to put across his new beliefs, we might have had some wonderful debates. Today he is still serving God in his own way with good works, and the disastrous marriage he made while he was our vicar has been annulled.

The first Methodist minister was Brendan Graaf, who was followed by Arthur Cozens in 1958/59. It was Quentin Smith who had started to build, with Ronnie Thornton's help, the A-frame church along Church Street in the 1960s. This was done in conjunction with the Presbyterians, who shared the costs and premises.

Following the Smiths were Ivan and Isa Carson, Ted and Sheila Houghton (Sheila taught at the school), Terry and Betsy Gillett, and Terry and Jean Isherwood. Then things 'fired up' somewhat when the Revd John Millns arrived in our midst. It took seventeen years for the congregation to learn to love him and accept the irascible ways of a bachelor clergyman.

One day he walked into Ron Thornton's office at Maidments in a thoroughly bad mood and proceeded to be very disagreeable. But Ron was up to it, saying he would not be spoken to in such a manner. John agreed and said he would walk out and try again. He escaped a murder attempt when Wim Potemans's boy attacked him with an axe, though even John's brusque manner was

no excuse for that. On a good day he could charm the angels out of heaven.

He preached wonderfully erudite sermons, more suited to the hallowed corners of Cambridge University, from where he had graduated, than to a bunch of farming 'oiks' in the Karoi bush, but in time many came to appreciate him. He was a one-man show, and could have been an actor of note – jumping from the pulpit to the organ and then to the lectern without missing a stroke, and pausing only to glare at the children and say, 'You there, stop your sniffing!'

John had been a missionary in Madras and was then given a parish in the Shetlands, ending his preaching days in Karoi before retiring to very comfortable quarters in Orpington in the UK. He could be very entertaining company, and when he left we were in two minds whether to be glad or sorry.

At his retirement, Maureen and Gordon Webster took over to become the first incumbents of the independence years. The Revd Margaret James succeeded the Websters. She would stay, for she was Zimbabwean born and her parents were well-known missionaries within the Methodist circuit. The government couldn't get rid of her.

Some Karoi residents of the 1960s may remember the first time they set eyes on George Kennedy. He stood out during the early years not just because of his red hair and blue eyes but because of his distinctive mode of dress – it was pukka colonial from head to toe: safari suit, knee-length stockings, and wide, hard-brimmed bush hat of the army type with one side buttoned up. Come to think of it, it probably was a remnant from his army days, a legacy from the past; it must have worn out somewhere along the line, but it was the hat that was particularly memorable.

George Kennedy.

George and his wife Myra will be remembered with affection as the protectors of Karoi residents, successors to the kindly 'Mum' and 'Pop' Mitchell of earlier years. They put themselves out and about voluntarily, without fuss or pretension, helping many along the way. The Kennedys, like so many others of their time, were products of good old-fashioned values. Karoi was a fortunate community indeed to have had two such 'god-parents' in their midst.

In bygone days they would have been described as 'pillars of society' – an apt expression, for they propped up a community and the church building, keeping it and everyone in good repair. Myra became the district nurse, with George always at her side driving the ambulance. They were faithful to their Christian beliefs, but it was their example that spoke louder than their words.

Demobbed in 1946 with 'Exemplary Conduct and Skilled Technician' written on his release certificate, George returned to his civilian job at the GPO's Department of Engineering.

His skill and interest was in clocks and other types of mechanical gadgets – he built a model train, with engine and carriages, that ran on tracks around his garden in Karoi, delighting the children who were lucky enough to ride on it. He also made the clock for Holy Trinity Church, which graced the tower and kept perfect time until they left.

The army had given him a taste for travel and awakened in him a desire to see more. Thus, in January 1950, he embarked on a new career with the East African High Commission, responsible for building a new route for telephones through the bush country and enabling small towns to communicate with each other and the city of Dar es Salaam.

After taking some leave he was posted to Lindi, a postal section 290 miles from Dar, in charge of a region covering 100 miles which included Mtwara. Having been alone all those years, there came the momentous meeting of two souls meant for each other.

Myra Sayers was born in Manchester. As 1945 approached, she turned eighteen and began her career as a State Registered Nurse. She applied to the Colonial Nursing Services and was sent to Dar es Salaam in Tanganyika. After a short while, a directive arrived for her to fly down to Mtwara, a two-sister bush station, to fill in for one of the sisters who was down with malaria.

Within these surroundings, her life was about to change forever when, six months later, she received a phone call from a fellow calling himself George Kennedy. It was Good Friday, the end of March 1956, and he told her that he would collect her in his Citroën and take her out to his camp for tea.

Over that Easter weekend, Myra recalls experiencing three amazing days when the two of them got to know one another. Easter Monday was her day off, and Myra was astounded when George proposed. Her reply was an emphatic 'Yes!' Could this be the quickest courtship in history?

Six months later they were married at St Bede's church in Bolton in the UK.

17. Tengwe

One of the examination papers set for the intake of young students enrolling at the Gwebi Agricultural College in 1958 required the writing of an essay entitled 'The Future of Young Farmers in Rhodesia'.

So impressed was the Principal, Dr Fielding, by the thoughts and ideas of two of the students that he submitted them to the Ministry of Agriculture for perusal. Pressure was brought to bear upon the Prime Minister, Sir Garfield Todd, who was equally impressed and forthwith sanctioned the idea of a scheme for young farmers, calling in the Land Settlement Board to take on the task of setting the wheels in motion.

The only available land suitable for growing tobacco was 100,000 acres in the northern province, between Sinoia and Karoi, that belonged to the BSA Company and was known as Tengwe River Ranch. Following negotiations to purchase it, a sale was concluded more successfully than had been expected: the BSA Company not only gave land to government in order that a Young Farmers' Scheme could be established but asked if they might float a £100,000 loan to assist twenty new young farmers. To each applicant they loaned £5,000 pounds at a nominal five per cent interest rate, repayable over five years.

The plan was that each farm should have 300 arable acres to enable the farmers to grow sixty acres of tobacco a year, in rotation. Each applicant was to be between the ages of twenty-three and thirty, which made for a very young community of farmers. Almost all had wives and children and, as nature took its course, many more children followed.

Mr A.J. 'Gus' Lehmkulu, the Senior Lands Inspector, was tasked with surveying the farms. This was no easy matter, as Tengwe was a very broken area. Ultimately the middle farms ended up being smaller than those on the periphery. It took three years to survey ninety-five farms, and then pits were dug and dam sites pegged.

Tengwe soils comprise mainly sand veld and sandy loams, categorised predominately as Class 2 and 3 types by agronomists. Twenty farms were to be made available to the Young Farmers' Scheme, with the remainder being be allocated under normal Land Settlement Board conditions. Later another farm was found to bring the number to ninety-six.

It all got under way in April 1961 under Mr Vic Danckwerts, Chairman of the Land Settlement Board. Farms were advertised, applications invited for both schemes, i.e. the young assisted and otherwise, and it was anticipated that the first could be installed by July 1961. Two hundred men applied and one hundred were interviewed.

Of the twenty successful applicants on the 'assisted' scheme, only ten were allowed to move on to their farms by the due date because not all the boreholes drilled produced a sufficient water supply. The others had to wait a further year until dams had been constructed. The second half moved on to their farms in 1962 along with fifteen others.

When UDI was declared in 1965, tobacco farming, hampered by the sanctions placed on Rhodesia, suffered many setbacks, and some farms not already settled were abandoned by their owners. These were re-allocated and split up among resident neighbouring farms.

Furthermore, the original site, intended to serve as the Tengwe township site, was changed to a more central position, after which the government built an 80-million-gallon dam that subsequently supplied the commercial and residential area with water. With this problem solved the structure of the township was planned.

As one of the first to arrive on his patch in 1961, Wilf Letcher set up his tent when all that surrounded him was bush and a self-made track. He called his patch Kamusha.

Soon after arriving he heard from a passing local who was looking for work that there was another *mukiwa* in a tent fairly close by. He went to investigate and found Colin Bray on land that he and Hazel subsequently called Dentrow, Dent being the name of the road on which they had met, and 'row' taken from Woodrow, the name of Ted Geoffrey's farm, where Colin had worked previously.

Other originals speedily followed. Neil Purdon was still a bachelor but was engaged to Zila Meikle, who soon became his wife; Hazel said they all travelled to Umtali for the wedding. The Purdons named their land Meidon – Mei from Zila's maiden name, and 'don' from the back-end of Purdon.

Peter and Anne Granville lived underneath the power lines on Cornucopia. The rest of the debutante gang were Derek and Deirdre Perkins on Tara, Nigel and Di Loney on Zimyewe, Richard and Elizabeth Harris on Sansegal, Ian and Val Ackerman on Datenda, John and Shirley de Neil on a farm whose name no one can remember, and Ronnie and Shirley Palmer on Payesa.

Colin Bray, apart from being one of the first to take up land, became very much one of the leading lights over the years. He was born in 1932. One of his questionable claims to fame was that he was among the last intake of boys at the Convent. He then went on to complete his education in Umtali. The three Colins – Sutcliff, Mason and Bray –

were already long-standing friends and came to be reunited in Tengwe.

Colin Bray had always wanted to farm, but his father wisely encouraged him to get 'a piece of paper' first, so he started an apprenticeship as a fitter and turner in Germiston through the company Simmer and Jack, an engineering company on the mine. While there he met Hazel, and the two married in 1956.

Colin, as everyone knew, was a friendly and gregarious kind of bloke who soon got to know everyone; he was also sports mad. He worked for a while for Ted Geoffrey on Woodrow farm, and then for Jack Quinton, before applying for a Tengwe farm. The Tengwe community, much like that of the post-war settlers of Karoi, developed in the same way – all of them young, enthusiastic and poor. Whether it was 1890, 1945 or 1960, they began life like all other Rhodesian farmers in a pole'n'daga hut and progressed from there.

The area of the Tengwe River Ranch, even in 1961, was still unbelievably wild. Had there been a good national road in the vicinity, a journey to the newly built Kariba dam would have been a fairly easy ride. At that time it was the biggest man-made lake in the world, and it was still filling up. It opened its power-generating stations in 1960, and eventually the waters covered 5,200 square kilometres, with a game reserve along its shores.

When the 'Danckwerts Delinquents' descended onto the plains, Tengwe was merely an extension of the national park. When the Brays arrived, they lost two dogs, one of which belonged to the Palmers, to leopards: they were boldly snaffled off the back of a truck in front of their eyes as they drove along the road.

On another occasion, one of the Perkins's dogs, also left in the care of the Brays, was caught up in a fight with a porcupine. When discovered the next morning, it was so badly punctured and in such pain that it was not expected to live, but patience won the day as each spike was carefully and gently withdrawn and disinfected; the poor creature did survive.

A few years later, a herd of six elephants was seen on Nigel Loney's farm and was subsequently culled by the Parks and Wildlife department. That same year a lion was shot, and Hazel bagged herself one of the claws which she had professionally set to wear as a pendant.

Despite their primitive appearance, homes were enhanced by gardens and whitewashed walls, and although the windows were unglazed, the interiors were very civilized and comfortable. Kitchens were separate from the main quarters, and in Hazel Bray's case, the bathroom housed an old-fashioned roll-top bath with clawed-feet that had once stood in luxurious splendour within the Grand Hotel, Salisbury.

Liz and Richard Harris lived with the Brays for a while until their own place was made habitable. One afternoon, Richard sent Liz to pick up a Nissen hut, in kit form, from the RMS depot in Karoi. Loaded on to the back of their truck it somehow got lost on the way home, and the men promptly set off to look for it. It was found only slightly buckled and bent.

Sundays were spent visiting friends to check up on progress. Anne Granville is remembered as a stickler for correctness, so one didn't just liberally 'drop in'. She had a pole placed across the entrance to the farm between the times of 12.00 noon and 4.00 p.m. – a signal that they were not 'at home' to visitors. Peter's father was the head of BOAC, which would perhaps indicate that English social etiquette had not been totally abandoned to accommodate the Rhodesian bushwhackers who waved such behaviour aside.

Dennis Prince and his wife Val are particularly remembered by many of those who were fresh-faced youngsters in 1961. Dennis had been a mere sixteen-year-old himself when he had first arrived in the Urungwe with his step-brother, Sonny Shakespeare, fifteen years earlier. He gave invaluable advice and help to the new inhabitants as they arrived, for by then he was farming on the edge on Shargezan.

Following the 'Danckwerts Delinquents' came the second batch of young farmers. There were eleven of them: Peter and Jill Dawson on Kemasembi, Kees and Erica Radermaker (Hollanders) on Kunaka, Colin and Pat Mason on Rugare, Robert Edgar on Mchowe Pools, Colin Turner on Chobeni, Colin Sutcliff on Nevern Place, Will Bowker on Glendene, Tony James on Driftwood, Pat and Charlie Parker on Taurus, Grenville and Nora Tapson on Grenora, and, last but not least, Danie and Cora Brink on Cordan.

Still others followed hard on their heels until the full complement of farms was taken up. The Tengwe farms were small (plus or minus 500 acres), which left many feeling frustrated after a time, bound by their limitations, and so they sold off to neighbours and found farms elsewhere. Neville Royston sold his to Charlie Parker.

The first Christmas Tree party for the children was held in the Brays' shed. Every effort was made to make it a special affair. Those were the days when the bush abounded with Flame Lilies, and armfuls were picked for decoration: it was a beautiful sight. Father Christmas arrived with his two fairies (the old-fashioned kind) by parachute, per kind favour of a sky-diving club in Salisbury.

This venue was used a few days later for a New Year's Eve party. It was a very wet season and the Mushowe river was in flood. Everyone had to 'walk the plank' that Colin had placed across the water for access to his shed. Deirdre Perkins wobbled over precariously and fell in, and had to be taken home to change her clothes. Consequently the community decided that a club, however basic, was necessary.

Twenty-one new residents held a meeting and made plans. Colin became the chairman of an organising committee and, sticking to tradition, the first improvised club building was built with – what else? – poles and daga. A permanent brick clubhouse became operational in 1965. While all these sporting facilities were being put in place, Colin Bray, who couldn't do without his weekly dose of cricket, played at the Karoi Club.

From the outset the community inaugurated the required associations – a Farmers' Association and Intensive Conservation Area – and local government fell under the Karoi District Council. Tengwe was no exception when it came to good services supplied by the RMS, who arrived without fail twice a week, transporting tobacco and maize – and even cattle by special arrangement. Without this service, the Tengwe community could not have survived.

There also seemed to be a need for a buying service. A small room was found and, under the aegis of the Mashonaland Farmers' Co-op, farmers ordered goods to be collected later. A crank-handled telephone was installed into the area in 1963, and was replaced by the STD system in 1970.

Commerce started almost on the heels of the first ten settlers with the opening of the Tengwe Agricultural Co-op. In 1964 an ICA house was completed, and the first CONEX

officer took up residence – Jerry Stocks, who was transferred there from Karoi.

A branch of the Women's Voluntary Service (WVS) was started in 1965, a branch affiliated to the national body. They took on the organisation and supervision of most of the entertainment – plays, film shows, Saturday club evenings, raffles and library – with the help of people such as Janet Hoets. They received help and donations of books from the Women's Institute Library of Karoi. A baby clinic was started to care for the health of the expanding young population – which could be visibly observed at one Christmas Tree party when 400 children were counted from 100 families!

The Electricity Board extended power to Tengwe in 1968 so that old paraffin fridges and lamps became obsolete – though they were kept for fishing and hunting trips. There were even streetlights in the township.

A correspondence school was started in 1968, and later the ministry agreed to the running of a government-aided school with one classroom. By 1967 it had become a fully graded government institution requiring two teachers.

In 1970, Tengwe boasted a garage and several houses, which accommodated traders who had started businesses in the industrial area. Tengwe Butchery was opened under the chairmanship of Bert Hacking with a local committee in 1970. A postal agency was granted in 1972 and was run from various outlets until in 1988, when a prefabricated postal building was set up, after which all mail was collected from post boxes.

The 'worshiping faithful' had hitherto held church services in their homes, but as 1972 approached the community felt it was

Tengwe Butchery.

time to build their own interdenominational church in the township. A variety of clergy and ministers of religion were invited to take services on a regular basis, and building funds were donated from each of the associations. The church always relied on donations for its maintenance. A 'wall of remembrance' was built in memory of those community members who had died, and a vast cross was erected in the grounds, hewn from a hardwood tree taken from Nigel Loney's farm.

The bush-war years of the 1970s brought with them a need for a casualty clearing station, which was built at the club. Banking facilities came initially in the form of agencies from Karoi, then, as the war escalated, all banking discontinued until they were reopened after independence.

In 1989, after a long wait, the farmers took matters into their own hands when they made plans to extend the tar road from the grid to the beginning of Tengwe Farm 1, to be continued to the Chanetsa turn-off, a distance of thirty-one kilometres.

Levies were raised by the Tengwe farmers. The total cost was to be Z$1 million, with 50 per cent donated by the European Community. Businesses were levied as well. Tonnages over roads at a fair calculation were formulated – non-negotiable and with no room for argument. Equipment was hired, gravel pits located and engineers employed to oversee the work. Money was collected at Z$12,000 per farmer, and the job was completed to everyone's satisfaction.

By 1991 only sixty-five farming enterprises remained in Tengwe. The war in particular had taken its toll. Farmers were murdered and farms abandoned. The younger generation left, either for greener pastures, or to further their education in other parts. Some returned and were called IDBs (In Dad's Bucks). There was great rivalry between these two groups – those who had made it alone and those who were fortunate enough to have Dad's expertise and financial backing.

From the outset the Tengwe community had been a close-knit body of people. They tackled everything with vigour and enthusiasm. Age refused to diminish them, and eventually many came to be known as the 'Geriatric Delinquents', renowned as much for their hospitality as for their friendliness. Many an anxious wife has been on tenterhooks until her errant husband returned home safe and sound – especially on a Thursday night – from the Tengwe Club.

A few Tengwe-ites attained fame by representing the country in various ways. Ian Alcock for the ZTA; Danie Brink went into politics and stood for parliament; and Nigel Loney worked for the police. Many shone in sport and achieved renown that way.

During the 1970s, Peter Dawson had invented a curing system that allowed forced air to be introduced to individual barns at a temperature which could be controlled as the curing progressed. Many farmers adopted the system and benefited from it.

The community was proud of them all, and their names and photographs had a place of honour on the bar wall. There was never any 'owner–manager syndrome' or formation of cliques: 'the community was too small for that nonsense', said Barbara Stirrup.

Tengwe farming scenes.

Coffee.

Maize.

Cotton.

Rhodes grass pasture.

Modro tobacco curers.

One of the Tengwe dams.

Tobacco.

Tengwe people.

Jonathan (Bobby) Hay.

Bundy Tatham.

Tony Walker.

Leith Bray.

Nick and Tessa Wiggins.

Paddy and Colette (née Johnson).

Janet and Doug Hoets.

Fred Burgess.

Rusty Burgess.

Helga Kagler.

Janet Wiggins.

Adrian and Annabelle Cross.

Doug Hoets and Willie Watson.

Tiger Tournament Ladies Team.

The Letchers: Mark, Wendy and their three children, alongside Granny Penny Lamb, all now in Australia.

Viv Field, Tiger Tournament.

Tengwe people now in Toronto.

Tessa and Nick Wiggins with Annabelle Cross, now in France.

At Tengwe Club.

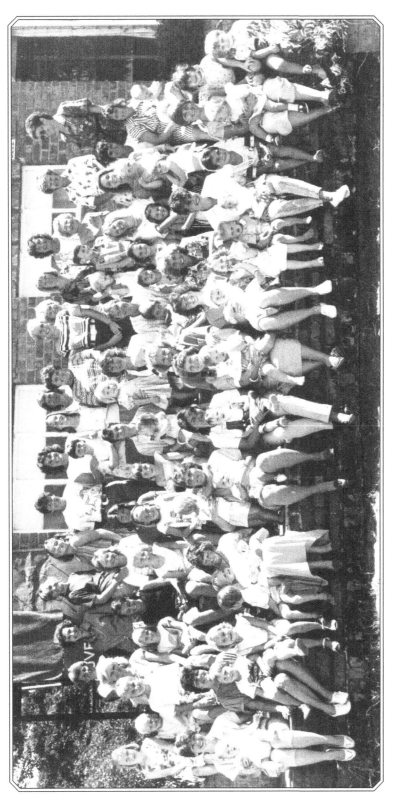

At Tengwe Club.

18. Ian Fraser

From the wide open seas of the Caribbean to the land-locked sand veld of Africa came Ian Alexander Fraser. He was the eighth child of a family of nine children, born at Cane Grove on the island of St Vincent in the British West Indies in 1924. His father farmed cotton, sugar cane and cattle.

He was fortunate enough to be part of a large extended family and was brought up in an idyllic and uninhibited island environment where the sea, the beaches and sunny days provided a lifestyle that was probably not much different from that of those growing up in Rhodesia at the same time.

Initially he was home-tutored by two older sisters until it was thought that he was ready to pass the entrance exam to St Vincent's Grammar School. After leaving school he found work as an overseer on Grand Sable Estate, which produced sea-island cotton, arrowroot, coconuts for copra, and cattle to provide oxen for transport and ploughing. During this time, life was one continual party, not to be taken seriously.

Then two things happened that gave him serious food for thought and galvanised him into a course of action that was to shape the rest of his life. First, he accidentally shot himself through the leg. This act of carelessness made him thankful for his narrow escape and helped him realise just how tenuous life could be.

Then, a windstorm and driving rain flattened twenty acres of cotton at the stage when the bolls were fully formed. Some quick thinking saved the crop, as he and his 'gang' managed to cut the sticks needed to prop up each plant to keep them upright.

He organised rum and bread for sustenance as he and his labourers worked in miserable conditions throughout the night. It kept them going and the job was completed 'by the light of a hazy moon' – though Ian was never quite sure whether the haze was due to the rum or to the misty, inclement weather!

He left Grand Sable Estate in 1942 for Trinidad to start as an apprentice engineer with the oil company Trinidad Leasehold Ltd. Once again his guardian angel – or fate, have it as you will – stepped in to intervene. This was wartime and, owing to the presence of German U-boats, the only mode of inter-island travel was by sailing ship. Ian had booked a place on a schooner for Port of Spain, Trinidad. However, he changed his plans when he met a friend who offered him a lift over on his yacht. Ian arrived safely at Port of Spain, but the dirty old schooner he had been booked on sank in a storm, with all passengers lost.

Three years later he had qualified as a pump-maintenance engineer and transferred to drilling with the same company. In 1952 he took leave and travelled to the UK by oil tanker, then flew to Dublin. In Galway he met an old tramp who had been in the West Indies and who presented him with a new, hand-wrought horseshoe nail, which he kept and later used to nail a horseshoe over the front door at The Ridges, his farm in Karoi.

The year 1953 brought adventure and Ian closer to his destination when he joined the South African crew of a yacht owned by Mr Flitton, a millionaire who had emigrated to South Africa. His yacht was called *The Cariad* (Welsh for 'darling') and was due to cruise the world. The crew was, in fact, made up mostly of Rhodesians; Ian stepped in when they became one man short.

They sailed via Cristóbal, Colón, an unhealthy den of vice and iniquity, where they had to wait to enter the Panama Canal. They continued on to Suva, Fiji, to make repairs, and then to Taio Hae Bay, Nuku Hiva, in the Marquesas Islands, where they were caught up in the doldrums for forty-six days.

Next they stopped at Tahiti, of Captain Bligh and the *Bounty* fame, the Cook Islands, Apia, in British Samoa, and Tonga, where a smiling Queen Salote, still fresh in people's minds after attending the Queen's Coronation in London, resided.

Sydney Harbour was a great favourite, and it was there that the crew learned that their journey was to be cut short owing to a death in the Flitton family. So it was that the journey home was by the shortest possible route, via New Guinea and Mauritius and back to Cape Town.

Ian's mother had a cousin, Vincent Ewing, who farmed on Glen Athol in Banket, Rhodesia, so he decided to take advantage of being in Africa and pay them a visit. He enjoyed the months of helping out in various Ewing farming enterprises and found himself staying on, running his own section.

During this time he met Fran Reid, a trained nursing sister from Scotland, at a dance held at the Blue Jay Inn in Banket. They subsequently married and moved to Karoi, when they bought the remainder of The Ridges farm from Dave and Jean Maxwell in 1958.

There, Fran started her own clinic and became well known for that and many other reasons, one of them being her 'home brews'. Always feisty and jovial, Fran was the life and soul of any party and had a formidable repertoire of stories about all and sundry.

One story she told was of Major D.D. Tate after dining at Kyogle. Jan Tate loved to entertain, despite the fact that D.D. usually disgraced himself halfway through the night.

No doubt she was used to it, and she did not allow anything to interfere with her candle-lit dinners.

The Major usually made it intact through to the second course, by which time he would try to 'keep himself together' in order to carve the meat. But gradually his head would fall and ultimately he would slide under the table out of sight. Whereupon Jan, hardly missing a beat, would calmly ring the bell for the cook to come, saying 'Remove the Master, Cookie', and everything proceeded as if nothing untoward had happened.

After Maurice (Simmy) Simpson, husband of Eve and father of Harry and Tom had died, Andrew van Zyl, Veronica Flight's father, worked as manager for Eve on Good Hope. One night he was invited over for a meal and he couldn't help noticing that the cat was ravenously helping itself to the roast waiting on the side to be dished up. Undaunted, Eve proceeded to carve and serve.

Brian McKay held a party one night in Pitlochry's grading shed and shot out all the fluorescent lights with a pistol. 'It must either have been Fran's 'home brew' or else it was the only way he could get rid of everyone', said Ian.

Stories about the shenanigans of the local 'jet-setters' were always rife, but Ian could never discover whether they were true or just made up to get everyone's curiosity going. Ian and Fran were invited to some of these parties, 'but nothing ever happened to do with keys and wife-swapping,' said Ian, sounding somewhat disappointed.

The only thing he did report was that at one party the life of a heavily pregnant Beth McKay was put in danger when she sat on a couch between Ray Hill and Sam Marnie. A heated argument developed, which turned into a fight, and fists and arms flailed around her 'bump'.

159

On one occasion following a social evening, Fran and Ian were tying chairs on to the roof of the car, which, in their befuddled state, they managed to tie to the doors as well. When finally they made their way home, the chairs slowly began to slide down over the windows. 'This fog is terrible', said Fran. 'Fog. Thank God!' Ian replied and drove slowly on.

Their neighbours were Barney and Muriel Wright on Folliot, Pat Hull on Protea, the van Heerdens on Kupeta, the Pembertons on Shingaroro, the Engelbrechts on Grand Parade, and the Coetzers on Easter Parade. Later came Stan and Deb Sheppard and the Williams-Wynns, who opened up Helwyn.

Pat Hull was known to have a hairy chest, but on one occasion it must have quite slipped his mind when he teased his workers about their relationship to baboons. One day, one of his gang had the guts to open up his shirt and shout out that his chest was as smooth as a baby's bottom in comparison to the boss's!

Many a boss has cast a lascivious, leering eye towards the wife of his manager, and Dennis Sanderson was no exception. Gary Smith 'did rather well' out of his wife's little fling with the boss, Ian said. When they left she had a larger herd of cattle than Dennis.

The owner of Easter Parade, before Stan and Deb Sheppard, was Gert Coetzer, who was married to Porky and Tom du Preez's aunt. Gert was renowned for his tremendous strength, and was one of two men who had earned the nickname 'Ka-Moto, Ma-Drum'.

One day he went over to Len Lundersted's to borrow some diesel. Len was just about to say that he would find some guys to help him load the drum on to the truck when he realised that Gert had already done it.

The other man with similar strength was Wessel van der Merwe, the first owner of Marshlands, who had also loaded a drum of diesel on to the back of a truck.

Pat Hull died in 1965. He had been bitten by one of his pet puff adders, the venom of which is particularly virulent. Pat survived the bite but it was said that the after-affects could bring on a blood disorder akin to leukaemia, which is why they think he died. Ian and Fran Fraser bought Pat Hull's farm, Protea, in 1974.

19. Immigrants to Marshlands

A brand new chapter began for many young farming couples at the beginning of the 1960s. Africa was beginning a new phase as nationalism took hold, and the colonial powers wanted little more than to off load their responsibilities on to emerging black leaders, whether or not they were equal to the task. Tribalism was still rife and could not be cast off that easily.

This was demonstrated almost on our doorstep, when political chaos boiled over into anarchy in the Belgian Congo in 1960, leaving violence, wholesale slaughter and bloodshed in its wake. Refugees fled through the borders of the Rhodesias into Karoi, where the Women's Institute set themselves up alongside the Women's Voluntary Service to receive, feed and comfort the French-speaking Belgians, who told stories of their experience. In a bloody campaign, Patrice Lumumba had declared himself President, only to lose his own life a very short time later through tribal opposition, a situation that typified many an African country that was granted independence.

Meanwhile, in sleepy Southern Rhodesia, two youngsters from Gutu descended on to the Karoi plateau, turning left where the topography levels out at the turnoff to the Chanetsa Road and one becomes aware that the highest point has been reached. My husband and I were heading for Marshlands, travelling anxiously along a rough dirt road and spewing out a cloud of dust in our wake.

It brought to mind a recent accident that had resulted in the deaths of Tommy Herselman and Attie Nel, two young men who had been close friends and had crashed head-on as they sped down the road. Their demise had stunned both districts, Karoi and Gutu, their unnecessary deaths brought about by playing chicken on a dirt road whose thick swirling dust had made visibility nil. Attie was one of the Gutu Nels, and on the day of his funeral the Gutu rugby team were scheduled to play an important league match. However, it had to be cancelled because all but one of the team were related to Attie; the only outsider was my husband.

The trees and thick bush flanking that long stretch denied the traveller a splendid view of the valley below. One old-timer, accustomed to the stark rolling prairies of the Orange Free State, used to say, 'Ag, man, I don't like being closed in – I like to see tomorrow coming.'

Mahogany trees towered among the mazhanjes, long-thorned albizias, msasas and mahobohobos, and here and there was the magnificent spread of a wild fig. We noticed just how much taller the trees grew here than in other areas, a tribute to the good rainfall. Look for a profusion of mazhanje trees, the fundis said, and there you'll find good tobacco-growing soils.

Understandably apprehensive, we wondered what we faced. We had noted the raised eyebrows when Karoi was mentioned, but tossed aside all the tales of dishonest employers who sacked a man on a whim. Being the proverbial beggars, we didn't have the luxury of choice. One bad season in Gutu had seen to that. It was enough that we had a job to go to, and as we approached our destination we sped along bravely in our tired-out green Zephyr, braced to face the slave-pits if necessary.

The expanse of Marshlands farm – three thousand acres of flat, sandy loam owned by Wessel van der Merwe, the Afrikaner known as 'Ma-Drum' – was to be our new home. Wessel had been a teacher in South Africa before buying Marshlands. At that time he was thinking of selling his property, but was leasing it to the Rautenbach brothers, Wessel and Gert, whose reputation had already preceded them.

Before long we discovered that we were to be the last of the primitive rustics. Our new home, though solidly built, was a shell, marooned and standing bare among trees. Inside, there was no sign of any plumbing – not a hint of a pipe, either in the bathroom or the kitchen, only a gaping hole in the bathroom wall indicated that once there had been a 'chemical loo' installed there. As I was heavily pregnant, those first few days tested my dignity with each trip into the bush to utilise the soil. A PK became a top priority.

For help we turned to Fritz Paulsen next door on Oribi Park. He gave us bricks and cement and the use of his builder, and in a very short time a 'little house' had been erected of such magnificent proportions, as so often happens if one has never built anything before, that it could quite easily have catered for the whole district.

It became known euphemistically as the 'Wee Palace'. It had been a close call: which would be christened first, the 'long-drop' or the baby? Gwen was born a month later. How every woman hated the long-drop. It was the first thing mentioned when early life was described and it was certainly prioritised in every list of requirements.

Our next priority was to supply water to the house. We adapted a water cart to suit our purpose: we merely thrust rubber hosing through the hole in the wall and joined it to the bath taps. This Heath Robinson solution held together satisfactorily to give us bathing facilities for two years, the cart trundling over to the dam each day to be filled. Years later, like most Rhodesians who couldn't afford to be particular, our bodies became riddled with bilharzia.

A Dover stove, another émigré from Gutu, stood in the kitchen, lonely and forlorn with a monstrous pot on top. Next to it was a table, so heavy that it would be going nowhere in a hurry. Many years later, Andrew, my son, still has it in his house – it's as heavy as a steam boiler!

So at last the wife was happy, and the husband, poor man, having done everything at her bidding, was at last ready to concentrate on his work. From the outset, Marshlands was a test of all one's sensibilities. Folk like the Rautenbachs were not thick on the ground where I had come from, and to this day I wonder how one should describe them, for they were not unkind people; Marie Paulsen said they were rough diamonds.

Lydia and Gerry Stroobach, whom we replaced, always remembered the looks of pity they saw on the face of anyone who happened to ask where they worked. At the time that they were employed, Wessel said that he didn't think that Gerry could cure tobacco, until it was suggested that each man would fill his own barn and cure it in his own way independently. When the time came to unpack the tobacco, and with the whole Rautenbach family looking on, it became very obvious that Gerry's barn looked and smelled better. Wessel's curing was definitely not as good, and the family disappeared quietly away.

The wildlife that ran across the make-shift ceiling at night unnerved me, as did just about everything else that lived around me, man and beast. I lay in bed at night, as stiff as the white-washed hessian hanging above me, listening to the vermin enjoying nocturnal high jinks, while Andries slept like a baby beside me. I kept a hockey stick close by, just in case anything should fall on top of me. Later, of course, we annihilated everything with poison. As each day arrived I would thank God that our job was intact; the turnover of employees was a constant worry.

Attached to one wall in our dining-room was a black celluloid contraption with a handle. It was the party-line telephone, which served us and a string of neighbours. One had to learn the party-line code: three short rings and one long for next door; one short and three long for the boss; and so on. The last digit told you the number of long rings and the second-last the short ones. However, once you'd mastered it, it was fine because the phones in those days never gave trouble, being regularly checked and maintained by the Post Office engineers. The party-lines also had the advantage of being able to interrupt conversations in an emergency.

On one occasion its ringing kept a visiting guest up well into the night. A bachelor, he had drawn the short straw and had to sleep on the couch in the lounge, but we had neglected to tell him about the party-line phone. He spent hours leaping off the settee to answer each and every ring. By morning he was exhausted, and he never asked for hospitality again!

Most of our furniture, which I hadn't then appreciated for its value, had been left in the Masai farm-house in Gutu, once the family home of Rhoda (Harris) Paulsen. It was out of the ark – or perhaps out of the trek – and would now have been greatly prized. One of the best pieces was a fine old four-corner bedstead supporting a 'riempie' base, which balanced on little wooden grooves, in a very precarious way, to the four posts. It took up the entire space in our guest room.

One night we were rudely awoken by shrieks of alarm when visitors found themselves tumbling in a pile on to the floor – they had turned over too forcefully causing the frame to move out of kilter and collapse. Fortunately, they thought it was hilarious

and it went down in their history book as a taste of 'wild country living'. We didn't get very many overnight visitors at that time, being too 'thick' to realise why!

Long before the name Rautenbach had become a household name in southern Africa, the earlier generation were already achieving notoriety in Karoi. The brothers were an unfathomable duo, who seemed to do little except drink the hours away with a group of hangers-on. Of course, they weren't the only ones that kept the pubs afloat: Karoi had a plethora of such types. Stories abounded about their wild exploits, all of which served to make daily life more interesting.

One of them concerned a neighbouring farmer who occupied Romford at the time. After he had tried to seduce one of their wives, the brothers took the law into their own hands. Waiting for his wife to be away, they lay in wait for him one night and dragged him to his home where they tied him to the bedposts and proceeded to score his 'crown jewels' with a sharp knife, all the while threatening him with castration if he tried his nonsense again.

The Rautenbach family were haemophiliacs, and had their roots in the Cape's Eastern Province. Haemophilia was said to be a fairly prevalent condition within the Port Elizabeth/East London region and to stem from George Rex of Knysna through his illegitimate progeny. George was supposed to have been an illegitimate son of George III; however, with the advent of DNA testing, this has proved incorrect.

Haemophilia is a condition that causes the sufferer to bleed severely from even a slight injury and is passed on to males through the female line. Sufferers learn to avoid tasks that could break open the skin, so the Rautenbachs, apart from the arm-lifting in pubs, lived a non-physical life. Nevertheless, it affected every manager and assistant who worked on Marshlands in the early days, for, while they avidly avoided all activity that would cause physical injury, Wessel and Gert expected their white employees to administer corporal punishment to any labourer who angered them.

Marshlands operated on a shoestring during those years. Well-equipped workshops with basic tools, farm transport and farm fuel were not available. The men repaired punctures with tools and repair kits from their private vehicles. Tyres were often packed tightly with dried grass in order to get vehicles from A to B. Fertiliser was quickly spread on to the soil before the money could be extracted to pay for it. Employees had to ask for their monthly wages and a day off was rare. It was clear that the Rautenbachs had a lot to learn about keeping their employees happy.

Labour shortages were always a problem, but they were more dire on Marshlands than anywhere else. Lorries were driven up to Petauke in Northern Rhodesia to press-gang men into working down south, but they didn't stay around for long. The managers were told to lock them in the sheds to prevent them from escaping. Not surprisingly, these reluctant workers left messages and lists of the names of decent bosses nailed to trees around the district whenever possible.

Labour conditions did improve later with the formation of the Native Labour Supply Commission, which brought contract workers in from Mozambique, Nyasaland and Northern Rhodesia. Half their wages were held by the company as a form of savings and was given to them as a lump sum at the end of the contract. It was a good system that served both parties well.

The women, wives of managers and assistants, hated the peak season of reaping time, which coincided with the rains, with a passion. During this time they rarely saw their husbands. January and February were testing times, with long, exhausting days working in discomfort. Sleep was short, meals were eaten mostly on the trot or standing under a dripping tree, as most of the workers walked or grabbed lifts on trailers to the lands.

Before long, every being on the farm would come down with one complaint or another, as the curing took them from hot and dry conditions to the cool, dampness of the lands. Fevers set in – from malaria and recurring low fever to coughs and bronchial ailments, not to mention snakebites and tick-bite fever.

From sparrow-call to well into the night, those who worked kept going until the last leaf reaped had been tied to a 'matepe' and was hanging safely in the barn. A 15-hour day was about average. Then a weary gang straggled home, utterly spent.

The manager himself, however, was not allowed to retire yet, for he still had barns to check before he could allow himself some much-needed rest. Often he was past eating and blessed sleep was uppermost in his mind. Some managers found it was the lesser of the two evils to sleep on the spot, on a camp-bed in the shed. For others, the four-hourly checking of barn temperatures coincided conveniently with feeding the baby. Tobacco rotted in the land if it stood in water and then became diseased, and everyone prayed for some good, hot sun, while wet, steaming nappies, on desperate occasions, hung beneath steadily yellowing leaves as they all dried together in the barns.

Dam building and irrigation was just a dream. Water supplies came from small dams no bigger than ponds and from boreholes. Both serviced seedbeds, households, compounds and cattle. If you were lucky, you had enough to dry-plant tobacco with. Empty oil tins were used as water containers and a good borehole was worth its output in gold.

There was a short period of breathing space between seasons. The old-timers spoke of the first decent rains falling in December, and sometimes planting the last of their tobacco just before Christmas; the entire crop could then be graded and sold by August. That interval would hopefully end in a holiday.

For the managers and assistants, the tobacco sales added spice to an otherwise humdrum life – a chance to escape, to see the result of months of hard work suddenly revealed in opened, neat, sharp-edged parcels of sweet-smelling bales. But although the reaping may have been finished, they were not quite done yet.

Confronted with millions of leaves the farmer and his workers were only at the beginning of the process. As each leaf was individually reaped, it would be handled again and again over the following months and exposed to different processes along the way: tied with string on to a 'matepe' and taken to a barn where they would hang in tiers on wooden beams, row upon row, from top to bottom where nifty, dextrous men scampered up and down like ferrets and attached them to hooks.

Once they had been flue-cured with wood smoke over about eight days, they were removed from the barn to make way for the next batch and stacked in sheds to await grading. Then, each bulk was untied and the leaves weighed into a 'scale', a daily quota, for each man or woman who stood at a table to arrange them into grades of size, quality and colour: orange, mahogany, spot, lemon and slate, diseased and scrap, all under sky-light roofing that gave off the best light. There was no artificial light from electricity in those days.

As the season progressed there was a noticeable easing in the atmosphere. Weeks earlier, life had been frantic, with hard task-masters egging labourers on in a frenzy; now that the crop was safely off the land, the tempo relaxed. Everyone was friends again, curses were less pronounced, and hatred for the boss had almost gone.

In the sheds, the mood had changed, supplanted now by a calmer, more placid rhythm – the murmur of happy voices, laughter and banter, the humming of a gentle lullaby, sung to sooth fretting babies on backs. By selling time, millions of leaves had been handled over and over again, and each was probably known by name.

The sun rises on a cold, winter's day, and the two-hour drive through mist to the auction floors for a 7.30 a.m. sale is very often not quite worth the free breakfast offered on the floors.

While our hearts pump in anxious anticipation, the line of important men approach steadily, one step behind someone gabbling apparently meaninglessly. The auctioneer bids his way past lines of neatly parcelled tobacco bales.

Did he realise what power he possessed as he trotted along? He could change lives in a moment, but he never failed to fascinate, even mesmerise, the onlookers. The whole performance seemed almost ecclesiastically reverent. He was the high priest whose power proclaimed our future through his imperfect utterings.

Well that's how we saw it at any rate. He could issue a life sentence or set you free. Ultimately, he would put money in the bank, and hopefully a smile on the boss's face. In those days, after a short wait you could drive straight to the bank and deposit a cheque – as long as there weren't too many stop-orders, which had precedence.

It was a unique system of selling tobacco and probably the fairest, although there have been many debates about it. At the start of each sale, the bales were ripped open – oh, what sacrilege after the time and trouble it had taken to produce such sharp edges and four perfect corners! But, as Robert Louis Stevenson said, 'To travel hopefully is a better thing than to arrive.'

Back at the farm, not all the workers were present: many had already gone on leave. They had taken their lump sums of accrued wages and boarded buses for the long journey home to the north and east – Nyasaland, Northern Rhodesia and Mozambique. These nationals were found to be better workers than the locals.

Sheds lost their neglected look with a new coat of whitewash, flues were repaired or replaced, boilers checked and serviced, cords or 'gwazas' of wood were chopped in flexitime and stacked into neat piles between the trees like miniature huts. This was the best time, the languid, easy-going hiatus before the preparations for the season ahead. Soon it would all start again. Meanwhile, money trickled in, debts were paid, and everyone breathed freely once more.

On Marshlands another season was about to begin. The men, having competed for an extra bonus according to best prices and best weights, waited impatiently for the results. The new young assistant accepted his extra £500 prize money – he had earned it; always honest, hardworking, reliable and uncomplaining. In the end Marshlands had been good to him, and his family and we were ready to move on.

Living around us were some of the original settlers: ex-servicemen such as John and Marjorie Hull on Renroc; Harry and Dorothy Coker, who had just sold Oribi Park to Fritz and Marie Paulsen but who still lived on the farm. Bob and Nan Riches lived on Sandara. Nan was a medical doctor – very useful to have as a neighbour. She was a godsend when Jackie Watson's baby came early. Further along were Harry and Betty Brown on Pumara and Paul and Joy Straarup on Tivoli, a sub-division of Renroc. Rod and Colleen Cawood were working on Renroc and so were Honk and Gina Hyde.

John Hull named his farm Renroc because initially it was the corner of that block: spell 'corner' backwards and you get Renroc, which was one of the most originally named farms in the area. John liked to be addressed as Mr Hull by the likes of whipper-snappers such as us. 'He was the only person I know who owned a solid-gold ingot,' said Marie Paulsen.

As far as pioneering pedigrees were concerned, Rodney Cawood outdid him because he came from 1817 and 1820 settler stock in the Eastern Cape. In Grahamstown one will find a Cawood Street and discover a plethora of interesting facts about the Cawoods and the Dells. Rod's maternal grandmother was a Dell and had a sister and twelve brothers. The former formed their own cricket team and travelled as far as Lindley in the Orange Free State to play cricket against some of their relatives. Rod retained that inherent love of cricket and played for Karoi and Tengwe.

Fritz and Marie Paulsen arrived from South Africa in 1958, and by the time we had become, first, neighbours and then tenants, Fritz was the proud owner of several farms: Deerwood Park, Deamour, and Baobab, where a baobab tree really can be found growing. He then bought Oribi Park and finally a portion of Nassau from Paul Venter. By the end of his life, Fritz had built 200 barns.

Fritz was the older twin brother of Koos Paulsen, and their father was the headmaster of a school in the Transvaal. He gained entrance to the University of Pretoria, graduating as a land surveyor. Marie, Fritz's wife, was a trained teacher, and like many Afrikaner housewives she was an acknowledged homemaker and baker of note.

The Methodist Women's Association learned many a new skill from her as we took on catering tasks for various functions. In preparation, several of us would gather in someone's kitchen and turn out hundreds of *koeksisters* and other pastries. I have never forgotten the subtle advice given on that first day: 'Remember, the dough should be cold and the oil hot, and as the fried dough hits the ice-cold syrup there should be a noticeable 'sppth' sound.

At the end of the block lived Harry Brown on Pumara farm. Our arrival coincided with the death of his wife, Roberta. The couple were childless, but not too long after Roberta's death Harry married Betty, Roberta's best friend, and to the delight of all the neighbours they had a daughter.

In 1964, John Hull sub-divided his farm into four sections. Lot 3 of Renroc was bought by Paul Straarup, who registered it as Tivoli after the famous gardens in Copenhagen, Denmark, the country of his birth. 'We were fortunate,' says Joy:

> We had found our dream farm with all the right criteria: we wanted it to be virgin land; it was flat and had good soil; it was covered in trees; and it had a satisfactory borehole. Fifty acres had been cleared and it was fenced, with a good road running along the boundary.
>
> Another advantage was that Montesuma, owned by Harry Wells, was on the boundary. His tobacco commanded top prices each year.
>
> My father was a builder. He and my mother decided to take early retirement

to help us. Mr van der Reit had a few original ideas himself. He made a room with sections of wood measuring 4 foot by 8 foot, which were transported by lorry to Karoi. Two of the sections had windows and one a door. This was erected in a day, even to the last piece of corrugated roofing. A long-drop was dug the day after, and water was carted in drums. Within twenty-four hours the two old people were set to go.

The next innovation was the house for Joy and Paul. They bought curved asbestos and rigged up a hut on a concrete slab, and closed one end in with brick and a window and at the other end with a French door.

Meanwhile, John Hull continued to develop another section. He built barns and a house on a piece of Renroc he called West Acre. He put Rod and Colleen Cawood there to run it. When the Cawoods left, Piet and Lettie Strydom bought West Acre farm.

Lot 4, always earmarked and kept by John for his nephew, Edward Hull, as a prime piece of virgin ground was the last piece to be occupied. It was registered as Virginia. John badly wanted Ed to have it, but there was one drawback – it had no water, and because it was so flat, a dam couldn't be built. Ed got there in the end, but was destined not to be there long.

The house that Mr van der Reit built for Mary and Fred Mulder on Nyamanda.

When John and Marjorie – who had no sons, only three daughters – left Karoi, the main section of Renroc was bought by Doug and Thea Cochrane, who had worked for the Hulls in Mazoe.

However, if one were to chose the most interesting couple there, it would be Harry and Dorothy Coker. The two met when Dorothy arrived in Rhodesia to take up a position as a governess to a well-known leading family in the country. During the war she had been one of the 'land girls' who had been recruited to work on the farms and parks in order to free the men to join up for service. It is only recently that their importance in the war effort has been recognised.

Harry was no oil painting; by the time I met up with them, Harry had become rather rotund – the epitome of Tweedledum or Tweedledee – with a gentle disposition. Harry cast his eye over Dorothy, who gave him her sweet, blue-eyed smile, and he liked what he saw. The two married, had no issue, and started pioneer farming alongside others after being allotted Oribi Park.

The couple were naturally very English, but Dorothy was more English than most. Dignified and 'proper' she exuded a shyness which was quite genuine. She was also pedantic, however, particularly when it came to business. This trait would have made her insufferable without a sense of humour, which she had in great quantities.

She knew to the last drop how much water they used in a year, much of it collected off gutters into tanks which she herself climbed into and scrubbed out once a year. Once she found to her dismay that she couldn't climb out and Charlie Hay, who lived next door, had to be summoned to help.

With Charlie pushing and shoving to no avail she was persuaded to take off all her clothes. 'Don't worry about me,' said Charlie.

'I won't peep', and she was saved. Mazhanje season arrived and the trees were laden with wild fruit. Dorothy harvested them, counted them, and dished them out to the children in the compound. Not one had more than another.

She ran a trading store which was known as the best store around. She and I became good friends, but clearly she didn't like my husband, who was an Afrikaner although he had had more education than she had. She was bigoted to the point of refusing to have a black man in her house or garden. Her years as a land girl stood her in good stead, for she mowed the grass, chopped wood, and did most of the strong physical outdoor work. Harry was happy to dust, sweep and iron.

The Nels of Gutu arrived in Karoi in 1962/3. Willie bought Buffalo Downs farm from C. P. Robertson, Hans farmed in Tengwe, and a third brother, Tommy, stayed behind. The Nels became as prolific and well known in Karoi as they had been in Gutu.

Willie's grandfather, Willem, made his way to Gutu from Craddock in the Cape Province in 1923. He fathered seven children – Maria, Gert, Jacobus (Koort), Mias, Pieter Schalk, who was Willie's father, Hendrick and William Cecil Rhodes (Toit). By the late 1950s there were as many as thirty Nels playing rugby for Gutu. The only one in the team who wasn't related to them was my husband, Andries Herbst. Among them were five W. P. Nels, which caused real confusion when it came to sorting out the mail.

Willie's father, Piet, had died at the age of twenty-seven, and his mother subsequently married Werrie Rademeyer. It was Oom Werrie who bought the former mica-holding grounds from Johnny Eden, where many members of his family came to be housed – hence the reason the farm Madadzi eventually came to be nicknamed Nel's Spruit.

The Nels weren't the only ones who were part of a mass exodus from Gutu. Most were Afrikaners: Essie and Soama Esterhuizen; Mossie and Katie Dryer (Katie was the sister of Frassie Moolman, married to Betty, whose grandfather, Martinus Martin, led the legendary Martin Trek from South Africa); Koos and Rhoda Paulsen; Phil and Betty Kruger; Hans and Wynand Bezuitenhout, with their wives Gerda and Dotsie.

Willie Watson worked in Gutu as a youngster before coming to Karoi. Neville, Daphne, Hugh and Monica Royston all came from Gutu. There were a number of the Swarts family – Gideon, Danie and Phyllis, who was married to Hans Nel. And, of course, my husband Andries Herbst and me. There were plenty more who didn't put down roots long enough to be remembered.

There were also imports from Northern Rhodesia in the form of Phillip and Margaret Gifford, Mr and Mrs James Watt Snr, with Roy and Ria, young James, Dave and Lyn (Watt) Kilborn, Dick and Eileen Bylo, Theo and Jose Venter, Karel and Colleen Kirstein, and Una and Dudley McKenzie, who arrived later from Chisamba.

Others came from Rusape and Inyazura: Jimmy and Veronica Flight, Margot and Neville Phillips, Harvey and Eth Ferreira, Dan and Mary O'Connor (not farmers), and Rod and Colleen Cawood.

Each group found their niche and either put down roots or moved on and made good.

20. Farmer Politicians

One old stalwart dared to boast during the early years that Karoi farmers were such a power in the land that it was surprising that none of them had become famous. That remark might smack of arrogance, but I believe it was said in admiration and it was justified as time went on.

It is true that there has always been an interesting collection of characters around the district since its inception. There were men of every class and every walk of life, but most preferred their independence, privacy and a peaceful way of life in the sub-tropical highveld to the restrictions of conventional urban life. The majority of those who landed in Karoi had just fought a war and many ambitions that they may have had would have been stymied by distance and bad roads. In any case, they were preoccupied with developing their new farms.

Nevertheless, leadership qualities were abundantly evident: a man has to have those traits to farm successfully. Those natural leaders who felt they could make a difference soon showed their mettle and went on to lead local committees, from which some graduated to higher offices when time allowed.

The rural and town councils, farmers' associations, tobacco boards and the Natural Resources Board were all acknowledged to be foundations on which to cut one's ambitious teeth. However, it was not until independence in 1980 that anyone from Karoi served as a president of the Commercial Farmers' Union or the Tobacco Association. Harry Wells was probably the first to escape to Salisbury, for the purpose of improving the marketing side of the tobacco industry in 1964.

Politicians from Karoi emerged much later. It was a strong conviction of what was fair and right that led Pat Bashford into the political arena. Gradually, through leadership roles in the farmers' and other associations, Pat became a fairly prominent figure. He and other opponents of the Rhodesian Front government established the Centre Party in 1968. Their overall aim was to promote multi-racialism and advancement on merit. Some might argue that this policy wasn't much different from the policy of the Rhodesian Front, except that the latter argued that the black man was not yet ready for majority rule. They advocated a slower approach to advancement.

Nevertheless, Pat Bashford and his party faithful fought tirelessly to counter what he believed were short-sighted policies of the ruling party. It was not an easy time, as he suffered the slights and disparaging criticism from the vast, right-wing majority.

Thomas H. P. (Pat) Bashford was born in London in 1915, a member of a large working-class Catholic family. He left school early and went on to train as a cabinet-maker, emigrating to South Africa in 1935. Two years later, at the age of twenty-two, he arrived in Salisbury with a minimal education and one shilling and four pence in his pocket.

Using his skill as a cabinet-maker, he obtained work with the National Housing Board until war broke out and led him to join up with the Eighth Army in North Africa. He returned to Rhodesia and married Margaret (Peggy) Horsfield, a member of a Pioneer family who lived on the corner of Cork Road, Salisbury, in 1940. That house is still there.

As an ex-serviceman, he was eligible to apply for a farm in Karoi, which he did in

1954. Pat's first farming experience came from market-gardening, after which he took a job in Trelawney as a tobacco assistant.

Peggy had been born in Salisbury in 1910. Her parents had come to Rhodesia from the UK in the 1890s. Her father, Jonathan Patchett Horsfield, worked for the Salisbury municipality for twenty-one years and then bought a farm near where Lake Chivero now is. She attended the Dominican Convent and then trained as a State Registered Nurse, after which she went to Queen Charlotte's Hospital in the UK to study as a midwife. Riding around the London slums on a bicycle, she delivered seventy-five babies to qualify.

Libby Garnett (née Bashford) recalls:

The year 1954 seems a lifetime away now. That was the year we Bashfords arrived in Karoi.

I can still hear the Christmas beetles singing and my father pacing through the hot, dry, virgin bush with an improvised divining rod that pulled towards the earth. And with that seemingly tenuous encouragement, our future was decided and the farm, later named St Brendan's, was bought.

In retrospect, I marvel at the gamble my parents took. There were five of us children, three already at boarding school. As my youngest sister so succinctly put it, 'we were rich of children but poor of money'.

A few local people arrived in search of work, and development began – a borehole, a road, and a thatched hut that was just capacious enough to house a double bed and a narrow, slatted bed for Trish, the youngest. I slept in the back of our dusty old Trojan truck, which was reversed up to the door of the hut every night. The haunting sound of night-jars still sings in my memory.

The bush was rich in game – baboons, wild pig, leopards, night-apes, hyenas and snakes. There seemed to be more insects around in those days – plagues of stink beetles, flying ants after the first rains, sausage flies and moths, all of which dive-bombed or hovered around our candles at night, drawn by the gentle warmth of the flame. Worst were the big, black, crusty-winged stag beetles with large antlers – they could be lethal.

I remember being bathed in a metal basin with water heated on an open fire. Oh, and I remember lovely succulent steaks cooked on it as well. We owned an old green pantry cupboard, which doubled up as an altar when the Catholic priest came to say Mass under the trees.

When all five of us were together during the holidays, we slept under sheets of asbestos propped up against trees; what a primitive existence!

I remember watching mud being sloshed into moulds as they made bricks, and loving the sensation of it squishing through my toes; those bricks became our tobacco sheds and our permanent dwelling place.

Picture a long building like a train, with a lounge at one end and a kitchen at the other. The rooms in between had high windows, and in the doorways were flapping swathes of hessian. The bathroom, too, was pretty basic, and an old Rhodesian boiler spluttered away outside as water heated, giving us an inexhaustible supply.

As the land was slowly stumped out, making way for crop-growing, Dad developed a great herd of Mashona cattle. Four years after arriving, we moved into a wonderful new house that perched among trees on a hill. Oh, the glory of a flush loo and a generator that gave us light – this was progress indeed! A dam was built in which we fished and pottered around with small boats.

As time progressed, more young and intrepid farmers arrived, opening up the land around us. They would buy vegetables and milk or use the phone or bath. There were the Johnstones, Flights, Pilchers, Donaldsons, Esterhuizens, Johnsons and Bartons. We also met mining prospectors and those most dedicated missionaries – the Jesuits.

They would call in to stock up on fresh produce and fuel before heading off into the depths of the Urungwe Reserve. In time, they built churches, schools and a hospital. These unsung heroes travelled the roughest roads, worked in the most hostile environment, making a huge contribution to the social and educational development of the local people.

Christmas was a very special time for us on the farm. The dams filled and spilled, and the world around us turned green. There were calves in the paddocks and mushrooms to gather by the basket-load. Wild orchids, gladioli and flame lilies lit up the bushveld.

A *mombe* would be slaughtered for the staff, and all the workers were given new shirts. There would be more mealie-meal than everyone could eat, loaves of bread, rapoko beer … and on it went.

On Christmas Day, the whole compound turned out to sing and dance on the front lawn, ululating and banging drums. It was their way of showing thanks, and usually there wasn't much lawn left by the time they danced back to their huts!

We attended Midnight Mass at the little Catholic church in the village, and I can still see those old faithfuls who made up the congregation: Chisholms, Staceys, Gaisfords, Featherbys, Mulders and Walshes. Father Thamm was our inspired parish priest for years and years.

I suppose all this might sound idyllic now, but all the while my parents, Peggy and Pat, worked tirelessly, always anxious about the rain that either fell in deluges or not at all – and anxious as well that debts might not be paid.

Mum was a trained nurse and midwife; every morning she kept a clinic, treating the sick, dishing out pills and handing out little tins of ProNutro to the toddlers. There were children with burns, cases of snakebite, stab wounds and leprosy, and babies to be delivered.

She also ran a club where the women were taught the basics of sewing and cooking and could learn about hygiene.

A little school was built, which about ninety children, all dressed in smart red uniforms, attended. There were prize-givings, at which there were gymnastic displays and bits of English poetry were proudly recited. Each child would say something like, 'I am stirring my porridge', 'I am standing up', or 'I am sitting down' – no one seemed to tire of the repetition!

My mother also ran a store, the social hub of the farm. A tailor treadled away on his sewing machine in a corner, and the customers propped up the counter, buying basics and swapping news.

She taught us all to read: our first schooling was through correspondence. It was all a bit haphazard, with many interruptions. However, it must have worked for all of us girls. Brenda, Heather, Trish and I are graduates of

Cape Town university. David, the only boy, was a star pupil at Gwebi Agricultural College.

I suppose one could say that Ian Smith's unilateral declaration of independence changed our lives, most particularly Dad's.

Black power became the watchword of the frustrated black population, and this quest for power led to our tragic war. It was difficult to watch as many shunned my father for his liberal views, but in hindsight I'm sure that many now admire that stance.

David, his son and our brother, was killed on active service on Christmas Eve 1976; Arnold Bathurst and Warwick Lilford died in that same tragic accident. Dad suffered a stroke shortly after that, and never fully recovered. He died in 1987.

With the loss of my farmer brother and the death of my father, St Brendan's became a liability. Mum sold to our neighbours, the Flights, and she died in Mutare in 1991. Her death marked the end of a traumatic era, to which she added sadness, more than words can express.

'Don't look back', they say. But how can one not? Nostalgia and random memories of Karoi and its wonderful people are all we have left, and they still walk across our dreams.

We still talk of Natalie Herud, who ran the library for many years with a style all of her own and who dished out news and sandwiches full of thickly erupting egg-filling.

We talk about Maidments, the family-run business that seemed to sell everything. We talk about the Kordonskis, who ran the butchery in town, and we remember the make-shift drive-in

The Bashford family in the 1970s.

cinema behind the hotel. We talk of the endless markets on the pavement outside the Farmers' Co-op.

We talk of the Club with its polo and rugby, its selection of amusing amateur dramatics and Christmas Tree parties. We talk, too, of the bush war and the way everyone rallied around, particularly in the most terrifying and tragic circumstances.

In short, we talk of a great town and country community in which we grew up during the most exciting and tumultuous times.

Peter Richards helped to found the new Rhodesia Party in 1972 and served as one of two Vice-Presidents. He contested the 1974 general election, standing against Danie Brink.

Not surprisingly, Peter admits, he was thrashed – his only claim to fame was that he was the only one of four RP candidates not to lose their deposits. Danie Brink, Tengwe, was MP for Lomagundi for one parliamentary term.

However, Peter distinguished himself later when he became ZTA President from 1994 to 1996, after which he handed over to Richard Tate when he was appointed Chairman of the TSL group. He served in this capacity for eight years until the group was indigenized.

Peter Richards.

Dennis Norman.

Dennis Norman went the classic route, and found himself destined to become the most significant of all Karoi farmer politicians when he entered the arena in 1980.

Dennis had farmed on Pelele on the Shola Road and began his apprenticeship by serving two years as Chairman of the Karoi Farmers' Association. He then did two years as Chairman of the Grain Producers' Association, followed by two years as Vice-President and two years as President.

However, before his term of office was up he was asked to serve in Robert Mugabe's first cabinet as Minister of Agriculture. It was a magnanimous gesture, designed to allay any fears that the white farmers who remained might have had, and assured them of the importance of their role in the development of the new Zimbabwe.

From then on, the farmers of Karoi were galvanised into a flurry of activity, taking on a more significant role in the affairs of national agriculture. Patrick Wells became a ZTA Councillor for the period 1990–96. Ian Alcock, Tengwe, was President from 1992 to 1994, followed by Peter Richards.

More recently within the political world, Roy Bennett, born and brought up in Karoi, entered the limelight at the beginning of 2001.

His political career had begun after he bought a farm in Chimanimani and was approached by the local chief to stand as their Member of Parliament for the ruling ZANU(PF) party. He agreed but later 'crossed the floor' after he had witnessed various nefarious activities.

He then joined the new Movement for Democratic Change party led by Morgan Tsvangirai. Roy's greatest asset, aside from his likeable and open personality, is his fluency in the Shona language.

Within a few years he had become a threat to the ruling party. He was jailed for fifteen months for pushing Minister Chinamasa in Parliament, and was later acquitted of charges of treason, but when further warrants for his arrest on flimsy grounds were issued, he escaped the country into exile. A lesser man would have been broken after this treatment, and his story is not yet complete.

21. Internal Affairs

In *The Guardians: A Story of Rhodesia's Outposts, and of the Men and Women Who Served in Them* (Books of Rhodesia, 1974), Joy Maclean writes:

> On a hot sunny day a young white-skinned boy was being teased by Lobengula. 'Have some beer. Go on, drink it. It is my royal command that you should taste some.' But Tomi was the son of a missionary, brought up to regard strong drink as evil, and he refused again and again. 'I command that you drink some,' Lobengula said, holding his own fly-ridden calabash near Tomi's lips. Suddenly the lad lost his temper and struck out at the King, hitting him with his hand. 'No,' he shouted. 'No, I will not.'

All within the audience of the King held their breath in a moment of deathly silence as Lobengula stared in shocked surprise. Not long previously a woman dancer had been beaten to death merely for murmuring in the King's presence. Surely now Tomi would suffer a terrible punishment. Instead the King broke into a great laugh and remarked 'The boy has spirit' and turning his attention elsewhere, he dismissed the lad.

Tomi who liked to tell this story to his children was the son of the Rev. Thomas, Morgan Thomas who with the Rev. William Sykes and the Rev. John S. Moffat and their wives, had arrived at Inyati in 1859. Moffat had known Mzilikazi in the Transvaal in 1829. Fleeing from Tchaka, Mzilikazi had wandered north with his people and reached Inyati only twenty years before Moffat himself. It was here that in 1875 Thomas Morgan Thomas junior

was born. Known for the whole of his life by the Matabele as Tomi, he and his brother, William Elliot Thomas, are thought to be the first born Rhodesians to become Native Commissioners, and Tomi claimed that he was the only person to have struck Lobengula and got away with it.

It is believed that W. E. Thomas joined the Native Department in 1895 and Tomi in 1897.

The Posselt brothers, Willie, who found the Zimbabwe Birds, and Harry were both early Native Commissioners. A relative, Frederich (Fritz) Posselt was the grandfather of Cynthia Posselt: in Karoi we knew her as Tinny Gifford, who was married first to the late Harry Simpson of Good Hope farm, and subsequently to Phillip Gifford of Amore farm.

Tinny's grandfather, born in Natal, joined the staff of the Transvaal Native Department and for a while served as Sub-Native Commissioner for the Sabi District. In 1908 he visited Mashonaland and accepted an appointment to the Rhodesia Native Department, being posted initially to the Salisbury staff of the Chief Native Commissioner. Over the next twelve years he served in Matabeleland – Belingwe, Wankie and Sebungwe. He served for ten years in Marandellas and was then transferred to Plumtree. He retired in 1941.

The earliest system of government set up under the Charter had no separate native administration. Once the Pioneer Column had been disbanded, Rhodes and Jameson had no shortage of material to choose from in finding men who would act as administrators. Many had rushed to make gold claims, but soon became disillusioned after finding little to bother about. Several of these men remained and were persuaded to join the new Native Department.

Until 1925 Miami and the rest of the Urungwe was administered from Sinoia. Ex-Pioneer Corps No. 113 W.H.Clarke was appointed the first Native Commissioner of Lomagundi in October 1894. He came from the Police Force of Manitoba, Canada.

In developing the administration of the law, and of rules and regulations, these men steered the country through its early course. One of their most important functions was the mammoth task of trying to reconcile, as painlessly as possible, two very different cultures. The Native Department was a great organization, from its birth and sturdy growth to its final, sad demise. Its story is impressive for the way in which the African people of rural Rhodesia were brought into the modern world.

In 1941, changes were made to the 1930 Land Apportionment Act that created national parks from the European and Unassigned areas, created townships for labourers in the urban areas, opened up new areas for white farmers returning from active war service, and established Native Purchase Areas for black farmers.

This readjustment meant that blacks in certain districts had to move, and many were obviously reluctant to do so. Despite the area being unhealthy and sparsely populated there were a number of kraals under Chiefs Dendera and Chanetsa that were situated on Crown land, and the people were moved to Urungwe Reserve in order to make way for the returned-soldier scheme for whites.

With wild bush, tsetse fly, mosquitoes and poor communications, along with other difficulties, the Europeans once more faced pioneering conditions. It was at this time, too, that the survey was started for the Kariba dam project.

It was officials from the Department of Native Affairs who were tasked to ensure that the movements of people were carried out smoothly and without acrimony. They patiently explained to the rural folk the reasons for the move and that the area to which they were to be transferred would be suitable, with good soils and plentiful water supplies. Their genuine interest in the welfare of the people in their care inspired such trust and confidence that the moves were generally carried out successfully.

Here are the recollections of one erstwhile 'cadet', whose career was destined to be short-lived because of the politics of the day.

1975: Karoi and My First Job, by Gerry van Tonder

Listening to the inevitable career-guidance lectures held at school in my penultimate year, one in particular, given by the Ministry of Internal Affairs, caught my interest. It offered, among other aspects, a predominantly outdoor career, which appealed to me, and also offered excellent long-term prospects for a young white male in Rhodesia. Added to this was the ultimate decider of an all-expenses-paid university degree. My academic qualifications ensured that I was indeed eligible, but I would have to work a year first to satisfy the Ministry of my long-term intentions.

I would start as a humble Cadet District Officer. Points were earned at the completion of various successful examinations, with African Language and Customs giving one point each,

Lower and Upper Civil Law two points, and the Bachelor of Administration degree four. Two years' service and four points would guarantee promotion to the rank or position of District Officer, so the three-year degree course would be time well spent.

My brother Jo had similar interests but more towards the Ministry of Agriculture. He completed his national service in 1974, and at the start of 1975 we were both posted to Karoi under District Commissioner Bob Ferguson.

I was nineteen years old, living in a country that was internationally isolated, where society was conservative, and the likes of me, a school-leaver, were naive about many aspects of independent adult life.

The new recruit to 'Intaf', 19-year-old Gerry Van Tonder.

The bush war was concentrated in an area called 'the north-east', which seemed far enough away to cause me little concern. It was a novelty to have my own automatic rifle where carrying a weapon in public was commonplace.

The small town of Karoi had derived its name from the Shona word for witch, *muroyi*, the prefix *ka-* being substituted for *mu-* to give the name its diminutive sense. The district itself, called the Urungwe, was arguably the largest and wealthiest Virginia-tobacco area in the country. Wherever one travelled in the large-scale commercial farming area, tall red-bricked curing barns bore testimony to the success of the golden leaf.

To the north, small-scale black farmers in the Vuti African Purchase Area produced the less capital-intensive Burley and Turkish varieties of tobacco. Together the whole industry contributed over 50 per cent of the country's foreign-currency earnings.

Tobacco and its by-products were therefore cheap, and most of the country's population enjoyed partaking of 'the weed'. I smoked Country Club Minors – small cigars with filters, the colour of rich chocolate and the size of a cigarette. I also enjoyed a pipe, especially after a long day in the bush, as I sat chatting with my District Assistants (DAs) around an open fire. My favourite tobacco was The Flying Dutchman, which came in a round, blue tin bearing a picture of a sailing ship.

Copper was being commercially exploited at Shamrock mine, to which I paid regular visits that were usually the highlight of my periodic field trips. It was in a very remote area to the north, bordering on the Urungwe hunting concessions – an oasis in the middle of the bush. The trip took several hours, and I passed initially through farmland where mica, a silicate mineral used for its insulation properties, could be seen glistening on the surface of the roads. Once there, I was provided with excellent accommodation in a guest lodge and fed royally in the clubhouse. We benefited greatly from our close proximity to the enormous man-made lake of Kariba – our own Riviera, as it were.

On Monday mornings at 8 o'clock we had team meetings with the District Commissioner, and newly appointed members were introduced to the rest of the staff. We didn't wear uniforms, just shorts, cotton shirts and lightweight boots. The DC, Robert Peter Kirkland Ferguson, was an affable man, loved and respected by all. The staff called him 'Sir'. Bob never wore a tie but was always smartly turned-out in a pale-green safari suit. He had light ginger hair and the ruddy complexion that usually accompanies such colouring.

As he was a heavy smoker, each jacket pocket was jammed with a 30-pack box of cigarettes, the backs of which were useful for jotting down notes. His racking cough left him breathless and puce in the face, but he remained undeterred and continued to puff away stoically, taking advantage of cheap fags.

Being a family man he drove a beige Peugeot station wagon which you could set your watch by. In a country beset by sanctions, the most common choice of vehicle was one of three – and they served almost as badges of recognition. The family man usually bought a Peugeot, the single youngster or little old lady bought a Datsun 120Y,

commonly known as the Rhodesian Rolls-Royce, and the farmer drove a Mercedes.

The Assistant District Commissioner was Peter Michael John Lombard, a conservative young man who never appeared in the standard safari suit but preferred the tweed-and-checked-shirt-with-old-school-tie appearance. His father was a retired army colonel, and this was unquestionably the source of Peter's approach to life and his job.

He took the latter very seriously, spoke Shona like a native, and didn't suffer fools gladly. He was precise and pedantic in all that he did, right down to the meticulously flourishing signature he produced. We were all wary of him, and the black members of staff gave him the nickname *kachoro*, a small wild berry that is very bitter. He was a fitness fanatic and jogged regularly with his Weimeraner dog running beside him. Peter gave me a lot of encouragement and continually pushed me to study and sit for various exams.[1]

The Karoi station didn't have a District Officer at the time, but the senior cadet, Ian Banks, took me under his wing and showed me the ropes. He was a softly spoken chap, thin, bearded and a confirmed bachelor.

My brother Jo came under the jurisdiction of Jacque Bouvey. He was a rather eccentric Hollander, whose cigar-smoking habits left him with a

---

[1] After independence, Peter managed the Enterprise Farming Co-operative, being responsible for the procurement of inputs for this very prosperous commercial farming belt not far from Harare. One day he unwittingly became involved in a domestic issue between two farmers. Tragically, he ended up being shot, and this left him permanently paralysed from the waist down.

constant need to clear his throat. Jack's throat-clearing was a ceremony in itself. With speech halted he would attempt to empty his lungs of all congestion while he belted himself on the chest with both hands. To a stranger, this was both odd and amusing. It was even more disconcerting when it was practised at high speed on a rural dirt road – Jack would let go of the steering wheel for this procedure and left the vehicle to the vagaries of potholes and corrugations. Then one said a prayer or two.

The accountant was Mr Johnson. He was not in his prime, and I never did discover his Christian name because even the 'boss' addressed him thus. He was a typical civil servant, obstinate and autocratic, and in complete control of the district's budget. If only we had them now. He had an unfortunate hunchback deformity which also affected his gait. His tiny wife was in charge of renewing the firearms licences, operated the switchboard, and dished out petrol coupons.

The remaining two white members of staff were the primary Development Officer, Axel McDonald, and his Field Assistant, John Chappell, another bachelor. Axel was a middle-aged odd-ball who, with heavy rimmed glasses, spent much of his time in the Tribal Trust Lands (TTLs) and was based up at the rest house in Magunje. John was a young, gentle giant who always ensured that he could operate legitimately in the remote areas bordering Kariba district where he could practise his favourite pastime of poaching. We were to meet again later in Mount Darwin.

Audrey Bryson was the DC's secretary, in addition to which she typed correspondence for the rest of us.

No e-mails then! She was an absolute hive of information and a great asset to the station.

Initially I was the only cadet, but was joined shortly after by Ian Banks, Ian Alexander and Bernard de Pins, a Frenchman whose English left a lot to be desired. He lasted only a few months but provided us with endless humour and some embarrassing situations, as his liberal and outspoken French manner collided head-on with Rhodesian conservatism.

Until 1980, the DC's office was the centre of civil administration in the district, where almost all functions were dedicated to the lives of the country's black people – from birth to death and all that goes on in between: civil law, deceased estates, trading authority and licensing, education, welfare, health, benefit payments, infrastructure, extension and development taxation, and animal husbandry.

In all, it decentralized government at the district level, and went hand in hand with a large dollop of paternalism. Absolutely nothing that happened in his district was permitted to escape the knowledge and attention of the DC.

The Land Tenure Act of 1969 replaced the various land-apportionment legislation that had been enacted after 1890. It divided the country into roughly equal and exclusive areas for the rural black and white populations, with further areas set aside for forests and nature reserves, national parks, African Purchase Areas for small-scale black commercial farmers, and so-called State Land for anything else not specifically categorized.

The large district of Urungwe contained several Tribal Trust Lands, reserves that were set aside for rural black people only, where subsistence farming was the norm. These formed the family home base, or *musha*, which meant much more than just the average home village. It represented the spiritual home – the place where the family spirit or *mudzimu* was domiciled.

The *musha* was the place to which black people were to go for their annual break from the city – to plough lands in which to plant the annual maize crop, to repair the pole-and-daga huts, to see to the welfare of their cattle, and to visit their extended family. Ultimately it was the place of their retirement and death.

The wives and children of most of the city dwellers stayed in the *musha*, as it was financially more expedient this way. There they grew their own food, and rural education was generally free. It was a simple, carefree way of life.

So it was into this environment that my work took me, where, even though I was the only white person for miles and miles around, I felt – and, indeed, was – content and safe as I travelled around and shared rudimentary accommodation with my staff in the TTLs.

Every three months was sub-office duty, when we, the entire District Commissioner's entourage (*mudzviti*) would literally up-sticks and take the office to the people. For a stretch of four weeks, my team and I would cover the whole district, calling at predetermined locations called sub-offices to attend to the civil needs of locals in that area. We would be out for three days, and then return to Karoi for the remaining two days of the week.

The de facto leader was Sergeant Nyoka, who had experience gained over many decades. He knew exactly what to do and when to do it. I was the head of the group, and along with two DAs and two clerks, we squeezed into an ancient Land-Rover that pulled a trailer carrying provisions and kit.

The sergeant and DAs each carried a World War II vintage .303 rifle and two magazines of ammunition. I had my FN and a hundred rounds. The clerks were unarmed. Vehicles had no mine protection, which was still the norm. Little thought was given to a possible terrorist encounter, nor did we post night sentries.

We would start at the south-west of Karoi, routing through the tobacco-rich farm lands of Tengwe and into the lower end of Urungwe TTL at Chief Mudzimu, then on in a northerly direction towards Chief Nyamunga and Headman Mbiza-zazenda, through to Chief Dendera and Chief Nematombo, ending up at the rest camp near Magunje.

Magunje was considered to be very civilized, with electricity and proper beds, but the temptation to return to Karoi and creature comforts was just too great – a cold Coke from a general dealer was a must after days of having nothing cold to drink, then home and a

Sgt Nyoka Zindoga and Jack Howman MP, Minister of Tourism and Information, in the Urungwe district.

hot shower, an ice-cold Lion lager, and a proper sit-down steak meal prepared by Dyason.

Mukwichi TTL lay to the east of the main Kariba road and was less densely populated, housing only Chiefs Chundu and Kazangarare. This part of the exercise usually incorporated the politically orientated Vuti African Purchase Area, a sprawling part of the district made up of small-scale farmers, most of them unable to sustain a viable commercial farming enterprise. Many were heavily in debt to the state-controlled banks.

Our sub-offices were three-walled square huts with thatched roofs; all had concrete bases. The Land-Rover would be parked in front of the open side, and this is where we slept overnight. Generally, though, we selected other places that afforded us privacy and scenic beauty. There were no toilets, and we washed out of buckets on a square of cement set for this purpose at one side.

In true colonial fashion, one of my DAs, normally Chanetsa, would set up my Hounsfield stretcher and make the bed with linen and blankets, which were always with me. I travelled with a metal trunk that contained all I needed for a comfortable stay in the bush – cooking equipment, crockery and cutlery. I have always adhered to the philosophy that camping does not necessarily mean having to rough it.

Towards evening, the hospitality from the locals would be phenomenal, as a steady stream of young 'maidens' brought bowls of *sadza* and *muriwo*, all presented in a bowl with the contents neatly rounded and smooth on top. Apart from the fact that I liked salt with my *sadza*, I found the portions were far too large, but it was polite and politic to accept the gift merely by breaking the mound in two. The *muriwo* would invariably be a meat-free relish – usually very tasty; meat of any kind was a luxury.

Sometimes Chanetsa would rummage through my trunk and open a few tins for the evening meal, but this was usually towards the end of the trip, after the boerewors and steak had run out. After a meal it was coffee and a pipe in front of the fire. I tended not to drink alcohol on these official trips.

Before all trips, the messengers were sent out to inform the chiefs that we would be calling. A few hundred people would be present and the proceedings would begin with a general meeting. The Chief and I would sit on chairs brought along from the school; everyone else sat on the ground.

Sergeant Nyoka would call *maoka* (hands) which would precipitate *kuombera* (clapping of hands), when all present would rhythmically, and in unison, clap. Occasionally, a woman would ululate, which many found amusing.

The Chief would welcome the *mudzviti*, and I would respond by raising specific issues pertaining to the area. There would then be an open, but very orderly, question-and-answer time, allowing the *sabhuku* (kraal or village heads) to put forward any concerns they might have.

In the more remote areas, these concerns often related to crop-raiding animals, especially monkeys (*tsoko*) and baboons (*mapfeni*). Vermin-control units did operate in the TTLs to address such problems, but as a token gesture of goodwill, I would invariably offer to try and shoot a few.

Once the real paperwork-part of the sub-office got under way, a DA and I, together with the complainant, would venture off to find some offending raiders. On one such occasion, in the remote western region of Urungwe, we headed towards a riverine thicket, dense with subtropical vegetation, where our guide assured us the rascals could be found.

We soon heard their chattering, and as I struggled through the undergrowth the DA shouted '*Hokoyo, Ishe! Uriri*' ('Look out, Sir! Buffalo beans'). Too late. I realized, much to my dismay and discomfort, that I had walked into the lethal vines of the buffalo bean, *Mucuna pruriens*. This vine carries hundreds of mustard-brown seed pods, each smothered in thousands of tiny bristle-like hairs that detach themselves from the pods at the lightest touch.

My uncovered legs and arms were soon developing welts that itched intolerably – the much-feared reputation of the buffalo bean had become a diabolical reality to me. Eventually, back at the camp, alternate applications of used tea-leaves and wood ash, and drenching water over several hours, brought gradual relief.

At every sub-office there were hundreds of applications for birth certificates. We spent many hours assisting mainly illiterate folk to fill in forms. In most cases these applicants were adults who had never had a birth certificate. In the absence of medical records or a baptismal certificate, an applicant had to have two witnesses to verify the date of birth.

We spent many a late night, working under the headlights of the vehicle, clearing up the backlog. The possession of an identity certificate was mandatory, and these we would issue *in situ* after taking an individual's fingerprints.

We were also paymasters to the low-income civil servants, such as dip attendants and chiefs' messengers. In certain cases, there were also individuals who received a small benefit allowance from government – one man as a result of having disabling leprosy. I forget his name, but will always remember him being brought to the camp on the rear carrier of a bicycle, his legs and hands totally reduced to stumps. He was one of the happiest people I have ever come across.

Peter Richards wrote this about Chimombe:

During the early 1960s, when we were on Chiwuwa, north Karoi, I kept hearing about an object that was regarded as very sacred to the people of the area.

The labourers were reluctant to talk about it openly, and what information we had was gleaned from my 'boss-boy', whose family had lived in the Zambezi Valley and who had been moved to Chundu's area when Mana Pools game reserve and its adjacent hunting grounds were promulgated.

According to his scant information, the object was made of iron. It was kept in a secret location watched over by a witch-doctor, and was known to the locals as Chimombe. It had apparently been located in the Valley inside a baobab guarded by the local *n'anga* when Chief

Dande's people still lived in the area. When they were relocated, Chimombe went with them, too. No white man was ever allowed to see it.

Several years later, when we moved yet again, to Ashton farm, I became very friendly with Aldrich Dawson, a retired Provincial Commissioner who had served as Native Commissioner in Miami in the early days, and asked him about Chimombe. He sent me an article that had appeared in *NADA*, the Native Affairs journal, years earlier. I have since mislaid it, but in essence it confirmed what I had discovered.

Apparently the object is a piece of iron that has three protruding legs, reminiscent of a three-legged stool. That is how I imagined it. The author of the article had either been allowed to view it or had been instrumental in its removal from the valley and its ultimate re-establishment in Chundu's area. The writer could only guess that its origins must have been some piece of derelict scrap metal left by an early explorer.

During initial survey work on the Kariba gorge, an object was discovered which conformed to what could only have been a small boiler from an early river steamer. This discovery confirms that metal objects were to be found in the vicinity of the river whose origins date from a much earlier era.

Peter Richards also knew Mandebvu Young, an elderly man living with, or married to, a black woman somewhere near Manyangau on the edge of the Chundu or Kasangarari reserve.

Distinctive by his flowing white beard, hence his name, a little unkempt but not startlingly so, he operated several trading stores in the local reserve and then built in the early 1960s that very large trading store on the hill overlooking the main road at Makuti.

He owned a Ford Thames Trader truck, and for the time that the Richardses were at Chiwuwa he collected and carted his tobacco, taking it as far as Lion's Den and from there by rail.

He appeared a lonely figure, and during the course of many conversations I gained the impression that he came from a well-known Scottish family and that he had siblings living in the UK.

He used to have recent copies of *The Times* and the *Daily Telegraph* in the cab, which led me to believe that he was an educated man who came to Africa and 'went bush', as they say.

He sired several coloured children of whom I know nothing, but within the last ten or twelve years, one of his sons was involved in a fatal accident on the road between Spring Fever and Rydings School. I seem to remember that a girl was killed in the incident.

22. Prelude to War – and Fear

Fear and death touched my life in 1966 when we lived on Montesuma farm. In a small way it was a prelude of things to come.

Let's set the scene: Montesuma lies due south-west of Karoi, some fifteen miles or so from the town as one travels along the Great North Road towards Chirundu. It was the season of 1965/66. UDI had been declared, and the farm was the property of that well-known figure, Harry Wells – farmer, businessman and entrepreneur of humble beginnings.

It was a huge set-up, with forty barns or more, and accommodated three tobacco sections. There were also several vast sheds and outhouses, all of which were built on top of a high ridge. To the side, on lower ground, was a small avenue of four homesteads that faced a grove of elderly eucalyptus trees – the wind had caused them to bend over the years, giving them an almost menacing character as they loomed towards our homes as if to keep us in our proper place, for, as we well knew, we were positively 'below the salt', not yet having 'arrived' as land-owners.

At this time, having farmed tobacco successfully in Karoi for several years, Mr Wells was beginning to lose interest in his farm and was drawn more and more towards the commercial side of the industry. Word had it that he had just sold Throgmorton House, a prestigious building – the highest building in Salisbury, they said – buying it one day and selling it the next for a huge profit without ever having set foot in it. How impressed we were by that story!

Mr Wells had decided to live in Salisbury to be on hand for his other more pressing interests: one was to look into the effects of sanctions on the tobacco industry, which ultimately led to the formation of the Tobacco Corporation. Thus he was looking for three ambitious, hardworking men, who would also have the courage of lions to take on a partnership with him.

It was a wonderful opportunity for all of us, with each one in charge of a section. Two were selected and, by dint of scraping together our meagre resources, two new companies emerged: Wells and Sicklemore (Pvt) Ltd. and Wells and Herbst (Pvt) Ltd., respectively. The third section was run by Andrew Schoeman, who was taken on as a manager.

As time progressed, being of a rather nervous disposition, Andrew began to live on tranquillizers, taking double doses the night before a visit from the 'boss' – it was general knowledge that Mr Wells had a fiendish temper and could put the fear of God into the Devil himself!

Also living on Montesuma was the farm mechanic, Bill Speldevinde, who was of Dutch-Indonesian extraction, his English wife, Cathleen, and her mother, whose name I've forgotten. Bill was a good mechanic and kept all the equipment and machinery in smooth working order.

So three families lived in that row of houses at that time, opposite those deeply depressing gum trees. Phoebe and Derek Sicklemore, being more senior, occupied the big house, slightly more elevated at the top of 'skid ally' – so called because on occasions we would go careering up and down the dirt track between the houses and the trees on the company motorbikes that each man had for use around the farm.

About three or four miles down the road opposite Coniston farm was another Wells-owned property called Ungwa, on which Eynon Deere and his wife, Janet, lived in a similar business arrangement. Eynon, like the rest of us, was allowed the use of Bill's knowledge and mechanical skill, so we saw a lot of him.

It would be hard to forget the sight of Eynon Deere charging madly among the gum trees on his motorbike with Phoebe Sicklemore hanging on for dear life behind him, shrieking first in alarm and then in delight as the ride became wilder and faster. For Phoebe it was probably the most liberating experience of her entire life, though to appreciate this spectacle fully one would have had to know Phoebe quite well, for she was 'awfleh ledi-like'.

The farming fraternity tend to measure their years in seasons: we are inclined to talk about the 1960/61 season rather than the calendar years of 1960 and 1961. So it is, for me, the season of 1965/66 that marked a turning point in the history of Rhodesia.

I dare say that it was then that we young Rhodesians took a giant leap into maturity. Suddenly, as a chain of events unfolded, we were forced to think more seriously about our future. I remember it being a very dry season, and we all did a rain dance for fun around the reservoir. It didn't bring the rain but it released the tension.

Only the chosen few had electricity at that time, and most of those lived in the village, so we thought ourselves very grand indeed to have access to a generator that gave us the luxury of electricity. Our husbands each took a weekly turn on generator duty, switching it off at 10.00 p.m., and as each man strolled up to the engine room they shouted loud obscenities, warning us that candles should be lit.

At that time, most of us lacked any real political awareness: how spoiled and cushioned we were from all unpleasant things. The wrangling between Harold

Wilson's British Labour government and our own, which culminated in the Unilateral Declaration of Independence on 11 November 1965, was the first of many disagreeable situations we were forced to take a serious look at.

Then came the incident that shook us to the core. We woke up to hear on the radio that Mr and Mrs Johannes Viljoen had been murdered in the night on their farm near Hartley. We realized that the dire warnings of terrorist attacks were now a frightening reality.

For the first time in our lives we thought of security. We had never locked a door or closed a window; Cookie was always there to look after everything. We hunted for keys to doors that had never felt a smoothly oiled turn in the lock. From now on they would be secured with every darned measure there was – bolts and padlocks, chains and hasps.

A few days later Phoebe Sicklemore summoned me to tea at the big house. It was a Friday, which was a favourite shopping day for most of us – everything would be fresh. The RMS truck would have arrived, bringing an abundance of fresh produce from Salisbury, including day-old chicks, cheeping away in ventilated boxes, that needed to be rescued before they expired in the heat.

Butchers made an extra effort to display unusual delicacies – sosaties, pickled pork and beef olives. They would have been up since 2.00 a.m., preparing huge orders of ration meat for farm labourers that had to be ready for the first customers to pick up by 8.00 a.m. The library would be open for the exchange of books, and, for those who were free to do as they liked, there would be tennis, bowls and golf to play at the Club.

I, too, liked to shop on a Friday, though in the morning. It was my custom to drive past the Speldevinde house – the ritual never altered – stop, hoot and yell, and somewhere through the dark depths of the open door a voice would call, 'Just the mail, please.'

On that particular Friday morning I made my usual stop but noticed that everything was closed up – tight as an armoury; not even a window was open. Clearly the Speldevindes were away. Thinking nothing of it, I drove on. But I did think it odd that everything was closed up. To this day, it amazes me how trusting we were of our staff, and we were hardly ever let down by them.

Lunchtime came and went, with a tired husband bent only on a 'siesta' rather than conversation. One remark from him, though, did make me thoughtful. Andries had wondered why Bill had not returned to the workshop after breakfast, though it was not uncommon for him to be absent from work as he suffered with bad migraines from time to time, a legacy of his naval war years.

At 4.00 p.m. I sauntered up to Phoebe with my two toddlers, Gwen and Sian for tea. Young Alison Sicklemore, four years old, was whiny and fractious at the lack of her mother's attention, and an exasperated Phoebe suggested that she pay a visit to Aunty Cathy, who, having no children of her own, always had time and patience to spare for difficult kids.

Alison trotted off and peace reigned – but it was short-lived. She returned within minutes, grumpier than ever. 'That was a short visit,' said Phoebe. 'Isn't Aunty Cathy there?'

'Yes, they are there, but they're sleeping,' said Alison.

At dusk, the working day finally wound down to a close, and as Bill had still not pitched up for the afternoon work, Andries and Derek decided to go and investigate.

The back door of the Speldevinde house was open and they walked in, calling cheerily – but this quickly changed to alarm at the scene that appeared before their eyes: Bill lay dead at the foot of an open refrigerator.

It seemed that, on arriving back at the house for breakfast that morning and hearing no sound from the bedrooms nor any sign of a cook, he must have decided to make his own breakfast, but had got no further than the fridge door before being clubbed on the back of the head with a 'simbi'. He would have known nothing after that.

By now thoroughly alarmed, the men investigated further, only to find that Cathleen lay dead on the floor in the bedroom, not ten yards away. A similar picture met their eyes in the old lady's room further on. Bill would have died never knowing that his wife and mother-in-law lay murdered some fifteen yards away.

A question now hung in the air: Was this the work of terrorists? With the Viljoen murder still fresh in our minds, we immediately assumed that it was. What do terrorists look like? We had no idea. Government droned on about communist-inspired insurgents trained in China and Russia, so were we to look for little slit-eyed yellow men or burly braying Russians carrying vodka bottles?

The men lost no time in checking up on us, their wives and children. In blind panic we hauled out our firearms. We locked ourselves in with rifles and revolvers beside us, the use of which was quite beyond me in those days, and fear ruled the next twenty-four hours.

But overriding those feelings were the horror that I had driven up to the house earlier that morning while a deadly scene was being performed, and the thought that those poor people had lain there dead all day as we had blithely gone about our daily business only fifty yards away. I should have realized that something was dreadfully amiss.

And then there was the horror I felt for little Alison Sicklemore, who had walked into a 'morgue' and thought that Aunty Cathy and Uncle Bill were just sleeping.

A panicky call soon brought the police, CID and reservists to our sides. Pretty soon we were surrounded by what seemed like battalions of uniformed men. They arrived by car, truck and helicopter from all sides. There followed a preliminary investigation and then the bodies were removed.

Afterwards the CID moved into the Speldevinde home to conduct an in-depth inquiry. I thought them very brave indeed, remembering that their cook had once made a shepherd's pie for the Speldevindes with pet mince. Had I but known it, I would have been doubly impressed, for that 'cookie' was charged with murder some days later. He had killed them for a mere 15/–.

So much for imaginary terrorism, then. But that horrific episode introduced us to what was to become a way of life for many Rhodesians – a life filled with tragic incidents that left those we knew and loved dead, and it was a campaign which seemed to last for ever.

A strange twist to this tragic event emerged some weeks later when I visited a neighbour, who told me this story: Before the Viljoens' murder, we had spent a weekend down in Gutu visiting family, and it was a shock to receive a call from the Gutu police advising us that a puppy that my two small daughters had played with had been found to have rabies.

According to the law, the police had to get in touch with anyone who had been in close contact with this hitherto bundle of canine delight, and they strongly recommended that we make an urgent visit to our GP for advice. Suffice it to say, my imagination ran riot, and after studying my two lovely girls for a few moments I decided that I could definitely see them frothing at the mouth.

In a panic, I searched for Andries but he was nowhere to be found. I phoned neighbours and asked breathlessly if he was there, telling them the full story. In the event, the matter was dealt with satisfactorily and then forgotten – or so I thought.

As often happens in remote communities where life can sometimes be lonely, dull and uninteresting, imagination does run away with people. Apparently the story doing the rounds at the time of the murders was that Andries, having been bitten by a rabid dog, had gone on the rampage and shot everyone on Montesuma!

It was no surprise when Harry Wells decided to sell Montesuma and terminate the partnerships after only one season. Indeed, we had no inclination to stick around on a set where we had experienced murder and melodrama at first hand.

Ungwa farm also came up for sale: Harry offered to back us if we bought it. It was a tempting thought, but we didn't feel ready. Nevertheless, our year with him had given us a financial boost, as well as experience that put us in good standing.

How strange life can be. Even sixty years ago, Africa tended to be a very small world, for who would have thought that Eynon Deere's charisma could have extended as far as the Eastern Cape. But let's not forget that our hero was one of life's mavericks and charmers.

Dyna Erasmus – as she was then: to us in Karoi she was 'Flo' McKay, wife of Tony – tells the story of when she was a scholar at the Diocesan School for Girls in Grahamstown, more years ago than she cared to remember.

She had never been to Rhodesia, and had certainly never heard of Eynon Deere, when suddenly the name confronted her daily, for it was emblazoned and embellished across the ruler and pencil box of her friend who sat next to her in class. After that however could she forget it? This remained the status quo until Heidi Louren's passion for Eynon had worn off. Thus Flo knew the name long before she met the man. She arrived in Karoi years later and finally met this mystical figure, who by then had married Janet Davies.

Eynon was a big man, full of bravado that hid a deep and underlying heartache beneath a façade of cheerfulness. To the outsider he was loud, jovial and charming, given to bouts of boozing and mad escapades, which often landed him in deep trouble. Without doubt he was one of Karoi's most colourful characters and could not be lightly dismissed. On a good day he was excellent company and in general he had a gregarious nature. In an ideal world he could have gone far.

Eynon and his brother, Alec, who did one stint in Karoi as an Assistant Native Commissioner, were orphaned as young boys. Neither recovered from their mother's senseless and tragic death and their father's disappearance. Bitterness ruled Eynon's life, making him a loose cannon.

Eynon attended several Rhodesian schools from which he escaped. Starting with Umtali, he went on to Milton, where he was remembered in a positive light for being an adept bugler as well as a skilled boxer. He ran away again and was sent to Guineafowl school, closer to Gwelo, where his guardian – his uncle, Jacky Deere – was the manager of Meikles.

During one holiday from school he visited his cousin, George Neaves, who was farming along the Kingsview road. He returned again in 1964 after working for various people, including the Goldberg brothers in Inyazura. From there he worked in that partnership with Harry Wells on Ungwa.

Many stories are told about the antics of Eynon Deere. Some are amusing and others are downright hair-raising, but all are remembered with a chuckle. Many were the occasions when Andries was asked to search for the errant Eynon late at night. It was never a difficult undertaking, except for one occasion. There were only three watering holes in town – the Club, the Twin or the Hotel – and Eynon was soon located at the Club, but he was far gone, and no amount of persuasion could get him into a car. Desperate to get to bed, but not having the ruthlessness to leave him, Andries eventually managed to drape the befuddled Eynon over the bonnet of the car and drove slowly back to Ungwa. Once there, he literally 'dropped him off'!

23. The Bush War

On 11 November 1965, Rhodesia had severed its ties with Britain by unilaterally declaring itself independent.

In retrospect, it was a fateful decision and one that has been the pivot around which Rhodesian/Zimbabwean affairs have revolved ever since. Before that act, the legal colony of Rhodesia had faced political disturbances from within and British interference from without. With the unilateral declaration, the country became an international outlaw, subject to sanctions and vilification. Then there followed years of endurance and great courage by both black and white civilians as a civil war slowly unfolded.

It was a war that threatened to destroy the vision of Cecil John Rhodes:

> The inevitable irony, one is tempted to predict, is that with the exception of the dead and maimed, the losers will have lost little and the victors will have won a mess of pottage.[1]

In retrospect, no one won that war, neither victor nor vanquished. If one views it from the vantage point of where we sit now, the very people who should have benefited have won little. However, without hindsight, such pearls of wisdom seldom deter man from going to war.

John Lovett continues:

> Rhodesians are in many ways well-suited to war. Two of the three main groups which make up the tribal structure of modern Rhodesia – the Matabele and the European – have a long colourful military history. The third group, the Mashona, although ironically providing many of the young terrorists in the present conflict, are in fact the antithesis of what the romantics like to call a 'warrior people'.

Our bush war was a silent, secret, unglamorous little war. By 1976 it had killed over 2000 people and injured a great many more. For a country the size of Rhodesia it had a tragic casualty rate and there were still more to follow.

There was scarcely a white person in Rhodesia who didn't know someone, a relative, friend or acquaintance, who featured on the casualty list. There was scarcely a rural African who didn't have first-hand knowledge of the terrorists and their savage methods. The war to the Rhodesians was a real and personal preoccupation.

There were more black men than white men in the regular government forces. The insurgents killed more black civilians than white ones. It was basically an ideological war between east and west and the prize was a strategically valuable piece of African real estate. This vast piece of real estate lends itself admirably to terrorist warfare; the wild and rough terrain, thick vegetation and numerous rocky outcrops, caves and 'dongas' provide good coverage, and camouflage in which to hide.

Rhodesia was in a unique constitutional category. It had been self-governing since 1923, with its own administration, judiciary and police. With the transfer to Southern Rhodesia in 1964 of almost the entire Federal army and air force, it became militarily self-sufficient. So Britain

---

[1] John Lovett, *Contact: A Tribute to Those Who Serve Rhodesia* (Howick, Natal: Khenty Press, 1978, 11.

had to negotiate independence with a Rhodesian government that was determined to resist premature change and to maintain the standards set through three generations of orderly white settlement.

From 1962 to 1965 the nationalists worked for the transfer of power by increasing pressure from within. They concentrated on creating disorder and lawlessness in order to coerce the British to intervene directly. Stoning, and burnings, beatings and murder became a nightly feature of township life. But this was political violence not terrorism. The weapons were clubs, pangas, petrol bombs and intimidation. It was not yet war. When the Rhodesian government declared their independence unilaterally, all that changed.

In Karoi, as in the rest of the country, people's attitudes towards the bush war were varied, and depended largely on their age and wisdom. For the youngsters, the effects of war were an unknown quantity. They envisioned only the adventure, comradeship and a romantic idea of heroism. They were ignorant of the consequences, the sorrow and the grief that would come to pass.

They would return from a stint in the bush and in no time at all they were ready for the next. Flo McKay said that Tony, her husband, so enjoyed his 'call-ups' that he was always well prepared a week ahead – his uniform washed and pressed, and every piece of clobber nicely laid out on the bed in the guest room.

If we are honest, most men generally relish that period in our history and the experiences that came with it. Given half a chance, they still talk about those days and will continue with their stories until the cows come home. It wasn't a love of killing – the

horror of that reality soon sank in when it began to happen. No, it was the experience of brothers-in-arms, comradeship and escapism that did it.

Most wars, they say, are made up of 90 per cent boredom. Nevertheless, it was a perplexing time. With many points of view being voiced, whether you were for or against the situation, every man and woman did their patriotic duty – from the leading opponents of the government to the geriatrics, everyone did their bit. One could even count one or two mercenaries from far away countries beyond our borders.

Farm homesteads had been targeted from the start, so by 1972, when the war proper had begun, the Karoi farming community were well organized, ready to face whatever was thrown at it.

Our homesteads were swiftly transformed into forts. We slept behind heavy security fences, locked and bolted doors, sandbagged or bricked-up windows. We created 'safe areas' within our homes in case of an emergency, usually around the telephones and Agric-Alert, a 220-volt, two-way radio system that used car batteries.

Every farm had one and it was linked to the police station, where each evening at 6.00 the voices of Peter Veck and others would be heard going through a roll-call. By day, farmers on the periphery especially went about their daily lives in mine-proofed vehicles as they ran the risk of detonating landmines on their travels.

The murder of the Viljoens on their farm, Nevada, near Hartley in 1966 was, for many of us, the official beginning of the terrorist war. Many of the civilians killed were farmers. 'Bright Lights' or members of 'Dad's Army' were stationed on farms for added protection – these men were not to be underestimated, for many had combat experience in previous wars: Dudley Duvenage and Colin Bray in Malaya, and ex-servicemen like Stuart Maclaurin, Dudley McKenzie and Dusty Laver, veterans of the Second World War. In Karoi the first farm to be hit was Doornhoek owned by Koen and Ruth Strydom who, thankfully, escaped unharmed.

A farmer's wife wore many hats in those days. Not only was she responsible for the welfare of her children, she ran the farm when her husband was away on his two-week stint.

From one day to the next, she worked under different guises – perhaps as a WVS member, providing meals to hungry security forces at the canteen, or as a member of a select team of nursing sisters at the Casualty Clearing Centre, where many lives were saved. Myra Kennedy, Karoi's District Nurse, along with Raie Wells and others, set up a Centre at the back of the Post Office.

Myra trained a team of medics to cope with emergencies on the spot. The school hall was the first venue for her lectures, and volunteers learned the basics though few lasted the course. Una McKenzie and Raie Wells were involved as they were professional SRNs; Dini Voorn, though unqualified, learned first-aid and was an invaluable asset.

These women were called out on a regular basis and any old time – during meals, late at night, or from church. The calls usually came from George Kennedy, Myra's husband, who drove the ambulance.

As the 'prepper', Dini arrived at the Centre first to open up. She got the operating theatre ready, sterilized instruments, made beds, opened windows, and then waited, fearful of what might turn up. June Veck was in charge of Karoi's blood-type register and residents were called upon to give blood if needed. Dr Chris Lewis was the GMO,

and his calm, unflappable demeanour saved many a life as he worked along side the nursing team.

A bigger team was sometimes required following a big contact in which many were injured; they took blood, set up drips, held a hand, and gave words of encouragement. No matter how small their contribution it was always of some help.

I was once given the harrowing job of washing a blood-soaked blanket in which a corpse had been wrapped. It had to be soaked in cold, salted water for days before it was then washed many times in a machine. It was not a job that anyone would relish, but someone had to do it and it was something that I, as a non-medic, could do to help.

Women reservists helped to run stations, releasing manpower for active service. Margot Phillips was manning the radio on Christmas Eve 1976 when she received the devastating news that a local PATU stick had been involved in an accident. She was given only the numbers of the 'dog-tags' so had to look up the names in the register.

That night David Bashford and Arnold Bathurst died; Warwick Lilford died of his wounds three weeks later; Adrian Herud, who had suffered head injuries, took months to recover. That was one Christmas that none of us will ever forget.

Apart from helping with catering, the WI also ran Operation Comfort, which provided essentials when homesteads were burned to the ground. In Karoi, there were three such incidents that I remember: the Gardiner home on Hazelmere, the Paulsens' on Oribi Park and the Johnsons' on Yawanda. All were left with nothing, yet they courageously proceeded to rebuild.

The Johnsons, Brian and Patsy, cleaned up their charred, sooty ruin and built another house alongside it, but they retained the ruin, which cleaned up well. It become a charming al fresco entertainment area, with climbing creepers and pot plants; one would hardly believe the distress it had caused. It was one way of getting up the nose of the enemy.

The WVS ladies ran the canteen. Farmers' wives ran it by day, and then Iona Shattock and Mary-Anne Haigh took over at 5.00p.m. so that the farm wives could get home safely before dark; Iona and Mary-Anne lived in the village. Gilly Hamilton Ritchie and Nell Whiting aided us during the school holidays. They were members of the WVS from Salisbury, and this allowed farming families to escape for that much needed rest and recuperation.

The name BSA Police had a resonance about it and had a proud history; it played a vital role in the development of our country. Once again, with the frontiers threatened on all sides, the demands on the police were tremendous. These gave rise to the introduction of women into the BSA Police.

Pam Clayton was Karoi's first WPO when Mike Farrell was Member-in-Charge in 1977. She became the Public Prosecutor when Les Donnelly was magistrate and she lodged with Mrs Herselman on 'The Hill' at the top of the Crescent. She also met her husband, Geoff Cooper, in Karoi when he was with 5RR (Rhodesia Regiment).

Then there were the active reservists, national servicemen who backed up the regulars. They had operational commitments

A BSA Police Rhino vehicle, 1975.

helping to defend targets such as base camps, road gangs, bridges, railway lines, convoys, and lonely farmsteads.

Many of them were volunteers in PATU (Police Anti-Terrorist Units). Later christened 'Hell's Angels', these 'sticks' used motorbikes that gave them a speedy, relatively silent approach and reduced the danger of triggering landmines.

A PATU stick.

Then there was the Police Reserve Air Wing; their elitist efficiency has been well documented by Jim Barker in his book *Paradise Plundered* (Harare, 2007). Finally, there were the specialist groups: Grey Scouts on their mounted steeds (Chris Bishop was one) and the Selous Scouts (Edward Hull and Chris Herud joined them).

Stuart Maclaurin was put in overall command of operations in Karoi. He had been the youngest colonel in the British army during the Second World War.

Another veteran at the station was Ian (Brick) Bryson, a full-time Reserve Section Officer involved in PATU training. At the age of sixteen he had run away to join the navy and became the youngest member to receive the Burma Star for his service in the Bay of Bengal.

Ian (Brick) Bryson, 1970.

But it wasn't all gloom and doom. There was plenty of levity and humour to keep the spirits up – though some of it was on the dark side, such as when Cedric Lamb arrived for duty carrying a coffin on his shoulders before going off on one stint. That got the wives into a real state!

Peter Whittle's stick – Ko Voorn, Siem Timmer, Andries Herbst and Colin Wiggle – found themselves in a predicament on one stint when they became lost, and they wandered around the bush like tourists.

Their bitching and continual cries of 'Where the f*** are we' were so repetitive that they soon realized just how ludicrous they would appear to anyone who saw them. After that they decided to call themselves the Fagawes. They even went to the trouble of having banners and medals made, and organized an awards ceremony.

The presentation of a Fagawe banner and medal.

It was the police who started the VATs (Voluntary Anti-Terrorist Tracker Units) with a heavy push from Allan Savory in the mid 1960s. These groups were the fore-runners of PATU. Several Karoi and Tengwe farmers formed sticks, keen to get fit and into peak condition in preparation.

Toby Saunders, who was a Tengwe farmer at the time and one of the first to volunteer, looked back on one of his group's first missions. He called it 'The Bunny Ambush'.

Immediately after the Viljoen murder in 1966, a group of us were sent on a 'sortie' down to the confluence of the Tengwe and the Sanyati rivers.

After hiding our vehicles, we chose an ambush site and then moved away to higher ground that overlooked it and prepared to spend the night in wait. Each man had been given a slot on the guard roster to see the night through.

Our stick consisted of five members: Jack Tatham, Glen Tapson, Doug Hoets, Kees Radermaker, and myself. Four of us were Rhodesians, born and bred. We had all done our national service and Jack had leadership training, as had I.

Doug Hoets was ex-RRAF, getting his wings on jets. Since childhood we had all been familiar with the bush and were not strangers to the usual pursuits of young Rhodesian boys who spent holidays camping, fishing and hunting.

Our military training focused on lay-ing ambushes, though not on any oper-ational level that had anything at all to do with insurgents bound on terrorist warfare, so we were not as raw as Jim Barker has suggested in his book.

It is certainly true that we were inadequately equipped, having between us one Sten gun and two magazines, one .22 Hornet plus ten rounds, a .38 Webley pistol and fifty rounds, and a miscellany of assorted sports rifles and shotguns, sleeping bags and our own rations, enough for two days.

Yes, we were raw owing to a lack of experience, and certainly nervous, for as yet we didn't know what we were up against. But, as usual, a sense of humour prevailed.

So there we were, in a good position after a long night. Guard duty was soon to end when suddenly we observed green flares rocketing up in our direction. This caused consternation and we reported it by radio. An hour later another green flare went up, seemingly even closer. Again we reported it. Between the first and second flare voices and footsteps were heard, all of which appeared to get closer and closer.

Jack woke everyone and ordered a 360-degree check. He then suggested that whoever had surrounded us would attack at first light, if at all, and that we should be ready to move as dawn broke, at which time we would open fire and retreat. However, in retreating Jack fell over an embankment and thought he'd been shot. Seeing this we all fell flat and someone shouted, 'Jack's down!'

Within seconds we disentangled ourselves and, like ferrets up a drain, raced for our vehicles, which made Glen so nervous that he couldn't even insert the key into the ignition.

A post-mortem revealed that what we had seen was more than likely a natural phenomenon. However, after further investigation, VAT Purdon reported a 360-degree kudu spoor at the site. None of us likes to think that it could have been a rabbit! Imagine the headlines in the *Herald*: 'Dad's Army Chased by Rabbits'.

It doesn't bear thinking about.

Ian Fraser, alias 'The Oracle', lived on The Ridges, a farm to the north of Karoi at the sharp end. He had a talent that was put to good use during the war, for he is a water-diviner, though dowsing is the correct term, he said. His skill came in handy in aiding the forces to locate a terrorist presence.

The use of the pendulum is not new, said Ian. It was used during the Second World War to discover the whereabouts of various groups of insurgents by cartography. Ian spent many hours poring over maps with a pendulum in the 1970s, and many of his reports did lead to follow-ups and eventual contacts by security forces.

One he will never forget was after he had reported a terrorist presence on the Shamrock Road. The RIP chap phoned to say he had seen new tracks at a spot that Ian had already indicated and asked for a new position. A later report came through to tell him that the convoy had been ambushed and one of our farmers had been killed by an RPG rocket. It was Bob Prince who was lost to us. He had been manning the machine gun on the back of a Land-Rover.

As Ian was over fifty, he changed to 'ground-coverage', a sort of secret service if you like, and what Fran, his wife, called the 'Millipede Patrol'. This also involved a neighbour, Hennie van Heerden, and the two of them spent many an hour driving out to the Vuti African Purchase Area, getting to know the farmers there. Over the years, they managed to gather information and become friends and advisers. If they hadn't, they wouldn't have survived.

At the height of the war, 'sit-reps' (situation reports) and roll calls became imperative, and in this way we would often learn of the death or injury of one of our community members. We might even be listening in on a farm attack as it was happening.

In 1978 four of Ian's workers disappeared,

and his map-dowsing showed the presence of insurgents near the boundary on state land. Headquarters could not be spared because they were preoccupied with another incursion.

Ian and Fran went to bed at 11.00 p.m. – attacks had usually occurred before that time. At 12.40 a.m. Ian was awoken by a single shot. As he woke Fran, all hell was let loose, as a hail of bullets hit the roof, the walls and the water tank.

Grabbing his FN and webbing he dashed through to Morag's room where he experienced another barrage of bullets. He fired twenty rounds in retaliation and the attack stopped. Then a huge explosion followed from the opposite side of the house. Fran was busy pressing alarms and reporting – she had changed into her smart house-coat, saying that if she was going to die she wanted to be well dressed for the occasion.

The next morning they counted 2,800 spent rifle shells, and several grenades had detonated in an attempt to kill them. It was a common tale that many a farmer throughout the country could tell. Most were just thankful to come out of it alive.

Lydia and Gerry Stroobach lived on Hill Top farm. They were a Dutch couple, and they decided to call it a day after receiving a letter warning them that their labour would be murdered if they didn't leave.

'I particularly remember our last trip to Salisbury,' Lydia recollects.

We had five of our Dobermann dogs with us. They had looked after us loyally during the hairy times. Walter was the most beloved, Gerry's right hand and best friend, who accompanied him everywhere, particularly at night when he checked the barns.

These dogs would lie in the lounge at night with the front door wide open,

Peter Stidolph had to wear a revolver in a field of magnificent tobacco with baby Kirsty.

and Walter would watch Gerry's face constantly, waiting for the signal that would alert him that it was time to go. It was only some kind of eye contact or a slight nod of the head, and the dog would quietly go out, run up to the security fence, circle it first and then the house. Gerry would stand dead still in the dark, waiting quietly for Walter to report that all was well.

What a bizarre time it was. I so admired the other women, who were all so much braver than I was. I carried my Uzi on my shoulder even to the vegetable garden.

I remember when Lynx mine was attacked, their turn-off was opposite ours on Hill Top. We were glued to the Agric-Alert, listening in on what was developing, and we even managed a smile when we heard the German-accented answering control: 'Yes, zey had put out ze candle in ze vindow.' The candles had to be placed so that the incoming stick could find the house.

We had placed five Adams grenades

at strategic intervals around the garden and one exploded in an electric storm one night. Gerry was reading on the veranda. What a shock and what a noise it made. Then it set all the others off as well, so we had our own little private war going on around us!

The war naturally affected all aspects of our lives, one of them being when tobacco quotas were introduced. Flossie Hoskyns was caught up in this and was forced to sell his farm. Brian McKay bought it and it was this homestead that was used as the local head-quarters of operations in the north.

Flossie had been, among other things, an officer in the British army and was made commander of operations – although he said that any one of his comrades could have done the job equally well.

Flossie provided another illustration of how ill-prepared they were at the start. He had set up an ambush near Cliff Wilcox's farm after a PATU stick had discovered tracks on Barry White's place. Ludicrous though it may seem, between them they had managed to dredge up a combination of one .303, one shotgun, and one air rifle. They subsequently discovered that they were to face eight 'terrs' in a camp only a hundred yards away, though they managed to kill and capture all of them. One man was lost, and he wasn't local.

Not many will forget the incident of the three miracles, which began with the unlikely but hilarious image of Piet Bosch, Slim Botha and Porky du Preez squeezed into the front cab of a bakkie as they made an early-morning start to Bambazonke (Salisbury).

The first miracle was that the three of them fitted into the cab at all: Porky, as his name suggests, was no sylphlike Adonis; Slim was a huge man, nicknamed with

irony; Piet – long, loose and gangly – was perhaps the thinnest of the three.

They had hardly travelled ten miles when they were ambushed, and that's when the second miracle happened. All three, with one accord, dived out of the cab windows, cleared the fence along the road in what could only have been by transcendental levitation, and threw themselves into the long grass out of harm's way.

The third miracle, of course, was that they had survived at all.

After a busy Friday morning's shopping, Charles and Sue Stewart of Nascot farm left their week's supplies at the Farmer's Co-op to retrieve later and went on to the Club to play their usual afternoon tennis. Meanwhile, security being uppermost in everyone's mind at the time, management noticed a suspicious-looking box lying unattended and called the police.

Taking no chances either, the police called the bomb-disposal experts, who duly arrived and blew it to smithereens. Blithely unaware of this incident and the fate that had befallen their box of groceries, the Stewarts left the Club in good spirits and trundled back to the farm, only to hit and detonate a landmine – which threatened them with the same end as their flour and baked beans.

However, on this occasion, fate was kind and their landing was soft. Sue was more incensed about the loss of her groceries than by her close encounter with death and the damage to the car!

In September 1978, not far from Karoi within the Urungwe TTL, a missile brought down a Viscount that was carrying passengers from Kariba to Salisbury. Joshua Nkomo, leader of the ZAPU nationalists, admitted responsibility for this dastardly act, claiming that it was a valid military target.

Anthony Hill, a former Karoi lad, whose parents Ray and Pippin had farmed Hillandale in Miami, had miraculously survived the crash along with a handful of others. On that same flight was Diana (née Thomas) with Hans Hansen, her husband. They, too, survived the double tragedy. Still mobile after the crash, they immediately went off to look for water, but while they were away the guerrillas came to the scene and shot the survivors.

Sadly, the second Viscount crash in 1979 caused a total loss of life. It was our Karoi PATU sticks who were sent out to the scene of devastation to gather up the charred remains.

The 'finale' to the war came on 7 September 1979, when the Karoi village was mortared.

We watched from our veranda on Chiltington as the sky was lit up as if by fireworks. With each explosion we ran inside – shades of two hundred years earlier when the hoi polloi had watched battles from the sidelines. What a view we had.

Ironically, most of the damage was done by the locals themselves when Neville Haigh and Derek Bennett rushed outside, guns blazing, and proceeded to shoot at all the power-lines. The headmaster, Pat Taylor, was out walking his dog and threw himself into a ditch, and he stayed there for the night. We could have sold the rights to Elstree Studios for another film – *Carry On Regardless*!

The following day Mike Lapham and I were married in the Methodist Church by the Revd John Millns.

Back row: Noel Blazey, Stan Sheppard, Jimmy Flight.
Middle row: Kees Bakker, Mike Carpenter, Peter Gibson, Barry White.
Front row: Dave Roper, Peter Walsh, Andy Messina (BSAP), Nigel Laney, Alan Coast.

24. Life after UDI

In retrospect, the 1960s, which had begun with a great deal of optimism, wound down to an inauspicious and inglorious end.

It has to be said that Christmas for the farmer in Africa comes at a very inconvenient time of the season. But one thing that doesn't change it is the importance of the weather patterns. It was always a busy, frantic time, and the weather was always at the core of the stress. Usually it can be generous and kind, the rains falling to allow plenty of time for crops to be planted well before Christmas. But there have been times when Christmas festivities have had to be completely overlooked, for the rains indulge no man.

Christmas on a farm demands that a *mombe* be selected and killed, cut up and apportioned to each worker. It demands that each worker receive double rations of maize-meal, along with treats of sweets and biscuits, and perhaps an advance on his wages to spend in the nearby farm store. Chibuku (sorghum beer) arrives by lorry in a tank, but the worker himself cannot even begin to think of celebrating until every necessary operation is up to date.

On Christmas morning, the children from the farm school would approach the big house in a rhythmic shuffle, kicking up dust or mud as the case may be, singing and dancing, hand-clapping and ululating in gestures of appreciation for the Boss's generosity. This usually ended with the Boss handing over a bag of small change to the supervisor to be shared among them.

As time went on, the building of dams for irrigation removed the greater risks of late rains or drought, and the development of modern chemicals, herbicides and pesticides to control weeds and disease added still more benefits. The last-minute, frantic efforts of hand-hoeing became a thing of the past.

Nevertheless, the first months of the new year were a lean time, as cash-flow stopped flowing, and necks ached from watching the skies until the crop was brought safely in.

There are pranksters in every society, and I thank God for them as they can bring light relief at a time when one's sense of humour is in danger of vanishing altogether.

One testing New Year's Eve, after the usual celebrations at the Club, the Miami crowd, as was their habit, went out to 'first-foot' the New Year at a neighbour's house. On this particular occasion they gathered at Fred and Merle Mitchell's place.

The season hadn't behaved as it should, and Fred had decided to work on New Year's Day. As the sun's soft gleam heralded the new dawn, neighbour Harvey Ferreira spied Fred's 'boss-boy' making his way to the house. Asking him what he wanted, the foreman replied that he had come to get his instructions for the day's work.

'What?' said Harvey. 'Work on New Year's Day? My good fellow, no one works on New Year's Day – it's a holiday. Go to the compound and enjoy yourself.' The foreman took his word for it and left. It was a very mystified and peeved Fred who arrived at the *mundas* sometime later to find no one there.

In another season, the first planting rains fell very late – on New Year's Day. Hours earlier, everyone had been partying at the Club when at long last the storms began, and all the men decided to go straight home to plant.

Brian McKay had started the night looking sartorially elegant in a dinner jacket and bow tie, but he looked decidedly the worse for wear by the time he had aroused his compound with everyone speeding off to the seedbeds to pull plants. However, when they arrived at the lands, he found that not one drop of rain had fallen. In farm parlance it's called 'sod's law': how often has it rained on one *munda* and not on the one alongside it?

As it does in Europe, the weather dominated our conversation. The 1967/68 season in particular turned out to be a regular box of tricks. The rains fell as if God had thrown them all down in one fell swoop but then continued for good measure, just to make sure that we knew about it. They went on and on, drenching the earth in continual deluges.

Jaundiced-looking tobacco stood knee high with reapers in water, and tractors and trailers, buried up to their bellies in mud, littered the tracks, where they remained immovable in various stages of deterioration for weeks. Meanwhile, indoors, racks of washed laundry steamed like cauldrons around the wood-burning Dover stoves, and shoes turned a mouldy green in cupboards.

The new branch of Standard Bank opened its doors, replacing Rebecca Khan's trading store. She had had to move to the Indian area because she was married to an Indian. That was one of the Rural Council's least glorious moments.

The Bank celebrated the opening with a cocktail party, and against a background noise of torrential rain we braced ourselves for the twenty-kilometre waltz home along a river of mud in a car that had developed a mind of its own – only to find that three barns had collapsed into a heap of bricks and sodden tobacco.

But that wasn't the end of that silly season. Some months later, in July, the district woke up to the after-effects of an uncharacteristic black frost. Tomatoes that had stood in regimental order the previous day, rosy and healthy, drooped in a slimy, viscous mess on the vine. In the vleis, trees stood as if victims of a third world war, and *mombes* lay stiff from hypothermia in the kraals where they had huddled together for warmth.

That season left its mark for a very long time. It took ten years for the trees between the Chikuti and the Poti rivers to fully recover. I remember it well, for I was giving birth to yet another daughter; the announcement placed in the Births column ran thus: 'Andries is delighted to announce an addition to his harem.'

UDI had been a shock. Sanctions took a while to bite, but shortages were going to be inevitable. Those with enough money set out to stockpile. Luxury items such as whisky and tins of salmon were quickly snapped up, and Marjorie Hull bought a whole case of Harpic!

Nevertheless, throughout the 1970s the government saw to it that we always had essentials, from food to spare parts. No pantry was empty, no one starved, and no farm ground to a halt for lack of necessary requirements.

When they did take effect, sanctions made the farmers more aware of costs. The industrial sector was galvanized into increasing productivity in an effort to manufacture items that could no longer be imported except from South Africa. Many new factories sprang up during the years following 1965, producing a variety of essential hardware products, spare parts and equipment, quite apart from clothing and foods.

Mothers everywhere blessed the appearance of foods such as ProNutro – a maize cereal responsible for many a healthy and sturdy Rhodesian child that was also a useful 'rat-pack' supplement for their PATU fathers when that time began.

Gone were all the Kellogg's Cornflakes and Quaker Oats; in their place, we bought Willards and Red Seal products. Whenever we travelled between Johannesburg and Salisbury we must have been an astonishing sight to foreigners who saw us boarding our plane clutching giant pots of Marmite and buckets of Quaker Oats! One Johannesburg businessman was alleged to have said in jest that he could have any Rhodesian woman for a tin of sardines and a jar of Marmite!

Tobacco farmers were hit still further when quotas were introduced in 1966/67. Many had to think of other ways of subsidising their lost earnings and began to diversify. Peter Adams went into pineapple production and the Saywoods into proteas and coffee.

A few turned to prospecting again. Johnny Eden mined tin on Nyangoma, Peter Gibson's place. Tungsten and wolfram had become sought-after because they were used in hardening gun barrels. Karoi's itinerants – Gillesby, 'Grobbie' Grobbelaar and Dick Shepherd – all worked for Johnny Eden and could be seen at the hotel daily, swigging down the toils of their labour.

It was at about this time that Grobbie took himself down to the Valley on a poaching trip and managed to bag half a dozen guinea fowl. He was caught red-handed and summonsed to appear in court. He pleaded not guilty, saying that he had shot them in self-defence!

Interestingly, however, by 1971 not one ounce of tobacco had been lost to sanctions, though the industry was beginning to recognise that the road ahead would be long and hard. The Tobacco Marketing Board set up a team to look into the effects of sanctions on the tobacco industry, comprising Sam Whaley, Harry Wells, Donald Bell, Ginger Freeman and Carol Heurtley.

Following UDI, Britain made it an offence, punishable by imprisonment or heavy fines, to buy or even manipulate tobacco from Rhodesia, or to assist the sales or export of tobacco in any way. The Tobacco Corporation was set up to take over the commercial side of the industry in order to protect firms from any action that the British government might take.

The biggest blow was when the country's three major customers – the UK, West Germany and Japan – who between them bought 80 per cent of the crop, immediately enforced sanctions. From then on everything to do with tobacco selling was shrouded in secrecy. Everyone concerned had to sign the Official Secrets Act. Ginger Freeman's biography is as good a read as any James Bond best-seller.[1]

Those involved in sanctions-busting became masters of subterfuge, assuming different identities with passports that enabled them to travel to several countries. They travelled miles to reassure their customers that they used the more obscure border posts.

They investigated possible barter systems and purchased a company in Europe to service and undertake the complex documentation involved in barter deals. The first deals involved textiles, fertilizers, motor cars and vehicle assembly kits. Inevitably there were confidence tricksters claiming that they could sell fantastic amounts of Rhodesian tobacco, the worst offenders being those from behind the Iron Curtain.

Research didn't falter either, and growers were delighted with the expansion of plant breeding at Kutsaga during this period. The production of disease-resistant varieties capable of producing higher grades and

---

[1] Peter Armstrong, *Tobacco Spiced with Ginger: The Life of Ginger Freeman* (Harare: Welston Press, 1987).

better-quality leaf looked to a brighter future – whenever that was going to be. But, inevitably, by the mid-1970s, the quality of tobacco had deteriorated, an indication that the war was beginning to take its toll on farmers who spent much of their time in uniform.

From the early 1970s life in the rural areas was dominated by call-ups, with more soldiering than farming being done. In general, the pattern was two weeks away on duty and two weeks at home, during which time it was a race for the farmer to rectify any problems and plan for his next absence. The call-ups for the men in suits in the city were as long as six weeks.

Karoi's busiest spot was around the vicinity of the police station which had become a hive of strategic activity. The old Nissen hut at the side of the rugby pitch was transformed into a WVS canteen to feed hungry men who were sick of living off 'rat-packs' and longed for a home-cooked meal.

It was the lot of the wives of these men not only to keep the farms working but to keep all other necessary services going as well. They rallied to the call of nursing, or feeding troops at the canteen, or joining the Women's Field Reservists.

They manned telephones and clerked in offices. In general, these were the older women, whose children had either flown the nest or were at boarding school. For Nan Maclaurin and Jean Fox it was their second taste of war within twenty years.

The flying club took on a new lease of life as interest was revived. Bert Hacking was the only survivor of the original enthusiasts of 1947. Thea and Doug Cochrane learned to fly, initially as a hobby; when the war escalated they trained for the Police Reserve Air Wing, which included 'spotting' and cross-country flying, flying Cessnas of various sizes. The activity of 'spotting', in

particular, was a dangerous pursuit, with the pilot having to concentrate on both flying and surveillance.

Thea was particularly proud of the occasion when she and George Donald came first in a training course. Others who joined the Air Wing were Cliff Wilcox, Peter Richards and Jim Barker, as well as the Tengwe three – Doug Hoets, Willie Watson and Danie Brink. The war began tentatively at first, and Section 3 was based at Coniston farm where Doug Cochrane was section leader.

One of Karoi's social personalities, Charles Postlethwayt, also a member of the Air Wing, crashed his plane and survived, but the injuries to his face left him badly disfigured. He died not long afterwards of a heart attack.

Charles was a lovely fellow – laid-back, easy-going and gentle. He was another great sportsman, a lover of cricket, tennis and golf. After he'd bought Longueil from Jack O'Hea, he spent a lot of money turning his farm into a private sports club. He created a nine-hole golf course, a beautiful swimming pool, and two tennis courts – gravel and lawn.

Marguerite and Charles were a generous and sociable couple. We young women, all with children clinging to our skirts, played tennis at Longueil every Wednesday and on many occasions attended weekend family parties. The children swam, the fathers played golf and the mothers played tennis, after which there was dancing.

The general pattern of community life during the 1970s changed little – life carried on in much the same way, except that we were kept busier and there was more to occupy our minds.

Travelling was curtailed to certain times of the daylight hours, preferably undertaken in convoys. Social life continued, but dinner guests arrived with their sleeping bags and stayed overnight.

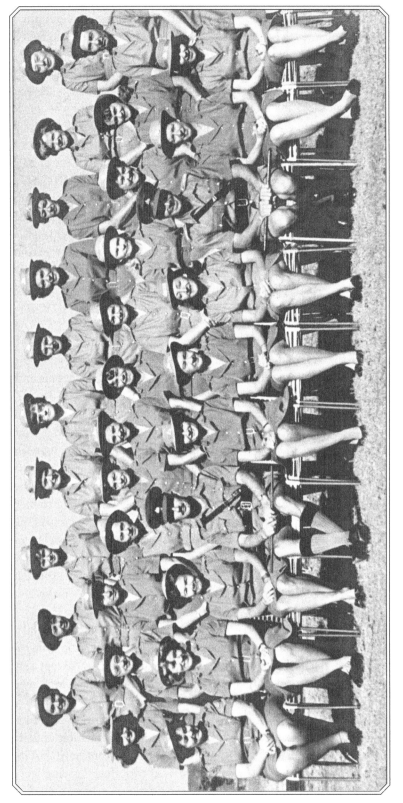

Women's Field Reserve – Karoi, 1969.

Back Row: W/F/Reservists E. F. Moolman; J. D. Straarup; T. J. Cochrane; G. B. Holmes; B. K. Fardell; S. M. Bailey; V. E. Flight; V. N. Howes; P. M. Mason; A. L. D. Postlethwayt.

Centre Row: W/F/Reservists E. E. F. Tapson; J. E. Fox; H. G. B. Kent; A. H. Stacey; J. M. Carpenter; A. M. Maclaurin; K. M. Bennett; J. Ferreira; P. E. Maclachlan; D. E. Marillier; T. J. Black; P. E. Gibson.

Front Row: W/F/Reservists M. Peirson; M. J. Grantham; M. Pope; C/Inspr. B. G. Thomas; W/F/ Reservists R. M. Taylor; D. H. J. Laver; A. A. Donnelly; R/Inspr. I. G. Bryson; W/ F / Reservists A. Bryson, V. P. Hacking.

At a twenty-first birthday celebration taking place on a farm, the festivities came under attack and everyone dived for cover; there were titters of nervous laughter after Andrew Ferreira remarked sarcastically, 'Gee, Mum, you didn't really have to organize a 21-gun salute you know!'

Stuart Maclaurin once again found himself donning a uniform – not quite as grand as his former braids, pips and stripes, but every bit as important. They gave him an office at the police station and from there he conducted the bush war activities in our district.

For a couple of years the Maclaurins and the Herbsts were neighbours when we leased Hunter's Lodge section of Four Winds from John New. I recollect an anxious morning when Stuart's cattleman came running over from Naba to ask for assistance with a cow that was having a difficult birth.

Stuart's herd had become highly pedigreed over the years, and Andries wasn't at all sure that he was qualified to handle anything quite as illustrious as a Maclaurin cow. He felt sure that only the bovine equivalent of a Harley Street gynaecologist would do. However, with some trepidation, he set off with visions of the likely headline in the next day's newspaper: 'Neighbour Sued for Murder of Pedigree Cow'. In the event, he returned home and launched into a vivid description of his morning's work, unable to hide the smug expression of satisfaction on his face. The foetus, in a breech position, had indeed been obstinate, defying all conventional methods of birthing. After hours of manipulating and pulling with ropes, death had seemed probable, if not inevitable.

What a pleasant surprise it was when a calf slithered out, like over-filled toothpaste from its tube, impatient to face the world. Then suddenly, like greased lightning, out popped another – Stuart's mother had been carrying twins, and Andries had saved them!

Nan Maclaurin had a passion for cats, and they draped themselves around every surface of the kitchen. One worried about hygiene. On one visit, we counted 99 – and that didn't include the nocturnal floozies who loitered around the barns.

Nan also had an interest in archaeology and spent time digging around the farm, mostly for fun. During the school holidays she and the children made several interesting discoveries – shards of pottery, tools and flints, including a collection of ancient relics among which were the copper crosses that turned up on farms all over the district in the early years.

This led to a visit from the archaeological department in Salisbury's museum, who confirmed that Naba farm stood on the path of the old Arab trade route. It was at Hunter's Lodge that Andries ploughed up four copper crosses.

Along Maclaurin Road, living directly opposite us, were Neville and Margot Phillips on Avalon. They had swapped their farm in Rusape with Dan Oosthuizen, the original owner of Avalon.

Then, when their neighbours, Paul and Maureen Philip, left Rufaro, Neville bought that farm and immediately sub-divided it, selling 1,000 acres to Joe Dabbs, who named it Star Cross. Joe was not much of a farmer, and it wasn't long before bankruptcy forced him to abandon his farm. His only real claim to fame was when he and his second wife lost their way in the Zambezi Valley for four days.

Eventually the Agricultural Finance Corporation asked Neville to buy back Star Cross. Margot also wanted Neville to buy Naba when it came up for sale after independence, but he wouldn't hear of it, saying that if they carried on like that they would be the only ones left in the district.

203

There is often one 'alien' that is completely out of place in a herd of cattle; they are wild and unpredictable. Neville had one of these genetic throwbacks, which had infiltrated into our herd – easily done when gates are left open at night by a worker who staggers back from a beer-hall in the dead of night.

Several attempts at moving it had proved fruitless, and eventually Andries told Neville that he would shoot it. Soon after this profoundly ominous statement, I found a very anxious Neville Phillips standing on our doorstep one morning. Could he please speak to Andries, it was absolutely imperative.

Neville was so laid-back that it was difficult to imagine anything that would ruffle his feathers. The story was that he had set out that morning, rifle in hand, with the express idea of ridding the herd of this renegade once and for all. Lining up the beast, he took aim and fired. The she-devil dropped in its tracks, but so did two others behind her. Needless to say, he was never allowed to forget that incident.

Weather, as usual, influenced everything. It helped us to differentiate one season from another as time passed. The season 1970/71 turned out to be a drought year, and with it came wild animals, making their way from the Valley looking for water and forage.

One morning, some of our labourers arrived to tell us that they had seen elephant spoor on the farm. Andries laughed and accused them of hallucinating. However, they insisted on showing us the spoor and, sure enough, there were the footprints to prove it – along with steaming mounds of dung and broken fences.

A phone call alerted Parks and Wildlife, who saw that these gentle creatures were gently steered back towards Makuti and the Valley beyond, a distance of at least 150 kilometres.

Lions never stopped being a nuisance, especially where cattle congregate. Brian Johnson (Yawanda) and Peter Pilcher (Laughing Hills) know all about them as their cattle were continually being devoured. Brian's cattle, in particular, were constantly grabbed by these predators, and he lost a fair number from his herd over the years that he lived on Yawanda.

That season, galvanized by hunger, wildlife gained the courage to venture farther and farther down into the heart of Karoi's farming land in search of sustenance. Elephant and lion were seen on Muchbinding, Dudley McKenzie's place, and on Coulson's a lone buffalo and zebra mingled with the cattle, but they were shot because they were creating havoc.

Neville Phillips was down in the Valley on a hunting trip and phoned Margot from the Chirundu Hotel one night.

'How's the shoot going, Nev?'

'Terrible! There's not much here.'

'Well, you'd better get home quickly. It sounds as if we have more game here than in the Valley!'

Saturday mornings on Hunter's Lodge were reserved for cattle-dipping. The herd would be rounded up into the kraal, where they waited, bellowing loudly, impatient to be free. On one very memorable occasion a heifer plunged into the murky, disinfected water and seemed likely to drown.

Noticing its distress, Andries, without much thought, jumped in to help it along, whereupon his cattle boys, not having paid much attention until they heard the boss swearing like a trooper, decided that they had better do the same and plunged in after him.

This left Andries floundering around in very little space trying to save not just one runt of a calf but two panicking herdsmen as well. My children, who were observing the whole performance from the sidelines, were delirious with delight – never had they had such an entertaining Saturday morning, nor could they wait to get home to tell me all about it!

That same year the Council realized that very soon Karoi would be approaching its Silver Jubilee, and despite a war being waged, they were not going to let it pass without some sort of celebration. The Rural Council, Rotarians and the Chamber of Commerce came up with a plan to commemorate Karoi's Silver Jubilee with a fund-raising project that they hoped would result in the building of some retirement cottages in the village.

Plans for the fund-raising were set in place by a committee comprising Bonny Laver, Bruce Humpage, Stuart Maclaurin – and eleven teenage princesses. These young girls were responsible for organizing fund-raising

events over a number of months, such as dances, guest artists, sky-diving exhibitions, dog trials, caravans and vintage-car rallies, all of which would culminate in a spectacular parade of floats, a Retreat Ceremony by the Rhodesian Light Infantry, and a Grand Ball.

The *pièce de résistance* was to come from light aircraft, used in ordinary life as crop-sprayers, that would emit the colours of the Rhodesian flag in a spectacular fly-past.

Unfortunately, the plan went slightly awry, as the predominantly green dye was released rather prematurely and floated gently down on to aghast spectators below, who included a very unimpressed Mrs Wrathall, the President's wife, who, dressed in a white ensemble from head to toe, was soon more appropriately attired in camouflage. She was not amused.

Lyn Hacking was crowned Queen for raising the most money, with Marina Watt and Viv Laver as runners-up. In all, the princesses raised $15,000 between them,

Artwork for the Karoi Silver Jubilee.

and building was able to begin immediately. The success of such a huge project was due not only to excellent organization and advertising but to overwhelming support from the local residents.

Karoi was a pretty little town in those days and kept in immaculate condition, always clean and orderly, but to enhance it for this momentous occasion, Betty Anne Gael had had extra flower beds dug and the place was awash with colour. Bougainvilleas of all colours were planted along the wide-open verges from the corner of Court Road right down to Checkers Motors, all donated by a well-known city gardener.

People came from all over the country to spend time in Karoi and to experience a taste of country life at its very best. The Karoi Hotel and the Twin River Inn, which had suffered economically from the closure of the Zambian border, enjoyed a brief revival as every room was booked up. The long and straight portion of the Great North Road through the Zambezi Valley had been turned into a military landing strip for the forces.

The Lions Club created a well-appointed caravan and camping park along the edge of the dam with an ablution block; the grass was mown, keeping it all in immaculate condition.

At the back of the town, running parallel to the main road, there is now a row of eight cottages in four semi-detached blocks. These are the Jubilee Cottages, the result of the Silver Jubilee fund-raising. Building began almost immediately afterwards, the first occupant moving in in January 1973.

Thirty-seven years later, Number 6 was a typical bachelor pad, the home of one of Karoi's rarer species, who surrounded himself with an accumulation of tools and useful accoutrements and jam-jars full of smaller hardware. Looking around his workshop-cum-lounge, it would have been difficult to associate him with English gentry, but that was exactly his background.

Flossie, as we in Karoi knew him, with his well-pronounced vowels and good manners, epitomized the elite and privileged class into which he was born – despite his shabby appearance and a Spartan home that lacked comfort but was uncompromisingly neat.

At the time of writing, Anthony Hoskyns, to give him his birth name, is a bespectacled, lanky octogenarian who was born into an environment in which his ancestors had lived for generations, where the eldest son of each generation took over as Squire of the Manor.

Over hundreds of years, a village grew from the needs of the estate – the carpenters, smithy, school, stone masons, and so on were simply extensions of the big house, developing in much the same way as the compounds on our farms did, when labourers, mechanics, builders, fencers, gardeners, maids and foremen needed a place to live.

The Hoskyns estate covered two thousand acres of land comprising fifteen farms, all with tenants on them, one of whom paid his rent in cheese. The Hoskyns family of North Perrott, Somerset, stems from an ancient lineage – but, said an unimpressed Flossie, so does half the population of Britain.

'Manor House', although no longer the property of the Hoskyns family, is now a school. It was built in the grand Gothic style, fashionable at the time, of fussy embellishments, with intricate arches, bay windows, chimneys and huge conservatories adorning the façades. In our world of minimalism it would be regarded as being 'a tad over the top'. During the 1920s, the household staff and estate workers numbered twenty-five, and the Squire really did own the village. He built the church, the school and the pub along with all the cottages.

Flossie attended Eton and then went on to Oxford, where he survived four terms. He did his national service and, as the second of four sons, his career was most likely to be found in joining the military. Then, quite by chance, Paget Hoskyns, Flossie's father, met Shalto Barnes, who was then running a mine in Miami, Rhodesia, and living at Waterloo farm. This significant conversation led to Anthony being sent out to Rhodesia after Paget had happened to mention that his son was at a loose end, having been sent down from Oxford.

Work was found for him with Ben Nichols in Banket, but dairying interfered too much with Anthony's weekends, which he liked to spend playing cricket. Later, through Brian McKay, Flossie obtained a job with John Impey, Karoi's acknowledged patron of cricket. A job with John allowed Anthony time to play cricket every weekend.

Mention the word cricket now and Flossie's eyes light up, for it is one of his obsessions. At Eton, and for his home village, he was an acknowledged asset with a bat and ball – indeed, were he to have been born in later times he could have made it his career.

Whether it's on the cricket field, in the snooker room, or on the tennis courts or golf course, Flossie shines. Endowed with great athleticism Flossie missed his true vocation. It must have been genetic, for Flossie's brother, Bill, became a world champion fencer, setting a record for appearances at the Olympic Games.

In 1961 Flossie learned that he had inherited money from a bachelor cousin, and this enabled him to buy Alec Watson's farm, Vermont. He asked Maidments to build him more barns and sheds and employed Tony Phillips, who had married Shalto Barnes's daughter, Philippa, to manage it for him.

During the time of the 1959 Nyasaland rioting, John Impey was away, and an emergency phone call from his wife Helena had everyone rushing over to see what had happened. A four-seater, single-engine plane had crashed on the farm.

It was owned by a man who was trying to get his sick wife to Salisbury for treatment. He had taken off from Blantyre in the late afternoon and in blind panic had lost his way and run out of fuel. On seeing what he thought to be a flat piece of ground, he had attempted to land – only to find that he was confronted with tobacco ridges, which capsized him. The workers had prized open the doors and pulled out the passengers who had miraculously survived.

Brian, with his usual brand of humour, got Flossie to photograph him with one foot placed on the aircraft in the characteristic pose of the big white hunter showing off his trophy!

Flossie grew the first irrigated crop in Karoi – forty acres of wheat. For that he won an ICA award.

Many wondered how Flossie got his nickname. His first car was an Austin A40 with wooden floorboards that leaked dust and was referred to as the 'vacuum cleaner' because it picked up bits of fluff – the female variety!

He fondly recalls that he won many a woman's heart through the good offices of his Mercedes sports car. A later Merc, acquired in 1964, became a familiar and integral part of the Karoi scenery over the next forty-six years.

For a short while after he had sold Vermont farm, Flossie went to live in Sinoia, working for Bruce Humpage who owned John and Bruce Motors in Karoi and had opened a branch in Sinoia.

The cricketers gave him a farewell party and presented him with every form of contraception they could lay their hands on. Then, in an attempt at decency, they added a new set of clothing which he was instructed to don immediately. No sooner was he in Sinoia than he was invited to a 'hat party'. 'What on earth is a hat party?' he asked. 'Oh, you just wear a hat,' someone answered.

Not yet sure to what lengths his Sinoia acquaintances might go, he decided on a compromise. Sewing three hats together, he wore them like a loincloth around his waist with a Dutch Cap on top of his head. Sure enough, everyone at the party was wearing a hat of some description – but they were also fully clothed!

On one April the First – and no doubt it was foolhardy of us, said Margie Herud – Chris, Marion, Adrian and I played an April Fool's joke on Gerald and Trish (Bashford) Hawkesworth.

We arrived after dark with a hot meal for everyone. We stopped at the security fence and waited for the Hawkesworths to let us in, just as if we were expected for dinner. We saw the curtains twitch and open a crack as one of them peered out. Gerald eventually came to unlock the gate and we laughingly piled out and went inside. Trish, who was evidently embarrassed, admitted that there must have been some mistake as neither she nor Gerald remembered inviting us.

At that point we also admitted to our prank and fetched the meal from the car, and subsequently a jolly good impromptu evening was enjoyed by all. We laughed heartily as they told us of their frantic rush to tidy up, wondering desperately what they might be able to feed us on. Now living in New Zealand, they often think of that evening with nostalgia.

On another occasion Margie decided that she would like to go to church with Natalie and Harold Herud one Sunday. It was a time of 'making do' and patching up. It was said that most farms in the country were held

together with the proverbial piece of tyre tubing and Triple X glue! Old-timers prayed like mad that their ancient appliances, clapped-out vehicles and cracking homesteads would outlive them.

So, on this particular Sunday, Margie went over to Maora to get her lift in Nat and Harold's trusty old Volvo – as familiar around Karoi as Flossie's vintage Mercedes. That car, like the house, was going to have to last them a lifetime; it had been patched up and nursed along in order to fulfil that expectation. In fact, the engine was perfect and hummed along sweetly long after the body work had disintegrated. It eventually ended up as a water-pump for Adrian's irrigation.

On this occasion, Margie was sitting on the back seat behind Harold, her feet on a plough disc that patched up the hole in the floor, put there so that the grandchildren couldn't fall through! After they turned off the Magunje road, they hadn't gone more than a few yards when they heard a loud clatter that brought the car to a skidding halt.

They leaped out to see the plough disc spinning down the tar and into the bush – if there had been a car behind them it would have caused quite a stir! Meanwhile, Margie had become covered in a layer of dust. Typically, Nat thought that it was hilarious and cautioned her not to go the same way as the disc.

After the service, they were just beginning to enjoy the conviviality of a social cup of tea when Simon, the caretaker, came to tell them that they had a leak and he had put a bucket underneath the tank to catch the fuel pouring out: the disc must have made a hole in it when it fell through. Wasting no more time they leaped into the car and sped off to Maora, this time saying an extra prayer or two in the hope that the Volvo would once again beat all the odds.

As if Karoi needed something more to set tongues wagging, there was an incident for which I was responsible and which a friend said made me a living legend.

One morning, a fresh-faced police constable arrived on the farm and handed me a summons to appear in court. Being quite used to my troublesome ways, Andries remarked with a sigh, 'So what have you done now?'

A day earlier, three Standard Three girls had rushed out of their classroom at close of school, sobbing in distress as though their hearts were broken. 'I wonder who's died,' I thought.

One of those girls was my daughter, and it turned out that the new teacher, a Miss Hammon, had accused all three of them of lying and cheating. Now, those are ugly words to fling around in class without getting to the bottom of the story, and I was incensed, especially when hearing about the treatment she had dished out to them, and more particularly after the guilty party eventually decided to own up to the charge four days later.

However, it was too late. The next morning, having simmered overnight to boiling point, I descended on the school like a prairie grouse in full flight. I stormed angrily into the classroom to confront the harridan who had abused my child and two of her friends, leaned over the desk and was about to grab her by her long black hair. She let out a blood-curdling shriek that could have woken every soul in Christendom and sent everyone scuttling off in all directions.

Needless to say, the kids who were brave enough to hang around were delirious with excitement; what a tale they could tell when they arrived home. But by then the story had inevitably been exaggerated ten-fold and I had almost become a mass murderer. You could have soured milk with the disapproving expressions that emanated from the po-faced, sanctimonious… – all of them standing on their high horses in judgment.

It was an incident that could have been avoided if it had been handled judiciously, but the headmaster, Pat Taylor, was a high and mighty 'grey man'. Nevertheless, I confess fairly and squarely to being a woman of infamy. For the record, contrary to what the children may have reported, I categorically deny harming, hitting or inflicting pain on said teacher.

A few days later, Andries and I drove into town to attend a tobacco sale. Word had travelled quickly, and as we walked on to the floors, several auctioneers, buyers and grower's reps all took a step back in false alarm, arms held up in front of their faces as if in self-defence. Serves me right, but I had to laugh.

That same week Dave Lazelle's new wife stepped out of her car and slapped a man who had taken her parking place. In her defence, she was pregnant, but there must have been something in the air that week.

Britain continued to treat Rhodesians as if they were headstrong adolescents. It was inevitable that, as time rolled on, the bush war, producing its atrocities, tragedies and sufferings, would have an effect on individuals and on the community. Like pieces of strong elastic we had begun to run out of stretch and it took its toll. When faced with reality we, the 'white supremacists', had to face the fact that we were losing the battle.

It was a bitter pill to swallow.

25. Karoi Library

Access to reading matter was of real importance in remote bush settlements long ago, and a library was deemed as imperative as a wireless set. The wireless, with hardly more than one channel to listen to, not only gave pleasure but provided education as well, and time did not hang quite so heavily on hands once the day's work was done. For the bachelor farmer or prospector it made all the difference in life.

Modern technology in its various forms – television, computer and Kindle – have almost replaced books and wireless sets, but not quite, thankfully. Fifty years ago and before, to be without a book or a radio was almost as unthinkable as being without the digital boxes of tricks used to-day – devices that vulgarise not only every modern home but often every room as well. It is a very courageous person who consciously decides to do without them.

Yet it is people who make a community, and the early settlers always had time to visit their neighbours, time to play card games, time to converse over a few convivial drinks at the Club, time to dance to music from the wind-up gramophone, and time to play badminton. It could perhaps be said that life was fuller then and that folk were the better for it, as society in general had to set about making its own pleasures.

To start with, the Road Motor Service was able to fill the gap that was created by the settlers being miles apart – not only through their efficient and faithful role as couriers of essential supplies but also because they were able to bridge the divide between families, friends and businesses in the outside world through mail deliveries.

The arrival of the mail was an occasion looked forward to with great excitement.

What would it bring? Letters from loved ones abroad or just from Sinoia? Rolls of weekly and daily newspapers and periodicals? Sometimes there was a tantalising batch of linen-bound books, strapped up on loan from the Queen Victoria Memorial Library in Salisbury. What a tremendous and valuable service that was.

The story of the Karoi library deserves a chapter of its own simply because it was at one time of such importance and featured so significantly within the fledgling community of Karoi. It topped the list of priorities when the Women's Institute planning committee was formed.

A so-called 'library' started with a few books on a cupboard shelf in the pole'n'daga hut that was built in 1946/47 as the humble beginnings of a social sports club. Before long it had outgrown that space and something far more substantial was needed – it now occupied an entire cupboard, which was housed in a corner of the new Farmers' Co-op, an insignificant building at the time.

It was not long before the library had to make more moves to other venues, before finally settling permanently on a piece of ground between the council offices and the Dutch Reformed Church Hall and Rectory. The huge sigh of relief from the Library Committee could be heard far and wide, for its journey to its resting place had taken fifteen years.

On the day that Mr Mitchell revealed the proposed layout for the town in 1948, the WI ladies had allowed themselves the luxury of buying a plot in readiness for the day when they had gathered enough capital to construct a library building. They had already given an interest-free loan of £200 towards the building of the community hall (the Gwen Scrase Memorial Hall) on condition that they be able to use one of the rooms as a temporary base, but before long they were on the move again – into a storage room at the back of Grantham's grocery shop in the Fraser Building. Mrs Russell later ran a tea-room there, but sadly this also proved to be of short duration when David Grantham died suddenly of a heart attack. David Grantham will be remembered for many reasons, but in the context of the library he will be remembered as a marvellous raconteur who had a gift for telling a story well.

Finally, in November 1962, Ronnie Thornton of Maidments began building the new Women's Institute library on the stand that the WI had acquired years earlier. Council declared that they would donate the land in view of the fact that the WI was a non-profit-making organisation and that the library would be enjoyed by the whole community.

By November of the following year, with the help of a grant from the State Lotteries, the books made their final move to rest proudly on wide, sturdy shelving within the walls of a building that then seemed spacious and roomy. No more cramped conditions – or so they thought. Over the next two decades two more extensions went up. At a celebration ball to mark the opening, each guest was asked to bring along five new books instead of paying for a ticket.

By the time Karoi was in its death throes, thirty-eight years later, the library staff had catalogued 22,000 books, and they proudly lapped up the cry of short-stayers, who, having left Karoi, never failed to mention that the main thing they missed was the library.

Duplicate copies of books were kept to start a library in Chikangwe township. Rooms were found in the Social Welfare Centre, shelving was erected, and a young student volunteered to keep the library open for a couple of hours a week in return for being able to use it as a quiet place in which to study.

However, within a year all the books had disappeared. The concept of borrowing and returning a book in good order did not seem to be understood and appreciated in that part of town. After that, duplicate copies were passed on to Karoi High School, where they were gratefully received.

The Karoi Women's Institute Library.

Over time, the library staff have notched up a tale or two to tell. Taking note of readers' tastes in books is as interesting as it is enlightening. The solidly-built, macho-type who developed a taste for Mills and Boon romances is just one curiosity.

Equally alarming was Ivy Curran's taste in the most bloodthirsty crime stories ever written. Ninety-year-old Ivy exuded shyness and timidity, but get her into the library and she would make a determined beeline for the crime and mystery section. She had a voracious desire for lurid and graphic murder. Not content with a gentle Agatha Christie, she would head straight for Patricia Cornwell, a former pathologist, whose graphic illustrations of the deed would have shocked even Doctor Crippen!

The Methodist Minister, Gordon Webster, mild and gentle, loved non-fiction crime stories, being interested in the psychological reasons behind the crimes. Then there was the farmer who was quite unaware of his bottled-up aggression as he strolled up to the desk and slammed down his books with such force that we assumed we must have upset him in some way. He would then saunter off, a beatific smile on his face to browse among the shelves.

My great favourite was Rene Grey, who enjoyed books with depth. 'My dear, I have to have something that I can get my teeth into.' So I slipped her a banned book that was supposed to have been hidden on the back shelves, out of reach and out of sight in case there was a surprise visit from the Censorship Board.

A week later, I anxiously awaited her reaction and she stood before me none too pleased. With her lips puckered as if she had just sucked on a lemon, and quite unlike her usual, friendly self, she carefully placed the book down on the desk. What a wealth of meaning in that gesture, I thought; she's

going to give me a real telling off. Drawing herself up, she pronounced loudly and in disgust, 'Hmm, very taken with his penis, wasn't he?'

It's amazing how well one gets to know people through their visits to the library. Penny-pinchers would sell their soul rather than pay a fine for the late return of their books. Fortunately they were lost among the generous, who far out-numbered them.

When the hard times began, hardback books were well-nigh impossible to come by, but it was to that kind majority that we turned for donations of best-sellers. It was then, too, that we saw the benevolence of the community who valued a good book.

Nevertheless, the intransigents were never satisfied: the dizzy blonde clutched seventeen books to her bosom and declared peevishly that we simply didn't have anything she could read. The cheerful and good-humoured were vastly appreciated and the unreliable and untrustworthy were irritating. Books – usually on a waiting list – would be left in waiting rooms all over the country and, amazingly, were returned to us by various receptionists or just by kind folk who said they would be passing through Karoi and would drop them off.

Members and non-members found the library a convenience for many reasons. It wasn't your average quiet, funereal institution of learning, where words were uttered in whispered or dulcet tones; no, it was probably the noisiest and friendliest place in the world.

Wedding plans were discussed there. Friends 'rendezvoused' there. Parcels were left there for collection by others. We spent hours listening to grievances and, God help us, dished out advice. We were guardians of confidences, very often taking on the role of counsellors. We witnessed wills and signed forms, acted as care workers, and drove geriatrics home when they had been left behind like forgotten parcels.

I once found a pension cheque denominated in foreign currency that had been used as a bookmark in a book that was returned. Working in the library was part of community service, an extra kindness that made up another aspect of rural life. For sheer entertainment, from the sublime to the ridiculous, it was worth every voluntary hour given.

On a number of occasions when we did a stock-take we would discover that whole volumes of books by well-known authors were missing. Among them were authors such as Peter Cheney, Agatha Christie and Louis L'Amour. Someone knew their worth as out-of-print books, but his or her identity was a mystery that was never solved.

When the cost of major repairs and maintenance became more than the kitty could stand, it was usually to one of the husbands that we turned. Ronnie Thornton was a really good friend of the library over the years and took care of most of the repair work.

Independence in 1980 brought tremendous changes. Government grants came to an end, as did the importation of hardback books, which became unavailable. As a result, our shelves filled up with paperbacks, which very quickly fell apart.

Natalie Herud, head librarian for many years, had a very obliging husband in Harold, who began to repair these lightweight substitutes. Each week he would cart away a whole suitcase of broken books to repair. After Harold died, Dusty Laver took over that task and then, when he became terminally ill, Alf and Joan Smith and I and my husband, Mike, went to him for lessons, but it was an onerous and thankless task trying to keep these books in one piece. Sooner or later they fell to bits again; like

darning socks, we were eventually repairing the repairs.

One of the library staff's biggest irritations was the irascible ninety-seven-year-old Mr Weigall; hearts dropped when Ed, his son, deposited him on the door-step. Throughout the morning, he would give us a piece of his mind. More often than not, it was also left to us to taxi him home when lock-up time arrived at one o'clock.

Somehow one couldn't blame his family for trying to forget that he was there, but he wasn't easy to overlook. He had a mixture of several disagreeable traits, and when he eventually reached the age of 102 we reckoned he had managed it on sheer fury, but not before he had scolded us all most soundly over the years – the same complaints and criticisms each week, all in outrageous anger.

'Why don't you have a phone?' he would shout. 'They do in England, and they have reliable clocks, too!' England was the perfect place to be. Didn't we know that libraries in England were free? 'Why, then,' I mumbled under my breath, 'are you not there?!'

Then came the morning when I reminded him, as gently and as diplomatically as I could, that his subs had been due for the last ten months. He was not short of a bob or two, we knew that. Enraged and amazingly agile for a man of his vintage, he jumped out of his chair, as geriatrics sometimes do, almost leapt over the desk and started to bang his fist – my goodness, nothing wrong with his fist! – shouting that I should know better than to ask him for money.

How could he pay his library subs? 'Don'cha know I've just had to pay twenty million [Zimbabwe] dollars for a new digital box for my TV? I've nothing left for the library. Anyway,' he said for the umpteenth time, 'in England libraries are free.'

Looking back, it was one of the most

hilarious mornings of my life. Natalie Herud and I could hardly contain ourselves; we laughed until we cried. However, I did have the last word. When the old man died, his son asked me to play the hymns at the funeral service, which I did as slowly and as fulsomely as possible, spinning out the moment of truth.

On the whole, we enjoyed the old-timers who enlivened our moments and regaled us with 'tales of yore' and their good old-fashioned opinions. A couple of old favourites were Pat and Peggy Bashford. They would come for Natalie's squishy egg sandwiches after an hour of shopping on a Friday morning, bringing with them their gentle, self-deprecating sense of humour and lively conversation. Pat could never get over the rising cost of things: he told us that when he had started farming he could buy an entire trailer for $47 but that morning he had had to pay the same sum for just for one bolt.

For many of the old-timers the library took the place of the club. It was probably the only time from one week to another that they ever left their homes or spoke to another human being other than their domestic servants.

I watched one morning as Una McKenzie's Mercedes reversed slowly down the driveway between the culverts and across the tar road, coming to rest on the verge on the opposite side. The thing was, Una wasn't anywhere near it – she was inside grabbing a book in double-quick time, which was her habit. She never did put the handbrake on. It was a case of stop … leap out … dash in … grab the first book … go. It was just as well that her car could manage without her!

The post-independence years gave us more entertainment on the whole. Some thought that our garden was worth using as a beautiful venue for photographs. A wedding party arrived one morning in all their finery – the bride, dark and dusky and beautifully dressed in the traditional white garb of a virgin bride. Hovering in the background were half a dozen bridesmaids and guests, all beautifully and traditionally attired.

I enquired as to their needs. The groom approached rather nervously and asked if I would permit them to use the library grounds as a backdrop for their wedding photos and would I join them in a group photo. Perhaps they felt obliged to ask. I told them to go ahead but politely declined being snapped. However, they insisted.

Somewhere in a sitting-room in Chikangwe, no doubt occupying pride of place, there must be a wedding photo of a charming, elegantly dressed black family, among whom stands a dowdy old white woman, looking awkward and very much out of place!

We once experienced a hit-and-run within six metres of the library door when Siem Timmer's bakkie was robbed of all his wages as we calmly looked on, unable to grasp what was happening before our very eyes. Siem was inside choosing a book.

Then life became political, and visits from the police started. They began to check up on us, convinced that we were a den of political iniquity. They were never able to disguise their deep distrust of us, particularly on a Friday morning when we made a real occasion of it and the sound of laughter resounded down the road. We went along with all the bluff – enquiries as to how they could join the library, etc.

We showed them around every nook and cranny, handed out the relevant forms to fill in – what a charade! We even gave them tea and cake to keep them sweet, and much to their chagrin they never could fathom out the cause of the levity that hid our supposedly nefarious business.

After 2002 the community began to slowly fade away: folk left and library membership declined with them.

The Women's Institute 50th Anniversary Celebration at the Library.

Bert Hacking, Ron Thornton, Margaret Fussell.

Piet and Nitsa Groot, Alf Smith, Ko Voorn.

One evening, some months after leaving the farm for good to live in Harare, I received a bizarre telephone call. The caller sounded rather desperate – as well he might when he had explained that he was locked in the library.

'What on earth do you mean, locked in the library?' I said.

'Yee-es, true, Medem. Please come and let me out,' he pleaded.

'I presume you mean the Karoi library,' I replied laconically.

'Yes indeed, Medem.'

'Well, I have to tell you that I am no longer living in Karoi, and I'm speaking to you from Harare. Anyway, how on earth did you manage to get locked up?'

'Medem, I came to exchange my books this morning,' he said. 'I sat down in the children's section and fell asleep. When I woke up it was dark and the library was locked.'

'So how did you find my phone number?'

'It was written on a list inside the drawer. Medem, please help me. My phone is about to die.' And with that the line went dead.

It was one of those hopelessly wet Zimbabwean nights, when phones go out of order at the first drop of rain, storms were raging throughout the entire country, and at the time the availability of fuel was but a distant memory. However, with perseverance

I eventually managed to raise my son, Andrew (Melek) Herbst, who was still living in Karoi, and against all odds he managed to get the Body in the Library (with apologies to Agatha Christie) released.

That was my swansong after forty-five years in Karoi. It couldn't have been more fitting or original: and, unlike Miss Marple, I never will let on who locked the body in the library.

From the start, the library had been run by an independent committee of WI ladies. One by one they died or left the district and other members took over. Over fifty years, much-beloved names have been associated with the library. Without doubt the longest-serving were Maureen Grantham, Natalie Herud, Tolleen Smith and Marion Thompson. Then there was Myra Kennedy, Joyce Ferguson, Joan Smith and me, and then came Monica Royston, Sylvia Versveld, Jill Thornton and June Veck.

In March 2010, I and two members of the last Executive Committee (the WI is now defunct) – the former National Treasurer and National President – travelled out to Karoi from Harare and cleared out an overgrown, neglected and very diminished Karoi Library. It resembled the state of much of the rest of the country.

26. The Arts in Karoi

From the very start Karoi always seemed to have a tremendous flow of creative energy about it. I have heard it said that there was more talent per square acre in the Urungwe than anywhere else in the country, and it came in a mixture of genres.

Perhaps living close to nature triggers an exceptional urge to recreate, as the soul is stirred into replicating all that surrounds us. The veld of the Urungwe with its many delightful quirky vegetative mysteries never failed to amaze and tantalise us.

A tumbleweed blown by a September wind dances its way over miles and miles of territory. Deserted swathes of landscape blackened by veld fires are miraculously transformed within days as if by the wave of a wand. Unbelievably parched matter allows a mass of seeds to germinate and grow, dressing cracked, arid soil that has felt no moisture for months with a layer of wild flowers and vegetation.

Throughout the months, God reminds us of His presence. There aren't many atheists who live in rural areas: they live too close to nature to ignore its greatness. The wonders of the earth unconsciously permeate one's being and, as each season follows the next and one becomes part of its changing pattern, the soul is stirred with each change of colour and sound. It's a poor soul who hasn't listened to the sound of exploding tree pods punctuating the cold, still, winter nights, spinning through the air and clattering noisily on the farmhouse's tin roof.

While Europe's seasons are pronounced and defined, Zimbabwe's change in subtle ways. Dry leaves and grass are designed by nature to show the springtime blossoms off to their best advantage – the coral lucky-bean trees; the delicate shades of lemon, white and pink Bauhinias delight the eye. Tabebuias burst into flower with eye-catching yellow trumpets – a brief explosion of brilliant hues more glorious than gold. Early jacarandas intermingle in their soft purple majesty. The last of the season's royalty, the flamboyants, spread their branches proudly and splendidly, holding candelabras of deep crimson and amber, reminding us that the seasonal rains and Christmas are almost upon us.

Everything has a season and its time of joy, so is it any wonder that the farmer who isn't even aware of his artistic soul stands obediently to attention at the request of his wife. Every demand is met, for it is more fun to construct something worthy that will gladden the eye than build a chicken run.

As time passed and the farms gradually became more established, artistic creativity showed up best in the beautiful gardens that were created and in the design and style of architecturally pleasing, renovated homesteads with interior decorations of every style and period. Even when resources were meagre, originality never failed when an innovative mind took over.

On her bush ramblings, Denny Gaisford once discovered an unusually malformed tree stump, shaped by a mass of boles, that immediately suggested to her the feathered body of an ostrich. With the assistance of the farm welder who shaped two long skinny legs, a long skinny neck with head and beak, she created an ostrich, which still stands on her veranda today.

Rae Hunt didn't like uniformity when she was renovating her house in Karoi, so she told the builder not to build straight walls. Hilary Macmillan put together a cluster of separate rondavels to form her homestead and wove it together with a green garden, most of it ground cover.

Rose and Peter van Breda built a spectacular double-storeyed African house, thatched and beamed with material off the farm. An intricate design in wood on different levels, amid a setting of exotic, thick-leafed plants, cycads and ornamental bananas, Strelitzia and palms, it was the epitome of a tropical paradise.

Elaine and Dave Roper both admired the Spanish look, which they later replicated more boldly in Harare. Mary Mulder's new house was an imposing double-storeyed Cape Dutch homestead.

The majority, though, were the typical rambling colonial homesteads, sometimes roughly built by the farm builder but comfortable and homely – the farmer is lucky enough not to have to worry about a lack of space. On the whole, farmers enjoyed exercising that side of their make-up – it made a change from building a new dip tank or a rabbit hutch for the kids.

Water was often a problem, particularly in the early days before dam-building became the norm. Janet Deere – whose Karoi life took her to live on many different rented farms until she and Eynon bought a home in the village – always managed to create a beautiful garden where ever she landed. Gardening was her *raison d'être* and without it she could not have survived the life she led. Her successors were always the lucky ones, as they inherited a ready-made garden.

There is nothing more soul-destroying than watching a garden slowly wither away for lack of water. In a bad year, severe droughts empty dams and dry up boreholes, and often the gardens are the last to be saved, for people and cattle come first. But following good rains, the urge to plant is revived and the task begins again.

Farmers, along with their wives, have often had to struggle against discouragement, but most never doubted the vocation that haunted their lives and led them to wrestle with nature time after time, always telling themselves that next year would be better – and usually it was.

But the years have tested our patience, and I have lost count of the times I have started a garden from scratch. Occasionally, in a rush of renewed vigour, the lady will add a little more of interest – features such as lily-ponds, pergolas, arches, terraces and miniature bridges add an extra dimension to the overall scene. Finally the garden is more magnificent than ever!

The bush war did have its positive sides: it limited the size of gardens. As farm life became more and more dangerous in the early 1970s, perimeter farms in particular became encased in high security fences, which halted the surreptitious enlarging of 'the yard' that every farmer's wife was guilty of. She had access to extra labour when the schedule allowed, she had all the space in the world, and, in many cases, her garden was her abiding and sole interest. So the park-like gardens became constrained by the fences that enclosed them.

After independence, funds for water supplies were once again made available and many new boreholes were drilled and dams constructed. Improved technology made it possible for boreholes to be drilled quicker and deeper than ever before. The deepest borehole in the district could be found on Chiltington farm: it was 300 feet deep but still produced only a pathetic dribble.

The area immediately surrounding the homestead is punctured like a kitchen colander after numerous failed attempts of different owners to find a good supply of water came to an end. Only after a good-sized dam was built on the Nyamanda river between Chiltington and Nyamanda farms, as late as 1993, was a thousand acres of land transformed into an irrigated paradise.

From this modern, post-independence facility came many further supplies of good irrigation. The crops benefited, as did the establishment of beautiful gardens. Margaret Gifford, however, seemed to succeed without copious amounts of water, winning the garden competitions year after year despite shortages.

Talent manifested itself more particularly in floral artistry, drama and music, not to mention the finer arts of pencil-and-ink drawing and painting in watercolours and oils.

Most of these artists were women; a few, very few, were men. Some husbands were lucky enough to discover their aesthetic side: David Roper worked with his hands to sculpt in clay, and some very masterly pieces he turned out, too.

Two of David Roper's sculptures.

Essie Esterhuizen wore many hats: besides farming, he bred roses, and with his wife, Soama, turned out a rough and naïve kind of pottery in different glazes baked in home-built ovens at the kitchen door. They also kept sheep for wool, and wove thick rugs and thinner materials for curtains. Both were extremely creative individuals, their home becoming a showcase for all they produced.

Peter Veck, son-in-law of Chiefie Maid-

ment, loved to grow exotic plants, orchids in particular. He used to show them off when they were at their best – on the shop counter, for everyone to admire. His artistry even went as far as gift-wrapping, and he often outdid the present within.

Peter participated in all the local flower shows, both in floral art and the single-bloom section of horticulture. In addition to this, he enjoyed drama and singing, having an excellent tenor voice that led to his being offered principal parts in musicals. He had been in a number of musical productions in Salisbury before arriving in Karoi. He was also a nifty ballroom dancer: his artistic talents showed up in many guises.

In all the clubs, whether within the bounds of gardening, floral arts or painting, enthusiasts learned as much as they were willing to absorb. Some found that they excelled, and they devoted as much time and effort as they could to serious improvement.

As the bush war intensified in the early 1970s, the Karoi ladies' art group gathered strength: many will tell you that art is a very calming pastime. Their first venue was at Shawnigan, Maureen Grantham's farm. Then they moved to Rosemary Slight's home on Church Street, and she was sometimes able to find a good teacher. Over subsequent months and years it expanded more and more to form a faithful bevy of enthusiasts.

During the 1980s and 1990s, watercolourists and artists painting in oils became numerous. They were mostly the older ladies whose children had flown the nest and who found that they had time on their hands. It was a soothing escape from boredom, but many discovered a true skill.

Charl Moller, one-time teacher at the school, and Forest Whenman had above-average artistic talent – they were naturals who went from strength to strength, eventually making art a successful career. In recent

Two of Joyce Walsh's paintings.

years, James McKay, Vivian Wesson and Sue Bishop, who paints under the pseudonym 'Soo', have all emerged as excellent artists.

Of the 1947 originals, Joan Newhook was probably the first who could claim to be a good artist; Liz Searle was also one and Joyce Walsh another. Joyce had been a very successful commercial artist in Bulawayo before marrying Peter in the 1950s.

She was a very accomplished watercolourist and painted landscapes – some fine ones of Kariba and the farm – but preferred to concentrate on flowers, which were her main interest. One year a number of her paintings were accepted by the Society of Botanical Artists for an exhibition at their annual showing in London.

Floral arranging was spearheaded by Betty-Anne Gael, supported by Joan van Heerden. They were succeeded by Kath Quail, who became the doyenne of floral artistry in Karoi. Kath had an array of enthusiastic acolytes, all of whom had great talent in this genre and kept the garden and flower shows going for many years.

Janet Deere, Elaine Roper, Daphne Royston, Veronica Flight, Elise Oosthuizen, Steph de Haas and Francis Pilcher all won accolades in various shows over the years.

Then the next generation, the young wives of the district, took their place, and a new crop of talent emerged in Debbie Black, Mandy Roper and Moira Saywood, to name just a few.

The art group grew and diminished as the community changed, which it did frequently. Its nucleus was made up of Maureen Grantham, Denny Gaisford, Rosemary Slight, Tawny Stidolph, Moira Saywood, Rose van Breda, Audrey Smit, Nesmay Laing, Raie Wells and Dini Voorn. They held exhibitions in the Club and sold much of their work.

Towards the last years, just before the collapse of the community, the art group gathered at the home of Rose van Breda. She made art fun and found good teachers who were willing to come out to Karoi. Sarah Fynn was one, the mother of Tamsin Barker. The ladies loved these lessons and had a wonderful time together, but one lesson will always remain etched in their minds.

During the 1990s, a Government Medical Officer arrived from Holland to take up a position at Karoi Hospital for a second spell. She was Dr Agnes Kalkoen, and accompanying her for this second term was her artist husband, Cornelius. He was well known as a contemporary artist in the Netherlands.

Rose was quick to draw him into the art club, asking him if he would give a lesson on figure drawing, with particular emphasis on the male body. Cornelius accepted with alacrity, saying that he himself would be the model. Needless to say, for these conservative ladies who were used only to painting vases of flowers and scenic views of the bush, it was a rude awakening.

As Cornelius divested himself of all his clothing, exposing his body in its entirety to a group of horrified farmers' wives, the reactions were varied. Even Dini Voorn, used to the liberal attitudes of Amsterdam and its red-light district, had to swallow twice and felt herself getting hot flushes when confronted with this spectacle.

For most of the ladies, the primary objective of drawing simply flew out of the window; others painted from memory as they concentrated firmly on the face, assiduously avoiding the lower half of the body. Only afterwards did a couple of the girls admit that they had noticed that Cornelius had not been circumcised! Nesmay Laing drew the model and just left out the genital area. It was to everyone's credit that no one fainted; all kept a stiff upper lip and later admitted that Rose had outdone herself this time; but hilarity was let loose afterwards!

There were others, such as Cathy Robertson, who stumbled on a love of photography, an art form that she discovered when she produced some marvellous shots of wildlife down in the Zambezi Valley. She was able to use them to illustrate her husband Kevin's book about the buffalo, an animal of which he was particularly fond.[1] Kevin was our resident veterinarian, who found time to farm, practise his chosen profession, write a book, and become a qualified safari hunter and guide.

The list of clubs to join in Karoi was endless. One could learn to ice cakes in the most professional manner, take dress-making lessons with Elise Oosthuizen, who had not only nimble fingers but green ones too. Her garden was always a joy of colour. As was her baking: cakes, tarts, rusks, jams, biscuits and crafts.

She turned out most of the local wedding cakes and, as if that wasn't enough, opened a cottage industry which she ran in tandem with her tea-room-cum-restaurant, and many a tourist and traveller had occasion to be thankful for a much-needed stop at Spring Fever, just north of the town.

One of the most audacious and ambitious projects to come out of the artistic talents of Karoi took place in 1990 when a promotional idea was formed, on behalf of the Zimbabwe Protea Association, by Cecily Saywood. The plan was to bring Zimbabwe-grown proteas to the attention of a commercial world of international flower traders, who thought that life started and ended in Holland.

Cecily's initial aspirations had not been quite as grandiose as they turned out, but the more she thought about it, the more ambitious it became. Armed with courage, she approached the venerable members of

---

[1] Kevin Robertson, *Africa's Most Dangerous* (Huntington Beach, CA: Safari Press, 2007).

the Royal Horticultural Society in Britain to ask for a stand on the famous and very prestigious Chelsea Flower Show, but she was told that she was a month too late.

However, she persisted and was eventually offered a 'flower arrangement' stand, which turned out to be a prominent site in the main marquee, far more substantial than she had bargained for, added to which was a comment that they were pleased to have 'Zimbabwe' competing in the show. So the first hurdle was overcome, and the Saywoods, along with the ZPA, were elated. The association offered cash and prize protea blooms.

Cecily chose her team carefully: Karoi's internationally recognised Kathy Quail as designer; Moira Saywood, Cecily's daughter-in-law, also from Karoi and also a gifted floral artist; Pam Harris as art judge; and Joyce Oliver, the PRO of the ZPA, as well as Cecily and Ken, her husband.

None of them had any inkling of the trials that lay ahead of them, which was probably just as well, for the dye was cast and there was no looking back. Criticism and scrutiny from the international floral world would be on them. Connoisseurs descend on Chelsea in their thousands over a few days in May every year to gaze in admiration at the artistry on display, both in design and horticultural skill.

The team decided that their design should be natural – taking a small piece of the Zimbabwean bush and transferring it, as if by magic, to a tiny spot in England. It was to take the form of a kopje, with all its interesting rock formations, nooks and crannies, within which natural vegetation of grasses, plant life and wild proteas would be growing. Magic indeed.

I was lucky enough to see it. It did look authentic – so realistic, in fact, that Queen Elizabeth, when she was taken round, asked the girls, 'How on earth did you cart all those granite rocks to Chelsea from Zimbabwe?' In fact, they weren't rocks at all but were made of papier mâché, so cleverly fashioned that they did indeed look natural.

The whole design was set up on the farm and then perfected. Once the girls were satisfied, they took each rock and made a mould of it, numbering each item according to a plan that would enable them to rebuild it at Chelsea. They carted every single piece of material they needed – each stick, stem, protea bloom and clump of grass, plus a large ant-eaten log – from Glenellen farm. They carefully co-ordinated the colours, matching flowers to the orange, grey and white reflected in the granite.

When packed, the whole consignment weighed a mere one and a quarter tonnes. In terms of its overall size, that was nothing.

Once their design had been prepared, they turned their minds to the cost of transport, bearing in mind that Zimbabweans had foreign-currency constraints in place at that time. That didn't help when the hiccups began.

An original offer of free transport by the air force was withdrawn, and the consignment had to be sent commercially. Once in London it was impounded by Customs because the addressee failed to claim it, on top of which there was a charge of £1,000 for demurrage.

Then they discovered that pieces were missing, but demurrage could be charged only on the whole consignment, so the bureaucracy and red-tape continued. Cecily borrowed a truck and found the warehouse for bonded consignments and, with the help of the forklift driver, found what she was looking for; with that, the fee was dropped.

From then on, the real work began. Joining their co-competitors on the show site, their days began at 6.00 a.m. and ended at 10.00 p.m. as they settled down to rebuilding their display.

For years, foreign-currency constraints had controlled and stymied all that Rhodesians and Zimbabweans sought to do. They curtailed all projects, so that we became masters of making do and cutting corners. The Chelsea group will never forget how they had to salvage, steal and rescue anything that looked useful.

They combed tips and refuse dumps for containers that looked as if they would hold water. They borrowed wheelbarrows and carted sand, donated to them by other stall-holders, receiving great kindness from everyone. Intabex directors, Roy and Phil Ingram, gave considerable assistance by allowing them the use of the Tabex flat in Wokingham, which eased the added strain of accommodation costs.

All their hard work, however, was

Kathy Quail's floral exhibit
that won a Gold Medal for Zimbabwe.

rewarded when the judges awarded them a Gold Medal. The Zimbabweans became well known at the show, and the workmen were as proud of their Gold Medal achievement as the ladies themselves. Kathy Quail had also entered her own floral arrangements, three in all, independently.

The National Farmers' Union (UK) offered them assistance, and Julia Clements, the well-known author of many books on flower arranging, congratulated them on their achievement, as did the Queen.

The team had not only put Zimbabwe and its proteas on the map but Karoi as well. They continued to exhibit for two more years, after which the costs became prohibitive without government assistance, which had never been forthcoming from the start.

All the early initiatives came from the Women's Institute, who had the advantage of numbers and had become expert organisers by the 1960s. So when it was proposed that the district should have a flower show, it was left to the WI to organise it. Joan Newhook, the most artistic and creative member, was the obvious choice as convener, and Maureen Philip and others eagerly assisted.

The month was February and the year 1960, and it was such a success that it continued to be arranged by the WI for a few more years. Then they relinquished the task and handed it over to a separate, independent committee of floral artists.

Betty Anne Gael, the sister of Chris Wilkinson, had started up the Floral Art Group in 1968, just before leaving Karoi to live in Salisbury when her husband, Chris, one of the local agronomists, was transferred.

This led to a brief hiatus until Kath Quail reopened it in 1972. During that time, Kath held regular meetings and demonstrations, but workshops were held in abeyance until she had qualified as a floral arts judge in

Cecily Saywood at the Glenellen stand
at the Chelsea Flower Show, 1991.

1995, after which she held six-week sessions of weekly floral art lessons until 2003.

Even then, she continued to teach in her flower room, which was well equipped and large enough to accommodate eight students at a time. Among them were a couple of enthusiastic black ladies who arrived by taxi every week to take part.

Kath said it was very rewarding to be appreciated by her past pupils when two of them wrote to thank her for teaching them skills they have used successfully in their present lives after losing their farms. One was Steph de Haas, widow of Arnold Bathurst, who left to live in South Africa and started a florist's shop, later winning a top award for her boutique.

Another, more recent, grateful former pupil is Debbie Black (née Phillips), who now resides in the UK. Richard, her husband, landed himself an excellent job as head gardener for a sheik, and Debbie has been able to use her artistic skills in flower arranging in her employer's mansion. She makes up to thirty arrangements daily – more, if there are functions – and has frequently been commended for her creativity.

Kath's personal achievements are numerous. She naturally regards the international successes to be the highlights of her career, of which the Chelsea Flower Show was the most outstanding. Kath and a team colleague, as judges themselves, were invited back the following year, 1991, to exhibit in the Floral Arts section.

This invitation was extended to them by Chelsea's ten judges who had judged the Glenellen stand the previous year. One of these judges was Julia Clements, Lady Julia Seton, OBE. The legendary Constance Spry and Julia Clements were the first artists to start teaching floral art during World War II. This was Julia's contribution to helping the wives who were left at home during the conflict. She died on 1 November 2010 aged 104.

In 1995, Kath was awarded 'Best on Show' at a floral art competition held in Bulawayo. The prize was two tickets to New Zealand to take part in the fifth World Association of Flower Arrangers (WAFA) competition the next year. Pam Harris accompanied her, but awards eluded them on that occasion. In 1999 Kath entered the sixth WAFA competition in South Africa, and this time was awarded 'Second Place'.

Her next 'bash' was in 2002 in Scotland. There, she said, she was almost on home ground, Scotland being the birthplace of her mother. She had a particular affinity with everyone around her and felt the spiritual presence of her late mother and excelled.

Her title was 'Outside Interests', where she depicted 'Sailing', with plant material taken over with her from Zimbabwe. She manipulated Agave leaves to suggest the sails of a yacht, and beneath she placed a combination of Sansevieria (mother-in-law's tongue) and twisted Flax leaves depicting the sea and waves on the horizontal.

For this arrangement she was awarded a Gold Medal, plus a special award for the use of foliage. Out of 800 competitors, a

Kathy Quail and 'Sailing'.

Karoi girl had one again excelled. Kath won twelve awards in Scotland altogether, and she believes very strongly that her mother's spirit guided her and gave her inspiration. Gavin Roper's wife Mandy also received a Special Mention.

Princess Anne, the Patron, opened the exhibition, and when her name was announced as one of the special award winners, Kath Quail felt totally overwhelmed. The aftermath was even more exciting, as she received floral journals from the UK and New Zealand with write-ups about her success; on the covers were photos of her award-winning arrangements. It made her glow with pride.

The Dramatic Society began in 1952, when Chiefie Maidment suggested – no doubt with Peter Veck, his son-in-law, foremost in his mind – that it would be good to put all the acting talent around to practical use. Peter had already done a fair bit of acting and singing in Salisbury before arriving to join the family firm in Karoi.

Once more it was the Women's Institute who took the initiative, and they produced Noel Coward's *Blithe Spirit*. The new club had not yet been completed so they built a make-shift stage with beer crates, testament

to the prodigious drinking habits of a small community!

The whole production was a resounding success, sparking up enthusiasm in many a local thespian's breast, and the dramatic society took off and never looked back. From then on, Karoi actors and actresses won local awards for 'best stage production' and 'best individual performance'.

Ruth Jacobson was an excellent actress who won the 'best actress' award one year. As a director, she put on an open-air production of *Bon Adventure* on their farm, Jacob's Ladder, one year. Other enthusiasts of that era were Susie Simpson, Ruth and Lionel Jahme, Derek Bennett, Tony Hoskyns, John Roebuck and Aileen Donnelly.

Flossie Hoskyns's moment of fame came when he took a leading part in *Dial M for Murder*, which was only superseded by a light-hearted skit in which he teamed up with Eynon Deere. It was a performance that took place three metres away from where Ian Smith was sitting.

The two men were dressed in 'drag', with balloons stuffed up their fronts as bosoms. Every now and again Flossie would drape his arm over Eynon's shoulder which would stray surreptitiously lower and lower to fondle the bosom beneath. It brought the house down, but Eynon was none too pleased!

It was, however, perhaps the two productions of *The Gay Nineties* that gave the most pleasure, probably because times were grave as the bush war escalated. Directed and produced by Ethne and Harvey Ferreira, with assistance from Helena Impey, in 1968 and 1970, both shows linger clearly in everyone's minds.

It was a revue, cabaret and burlesque, of what was popular in the Britain of the 1890s. Who will ever forget the picture of Cliff Wilcox doing a rendition of *Burlington Bertie*, looking so much the part in his shabby, ill-fitting dinner jacket, trilby hat and walking stick. The audience watched from individual tables where waitresses served drinks and an excellent dinner.

Dolan Hampson and Dusty Laver were often called on to compere; they were adept at filling in awkward pauses with light-hearted, witty ad-libbing and jokes.

The Club took on the ambitious challenge of Gilbert and Sullivan operettas. The principal parts in *H.M.S. Pinafore* were taken by Marietta Brayne-Skilton, Peter Veck, Gerry Hughes, Robert Anderson, Ewa Kordonski, Veronica Flight and Vic Athenides. The casting was good, for we will never forget the incongruous sight of the statuesque and stately form of Veronica Flight (as Mrs Cripps, 'Little Buttercup') towering over her stage-husband Vic Athenides, who was short and stocky.

At its population peak Karoi had a wealth of musical talent, not just on the stage but as musicians as well, in musical and production directors Norah Thomas, Anne Carberry and Ann Wellsted.

Later still, we landed another 'nightingale' when Ted Milton (the former Federal Hang-man) remarried and brought his new wife, Joan, into out midst. Joan was well known in Salisbury's musical circles, and until she retired she gave us several renderings with her splendid soprano voice. When Margaret and John Whenman, the District Commissioner, arrived, they, too, added their talents to the stage.

Kelvin Weare arrived in Karoi in November 1978. He produced a very courageous play in the early days of independence, which was entered into the national drama competition. With independence and change in mind, Kelvin decided that Athol Fugard's play *Sizwe Banzi Is Dead* would be appropriate. With a cast of two, requiring one black actor and one white, the two roles were given to Shane Shem Chitunhu, a black teacher from Rydings, and Des Hill, a postal engineer.

The play was a difficult one, comprising much narrative and dialogue and requiring hours of learning. Perhaps it was too ambitious. Both actors had done their utmost, but the play itself didn't capture the local imagination, although it had its humorous moments.

In particular, it was not appreciated by the British adjudicator who was not au fait with the Rhodesian/Zimbabwean way of life. Neither had she grasped the stout effort for change. Fifty per cent black was not good enough, and she was very critical. After that no more effort was made to participate at a national level. We all felt that the need to be politically correct for the sake of it had stymied the natural flow of local dramatics.

Bebe Mostert produced some good, light-hearted variety shows throughout the following years. She once used her husband, Nick, in a part that could have been tailor-made for him, when he stood on stage and narrated with effortless and characteristic dry humour one of Herman Charles Bosman's classic stories – learned by heart.

Nick, a typical Afrikaner Boer, looked so much the part, being large, burly and slow speaking, and could hardly have been mistaken for anything other than what he appeared. He had the required accent and the khaki, everyday garb of a straw-chewing yokel. All he had to do was be himself. And he did it superbly. He became a true Bosman character, straight out of the book.

27. Independence

Independence in 1980 brought with it many radical changes, in both behaviour and attitude. It was a difficult time, but at least there was peace, however tenuous.

That season of 1980/81 brought good rains – they fell in abundance as if to expurgate the war-torn land of its battle-weary endowment. The black people saw it as God's way of washing the blood from the earth, but it was not quite as easy to expel the inner grieving and physical scarring, suffered in the name of freedom and in defending a way of life.

Thus the settling-down period began, which saw displaced war veterans on both sides having to be infiltrated carefully back into civilised society after years of living an abnormal existence. Fighting men, both black and white, had to overcome their differences and reconcile themselves to peace and the rule of law.

ZANLA and ZIPRA war veterans had been tempted by many promises when they joined the freedom campaign. Now they anticipated free education, places at universities and technical colleges, apprenticeships and career training, all of which would render them employable in order to start a new life. That was the plan, anyway.

Concurrently, there was a third exodus of white Zimbabweans, heading for various border posts and airports. The first emigration of whites had come after the break-up of the Federation in 1963. These were British nationals, civil servants mostly, who were thinking primarily of their future pensions, and had never fully embraced Africa and still talked of Britain as 'home'.

The second wave left at UDI – and who can blame them when they thought of frozen bank accounts.

Robert Gabriel Mugabe, the newly elected Prime Minister, was an unknown quantity, an enigmatic surprise, who, in his first speech to the nation, put initial fears to rest when he spoke of reconciliation.

In an effort to appease the white farmers, he had hand-picked two of them and brought them into his Cabinet in important ministerial portfolios – Dennis Norman and David Smith. Dennis was a Karoi farmer who farmed on Pelele farm along the Shola Road. Now, surely, we could anticipate a bright future that would benefit every Zimbabwean, but the independence years of the 1980s hardly improved our lot.

As outcasts during the UDI years, we had remained fairly static, although I would venture to say that we had managed pretty well and, despite sanctions, were leading producers of agricultural and manufactured goods on the African continent. So now that the world was open to us again, we would surely go ahead in leaps and bounds.

We hungered for stability and a vibrant economy which would lead to a boom. We longed to be the part of the international community that saw a stable economy, but as the 1980s came to a close, the country had become noticeably more and more poverty-stricken, with a massive dearth of the goods that were necessary to run our farming enterprises.

But life had changed little on the land. Tobacco growers were more concerned about the onslaught by the World Health Organization as the anti-tobacco lobbyists began their campaign, and we wondered if the long-term future for tobacco would be on the decline.

Spares became harder and harder to locate for our tractors and equipment, and the farmer as usual fell back on resources he never knew he had as he became more and more adept at making do.

By 1990 just about every farmer drove a clapped-out vehicle that was well past its sell-by date, and his farm was held together with wire, tambo (string), glue or strips of reken (tyre tubing). I remember having to borrow Piet Groot's spare wheel to make a trip to Harare on one occasion because tyres were unobtainable.

However, our children were well educated and the severe monetary restrictions could be circumvented if one applied to the Reserve Bank for tutorial fees to pay to study at colleges and universities out of the country, and mostly this was forthcoming. Shortages were overcome by stock-piling, laying out enormous amounts of money.

Farm schools were deemed unnecessary and many were closed down. We ran one with Grippos next door. We paid one teacher and the Mortimers paid another and then we shared the cost of the books and pencils. We were castigated for not having flush toilets.

We were bombarded by new policies, but if one waited long enough they surreptitiously faded away when it became clear either that they were impractical or that they affected the powers that be more severely than any-one else.

At one stage, for instance, it was suggested that the all youths, including whites, should be made to do a spell of annual national service, but this idea was quickly dropped when it was pointed out that perhaps the *mukiwa* youth could not be trusted, espe-cially after a bombing at the Thornhill base near Gweru.

The bonding of trade apprentices led to an exodus of school-leavers who weren't happy to tie themselves to one company for what seemed to them at their age a life-time sen-tence. Thus the brain drain began to gather

momentum: it showed just how important education and training was to the majority. People could put up with most things if their children were getting a good education and had access to good health facilities.

During the mid-1980s we were made alarmingly aware of a frighteningly new scourge called HIV-AIDS, deemed at first to be so terrifying that it was better ignored and over-looked. To the government it simply didn't exist.

One of Karoi's GMOs, a Belgian doctor, Frank Le Bacq, very quickly recognized early symptoms among the hundreds of indigenous patients that he saw every day in the Karoi hospital. He began to write papers on his findings and sent them to government for perusal. They were never acknowledged.

But he did address the farmers at farmers' association meetings. He warned that within five years there would be a shortage of labour. It seemed a gross exaggeration at the time, but sure enough it happened – not quite as quickly as he had at first thought, but certainly within eight years farmers found that that they needed to employ more and more workers to make up for daily absentees caused by illness.

Before independence, workers had been strong and in good health: it would be a rare day if anyone was absent. Now they were noticeably weaker and malnourished. Unfortunately government had stopped the practice of weekly food-rations, condemning it as being paternalistic. The farmer didn't mind – it was less work for him – but it was obviously detrimental to the well-being of his labour force.

Shorter working hours at peak season led to rotting tobacco and spoiled crops. Thus the 1980s and 1990s saw us limping from one crisis to another.

In an effort to help stem the spread of

HIV-AIDS, the Zimbabwe Family Planning Association, working in conjunction with the WVS, tried to do their bit by running training courses for farm health-workers: lectures were held giving advice and understanding of how the virus worked. At that stage we were all rather ignorant about it. Contraceptives were given out freely and workers were shown how they worked.

I remember one amusing story told by farmer's wife, Monica Renwick, who used to give us lectures. She started off by demonstrating to her cook how to use the condom, telling him that it would prevent him and his wife from getting the new virus.

She inserted her thumb into it to illustrate its correct use, naively unaware that he wasn't sufficiently clued up to know where it should have been placed. Some weeks later she happened to notice that his wife was very much with child again.

'Kefas,' she said, 'I see that your wife has a bokis. Didn't you use the "into" as I taught you?'

'Ee-e, Medem. That thing, no good. I put on my thumb as you said, but there she has a bokis again.'

The damage done to the tobacco industry by the UDI sanctions continued to be felt even as late as 1985, with the majority of importing countries still not buying flue-cured Zimbabwean tobacco, even though growers were producing the correct style once again. The 1986/87 season was the most difficult and least profitable for forty years.

However, from then on it did improve slightly. In modern terms, Zimbabwe is one of the few countries whose tobacco is 'clean'. The 1990s were fast proving to be a 'green' decade, with health and environment considerations becoming paramount.

In 1990 the government accepted advice from our leading economists, who urged the opening up of the economy. After this, massive improvements were made in all sectors. They named it ESAP: the Economic Structural Adjustment Programme. Later, with irony, some began to call it ESAP's Fables.

As a result, the season of 1990/91 saw farmers selling their tobacco at prices that they hadn't seen in years. They boasted of their new-found wealth – which was not very wise. It did not go unnoticed that the green-eyed monsters hovering in the background began to covet what they had been promised but not yet received.

Besides, inflation was starting to creep up insidiously, and the Zimbabwe dollar was allowed to devalue over ensuing years. Until then, it had remained almost static. At Independence in 1980 it had been more or less on the same level as the British pound. In 1990 the rate was 5 to 1, but by 1997 it had crept up to 16 to 1. From then on, it was often in free fall. Were we never to be secure again?

Unused farms were to be had for the asking once the war was over. They had been abandoned for many reasons, but mostly because they were on the periphery of a dangerous area where they were continually attacked during the bush war. In 1980 they remained unused, for not many had enough faith in the new Zimbabwe at that stage. Some of those farms to the north of Karoi were bought legitimately by black farmers.

Over the years since Cecil Rhodes had bestowed William Harvey Brown with Nassau in the late 1890s there have been many changes in the divisions of land. Piecing them together and trying to make sense of them is as complicated as doing a jigsaw puzzle.

Peter Walsh had run the gauntlet over the years to arrive at a point where he feasibly had enough land to keep himself and Joyce plus two of his sons, Matthew and Steve, farming alongside him. He explained:

My introduction to Rhodesia came in 1949 when I met some Rhodesian farmers in Beira. I had been crewing on an English yacht on its way to Australia when the owner fell ill and died.

I eventually managed to get the boat back to Beira and was contemplating my next move when the Rhodesians suggested that theirs was a land of golden opportunity. I took them at their word and made my way there. I served my time and landed a job as a manager in Banket.

On one of my leaves in Durban I fortuitously met a Bulawayo girl, Joyce Newton, and we eventually married. We moved to Karoi in 1961 where I leased Oribi Park from Harry Coker, an original settler, and then the following year leased from Dennis Hook, who was then on Rydings farm and had built all the barns and sheds which were ultimately to become Rydings School in 1981, just after Zimbabwe's independence.

Before I purchased the subdivision of Nyamabidzi, owned by George Potter, who was also an original settler, the Land Bank had foreclosed on Johan Crause. He had bought a subdivision of Nyamadidzi and named it Wag'n Bietjie (Wait a Bit) and then declared it to be an unviable proposition. Perhaps in retrospect Mr Crause was correct. The Land Bank was happy to sell it to me.

Although it was small in size, when I asked CONEX for a quick survey they came back saying that it had 600 acres of arable along with a new borehole rated at 800 gallons per hour. However, it turned out that CONEX were 100% out – only 300 acres were arable, and

when Johnny Bennett came to help me install the piping for the borehole we found a reamer stuck half way down! Eventually we got 150 gph.

So our start was not an auspicious one. It was all very frustrating and sad, and had I known the Latin term then, I would have quoted the Queen and called that season our *annus horribilis*. However, we persevered, as so many have before and since.

We named that portion Fiddlers Green and were then able to add Hesketh Park section, which belonged to Bert Hacking, to our lot, which gave us a little more elbow space.

When Bert Hacking bought Hesketh Park he had applied for extra land nearby on the grounds that what he had was unviable for settlement, meaning little arable and no water.

This he sub-divided and sold off later, mostly in the 1960s: Chitiwafeni (Place of Baboons) to Jack Crees, who in turn sold to Dusty Laver, who then sold to me. That was Lot 1 and 2 Chitiwafeni. Lot 2 was split between Johnny Bennett and myself. At the last moment, Bert retained the wedge between Happy Valley and Mushi Park as a timber reserve.

My share I joined to Fiddler's Green, and the rest of the subdivision was sold to Alan Coast, Westlands, and Dave Roper, Rocklands. All in all, our Bert was a canny lad.

A rather interesting counterpoint to the above occurred when Pat Bashford was granted his farm, St Brendan's. He thought it was too large for one man and returned half to the Land Settlement Board.

Adjacent to us was a farm that had once been the experimental farm and was subsequently bought by Syd Baxter. I acquired that from his widow after he died.

Lastly, we bought Troon from Neville Wright and later merged it with what Syd had named Independence to form Troon estate. This was, in fact, the last consolidation allowed by the new Zimbabwean government before the policy that if a farmer wanted to sell his farm he had to first acquire a Certificate of No Interest from the government.

Thus Peter, who had four sons, had acquired enough land on which to place them if they became interested in farming.

The acquisition of land over the years was a confusing practice. Over time, the original properties were sub-divided, names were changed, and portions expanded and contracted as they were purchased or sold – shades, perhaps, of a Europe in which national boundaries changed many times after the Middle Ages.

Noel Bichard, another original settler, had sold Wingate to Peter Adams, who had sub-divided it, creating Troon. When Peter Adams left at independence in 1980, Neville Wright bought the remainder and Wingate reverted to its original state. Peter Walsh said that he was lucky in his neighbours: Peter Adams, Alan Coast, Bert Hacking and Billy Postlethwayt.

Billy had a number of firsts to his name. He was one of the first five settlers, the owner of the first telephone in the block, much used by everyone, and notably the first television, with a forty-foot mast some distance from the house to which he had attached a large 'bobbejaan spanner' (a wrench). When the reception was poor, he would scurry out and turn it around until Anne, his wife, who was hanging out of the window, shouted that the picture had improved.

Billy was also the first driver to miss the bend on which a hazardously low-level bridge had been built, and therefore landed in the spruit. He had been celebrating some occasion rather too enthusiastically. His son Charles replayed the scene a couple of years later, and when he was asked what had happened he just shrugged and replied: 'I don't really know. I just found that I was unable to lift my arm and turn the steering wheel'.

Karoi's sons began to trickle back to the farms. They had been at colleges and universities overseas and in South Africa. They had trained at technical colleges and done apprenticeships, but the call to return to the land in the country of their birth was still as strong as ever.

A farm has always been recognised as being a farmer's pension, the security for his old age, particularly if he had a son to take over from him; so now we began to see 'the return of the native'. The most senior of the second generation was Paddy Barrett-Hamilton. Then, apart from Matthew and Stephen Walsh, there was Ian and Robbie Cochrane, and the four sons of Ken Saywood – Neil, David, Peter-John and Tony.

Chris Wilcox returned to Mpofu River, Kevin Mitchell to Kevlyn, Marshall and Gavin Roper to Rocklands, Ian White to Landithy, Glen and Ian Barker to Trezona/Nyahoa. Edward, Ray and Andrew Flight came back to Lanlory, Adrian and Chris Herud to Maora, and Jimmy Jr, Roy, Alan and Doug Watt to Montesuma.

Although Neville Phillips had only daughters, all four of them returned to live in Karoi having married boys who were keen to farm. Moira married the widower Alec Gardiner after Trish died. Jennifer married Bill Bales-Smith, Cathy married veterinarian Kevin Robertson, and Debbie married Richard

Black, who was also reared in Karoi. A deficiency of the male of the species within the Phillips family has long since been rectified, as a plethora of grandsons made their way into the world. Neville at last had some support.

Many others returned: Glen and Ian Barker, Grant Pilcher, John Harvey, Stewart and Peter McKenzie, Anthony and Jo Wells, James and Scott McKay, Rory Richards, Hennie and Gerry Terblanche, and, later, James and Alexander Stidolph and their cousin Neville, Andrew Herbst, Kevin Smith, Ian and Robin Gifford, the young Nels, Oosthuizens, Strydoms and many more.

Piet Groot spent years expanding his small empire. He wrote:

I came to Karoi from Inyazura and settled on an undeveloped piece of land that I bought from Jock Rutherford, who had 3,600 acres called Chedza.

Jock was a bit of a character and had no idea of what farming entailed. The Land Settlement Board forced him to sell part of his farm, which I eventually bought and called Trianda. A year later he had to sell another portion, which Hendrik Viljoen bought and named Claudia.

That left Jock with the remainder of Chedza, but later he was forced to sell that as well. As it was wedged between Trianda and San Michele, we bought it so as to make one farm.

San Michele, bought some years earlier, had once belonged to Paul Renwick. Chabwino also came up for sale after Lindsay Gripper left. Jack Gauche, who had bought Blockley from A.B. Roberts, suggested that we should buy it together just to keep squatters off, but he pulled out of the deal and so I

bought it and then sold it to the government two years later.

Jack Gauche then sold Blockley to Hugo Blignaut, who built the Blockley dam – one million gallons – in which he had 10 per cent share, as it bordered Chedza.[1]

Piet, a well-known and established breeder of Brahman cattle, bought Chabwino and put cattle on it. He was originally from Holland and married to Nitsa, who came from Greece. The couple had two sons, Petrus and Christo: we used to say that Petrus was the Dutch son and Christo was the Greek one. They were valuable and close neighbours.

Both sons joined their father in farming ventures: Petrus, a B.Sc. Agric. graduate from Pietermaritzburg, started a state-of-the-art poultry/chicken production line on San Michele. Following in his father's footsteps, he began to build up a breeding herd of cattle. Christo graduated from Blackfordby as top student. He grew tobacco on Claudia – but not for long. The Ides of March were already creeping up to halt any dreams they may have had for a future in farming in Zimbabwe.

About two years into Independence, Morag Fraser, of The Ridges Farm, still single at that stage and being a bit of a career woman, was working in the UK. Later she returned to marry Ray Flight and live in Karoi.

One evening she was socializing in a pub in the heart of London and made her way up to the bar to order drinks. The barman was a black guy who kept studying her face as if he knew her

Eventually he said, 'Do you by any chance come from Zimbabwe? Your face looks

---

[1] Chabwino and Demavand had also been part of Blockley – historically interesting, as all were part of William Harvey Brown's Nassau.

familiar. 'Yes,' she said. 'I come from Karoi.' To which he replied, "Thought so – so do I,' and he began to laugh.

He explained that he had been a 'freedom fighter' in the area during our bush war and told how he and his *shamwaris* had often watched Morag and her sister, Alison, horse-back riding around the farm, adding that they could have shot them dead at any time they chose.

Clearly after the fighting had stopped he had seen his opportunity, taken his hand-shake and made his way to Britain. It was an interesting and strange encounter.

Left to right: Sitting: Jill Thornton, Monica Royston.
Standing: Ron Thornton, Hugh Royston, Mike Lapham.

Left to right: Sitting: Mike Lapham, Peter Walsh.
Standing: Ted Kordonski, Peter Pilcher, Francis Pilcher, Ewa Kordonski.

28. The *coup de grâce*: Farm Invasions

Il y a deux choses auxquelles il faut se faire sous peine de trouver la vie
insupportable: ce sont les injures du temps et les injustices des hommes.
There are two things to which we must adapt, lest we find life unendurable:
the injuries of time and the injustices of man. (Sebastien Chamfort, 1741–94)

And so began the demise of the community as we knew it. The 'rose' was fading and disintegrating before our eyes. We saw history repeating itself, for we knew we were not the first people to experience the plunder, destruction and take-over of land that has occurred throughout the ages.

Some say that history is just 'boring ol' stuff', full of dry, mouldy facts, as inconsequential as the past, so what's the point of keeping it alive? Not at all, says the historian, who stands his ground.

Apart from the telling of a good story, history is supposed to prevent the repetition of failure. We are meant to learn from it. Although Zimbabwe's most recent perpetrators felt justified by taking the course of action that they did, part of their action was about indulging in sweet revenge. Avenging ruthlessness does have a habit of coming back to haunt one, however. Two wrongs never make a right.

It all started with a soiled piece of paper called a Section 8, looking anything but official. It was handed over by an equally scruffy individual, paid to deliver it on foot from its place of origin. The words gave the owner ninety days to vacate his farm. Never in modern history was a body of people so confounded and caught unawares as the white farmers in Zimbabwe were towards the close of 1997.

Insult was added to injury when groups of paid political rabble-rousers began to target various farmers in an effort to 'jambanja' them off their land by 'toyi-toying'

frenetically to the beat of drums throughout the night.

Jambanja comes from the Shona and indicates noise, chaos, terror; it came to be used to describe the method of frightening people into leaving their farms. This unrelenting, mesmerizing cacophony was guaranteed to drive away the devil himself – that was its purpose – but it had a counter effect and at this stage the farmers' resolve hardened and no one was prepared to be frightened away quite so easily.

The first farm in Karoi to be to be victimized was Lanlory, where Jimmy and Veronica Flight lived. Friends and neighbouring farmers converged on the place to give moral support just by being a presence.

This became a course of action which was to continue throughout the whole campaign, and was the only source of support and comfort for victimized farmers, for there was no other means of help. The police had their orders and would not intervene.

The plot to rob the country of titled land that had been worked and developed over decades by generations of white farmers was not taken as seriously as it should have been at first. Did the 1979 Lancaster House constitution not have built-in safeguards for its minorities? Did this not protect us from what was brewing up all about us?

Lord Carrington, the British Foreign Secretary at that time, had said that measures would be put into place to safeguard the rights of any minority group: 'This is one of the essentials if there is going to be a settlement … that the white population in Rhodesia must feel that their interests are safeguarded.'

Many could have told him then that this would not be worth the paper it was written on. However, not many were aware that this safeguard would fall away within ten years. It was in the small print that no one bothers to read but turns out to be the most relevant part of a contract. Just what was supposed to happen after that period was never discussed.

The sober truth, which we viewed as inconsequential at the time, was glossed over and never referred to again. In our naïve ignorance we continued to plough profits back into the ground, continued to develop and build, blissfully unaware that we had no future.

It was no wonder that the Polish ambassador was later heard to remark that the white farmers in Zimbabwe should have realized that they were on borrowed time – it was written in the winds, the sands of time that blew over this confounded country.

Following the presentation of hundreds of Section 8s and Section 5s (preliminary notices of acquisition) of dubious legality, which many largely ignored or temporarily fended off, the government stepped up its campaign to hurry it up.

In Karoi, anxious farmers ran around like headless chickens and lawyers rubbed their hands in glee. They did earn every penny they made, but no one could win against a government that had no respect for the law; at every turn they managed to confound us.

Jeremy Callow, our own man of law, ran himself ragged as he sat in court or sought to bail out farmers who had been arrested and jailed on trumped-up charges. Eventually he could take no more and left the country because the stress was affecting his health.

Each farmer felt that his own case was more deserving than another. Wiser men decided that it was more sensible to hold on to the money they had rather than waste it in the courts. They left gracefully. As it turned out, they were right, for although the majority who went to court won their cases, no one was willing or able to enforce the law. It was a complete and utter travesty.

However, before all this became apparent, farmers filled in reams of inconsequential forms, and wasted time and money driving up and down to Harare in an effort to meet up with anyone who might help. In the end, these were mere lackeys and had no jurisdiction at all.

There were meetings, with guest speakers addressing the floor and dishing out advice that was largely academic, but no one had a formula to solve the problem. Perhaps the best advice, given by the CFU, was that there should be no retaliation with firearms. Life was sacred and should not be lost.

Nevertheless, we all felt abandoned. Years earlier, at Kenya's independence, Britain had compensated their white farmers for the land that was confiscated. Zimbabwe's counterparts received no such support. It seemed patently obvious from the media that the world had already judged and damned us, deciding that all Zimbabwe's white farmers deserved everything they got.

So what was the catalyst that turned the tide? What ignited such anger and hatred that caused the nightmare to come, for which we were so unprepared? Was it all the result of the white man's arrogance and intransigence? Or was there something much deeper?

The shortage of land was one reason given. Ludicrously, it was said that the best land had been occupied by the colonizers and the worst allocated to the indigenous people.

Frankly, there was very little difference between any of the land in the country at that time. Of course there are badlands on every farm: it is rare to find any farm that is one hundred per cent arable. Over time, bad husbandry exhausted much of the land that was occupied by rapidly increasing numbers of indigenous people, so the contrast could be noticed.

As for the argument that there was a shortage of available land, that, too, is inaccurate. Plenty of land had been offered voluntarily since independence by farmers who, for one reason or another, had no further need of their farms, often because they had no male issue interested in farming it.

In 1980 Britain had provided millions for the government to buy land when it came up for sale – on a willing buyer, willing seller basis. The government had the first option to buy it and, if they did not wish to, issued a Certificate of No Interest. The vast majority of farmers received such certificates when they wanted to put their farms on the market.

Jimmy Flight had been the first to experience these tactics, but it was Anthony Wells who was the first to lose his farm. His rude awakening came when he was forcibly led in a crude, undignified manner by his nose like a bull in a sales pen around the perimeter of his farm, Maunga. He moved into town the next day.

Slim Botha decided that he was going to go quietly, like a lamb to the slaughter; no histrionics and drama for him. Through the grapevine he received word that the rabble were approaching. Grabbing his guitar he sat on his stoep and strummed away calmly.

'Ja, man, what do you lot want?'

'We've come for your farm.'

'OK, you can have it. I'll start moving my *katundu.*

So Slim and Marie began the mammoth task of packing up an accumulation of decades – machinery, farm equipment, tractors, cattle and household furnishings. Truck-load by endless truck-load left the farm and was off-loaded on to land in Banket, owned by cousins, until finally Slim was ready to say *totsiens* to his farm. But it had all been too much. That night he suffered a massive heart attack and died.

By September 2000, Karoi farmers, residents and farm-workers had had enough of the anarchy and demonstrated outside the police station in protest at the criminal acts being perpetrated on farms. They were confronted by the Member-in-Charge, flanked by so-called war veterans.

The war-vets had no legal or official status and no mandate from the people. In terms of negotiation they did not exist, and while they camped on farms they were trespassing squatters; if they committed acts of barbarity, they were criminals. To acknowledge them as the police did was to condone illegality.

Like the friends of those beaten, raped and murdered earlier that year in other districts, Karoi was appalled by the savage and senseless attack on Marshall Roper by one of his workers, who wielded a machete while he was working in the land. What was even more shocking was that while Marshall's face was being sliced open, the Member-in-Charge of Karoi's police, flanked by his war-vets, observed the whole performance from the sidelines.

Marshall used his cell phone to call his friends for help. They came swiftly to support him. He was rushed off for medical attention while many of his friends chased the assailants off the land. The attack on Marshall provided evidence that 'land reform' in Zimbabwe was being orchestrated for personal gain, and his picture appeared on the cover of *The Farmer*. Karoi became synonymous with evil that day. One could smell the odour of malevolence.

It was a bizarre and crazy time. It was like the Wild West – all that was needed were a couple of wagons, some bows and arrows, and a few colt pistols firing away. But as time rolled on, it all just became another way of life. Where else in the world would you greet your friends and acquaintances with

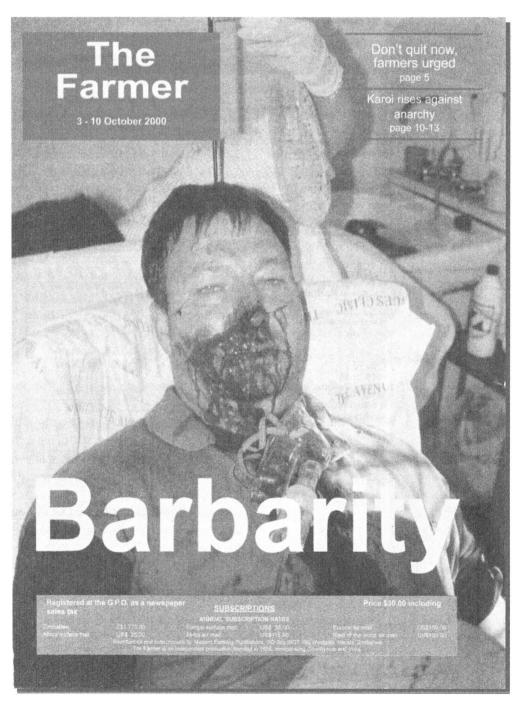

the words, 'How are your war-vets today?' Where else can some arbitrary person take a fancy to your property and demand that you leave it so that he can take it over?

Whether passively or as a result of aggression, Karoi farmers left with a sad inevitability, broken by despair. Following in their wake were the traders and the commercial sector. As the farming stopped, the businesses closed, until only Karoi Engineering remained, its management left to Hilary and Hazel Townsend.

Ray never did have much interest in his father's business: his chosen life was the bush and hunting, which had all begun when the Rural Council asked for his assistance with animal control. Then he joined hunters Alan Lowe and Fritz Meyer, who offered him an apprenticeship. Both of them later died: one killed by an elephant and the other suffering a heart attack after hunting a buffalo.

These days Ray is doing what he loves: he owns two camps in the Valley which rely on foreign tourists to keep the business afloat. He has one of the Hill brothers – son of Sandra (Coast) and Des Hill – apprenticed to him.

Over ensuing months, land that had become the most productive in Africa took on an appearance of desolation, forsaken and abandoned as if having suffered a medieval scourge. Barns stood ghostlike, isolated in their neglect, their doors, roofs and windows ripped out.

Only five years earlier I had looked down from Chris Bishop's Cessna on to a thriving and productive industry, with verdant pastures energized by nature's life-blood. As far as the eye could see, water irrigated the earth, harnessed in dams built mostly after independence.

The inventive pivot circle, which enabled vast acreages of winter wheat to be sown during the dry months, allowed tobacco production to be doubled, as first one crop was planted and irrigated and then a second, sustained by rain. From a birds-eye view one had the privilege of seeing progress at its best. It was a sight to gladden the eye.

It had taken about sixty years to accomplish what I had looked down on, but less than ten to destroy it. To see it now, unused and unproductive, the shredded remains of plastic flapping here and there in the breeze, is a sorry, depressing sight indeed, one that speaks more eloquently than words.

It speaks of tyranny and outrageous disregard for development. It speaks of waste and ignorance and, above all, of disrespect for the fostering and nurturing of a country. It shows disdain for man's effort, as he wrestled with the land over time. It diminishes achievement and accomplishment. Worst of all, what was done was done with purpose and malice.

Karoi, once a vibrant, bustling town, became a shadow of its former self. Its character and charm, neatness and cleanliness have been slowly eroded away. The market that had sprung up among the trees in the park encroached further into the cemetery.

Eynon Deere, whose last wish had been to be buried under a tree in a secluded and private corner where the dead lie peacefully, now lies hardly a metre from the blacksmith's pile of metal shavings.

Litter lies among the rubble of broken pavings and shattered cement. Trees that once lined streets, the pride and joy of Pat Taylor (headmaster), who kept a beady eye on them as if they were his own, are deformed, their branches lopped off for firewood.

Flamboyants that George Kennedy planted at the post office, breathtaking in their full bloom come November, have reached the same inglorious end. Rose

Walk, pride of Charlie Slight, the last white Secretary of the Rural Council, has, too, disappeared.

Every farmer remembers where he was and what he was doing on the day he received his Section 8. After the notices were served, a list of the names of the farms to be acquired was published in the *Herald*, and within hours the banks swiftly thrust in their swords, calling in loans.

The day on which the farmer left his farm forever would probably have been the day he was at his lowest ebb. Ahead of him was no compensation to soften the blow. He was just expected to get on with his life with a fictitious fortune in his pocket and find employment he had no heart for. No more job satisfaction for him. Those who had professional training to fall back on were lucky indeed.

In the end, that final journey came almost as a relief, bringing with it an absurd and unexpected feeling of freedom. The grief still had to be dealt with, just as a new life had to be discovered, but that date and that feeling of hopelessness will remain forever etched on his memory.

It takes great strength of mind not to wallow in self-pity, not to hit out in anger, or whine and become embittered. Men wept, men cursed, and tears mingled with the bitter taste of sorrow for it was a loss of huge proportions.

Yet, in due course, those very people with good, strong blood in their veins, despite having lost everything, have managed to overcome the adversity just as their pioneering forefathers did. After a brief period of self-indulged pity, grief abates and enables one to start thinking straight once more.

It just took one self-opinionated Brit to give his ignorant opinion on a BBC phone-in chat show to anger me into recovery: 'The trouble with those white Zimbabwean farmers is that they're just waiting for someone to rescue them.'

Only two people I know from other countries have ever bothered to ask me questions and have been genuinely interested in listening to the very improbable story we can tell. Only two people posed the question with any concern: 'But what *did* the farmers do when they were driven off the land?'

Each, of course, has his own story to tell. They are many and varied. Some left with everything and others with nothing. Some are still on their farms, but it is a very tenuous situation and not guaranteed to last. There is no general rule. One is left to the vagaries of capricious minds and circumstances.

Displaced white Zimbabwean farmers gradually made their way to all corners of the globe. The world looked on – it was just another diaspora, one that had overtaken many peoples through the centuries. They headed to Australia and New Zealand, South Africa, Britain, Canada and America. Some returned to their European roots; others tried their luck in Zambia and Mozambique. The brave and courageous went to Iraq and Afghanistan, mercenaries who put their lives at risk for large amounts of money for a new home and to educate their children.

A few stayed just where they were, finding land that had been bought as far back as the early 1980s by black Zimbabweans who were willing to lease a portion to them. One ex-farmer admitted that losing his farm was the best thing that ever happened to him. But many have stayed in the country to eke out an existence because it is their homeland.

We will remember the day that we were warned of an impending first visit by warvets as a bit of a farce. A clapped-out Ford Anglia trundled up the road, coughing and spluttering like an old man in the last stages of TB. We had told Langton, our gardener, to lock the security gates and not let anyone in. The vehicle finally made it, stopped and hooted.

'Bugger off!' shouted Langton, to no avail.

'Better let them in,' said Mike. 'The sooner they come, the sooner they go.'

The two men – Mike and Drew, my son – took the happy hopefuls to the office to hear what they had to say. They wanted a letter offering them half the farm. This was done, with a proviso saying it was given under duress and in protest. They went off well content – or rather they tried to go, but their jalopy just wouldn't start. Much to their embarrassment and chagrin, they had to ask for a push to get going. Mike and Drew were only too happy to oblige.

Hyperinflation followed. The 'fat cats' were quick to take advantage of the status quo, loath to do anything about rectifying the economy. By 2006/7 Zimbabwe had become the laughing stock of the world. We had more millionaires per square yard than in any other country throughout history – even my gardener was one.

Shops emptied, queues formed and if you saw one you joined it, not knowing what rare commodity you might find at the end. Prices of available goods changed from hour to hour until the Stock Exchange closed and the Reserve Bank and the government called it a day. The country was bust.

Once the farmers had left Karoi, many businessmen shut up shop. Dini and Ko Voorn left to live in Holland, where Dini's compatriots think her to be a foreigner because she speaks Dutch with an English accent and English with a Dutch accent!

Most of us moved to the city. It is difficult to transplant an old *mukiwa* whose roots are firmly entrenched in the African soil. Uproot us and we would surely wither and die. Besides, truth to tell, we like living among the black people and would miss their natural, spontaneous friendliness. However, there are still one or two bush-whackers who insist on living on leased land to the north of Karoi near Vuti.

Wild horses would not be able to move Paul and Sheila Stidolph; their farm was the very last to be invaded. About three years ago they returned from a trip to the city only to find a boom placed across the entrance to Grand Parade. The new man was an army general who said that the place was now his. Sheila looked him in the eye and said, 'To get rid of me you'll have to put me into a box first,' to which he replied sarcastically that he could certainly see that she was very attached to her home and farm.

For a number of days the Stidolphs were kept locked within their security fence. Only after dark was it safe for Paul to cut the wire at the back of the yard and climb out in order to walk to the main road through a back route. There one of his sons was waiting to hand over provisions that would keep them going.

For many months Paul had been like a man possessed, spending a great deal of his time travelling to various government departments; he spoke to Governors, MPs, police and magistrates – anyone who would listen. He was like a wire-haired terrier with a bone that he wouldn't let go.

One of the ministers was so intimidated by Paul's daily visits that he was afraid to leave his office to 'spend a penny', and on the day that Paul was at the courts he came face-to-face once more with his old adversary, the magistrate.

'Mr Stidolph,' he said, 'we will have to make one of our offices available to you as you spend more time here than I do.'

So, for the many hundreds, life began anew. Those who emigrated to new countries had the hardest time, for they felt they had lost their identity. The tight-knit community they had always belonged to had gone, and with it had gone their status. Now the world had become an impersonal place. Suddenly they had become just one of many and they had to prove themselves all over again.

No one knew how successful they had been in their former life. No one cared a jot, nor could those strangers grasp the meaning of what had happened to them. They were confronted by a world of materialism where folk were judged by their outward possessions.

In 2009, the British government undertook a 'repatriation' scheme for aged British citizens in Zimbabwe who were literally destitute. It lasted only a few months, but did alleviate the plight of those in greatest need.

The consequence of taking land away from commercial farmers in order to resettle small-scale farmers will not sustain a population the size of today's Zimbabwe.

When the colonizers arrived here, they came with new ideas and innovations that were eagerly adopted by the indigenous people. Throughout the early pioneering years, there was little that the native population would have envied, though Lobengula had been quick enough in coveting fire-arms, exchanging them for land.

As time went on there was no question of discarding telephones, abandoning road-building, hospitals, schools and modern drugs simply because they were the products of colonization. All of them are in fact symbols of all that the present leaders purport to resent and find offensive.

Our leaders lose no time in denigrating colonialism, but they have no intention of giving up their gas-guzzling conveyances, nor will they desist from building their cathedrals of opulence.

Ironically, the one imperative they do reject is individual title to land – the piece of paper that bridges the present and the future, links the bank to land development, the farmer, the best farming research, and turns the land it represents into an asset.

It is an iniquity that must be corrected, for it is the one device that secures capital investment and accumulation, and ultimately makes a massive contribution to a country. By destroying this concept, the prosperity of this country is likely to fail.

Out of this tragedy also comes the destruction of a system and relationships between members of the commercial farming community, not the least being the better understanding that had developed between the farmer and his workers before the land invasions began. The commercial farm-workers were also significant victims of the infamous land-grabbing campaign.

A postscript

I will give Cathy (Chisholm) Oldreive the last word.

She and her husband, Brian, ex-Karoi, started the idea of 'zero tillage' farming in Bindura. Today they run Foundations for Farming, which trains small-scale farmers to use those same methods.

Cathy's brother, Ian Chisholm, his wife, Christine, and their children, Samuel and Ruth, were travelling back from Kariba soon after 'Tebbie' Terblanche had been jambanja'd from Moy farm in about 2004.

They saw the gate open and the kids begged to be shown around the place where their Dad had been born. The house was open and appeared unoccupied; no one was around, so they walked in.

From nowhere a female 'war-vet' appeared and asked what they were doing in 'her' house. Ian explained that his Dad was the one who had opened up the farm and had built the house and all the barns, where he himself had been born.

They were truly flabbergasted and very sheepishly allowed them to tour around.

Cathy said:

Since the land distribution exercise, much has been said about greedy white farmers taking over land from the black folk. Well, as I recall it, there were not many Shona people in the area in the 1940s.

The Urungwe had only recently been cleared of tsetse fly and, because the wealth of the black people was measured by the number of cattle each person owned, the area was sparsely populated.

The Shona were also unwilling to work on the farms and were just as happy to cultivate enough land on the periphery of Karoi to provide for themselves and their families.

As the tobacco industry grew and prospered, migrant labour had to be brought in from beyond the borders to subsidize this deficiency.

There is a very incorrect perception that all the infrastructure on commercial farms evolved from nothing. While I do think that redistribution needed to take place, I'm greatly saddened that there is no recognition of the huge part that the commercial farmers played in the development of this beautiful country.

It is wrong that we are portrayed as selfish, self-seeking individuals who just sat on our verandas and drank tea.

29. An Initial Register of Karoi Farms

Many of the farms were named by the surveyors before being taken up by landowners who, in many cases, renamed them because they already had a name in mind. Later, when farms were sub-divided, each piece was renamed once more. Over the years, farms have changed their boundaries and their owners several times. For example, Nassau, which belonged to William Harvey Brown, was divided into two after his death when Robert Leask decided to buy one half which he re-registered as Coldomo. Years later, Coldomo was sub-divided into Lot 1, bought by J. Thompson, who named it Chinyerere; Lot 2, bought by Neville Canon, became Musha Wedu; and Lot 3 became Asuahi Valley when it was bought by Paul Rawson, who rented it out not having any inclination towards farming.

The naming of a farm was often obvious: perhaps because it sat between two rivers, or had particularly pronounced features, such as was the case with Granite farm, or Rocklands. It might have found to have luxuriant growth of a particular tree, such as Mwala or Maora, or a copious number of animals, such as Pangwarati (home of the sable) or Oribi Park. Others were named for sentimental reasons – after a place of birth or a happy event.

Perhaps the most original name was Renroc, named by Marjorie and John Hull. Spell it backwards and it gives you 'corner', which is exactly what it was at the time: the corner of the block.

Miami settlement land was eventually surveyed and divided into farms:

Miami 1: J. Barker on Nyahoa.   Miami 2: C. Wilcox on Mpofu River.
Miami 3: B. White on Landithy.   Miami 4: F. Mitchell on Kevlyn.

Farm name	Comments
Amore	Original owned by Dan Groenewald, ex-serviceman. Sub-divded to form: Lot 1, Siwa, bought by Marshall Duguid and named after the river close by; Lot 2, Shangrila owned by Tommy Herselman; Lot 3, Derepat, owned by Phil Kruger. Phillip Gifford bought the remainder still known as Amore.
Andrilen	Original owner H. Louw. Sub-division of Devondale. Subsequent owners A. Visagie and then Laver/Griffiths.
Ansdell	Ex-serviceman allocation to L. J. Harris. Subsequent owners A. Bathurst and then George Bennett.
Ardingly	Ex-serviceman allocation to Sam Marnie, who sold to Adrian Herud.
Arden	Once part of Karoi farm, owned by Le Roux brothers. Named after the river Karoi. Owned by C. Niemandt.
Ashton	J. Carpenter. Peter Richards.
Asuahi Valley	Sub-division of Coldomo, bought by Paul Rawson, who named it after a valley in Spain. Still owned by Franca and Charlie Spiegnese.
Avalon	Ex-serviceman allocation to Dan Oosthuizen, who later swapped with Neville Phillips for a farm in Rusape. Avalon: Isle of Apples, a Celtic Paradise.

Baobab	Named after a baobab tree that grows there, quite out of place. Bought by Fritz Paulsen.
Basella	Sub-division of Blockley, owned by Patrick Wells.
Blockley	Sub-division of Nassau bought by A.B. Roberts in 1940.
Boland	Sub-division of Maora. Bought by Esterhuizen.
Bonanza	Sub-division of Shawnigan. Bought by Le Roux brothers – a second pair; they may have been descendants of the original Le Roux brothers on Karoi farm during the 1920s. They occupied it only for a short while. It was then brought back by David Grantham, Jr, to join up once more with the original Shawnigan farm.
Bonnyvale	Sub-division of Chisapi bought by Bert Hacking. Subsequently purchased by Doug Cochrane, who sold to Phil Kotze, who then sold back to Sam Barrett-Hamilton's son, Paddy, on Chisapi. Thus Chisapi became one entity again.
Broad Acres	Ex-serviceman allocation to Ernie Went. Later sold to James Upton and Alec Cummings in a partnership. Then to K. Kirstein and R. Watt, and finally to Kingsley Edwards.
Buffalo Downs	Crown land bought by C.P. Robertson in the 1930s. Subsequently sold to Willie Nel. Two explanations for its name – the obvious one being the prevalence of buffalo in the area, the second after a favourite dog, reputed to have had the strength of a buffalo. The upper part always known as Aerodrome farm by the neighbours but not registered as such.
Buttevant	Ex-serviceman allocation to Guy du Barry. Sub-divided twice: Mike van der Merwe bought Lot 1, New Haven; then Ron Hayes. The remainder later bought by Coulson (Snr). Home section later bought by James Watt.
Caveat	Sub-division of Nassau owned by P. Venter. Sub-divided again to create Kia Lami: F. Paulsen; H. Royston.
Caversham	Original ex-serviceman allocation to Sonny Shakespeare. Named after step-father's place of birth, a small village near Reading in the UK. Sub-division bought by Geoff Lockett and called Romford. Later bought by Pringle, then Jack Tatham and son.
Ceres	Original ex-serviceman allocation to H. S. Hay. A piece/sub-division sold to Harry Wells to join Montesuma. The remainder later sold to Jackie Waddle then to Richard Black.
Chabwino	Sub-division of Chedza owned by Jock Rutherford and bought by Edward Arro. Later purchased by Piet Groot.
Chanetsa	Sub-division of Chelvern owned by Des Evans.
Chedza	Original ex-serviceman allocation to Jock Rutherford. First sub-division bought by Piet Groot called Trianda. Later Piet bought the remainder of Chedza and Claudia, which was a sub-division of Chedza owned by H. Viljoen.

Chelvern	Crown land bought in 1930 by Des Evans. Later purchased by Jimmy Graham. Sub-divisions are Little Gem and Chanetsa.
Cherodzo	R. Purchase.
Cheti	Original ex-serviceman allocation to Alistair Laing.
Chigangas	Crown land bought in 1924 by G. G. Olivier. It was never farmed and subsequent owners are unknown.
Childerley	First owned by Dennis Sanderson and subsequently by Jan 'Slim' Botha.
Chiltington	Sub-division of Grippos and a portion of council land. Original owner Ann (Susie) Simpson. Named after a town in Britain. Bought later by James Upton and finally by Andries Herbst.
Chinyerere	Sub-division of Coldomo, bought by Jimmy Thompson, then by Hugh Royston.
Chiombi	Bought by D. Stotter and C. Lamb in partnership.
Chisanji	Part of which was Toro, named by the surveyor and subsequently bought by John Impey.
Chisapi	Ex-serviceman allocation to Sam Barrett-Hamilton. Later sub-divided into Lot 1, bought by N. Blazey and registered as Red Leaf; Lot 2, Bonnyvale, to Bert Hacking, then to Doug Cochrane, who sold to Phil Kotze, who then sold back to Paddy Barrett-Hamilton. Thus Chisapi became complete once more.
Chitiwafeni	Meaning 'Place of Baboons'. Sub-divided by Bert Hacking. Subsequent owners: Jack Crees; Dusty Laver; Peter Walsh. Lot 2 was split between Johnny Bennett and Peter Walsh.
Chiwuwa	Ex-serviceman allocation to Shalto Barnes. Named after the river of that name.
Chumburukwe	Ex-serviceman allocation to E. R. Thomson. Named after the river close by. Subsequently owned by Sonny Roberts, the van Zyl brothers, and finally by J. Winward.
Circle 'S'	'Swifty' Rautenbach.
Coldomo	Sub-division of Nassau in 1916. Bought by Robert Andrew Leask who named it after his home farm in the Orkneys. Later further sub-divided into Chinyerere, Musha Wedu and Asuahi Valley.
Collingwood	Collis, Haasbroek.
Coniston	Ex-serviceman/original. William (Billy) Postlethwayt. Named after his place of birth in the Lake District of England. Later purchased by Mike van der Merwe.
Craigdhu	H. McFadjean.

Deamour	E. Kruger. Sold to Jacobus (Koos) Paulsen.
Deerwood Park	Crown land. Sub-divided in 1960. Lot 1 bought by Brnjac, Lot 2 by Fritz Paulsen. Sub-divided once more in 1961. Lot 1 to Piet Kloppers, Lot 2 to Wessels.
Demavand	Sub-division of Blockley.
Derepat	Sub-division of Amore, owned by E. Kruger.

Dixie	Lilford, half of St Brendan's returned by Pat Bashford. Named by owner Guy Lilford after his mother, May Wentworth Dixie.
Doornhoek [Thorn bush]	Koen Strydom, then D. Younghusband. Subsequently sold to government.
Dugane	W. Edwards. I. Stringer.
Dundazi	Original/ex-serviceman's farm: David Cockburn. Sub-division bought by Lazelle, Hunt, Terblanche.
Dunromin	Sub-division of Sapi Valley.
Easter Parade	Stan Sheppard. Bought from Gert Coetzer.
Elephants Walk	Lessing.
Elka	Sub-division of Nassau owned by Lubbe (nothing to do with Ben Lubbe). Subsequently owned by Paul Venter, Piet Nieuwoudt, Peter van Breda.
Enthorpe	Sub-division of Rydings farm. Subsequently owned by R. Robinson.
Eureka	Owned by M. Timms, who never farmed it. Leased first by J. Grobbelaar and then B. White.
Experimental Farm	Sold to Syd Baxter at the break-up of the Federation. He named it Independence.
Fiddlers Green	Peter Walsh. Sub-division of Nyamabidzi, owned by George Potter. Formerly known as Wag'n Bietjie owned by J. Crause.
Folliot	Original/ex-serviceman Barney Wright, son Chris Wright. Sub-division bought by Dave Younghusband.
Four Winds	Sub-division of Hunter's Lodge, owned by Frank Lucas, ex-serviceman, and sold to John New, who sub-divided it after he and his wife, Beryl, divorced. She retained the home section, which she called Four Winds, and John kept the remainder called Hunter's Lodge. Both pieces were later bought by Dick Bylo and then by Mike van der Merwe.
Furzen	Ex-serviceman allocation. Eric Pope never saw active service but qualified as an ex-serviceman.
Futvoyes	Ex-serviceman allocation to David Walker, then Mark Foster, Joachim van der Sluis.
Gainlands	Ex-serviceman Bill Gains. Subsequently bought by Lionel Jahme.
Garahanga	Sub-division of Moniack, bought by Peter Moore. Name derived from 'Place where the Guineafowl live'. Later owned by Moolman, father and son.
Garika	Peter Davies, then Anthony Walters.
Geluksvlei	Jan 'Slim' Botha.
Glenellen	Sub-division of Pompey. Arnold Miller de Haan, ex-serviceman. Bought by Ken Saywood. Glenellen was the name of Ken Saywood's farm in Hout Bay, Cape Town. He later bought the remainder of Pompey.
Glenurquart	George Purchase.

Good Hope (Goed Hoop)	The original name, according to one early map, became anglicised later, acquired in 1923 by Willie Schultz. Subsequently bought by Maurice Simpson. Continued to be farmed by widow, Eve, and eldest son Harry, who married Cynthia Posselt. After Harry's death, younger son, Tom, and wife, Kay, took over the farm. Still farmed by Kay Simpson, widow of Tom at the time of the farm invasions.
Grand Parade	Bought in 1925 by Jack Goldberg, original owner, who also owned Grand Parade mine in Miami, opened up in 1919 and named after the winner of the Grand National. Mr Goldberg may have won money by betting on that horse. Subsequently bought by Engelbrecht brothers, Andries and Schalk. Sold to Peter Stidolph.
Granite	Bill Morris, ex-serviceman. Named after the granite that dominated the area.
Gremlin	Original owner J. K. Mitchell. Subsequently sold to Richard Sims, then to Peter van Breda. Sub-divided in 1964: Lot 1 bought by Mike van der Merwe, which he called New Haven.
Grippos	Gerald Marillier, ex-serviceman.

Halstead	Robbie Watson, ex-serviceman. Then Kevin Robertson, the vet.
Happy Valley	Sub-division of Chitiwafeni.
Harmonie	Serfontein.
Hazeldene	Crown land. Gerald Turner.
Hazelmere	Fred Rae, father of Ralph, Pat Niemandt, Alec Gardiner. Named after Fred's place of birth in the Lake District, UK.
Helwyn	A. Williams-Wynn.
Hesketh Park	Bert Hacking. Made up of five sections: 1. Main section; 2. Northlands; 3. Westlands; 4. Eastlands/Matonga; 5. Southlands. Rocklands sold to Dave Roper in early 1960s. As the name suggests, farm made up of rocky granite outcrops. Dave also bought remainder of Peverell Place from Frikkie Herselman. Subsequently part of that was sub-divided and known as Sundown owned by Roy Ayers. Hesketh Park subsequently bought by Peter Walsh.
Highdale	Gordon Johnson.
Hill Top	Originally part of Miami Estate, Captain Boshoff. Then Andries Engelbrecht, G. Stroobach.
Hillandale	Originally given the name Sunspot by surveyor. Ex-serviceman allocation in 1947 to someone whom none can remember. He pitched his tent, drank away his two thousand pounds, and then left, leaving his tent behind. Subsequently, in 1950s, Ray Hill, ex-serviceman, took over. A strip of Sangalalo was added to it because the original was deemed too marshy to farm with great success.
Hunter's Lodge	Ex-serviceman allocation, Frank Lucas.

Idlewood	Once part of Musha Wedu, Neville Canon. It has been suggested that the Miami landing strip was on this land (not confirmed).
Impala Plains	C. McAllister, then Rory Duffin.
Independence	Former experimental farm sold to Syd Baxter.
Ingwenya	A. Gidley.
Inverness	Willie Smyth. Sub-divided: Lot 1 bought by N. Quail; remainder bought by C. Lamb.
Inyati	Meaning 'Buffalo'. Owned by Lionel Tiltman, who built a pretty little house on a hill in which he kept both his mistress and his wife.
Jacob's Ladder	Sub-division of Musuku farm bought by Lionel Jacobson. Lionel was Jewish, hence the Old Testament name.
Janetville	Owned by C. Stewart who combined it with Nascot.
Jenya	Ex-serviceman allocation to Sims. Later, Sid Scolnik, Jewish.
Kachichi	H. Ferreira. Sold to government after independence for a co-operative.
Kangerie	Richardson.
Kankombe	R. Wheeler, C. Lamb.
Karoi	Named after the river on which it stands, owned by the Le Roux brothers in 1923.
Kasimure	Hugh Dewar, J. Graham, Lightbody.
Kent	Once part of Rekomitje, Miami Estates, Captain Boshoff.
Keppoch	Sub-division of Gainlands, bought by A. McDonald. Sold to Piet Bosch, who sold on to D. Mackenzie. Named after a tree.
Kevlyn	Fred Mitchell. Named after his two children, Kevin and Lyn.
Kia Lami	Sub-division of Nassau, owned by Paul Venter and sold on to Fritz Paulsen and then to Hugh Royston.
Kilrea	Sub-division of Blockley. Patrick Wells.
Kiplingcotes	M. Featherby, named after his home village in the UK.
Kupeta	H. van Heerden. Dave Stirling.
Kyogle	Ex-serviceman allocation to D.D. Tate. Subsequently bought by Thomas du Preez (Snr), uncle of Tom du Preez, Jr.
La Pieta	Sub-division of Scorpion farm bought by Pieter de Wet. Subsequently bought by Frank Donnelly.
Lancaster	Ex-serviceman allocation to Peter Groenewald. Named after the Lancaster bombers he flew in the war. Subsequently bought by Ria Watt, widow of Roy. She subsequently married Bert Hacking.
Landithy	Crown land, B. White.
Lanlory	Crown land, Jimmy Flight.
Langholm	'Mandebvu' Young.
Laughing Hills	Crown land, P. Pilcher.
Leconfield	Ex-serviceman allocation to P. Fisher, later sold to M. Gaisford and Rory Fraser.

Linda	Next door to Nyarenda, both owned by E. R. Thomson.
Little Gem	Sub-division of Chelvern, owned by Peter Burgess, 'the one-armed bandit'.
Longueil	Ex-serviceman allocation Jack O'Hea. Named after a small Canadian town (correct spelling is Longueuil) where his mother was born, now a suburb of greater Montreal. Sold to Charles Postlethwayt, son of Billy, and then to Peter Richards.
Loughry	Peter Lindsay. Noble.
Madadzi	Johnny Eden. Werrie Rademeyer, step-father of Willie Nel, as a result of which it became known as Nel's Spruit.
Mafalo	Ex-serviceman allocation to Geoff Holland, who sub-divided. Two sections bought by Gigi Falzoi and the remainder by Rupert Hawley, who registered it as Tollington.
Mahuti	Ex-serviceman allocation to Zak Olivier.
Mani/Mlichi	Ex-serviceman allocation to H. Ormerod. Named after the river Mlichi, which is on the boundary. Mani subsequently sold to Peter Armstrong, then to J. van der Sluis, then to Alan Fraser-Bell.
Manyangau	Jannie Grobbelaar; Dave Chadwick; Dave Stirling.
Maora	Ex-serviceman allocation to J. Blanckenberg, subsequently bought by Harold Herud, inherited by Chris Herud. Named after the Maora tree in abundance on the farm. A sub-division was Boland, bought by Esterhuizen.
Marmi	Lund. Then Morris Bell, who won awards for his rowing prowess. Sub-division bought by MacMillan.
Marshlands	W. van der Merwe. Then sold to Rautenbach brothers.
Maseru	Serfontein
Masterpiece	Crown land 1924, bought by D. G. Hartman. Never occupied. In the middle of nowhere.
Maunga	Ex-serviceman allocation to Jack Wilson. Subsequently bought by A. Wells.
Miami Estates	Captain Boshoff. Comprising Grand Parade, Hill Top, Kent, Rekomitje AA, A, and B (Omega, St Mawes, Chiwuwa and a part of Grand Parade).
Milverton	Ex-serviceman allocation to Bob Kind. Named after his former farm in Chakari, bought by father of Ben Lubbe. Subsequent owners: J. Gottwald; Alf Smith.
Momba	Ralph Ray, Nico Smit.
Mondoro/Welkom	Crown land, Mossie Dryer. Sold later to Eric Johnsen.
Moniack	Ex-serviceman allocation to C. Gair.
Montesuma	Ex-serviceman allocation to Aubrey Lewen. Sold to Harry Wells in 1954. Well named, after the Mexican ruler of the legendary kingdom of gold.

Morewag	Crown land, Mike Bennett then M. Greyling. Name from the Afrikaans: 'Tomorrow waits' or 'Expectations'.
Moy	Ex-serviceman allocation to Alexander Chisholm. Named after the family estate in Scotland.
Moyale	Ex-serviceman allocation to Douglas Fox. Named after an East African town that was split by the Kenya/Ethiopia border where he was stationed during the war as a Platoon Commander in the Kings African Rifles.
Mpofu River	Crown land, bought by C. Wilcox.
Mshalla	Ex-serviceman allocation to W. D. England, who picked up the name in the Middle East when he was buying wheat for the 8th Army. The Arabic words mean 'God Go with You'. Subsequently bought by Don Stotter, Nephew of Mary England.
Muchbinding	Cliff Garside. Later owned by Dudley McKenzie.
Mukanga	R. Stockhill.
Mukuyu	Crown land. Jimmy Hamilton; Buddy Donaldson.
Munande	Once a part of Karoi farm, Cornelius Niemandt.
Musha Wedu	Sub-division of Coldomo. Sold to N. Canon, N. Royston.
Mushi Park	Sub-division of Chitiwafeni bought by Johnny Bennett.
Musuku	Ex-serviceman allocation to Glover. Subsequently to W. Stegman, Brink, A. Rama.
Mvagasi	Mike Reynolds.
Mwala	Ex-serviceman allocation Jimmy Pearson. Named after the Mwala trees found on the farm.
Myrlen	Len Lundersted.
Naba	Ex-serviceman allocation to S. Maclaurin. Sold to V. Versveld in 1980. The name is believed to be Indian.
Nascot	Owned by Peter Gibson, then Charles Stewart, who combined it with Janetville.
Nassau	Twenty-four thousand acres of land granted to William Harvey Brown by Cecil John Rhodes in 1896, which he named after his place of birth. First sub-division of 12,000 acres bought by Robert Andrew Leask in 1916 and called Coldomo. Second Sub-division bought in 1940 by A.B. Roberts. It was divided equally between A.B. and Margaret, his wife, and registered as Blockley. Subsequently Jack Gauche bought the remainder of Blockley and then sold to Hugo Blignaut.
Nduba	Ex-serviceman allocation to Hugh Neil. D. Kilborn.
Nebo	Crown land. Matiens du Preez (father of Porky and Tom). Nebo is a town mentioned in the Bible.
New Forest	Ex-serviceman allocation to Francis Heron. Awa du Toit. Peter van Breda.

New Haven	Sub-division of Gremlin, bought by Mike van der Merwe from R. Sims. The name indicates a place of sanctuary.
Ngwee	Crown land. Derek Marillier.
Nicotiana	Charles Stewart.
Nyahoa	Jim Barker.
Nyamabidzi	Ex-serviceman allocation to George Potter. Sub-division called Wag'n Bietjie bought by J. Crause. Taken over by Peter Walsh, who changed the name to Fiddlers Green. Remainder subsequently sold to Bakker brothers, then to Karel Kirstein and finally to Sven Johnsen.
Nyamahamba	Ex-serviceman allocation to Lewis A.P. Thomas. Named after rivers close by.
Nyamahapi	First owner was called Brown, who died after being struck by lightning while talking on the phone. Bought by Cedric Lamb and Don Stotter in a partnership.
Nyamanda	Ex-serviceman allocation to Jimmy Oxenham and subsequently bought by Fred Mulder. Named after the river that runs along its boundary.
Nyamapipi	Owned by G. Marillier (Snr); Collis, Gert Willemse; C.T. Lamb.
Nyangoma	Ex-serviceman allocation to Peter Gibson. Named after the river on its north eastern boundary. Nyangoma, Shona for 'River that sounds like a drum'.
Nyaramanda	Ex-serviceman allocation to Paul Renwick.
Nyarenda	Ex-serviceman allocation to Thomson, whose wife is buried on the farm. Subsequently owned by Wilfred Smith.
Nyodza	Noel Bichard. Named after the river close by. Later sub-divided, Lot 1 bought by Harry Wells and the remainder sold to Peter Adams, who called it Wingate.
Omega	Ex-serviceman allocation to Frikkie Taute. Thus named because it was geographically the last surveyed property to the north.
Oribi Park	Ex-serviceman allocated to H. Coker. Named after the oribi in abundance in the area. Sub-divided and joined on to Marshlands, owned by Fritz Paulsen.
Padenga	Dr Bathurst.
Pangwarati	'Home of the Sable'. Ex-serviceman allocation to Lionel and Paddy Searle. Bought by A. Gravenstein.
Pelele	Original owner Potgieter. Clift. Dennis Norman, according to whom it was the last farm to be surveyed in Karoi before the outbreak of World War II, before the withdrawal of surveyors, who had finished their work.
Pendennis	Crown land, 1924. Original owner Captain Whitby. Never farmed and was bought by A. Hess.
Penstock	Crown land. Mike Bailey.

Peverell Place	Ex-serviceman allocation William (Bill) Rayburn. Sold to Frikkie Herselman, who sub-divided it into seven sections. Bert Hacking bought three of them.
Pitlochry	Ex-serviceman allocation to Ian Laing. Named after family home in Scotland. Bought by Brian McKay in 1954.
Pompey	Ex-serviceman allocation to Arnold Miller de Haan. Named after Portsmouth, nicknamed Pompey, after it was razed to the ground during World War II. Arnold met his wife, Jackie, there.
Pumara	Ex-serviceman allocation to Harry Brown.
Protea	Pat Hull. A portion bought by Alex van Leenhoff. A sub-division bought by Ian Fraser to join on to The Ridges.

Quo Vadis	E. Kruger

Rendezvous	Sub-division of Coldomo. John de Lange. Taylor/Pye.
Renroc	Ex-serviceman allocation to John Hull. Subsequent sub-divisions: Lot 1, Virginia, kept for his nephew, Edward Hull. Lot 2, West Acre, bought by Piet Strydom in 1970. Lot 3, Tivoli, bought by Paul Straarup, a Danish national, hence the name. Remainder bought by Doug Cochrane.
Rhukwedza	Tienie van Rensburg.
Richmond	Original owner A. Bennett.
Ridges, The	Ex-serviceman allocation to Dave Maxwell. Sub-divided: Lot 1 bought by Gert Coetzer and remainder by Ian Fraser.
Rocklands	Sub-division of Chitiwafeni, bought by Dave Roper, which was originally part of Peverell Place owned by Bill Rayburn.
Rockwood Estate	Geoff Bennett.
Rufaro	Previously called Sherwood farm. Bill Soames. P.Phillip. N.Phillips. P.Gifford.
Runnimead	Ex-serviceman allocation to Cedric O'Hea. Then sold to Neville Quail.
Runora	Sub-division of Shambatungwe. Noel Pickard.
Ruwanzi Ranch	Ex-serviceman allocation to 'Bez' Bezuitenhout.
Rydings	Ex-serviceman allocation to G.H. Lea. P.Mitchell? Dennis Hook. It later became the property on which Rydings School was built.

Sable Ridge	T. Neilsen. He and his wife both died in a car accident. Farm subsequently left to son, Mike Neilsen. Subsequently bought by Christoffle Paulsen.
St Brendan's	Ex-serviceman allocation to Pat Bashford but only taken up in 1954. Later bought by Edward Flight. Other half of St Brendan's was given to Guy Lilford, which he called Dixie.
St Mawes	Lessing.
Sandara	Bob Riches.
Sangalalo	Means 'Happiness'. Bought by Colin Duff, then by Peter Stidolph.

San Michele	Paul Renwick. Later bought by P. Groot.
Sapi Valley	Tucker, who swapped it with Dolan Hampson for Waterfalls farm on the edge of Salisbury.
Scorpion	Ex-serviceman allocation to Sydney Jenkinson. Subsequently bought by Harry Stanford, who sub-divided a portion and sold to Pieter de Wet, who called it La Pieta.
Shambatungwe	Ex-serviceman allocation to Richard Scrase, named after the river on its border. Subsequently bought by Pieter de Wet, who sub-divided it, selling one piece to Noel Pickard, who registered it as Runora.
Shargezan	Crown land. Dennis Prince.
Shawnigan	Ex-serviceman allocation to David Grantham.
Sherwood Forest	Original name of Rufaro farm. Bill Soames. P. Phillip.
Shingaroro	I. R. Pemberton
Shola Park	Original owners Terry and Emma Gidley. Then Willie Smyth. According to Dennis Prince, a nephew of the Gidleys, they eventually divorced and Emma became 'a loose woman'.
Spring	Ex-serviceman allocation to Zook Nesbitt. Later bought by Jimmy Corbet; J. Stegman; Piet Oosthuizen; Alan Parsons.
Springbok Heights	Original owner thought to be Pretorius. Farm named by surveyor Alex Fry in 1952 after two consecutive wins by the Springboks over a visiting touring team in which both his brothers played.
Star Cross	Sub-division of Rufaro. First owner Joe Dabbs.
Strathyre	Original owner Watson. Subsequently bought by B. McKay.
Sunspot	Original name of Hillandale. Ray Hill.

Tarquinia	Ex-Serviceman allocation to Paul Pearson.
Templecombe	Ex-serviceman allocation to David Stacey. Named after the village in England where his father came from.
Toekoms	Afrikaans for 'The Future'. Gil Pretorius.
Toronanga	C. Holmes.
Torwood	Crown land. Sanderson's father and son, Dennis.
Travios	Jack Waddle. Dave Richardson.
Trokiadza	J. Aston.
Troon	Sub-division of Wingate, bought by Neville Wright. Then sold to Peter Walsh.

Uitkyk	Afrikaans for Outlook. W. Bezuitenhout.
Umgarati	'Sable'. Ex-serviceman allocation to C. McLaughlan.
Ungwa	K36. Originally allotted to J. Fraser-Bell. No development. Next owner Ronnie Callon, who sold to Harry Wells.
Utopia	'Sakkie' Orangies.

Vermont	Ex-serviceman allocation to Alec Watson. Subsequently bought by Anthony Hoskyns, then Anthony McKay and finally Brian McKay.

Vuka	The name means 'Wake Up'. Ex-serviceman allocation to Trevor Harvey.
Vuna	Meaning 'Harvest'. Kremer. Sub-division of Impala Plains belonging to McAllister.

Wajetsi	Not occupied until 1956, when Lionel Searle and Liz married and moved there.
Waterloo	Owned by Captain Boshoff and managed for him in the early days by Frank Dalkin. Frank subsequently bought the property before moving to Enthorpe. He then bought Scorpion from Harry Stanford. Final owner P. du Toit.
Wingate	Also known as Nyodza. Ex-serviceman allocation to Noel Bichard who sold on to Peter Adams, who sub-divided to create Troon, bought by Neville Wright.
Wirral	Sub-division of Pendennis.
Woodlands	George Neaves then sold to Mike Ricquebourg.

Yawanda	Brian Johnson.
Yeadon	Crown land. George Donald.

Zakanaka	Lewis A. P. Thomas. Sold to W. Nel, Buffalo Downs.
Zamora	R. Cawood. Sub-division of Loughry.
Zebra Downs	Arthur Bishop and subsequently his son, Chris Bishop. Named because of numerous zebra roaming around.

Index

Acknowledgements and Sources

There are a great many people to thank for taking the time to reminisce about a bygone era which the world will not see again. I am indebted to all of them.

Most are mentioned as their recorded memories appear in the book. Others have helped by giving interviews, and others still have just dropped their little gems of knowledge in passing conversations. All have been instrumental in helping to record this age of Rhodesian/Zimbabwean history in relation to Miami, Karoi and Tengwe. Already, in some cases, we have left it far too late, for much has been lost as the real 'old-timers' have passed on.

While every effort has been made to ensure that facts are correct, your indulgence is asked in advance for any discrepancies, distortions or mistakes that may have been made. The frailties of the human mind can play tricks.

Where possible I have tried to verify everything by making use of the National Archives of Zimbabwe and by reading various books and journals. Should there be any glaring mistakes I would like to be informed so that they can be rectified.

It was indeed fortuitous that, as Karoi's Women's Institute Archivist, I had already been able interview Maureen (Leask) Grantham, Mary and Peter England, and Greta MacDonald and Patricia (Tish Marillier) Duguid before their deaths.

Mrs Edna (Taylor) Thomson and her daughter, Hilary Dowling, both now living in Britain, have done a splendid job in getting Edna's reminiscences of Karoi to me, of which I'm most appreciative. Edna, now in her nineties and blind, recorded her memoirs orally onto a Dictaphone, which was then written down by Hilary, and sent to me by e-mail along with photos. A stout effort indeed. And my appreciation.

Thanks also to the late Mr Harry Wells and his daughter, Alex Sheppard, for permission to use excerpts relevant to Karoi from a biography that she wrote about her father. Gratitude also to Mr Alex Fry for allowing me the same latitude for excerpts from his book.

Special mention and thanks also go to Rita Leask Mills.

Further thanks go also to:
Brian McKay, Althea Dewdney (Deacon), Avril Chisnall (Deacon), Janet(Paterson) Wiggins, June Maidment Veck, Jill Maidment Thornton, Rob Truscott, Sarah Fynn, Catherine (Chisholm)Oldrieve, Ian Chisholm, who sent some recollections the day before his untimely death. Jean Graham, Hazel Bray, Libby (Bashford) Garnett, Sylvia Bishop, Denise Gaisford, Ko and Dini Voorn, Robyn (Toby) Saunders, Ian Gibson, Peter Richards, Maureen Philip, Honor Duff, Anthony (Flossie) Hoskyns, Margaret (Simpson) Herud, Gwen (Southey) Adams, Lex Southey, Peter Walsh, Lydia Stroobach, Maartje Bakker, Ian Fraser, Tawny Stidolph, Jimmy Flight, Kath Quail, Cec Saywood, Paddy Barrett-Hamilton, Ray Townsend, Hazel Townsend, Jimmy Upton, Dennis and June Prince, Wendy Miller de Haan, Helen Kennedy Fox, Marie Paulsen, Joy Straarup, Willie Watson, Brian Johnson, Pearl Roberts McClaughlin, Gerry van Tonder, Barbara Stirrup for information on Tengwe, Mike van der Merwe, Penny Lamb, Nat Stotter, Janet Deere and Flo McKay.

Lastly, but not least, my gratitude to Roger Stringer, my editor, who never gave up on me.

Published sources consulted

Armstrong, Peter *Tobacco Spiced with Ginger: The Life of Ginger Freeman* (Harare: Welston Press, 1987).

Black, Colin *The Legend of Lomagundi* (Salisbury: North-Western Development Association, 1976).

Bower, Tom *Tiny Rowland: A Rebel Tycoon* (London: Heinemann, 1993).

Brown, W.H. *On the South African Frontier: The Adventures and Observations of an American in Mashonaland and Matabeleland* (Bulawayo: Books of Rhodesia, 1970, reprint of 1899).

Clements, Frank, and Edward Harben, *Leaf of Gold: The Story of Rhodesian Tobacco* (London: Methuen, 1962).

Danckwerts, Brian *A Century of Polo in Rhodesia/Zimbabwe* (The author, 1995).

Davies, Marjorie Dick *Twin Trails: The Story of the Fynn and Southey Families* (Salisbury: K.B. Davies, 1974).

Douglas, R.G.S. 'Two early Portuguese in the Mutapa State', *Heritage of Zimbabwe* (1986), 6: 41–6.

Fry, Alex *How I Won the War: Personal Accounts of World War II* (Durban: Just Done Productions, 2007).

Howell, James 'The Legacy of Roger Barclay-Smith', <http://www.gonvilleandcaius.org/Document.Doc?id=178>.

Lovett, John *Contact: A Tribute to Those Who Serve Rhodesia* (Howick, Natal: Khenty Press, 1978, 11.

Maclean, Joy *The Guardians: A Story of Rhodesia's Outposts, and of the Men and Women Who Served in Them* (Bulawayo: Books of Rhodesia, 1974).

Ransford, Oliver *Rhodesian Tapestry: A History in Needlework* (Bulawayo: Books of Rhodesia, 1971).

Robertson, Kevin *Africa's Most Dangerous* (Huntington Beach, CA: Safari Press, 2007).

Smith, R.C. 'The Africa trans-continental telegraph line', *Rhodesiana* (1975) 33: 1–18.

Tabler, Edward *Pioneers of Rhodesia* (C. Struik, 1966).

Tracey, Hugh 'Antonio Fernandes: Rhodesia's first pioneer', *Rhodesiana* (1968), 19: 1–26.

Maps on the following pages

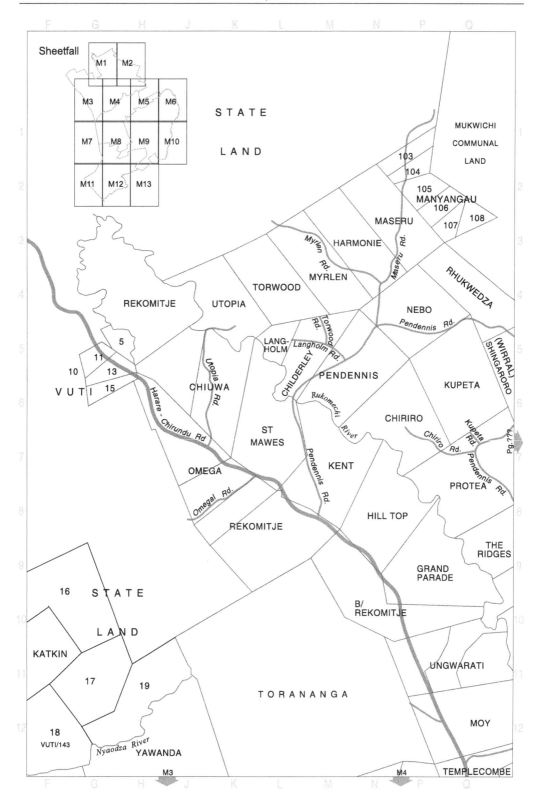

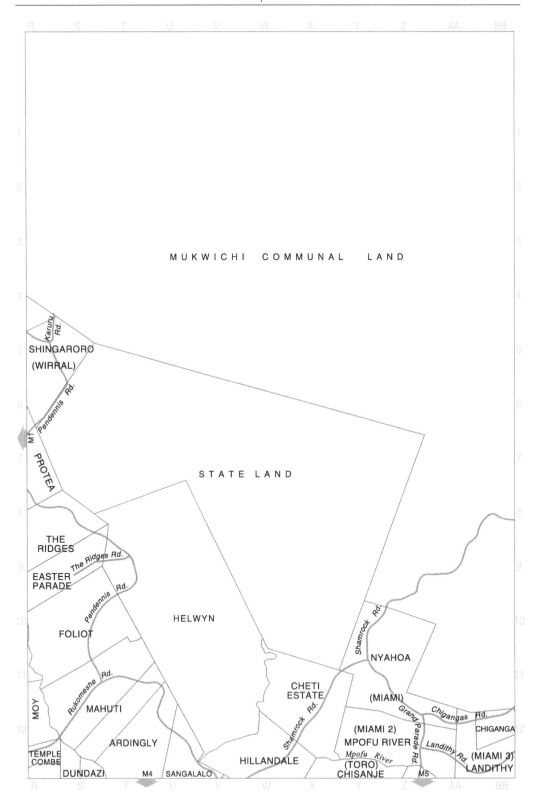

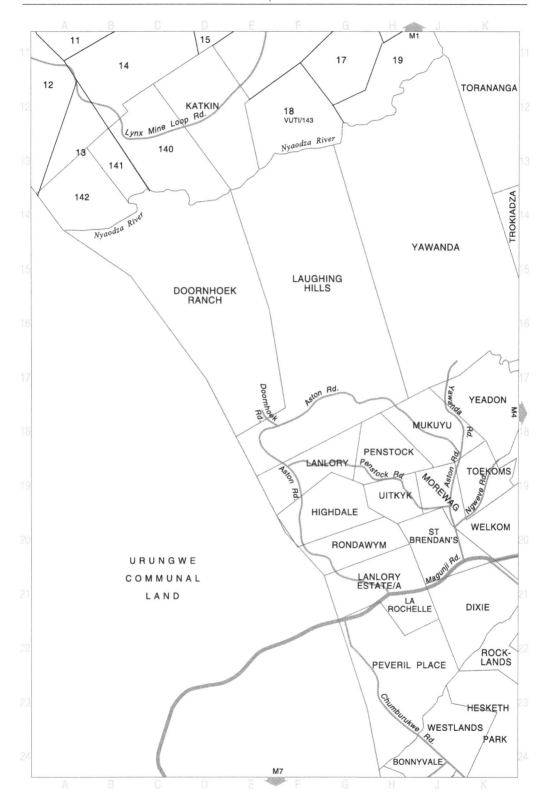

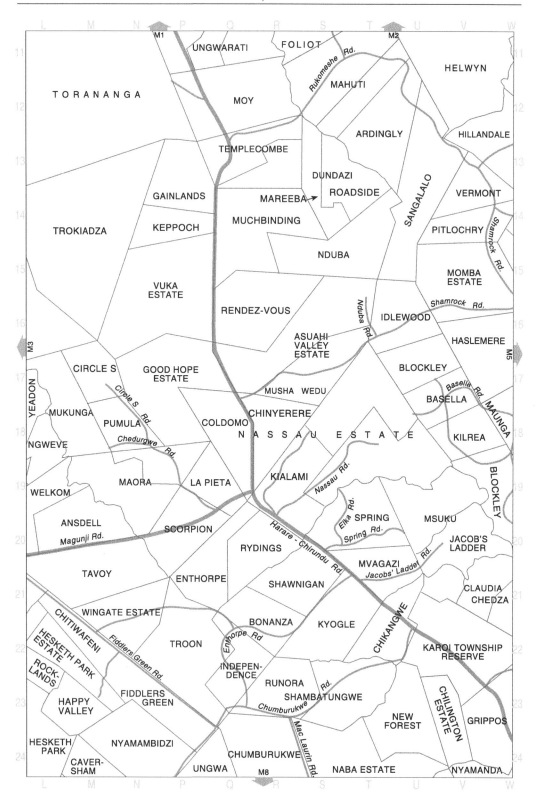

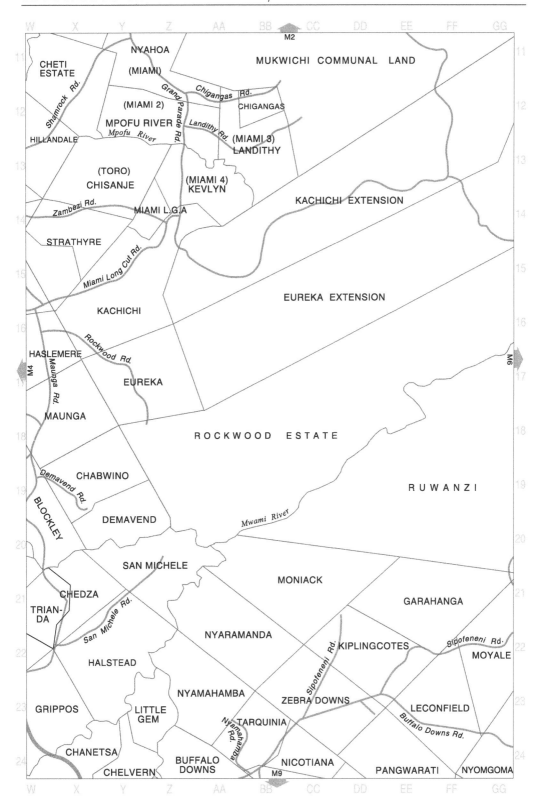

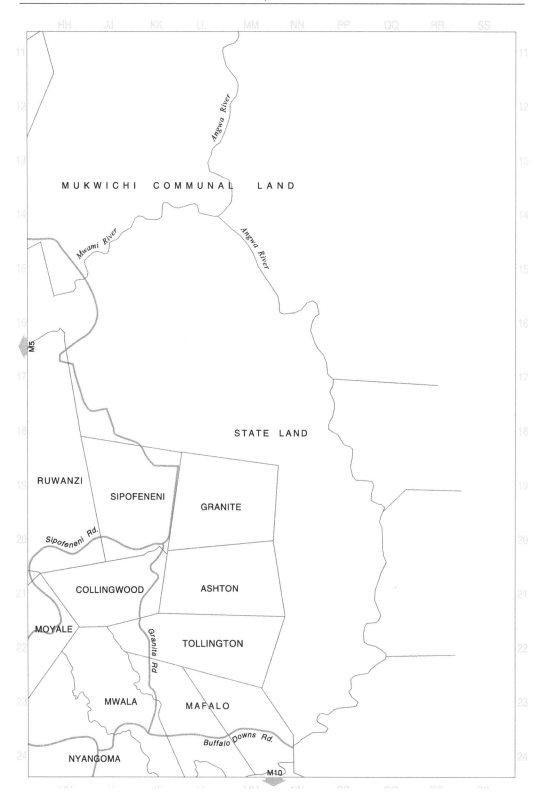

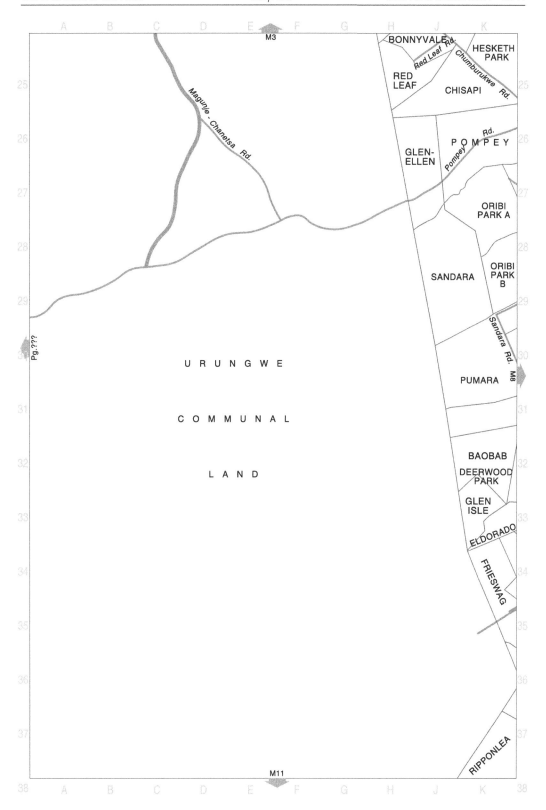

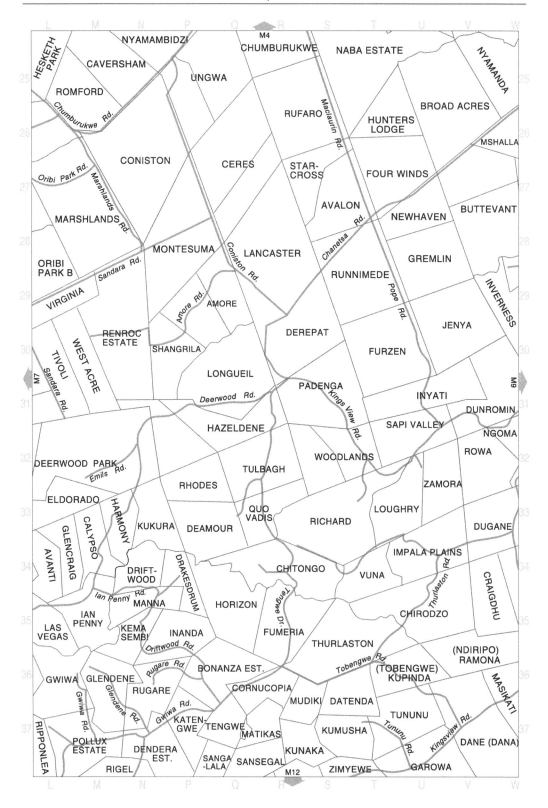

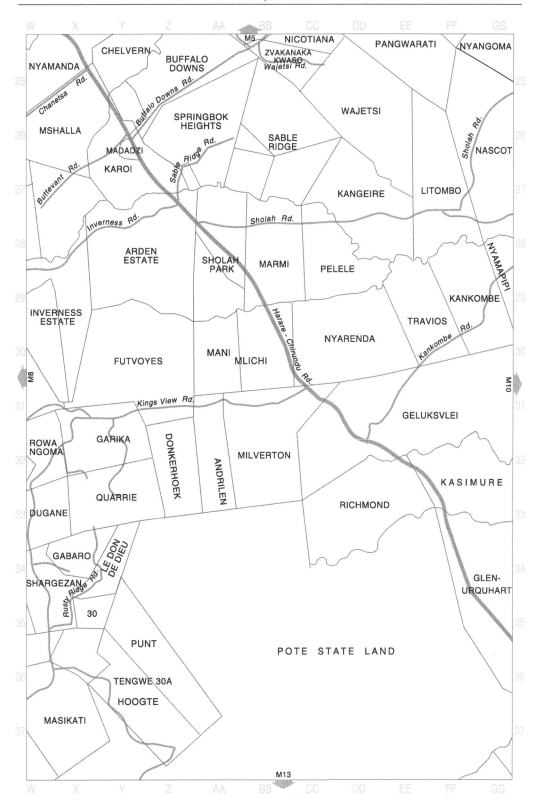

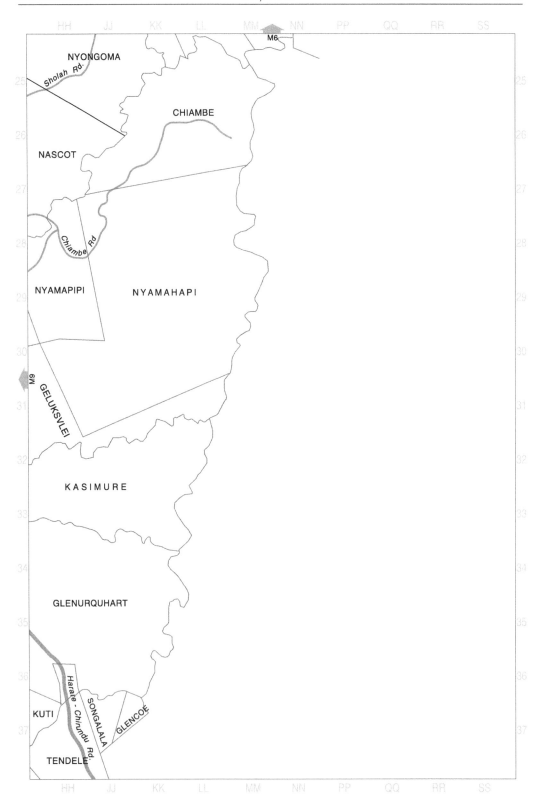

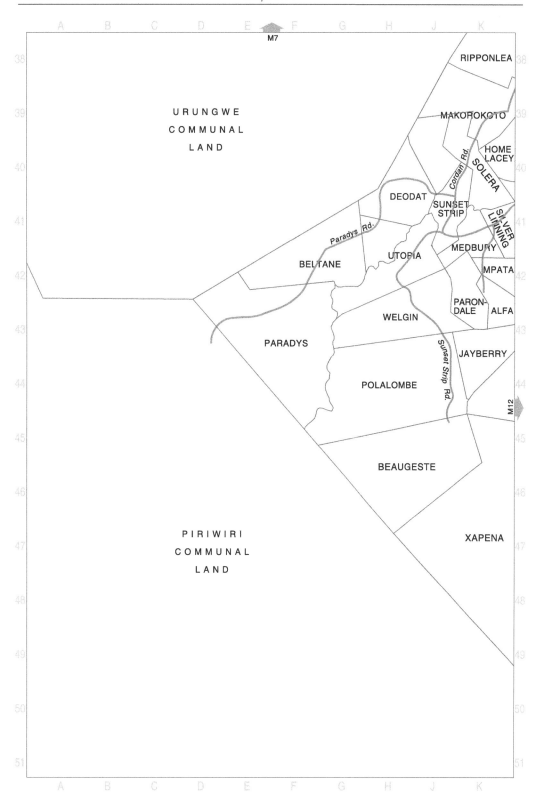

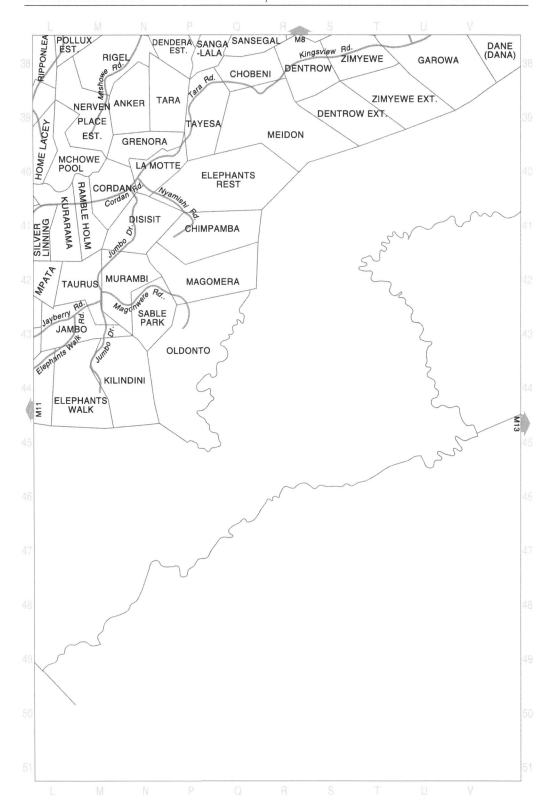

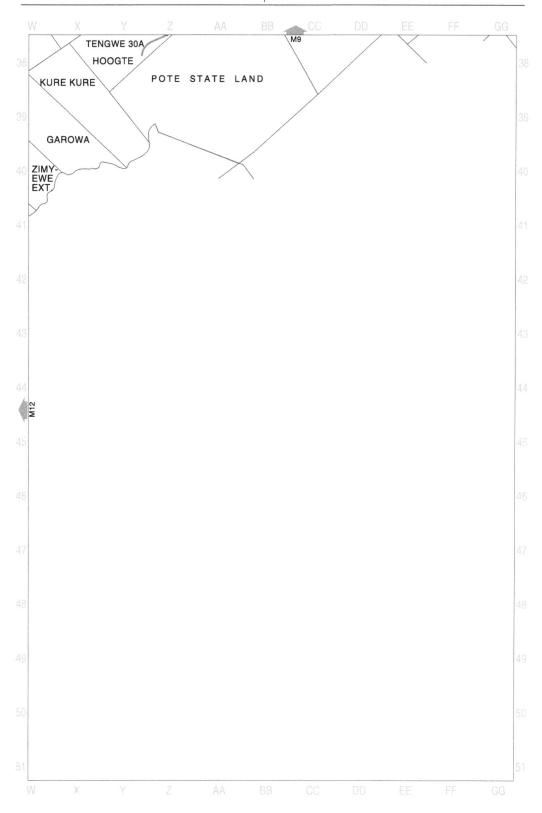

Farm name	Map	Grid ref.	Farm name	Map	Grid ref.	Farm name	Map	Grid ref.
Alfa	M11	42K	Chitonga	M8	34R	Furzen	M8	30T
Amore	M8	29P	Chiuwa	M1	6J	Futvoyes	M9	30Y
Andrilen	M9	32AA	Chobeni	M12	38Q			
Anker	M12	39N	Chumburukwe	M4	24R	Gabaro	M9	34X
Ansdell	M4	20M	Circle S	M4	17M	Gainlands	M4	14P
Arden Estate	M8	28Y	Claudia	M4	21W	Garahanga	M5	21EE
Ardingly	M4	12T	Coldomo	M4	18Q	Garika	M9	32Y
Ashton	M6	21LL	Collingwood	M6	21JJ	Garowa	M12	38U
Asuahi Valley			Coniston	M8	26N	Geluksvlei	M9	32EE
Estate	M4	16S	Cordan	M12	40M	Glencoe	M10	37JJ
Avalon	M8	27R	Cornucopia	M8	36R	Glencraig	M8	34L
Avanti	M8	34L	Craigdhu	M8	34V	Glendene	M8	36M
						Glenellen	M7	26J
Baobab	M7	32K	Dane/Dana	M8	37V	Glen Isle	M7	33K
Basella	M4	17U	Datenda	M8	36S	Glenurquhart	M10	34HH
Beaugeste	M11	46H	Deamour	M8	33P	Good Hope		
Beltane	M11	42F	Deerwood Park	M8	32M	Estate	M4	17P
Blockley	M5	19W	Demavend	M5	19Y	Grand Parade	M1	9P
Blockley 1/B	M4	17U	Dendera Estate	M8	37N	Granite	M6	19LL
Bonanza Estate	M8	36Q	Dentrow	M12	38R	Gremlin	M8	28U
Bonnyvale	M3	24H	Dentrow Ext.	M12	39S	Grenora	M12	39N
Broad Acres	M8	25U	Deodat	M11	40H	Grippos	M4	23W
Buffalo Downs	M9	25Z	Derepat	M8	30R	Gwiwa	M8	36L
Buttevant	M8	28V	Devondale	M10	34AA			
			Dixie	M3	21K	Halstead	M5	22Y
Calypso	M8	34M	Doornhoek			Harmonie	M1	3M
Caversham	M8	25M	Ranch	M3	15D	Haselmere	M4	16V
Ceres	M8	27Q	Drakesdrum	M8	34P	Hazeldene	M8	32P
Chanetsa	M5	24X	Driftwood	M8	34N	Helwyn	M2	10U
Chedza	M5	21X	Dugane	M9	33W	Hesketh Park	M3	24K
Chelvern	M8	25Y	Dundazi	M4	13S	Highdale	M3	19F
Cheti Estate	M5	11X	Dunromin	M8	31V	Hill Top	M1	8N
Chiamba	M10	26LL				Hillandale	M2	12W
Childerley	M1	5L	Easter Parade	M2	9R	Home Lacey	M12	40L
Chigangas	M2	12BB	Eldorado	M8	33M	Hoogte	M13	38Y
Chiltington			Elephants Rest	M12	40Q	Horizon	M8	35Q
Estate	M4	23V	Elephants Walk	M12	44M	Hunter's Lodge	M8	26T
Chimpamba	M12	41P	Enthorpe	M4	20Q			
Chinyerere	M4	18R	Eureka	M4	17Y	Ian Penny	M8	35M
Chirodzo	M8	35U				Idlewood	M4	16U
Chiroro	M1	6N	Fiddlers Green	M4	23N	Impala Plains	M8	34U
Chisanje	M5	13Y	Foliot	M2	10S	Inanda	M8	35N
Chisapi	M7	25J	Four Winds	M8	27T	Independence	M4	22Q
Chitiwafeni	M4	22M	Frieswag	M7	34K	Inverness	M9	29W

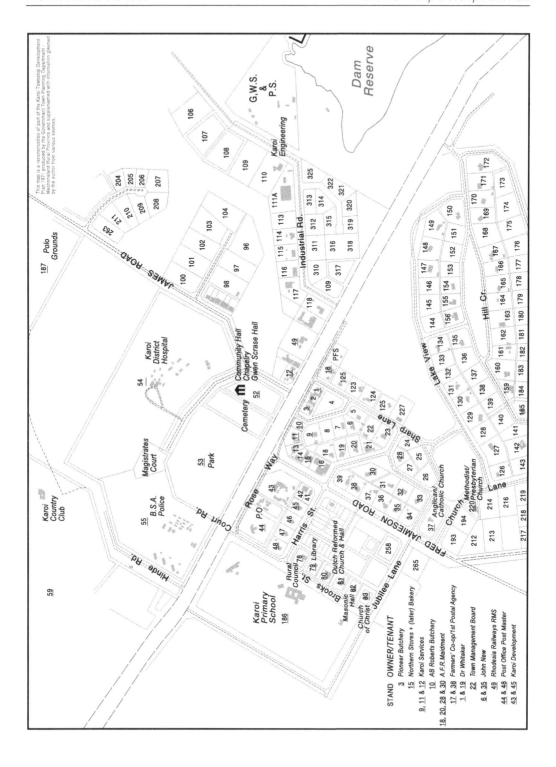

This map is a reconstruction of part of the Karoi Township Development Plan 1971 produced by the Government Town Planning Department, Mashonaland Rural Province and supplemented with information gleaned by the author from various sources.

STAND OWNER/TENANT
3   Pioneer Butchery
15   Northern Stores + (later) Bakery
9, 11 & 12 Karoi Services
10   AB Roberts Butchery
18, 20, 28 & 30 A.F.R. Maidment
17 & 38 Farmers Co-op/1st Postal Agency
1 & 19 Dr Whitaker
22   Town Management Board
6 & 35 John New
49   Rhodesia Railways RMS
44 & 48 Post Office Post Master
43 & 45 Karoi Development

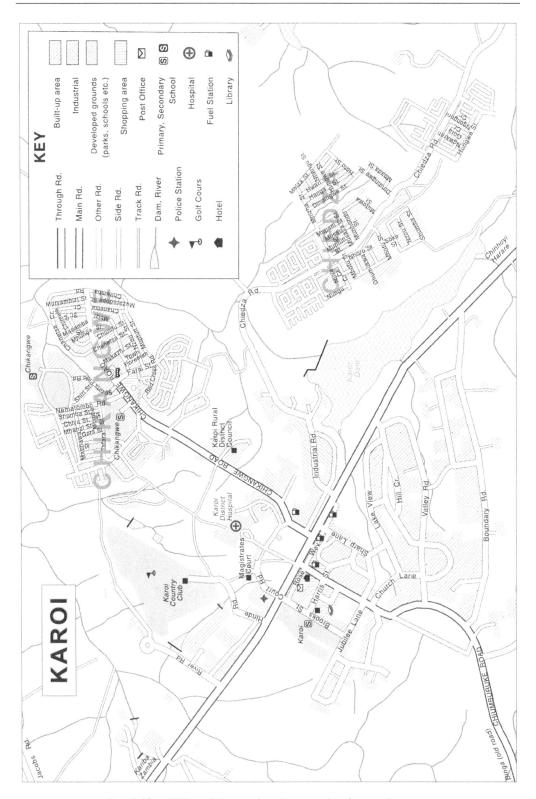

Compiled from 1996 aerial photography with some up-dates from satellite images.

Lightning Source UK Ltd.
Milton Keynes UK
UKOW07f1833261115

263616UK00010B/256/P